Information Security and Cryptography

Series Editors

David Basin ⓘ, Department of Computer Science, ETH Zürich, Zürich, Switzerland

Kenny Paterson, Department of Computer Science, ETH Zürich, Zürich, Switzerland

Editorial Board

Michael Backes, Department of Computer Science, Saarland University, Saarbrücken, Germany

Gilles Barthe, IMDEA Software Institute, Pozuelo de Alarcón, Spain

Ronald Cramer, CWI, Amsterdam, The Netherlands

Ivan Damgård, Department of Computer Science, Aarhus University, Aarhus, Denmark

Robert H. Deng ⓘ, School of Information Systems, Singapore Management University, Singapore, Singapore

Christopher Kruegel, Department of Computer Science, University of California, Santa Barbara, Santa Barbara, USA

Tatsuaki Okamoto, Okamoto Research Lab, NTT Secure Platform Laboratories, Musashino-shi, Japan

Adrian Perrig, CAB F 85.1, ETH Zürich, Zürich, Switzerland

Bart Preneel, Department Elektrotechniek-ESAT/COSIC, University of Leuven, Leuven, Belgium

Carmela Troncoso, Security and Privacy Engineering Lab, École Polytechnique Fédérale de Lausa, Lausanne, Switzerland

Moti Yung ⓘ, Google Inc., New York, USA

Kui Ren, University at Buffalo, Buffalo, USA

Information Security – protecting information in potentially hostile environments – is a crucial factor in the growth of information-based processes in industry, business, and administration. Cryptography is a key technology for achieving information security in communications, computer systems, electronic commerce, and in the emerging information society.

Springer's Information Security & Cryptography (IS&C) book series covers all relevant topics, ranging from theory to advanced applications. The intended audience includes students, researchers and practitioners.

David Basin · Cas Cremers · Jannik Dreier ·
Ralf Sasse

Modeling and Analyzing Security Protocols with Tamarin

A Comprehensive Guide

David Basin
Department of Computer Science
ETH Zürich
Zürich, Switzerland

Cas Cremers
CISPA Helmholtz Center for Information Security
Saarbrücken, Germany

Jannik Dreier
Université de Lorraine
Vandœuvre-lès-Nancy, France

Ralf Sasse
Department of Computer Science
ETH Zürich
Zürich, Switzerland

ISSN 1619-7100   ISSN 2197-845X (electronic)
Information Security and Cryptography
ISBN 978-3-031-90935-1   ISBN 978-3-031-90936-8 (eBook)
https://doi.org/10.1007/978-3-031-90936-8

© The Editor(s) (if applicable) and The Author(s), under exclusive license to Springer Nature Switzerland AG 2025

This work is subject to copyright. All rights are solely and exclusively licensed by the Publisher, whether the whole or part of the material is concerned, specifically the rights of translation, reprinting, reuse of illustrations, recitation, broadcasting, reproduction on microfilms or in any other physical way, and transmission or information storage and retrieval, electronic adaptation, computer software, or by similar or dissimilar methodology now known or hereafter developed.
The use of general descriptive names, registered names, trademarks, service marks, etc. in this publication does not imply, even in the absence of a specific statement, that such names are exempt from the relevant protective laws and regulations and therefore free for general use.
The publisher, the authors and the editors are safe to assume that the advice and information in this book are believed to be true and accurate at the date of publication. Neither the publisher nor the authors or the editors give a warranty, expressed or implied, with respect to the material contained herein or for any errors or omissions that may have been made. The publisher remains neutral with regard to jurisdictional claims in published maps and institutional affiliations.

This Springer imprint is published by the registered company Springer Nature Switzerland AG
The registered company address is: Gewerbestrasse 11, 6330 Cham, Switzerland

If disposing of this product, please recycle the paper.

Preface

Security protocols, as an object of study, have been likened to fruit flies as studied in genetic research. The objects under consideration are small, ubiquitous, and exhibit surprising complexity. For security protocols, even relatively simple protocols may have surprising behaviors. And as they serve as the cornerstone for security in distributed settings, like within the Internet, their proper functioning is critical.

TAMARIN is an open-source analysis tool for security protocols. Given a specification of a protocol, a threat model describing the capabilities of possible adversaries, and the protocol's desired security properties, TAMARIN either verifies the protocol or can provide counterexamples witnessing attacks. TAMARIN is a robust and powerful analysis tool: it has been under development for over a decade and has reached a state of maturity where it can be applied to model and analyze a wide range of real-world protocols. It is now one of the leading tools in this domain, with a large, active user community spanning both academia and industry.

TAMARIN's foundations are based on decades of research in theoretical computer science, covering topics such as symbolic reasoning, deduction, and equational reasoning. While this book provides a high-level overview of TAMARIN's underlying theory, its emphasis is on applications: how to apply TAMARIN to security problems that matter. In writing this book, our objective is thereby to help both researchers and practitioners to gain a general understanding of how Formal Methods tools like TAMARIN can be used to analyze and improve the quality of real-world security protocols. Moreover, we specifically showcase TAMARIN and provide guidance on its usage. In this sense, this book provides a user manual for TAMARIN. But it goes far beyond that, highlighting TAMARIN's underlying theory and its use in modeling and applications. This includes:

1. How to specify the cryptographic core of protocols in a way amenable to automated reasoning.

2. How to model adversaries who try to defeat the protocol, for example adversaries who control the network and actively spoof messages, malicious insiders, or adversaries that can compromise agents.

3. How to formalize security properties, for example to specify that keys are secrets or that agents have authenticated each other's identity or agree on critical data like cryptographic keys.

4. How to use TAMARIN to analyze protocols, namely to prove that the protocol as specified (1), when running in the adversarial environment (2), satisfies its security properties (3). Alternatively, when the protocol is not secure, to use TAMARIN to find attacks that witness this.

Extended examples are given that illustrate TAMARIN'S use and illuminate those features that are helpful for expert usage.

Intended audience and usage

This book emphasizes practical aspects of security protocol verification. Its intended audience is security researchers and engineers who work with such protocols and wish to learn how to rigorously specify and analyze them. This includes information security students learning about these protocols, industrial practitioners who design their own proprietary protocols, engineers involved in protocol standardization and related activities, and even teams that evaluate protocol designs in some fashion. We have written this book with this diverse audience in mind. As background, we assume some basic knowledge of formal modeling, e.g., modeling systems as state transition systems, as well as applied cryptography and its applications. However, we have kept other prerequisites to a minimum.

This book can be used for teaching, either within a course on security protocols or as part of a more general Information Security course. Parts of the book have been used in both bachelors-level and masters-level courses at European universities including ETH Zürich, Saarland University, and Université de Lorraine. It has also been used for industry courses and self-study. We recommend that self-study readers who are interested in using TAMARIN hands-on should read at least the first four parts of the book, through Chapter 11.

Supplementary material for the book is available online [12]. The TAMARIN tool itself is available for download at https://tamarin-prover.com. The book's website also provides all the TAMARIN input files containing the examples presented in the book as well as other resources including teaching material, slides, problem sets, and worked examples. Most of this material is available under a CC-BY license, enabling re-use as long as the source is attributed.

Finally, TAMARIN not only has an active user community, it also has an active developer community. It is a living system, undergoing evolution and improvement.

This has implications for this book in that there may be minor deviations from what is described here and what the current version of the system supports. For example, there may be improvements to TAMARIN's user interface, whereby TAMARIN's actual output may differ slightly from what is presented here. Or automation support may be improved, leading to new options and commands. While we will work to keep this book up-to-date going forward, for the latest features, the reader may consult TAMARIN's documentation available at the URL https://tamarin-prover.com, mentioned above.

Acknowledgments

Work on TAMARIN has been ongoing for over a decade and has been a truly international effort spanning many countries. Its development started at ETH Zürich as a successor to the Scyther tool, and afterwards additional groups joined at the University of Oxford, the CISPA Helmholtz Center for Information Security, CNRS, Inria, and Université de Lorraine. We would especially like to thank Benedikt Schmidt and Simon Meier for their pioneering work on the theory underlying TAMARIN at the project's start and for building the first implementation, much of which is still in use today.

We also thank the following security researchers and colleagues for their substantial contributions to TAMARIN and its applications: Mathias Aurand-Augier, Deni Begai, Katriel Cohn-Gordon, Yann Colomb, Véronique Cortier, Adrian Dapprich, Alexander Dax, Martin Dehnel-Wild, Stéphanie Delaune, Charles Duménil, Ilkan Esiyok, Sofia Giampietro, Lucca Hirschi, Xenia Hofmeier, Yavor Ivanov, Charlie Jacomme, Robert Künnemann, Elise Klein, Steve Kremer, Felix Linker, Philip Lukert, Kevin Milner, Kevin Morio, Maïwenn Racouchot, Saša Radomirović, Lara Schmid, Christoph Sprenger, Cedric Staub, Wenjia Tang, Hugo Thevenin, Valentin Thiebaux, Yuri Valentin, Jorden Whitefield, Felix Yan, and CISPA's Scientific Engineering team. Moreover, we thank the many members of our groups for their feedback on parts of this book.

Finally we thank Emma Basin, Solvej Basin, Daniel Cremers, Nathalie Cremers, Yen Ha Dang, Alix Dreier, Lilou Dreier, Oscar Dreier, Mathilde Gilbert, Lone Kølvrå Rønberg, Fritz Sasse, and Heidrun Sasse for their emotional and logistical support, and enduring patience during this multi-year project.

Contents

Part I Introduction and Motivation

1 Introduction 3
   1.1 The setting 3
   1.2 Tamarin 5
   1.3 Application domain 9

2 An Example 11
   2.1 A simplified version 11
   2.2 The real deal 14
   2.3 Summary 25

Part II Modeling Foundations

3 Modeling Foundations 29
   3.1 Multi-set rewriting 29
   3.2 Semantics of rules 39

4 Modeling State Machines 43
   4.1 A simple challenge-response protocol 45
   4.2 Further concepts 49

5 Specifying Trace Properties in TAMARIN 53
   5.1 Syntax 54
   5.2 Semantics of trace formulas 56
   5.3 Secrecy on a toy example 57
   5.4 Authentication on the toy example 59
   5.5 Modeling a public key infrastructure 60
   5.6 Simplified Signed Diffie-Hellman Example 60
   5.7 Modeling malicious or compromised agents 62
   5.8 Flavors of secrecy 65

	5.9	A hierarchy of authentication properties 66
	5.10	Additional features for specifying properties 72

Part III The TAMARIN System

6 **A First Glimpse Under the Hood** 81
    6.1 Running TAMARIN 81
    6.2 How TAMARIN works 86
    6.3 How dependency graphs relate to traces 90
    6.4 The constraint-solving algorithm 92
    6.5 Dependency graph visualizations 101
    6.6 Heuristics 104
    6.7 Handling equations 107
    6.8 Adversary deductions 109

7 **Built-in Equational Theories** 121
    7.1 Syntactic built-ins 122
    7.2 Algorithmic built-ins 125

8 **Pre-computation and Deconstructions** 131
    8.1 Pre-computations and sources 131
    8.2 Sources lemmas 135
    8.3 Auto-sources 135
    8.4 Using sources lemmas 136

9 **Lemma Annotations** 141
    9.1 Induction 141
    9.2 Reuse and hiding 144
    9.3 An example: a simple hash chain 145

Part IV Using TAMARIN in Practice

10 **Basic Modeling** 151
    10.1 Modeling with state facts 151
    10.2 Macros and conditional blocks 160
    10.3 Threat modeling 163
    10.4 Channel types 167
    10.5 How do I know my model makes sense? 169

11 **Common Workflows** 171
    11.1 TAMARIN's user interfaces 171
    11.2 Exists-trace lemmas 175
    11.3 Further workflows 177
    11.4 Error messages and solutions 179
    11.5 Guardedness of lemmas 187
    11.6 Termination and memory exhaustion 188

11.7 Extensions and tools 193
11.8 Common questions 193

12 Case Study: 5G-AKA 195
12.1 Overview of 5G-AKA 195
12.2 Modeling 5G-AKA in TAMARIN 199
12.3 Conclusions and general insights 213

Part V Advanced Topics

13 Observational Equivalence 217
13.1 Observational equivalence in TAMARIN 217
13.2 Modeling and analysis workflow 219
13.3 A simple voting protocol 220

14 User-Specified Equational Theories 231
14.1 Subterm-convergent equational theories 231
14.2 Beyond subterm-convergence 232
14.3 Current limitations for equational theories 233

15 Advanced Modeling of Primitives 235
15.1 Digital signature schemes 235
15.2 Other primitives 244

16 Reducing Proof-Construction Time 249
16.1 Changing priorities of facts using label prefixes 249
16.2 Changing priorities using + and - modifiers 250
16.3 Tactics 251
16.4 Oracles 254

17 Analyzing Protocol Families 259
17.1 Noise Protocol Framework 259
17.2 Analysis approach 262
17.3 Example results for Noise 265

Part VI Outlook

18 Impact in Practice 269
18.1 TLS 1.3 269
18.2 5G-AKA 271
18.3 EMV 273
18.4 Summary 276

References 277

Part VII Appendix

19	**Dependency Graph Example**	291
20	**Syntax**	295
21	**Exercises**	305
	21.1 Simple Protocols	305
	21.2 A Large Protocol: PACE	312
	21.3 Solutions	315
Index		319

Part I
Introduction and Motivation

Chapter 1
Introduction

1.1 The setting

Security protocols provide a basis for secure computing in distributed environments. We use them daily, without much thought. For example, we use TLS every time our browser connects securely to a webserver on the Internet or our devices download software updates. We use IPSec to create virtual private networks, SSH for secure remote login, and the Signal, WhatsApp, and iMessage protocols for messaging. Behind the scenes we may be using Kerberos, OpenID Connect, or OAuth2, for single sign-on or access delegation. And when we make payments with our credit cards, perhaps stored on our phone, we are using the EMV protocol of Europay, Mastercard, and Visa.

What these protocols have in common is that they provide services that must meet stringent security requirements, for example, authenticating entities, exchanging secrets, setting up secure channels, or making secure payments. They accomplish this (or so we hope) using cryptography. For this reason, security protocols are also known as cryptographic protocols although, strictly speaking, the class of security protocols is larger, as they may use other means than cryptography to achieve security, for example, security measures in the physical world.

As the above examples suggest, the applications that employ security protocols are often security critical and they must therefore operate correctly. For example, only authorized parties should be able to log in, access resources, or make payments with our credit cards. Unfortunately, security protocols are difficult to get right, and the security community has seen countless protocols proposed and implemented, only to be broken afterwards. Less well known is that many flawed protocols are not "broken" in a technical sense for the simple reason that they lack a clear specification of what they should actually do in the first place!

This last point is critical. Protocols are distributed algorithms and security protocols are, by definition, designed with security objectives in mind. But like many algorithms, they are often implemented in practice without a proper specification of their objectives. Lacking a specification, the question of whether a security protocol achieves its objectives cannot be answered, as the question itself is ill-defined. It is like asking "is this program correct?" without first stating what the program should do.

In addition to the necessity of specifying a security protocol's intended properties, one must also be precise about that protocol's threat model, that is, which kinds of adversaries the protocol should resist. This is critical as one should assume that a security protocol is operated in hostile, adversarial environments, reflecting the sad reality where there are indeed hostile, malicious adversaries out there. Without a specification of what the adversary can do, the question of security is again ill-defined. For example, data on a computer might be secure (e.g., unreadable) against a network adversary when access is protected by a properly functioning Virtual Private Network, but completely insecure against an adversary who can gain physical access to the computer and extract and analyze its hard drive. In the case of security protocols, we typically consider powerful adversaries who can actively interfere with the protocol and who can even corrupt agents, learning their secrets. We will see that even in such cases, it is still possible to achieve some security properties.

Specifying a security protocol, the adversary, and the desired security properties is just the starting point. We ultimately want to know whether the protocol is actually secure in this setting. Note in this regard that testing or simulation is insufficient, as such methods only check whether the protocol satisfies its specification for some *selected* test cases and selected adversary actions. In contrast, security should entail that the property holds for *every* possible execution (or concurrent executions) between agents running the protocol in combination with *any* possible interference from the adversary.

This distinction between the analysis of *some* versus *all* scenarios is significant, and a clever adversary will do everything within its powers to defeat a protocol, including actions that we as testers might not envision. The strongest guarantees come from a rigorous mathematical proof that covers all of the infinitely many possibilities. Alternatively, when the protocol is insecure, we would like to get a counterexample — in the parlance of security, an *attack* — showing why the specified property does not hold. Effectively carrying out this kind of analysis on real-world protocols requires appropriate tool support to handle their complexity.

Let us summarize the above discussion. Figure 1.1 provides an abstract account of this setting. The protocol correctness problem is defined by giving:

1. the description of the protocol, depicted here by Alice and Bob exchanging messages,
2. a threat model describing a class of adversaries against which the protocol should be secure, depicted here by the set of devils, and

1.2 Tamarin

Fig. 1.1: Setting for Security Protocol Verification

3. a specification of the protocol's desired security property, depicted here by the adversary not being able to see, say, a session key that has been set up by the protocol between Alice and Bob and is intended to be confidential.

Given a mathematical formalization of these three things, the objective is to establish the protocol's correctness, depicted in Figure 1.1 by the $\models$ relation. Namely, for all adversaries in the class of adversaries considered, no matter how the adversary interferes with the protocol's runs (depicted by the messages exchanged in the figure), the protocol still has the desired security property. And when this is not the case, we would then like to obtain a counterexample. Tools such as TAMARIN, described next, help us with this analysis task.

1.2 Tamarin

1.2.1 A model-checker based on constraint solving

We start by describing the wider context of Formal Methods tools. Formal Methods is that part of computer science concerned with assigning formal meaning, also called a semantics, to systems, so that one can rigorously reason about their behavior using mathematics and logic. The Formal Methods community has built associated tools that support the specification and analysis of a wide range of systems, from hardware to software. Examples include circuits, sequential programs, concurrent systems, and protocols. In some critical domains where mistakes are particularly costly, such as hardware development, the use of verification tools is not just well established, it now is commonplace [3].

Verification tools are commonly classified as either theorem provers or model checkers. Theorem provers construct explicit proofs using the rules of a formal logic, such as first-order logic or higher-order logic. In contrast, model checkers use algorithms to determine provability and they often return counterexamples when properties are not provable. However, this classification is somewhat rough. TAMARIN, in particular,

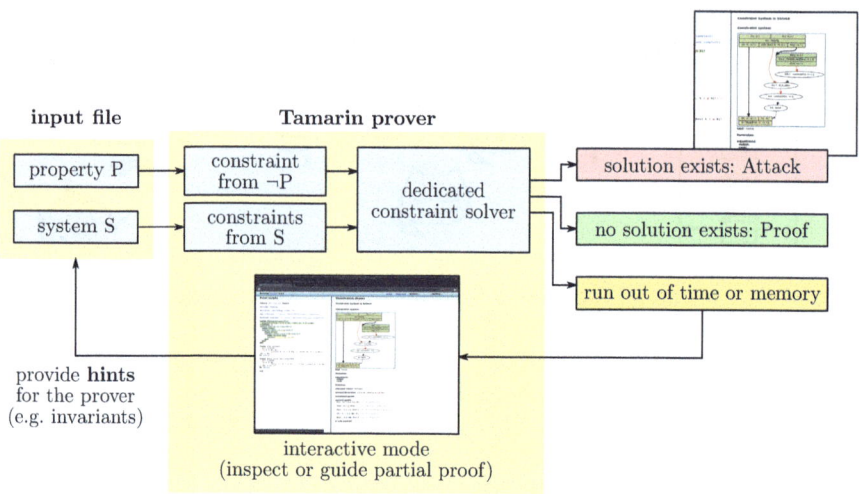

Fig. 1.2: TAMARIN Schematic

both constructs proofs and uses algorithms that help automate proof construction and counterexample finding.

Turning now to TAMARIN, Figure 1.2 illustrates its usage, which is typical for a model-checking tool. TAMARIN takes as input a specification of a system S, which is also known as a *model* as it constitutes a mathematical model of the system. For security protocols, S would comprise both a protocol model and an adversary model. TAMARIN also takes as input a specification of the desired property P. Note that we use the terms specification and model mostly interchangeably as our models constitute behavioral specifications of the protocol and adversary.

At its heart, TAMARIN is a constraint solver that searches for behaviors that are consistent with the system description S and the negation of the property P. These are system behaviors that violate the property and hence represent attacks. As the underlying verification problems are undecidable [62], TAMARIN cannot provide a decision procedure that terminates on all inputs. Hence there are three possible outcomes when running the system, depicted in the figure.

1. TAMARIN finds a behavior satisfying all the constraints. This represents an attack on the protocol.

2. TAMARIN produces a proof that the constraints are inconsistent. This means that there is no possible attack and the protocol is therefore secure. This proof can be produced automatically, or interactively with user support.

3. TAMARIN fails to terminate and so the result is inconclusive. We do not learn which case holds: whether the protocol is secure or there is an attack.

1.2 Tamarin

TAMARIN's underlying proof rules provide a semi-decision procedure for constraint satisfaction. Hence, if there is an attack on the protocol and if TAMARIN were to be run long enough (perhaps with user guidance), then it would terminate with an attack (Case 1). However, in some practical cases, for both falsification (Case 1) and verification (Case 2), TAMARIN may run out of memory or the user may run out of patience and the results are then inconclusive (Case 3). Fortunately, TAMARIN provides means for the user to inspect proof states and influence how proofs are constructed, which can enable, or speed up, termination.

1.2.2 Modeling languages

As explained in Section 1.1, reasoning about a protocol's correctness requires specifying the protocol, the adversary, and the protocol's desired properties. To support this, TAMARIN features two expressive modeling languages. The first is a language for system modeling based on multiset rewriting with equations. This language is Turing-complete and can formalize any system, including its adversaries, that can be modeled as a transition system with a computable transition relation. This is very general and can be used to formalize distributed systems such as protocols where (i) a state of the transition system is a multiset that models the distributed states of each of the protocol participants, the adversary, and the communication channels, and (ii) the transitions model how the state can evolve, e.g., as messages are sent and received by the different participants and the adversary. Moreover, one may specify equational theories, which are useful for formalizing cryptographic operators via equations. For example, for security protocols based on Diffie-Hellman key exchange, one would leverage equations expressing properties about modular exponentiation, such as $(g^x)^y = (g^y)^x$.

TAMARIN has a second modeling language for specifying properties of protocols, based on sorted first-order logic, supporting quantification over time points. This logic is interpreted over the finite traces of the transition system specified using multiset rewriting. One uses it to specify properties like "if the initiator A accepts a session key at some time point (during a run of the protocol) then the adversary has not learned it at any other time point." This logic is expressive and can specify, for example, a wide variety of *safety properties* expressing that nothing bad can ever happen during protocol execution. Hence, in combination with the system modeling language, one can express nuanced notions of security where properties hold even when the adversary is a malicious insider, or can compromise agents in different, precisely defined ways.

TAMARIN also offers an alternative input language for modeling systems through its SAPIC module [34, 79]. This language is based on the applied-Pi calculus [1], however its detailed explanation is beyond the scope of this book.

Finally, TAMARIN can be used to specify a *pair* of systems and to verify that they satisfy a notion of equivalence called *observational equivalence*. This equivalence is useful for expressing security properties such as strong notions of secrecy, privacy properties (e.g., of voting and auctions), and game-based notions such as ciphertext indistinguishability in the symbolic setting. We will describe observational equivalence and its applications further in Chapter 13.

1.2.3 Usage in protocol and system development

TAMARIN is not just a research tool. It has been designed to help engineers build better security protocols and systems. We provide here some general comments on where TAMARIN can be used in the system development process.

TAMARIN's focus is on analyzing designs, not implementations. It is therefore invaluable when *developing* security protocols. In particular, TAMARIN provides protocol designers with a way to analyze their proposed protocols and find and correct any errors during the protocol *design phase*. The tool also supports exploring design options and comparing design alternatives; we will give an example of this in Section 17.1. TAMARIN naturally has an important role to play in the *system verification and validation phase* as its proofs demonstrate that the protocol, as designed, satisfies its specification, no matter what the adversary does, within the adversary's specified capabilities.

We emphasize that TAMARIN provides design-level guarantees, and an implementation may deviate from its design or introduce new errors that adversaries can exploit. Establishing the conformance of implementations to TAMARIN models and, more generally, carrying out code-level verification is outside of this book's scope. However, note that it is possible to use TAMARIN models for these purposes. Namely, one can (1) automatically translate a TAMARIN protocol model into behavioral specifications for the implementations of the different protocol roles and (2) verify implementations of the roles (e.g., clients, servers, etc.) against these specifications as well as verify the absence of other kinds of errors such as memory corruption or the leakage of keys. For details on how this is done in a sound and effective way and examples of applications of this approach, including verifying the official Go implementation of the WireGuard VPN key exchange protocol, we refer the reader to [5].

Finally, TAMARIN, and tools like it, can play an important role in *standardization and certification*. Using TAMARIN necessitates a high degree of specification hygiene in that the protocol, the adversary, and the desired security properties must all be formally documented. The proofs then provide rigorous, mathematical evidence that the properties hold. Indeed, there have been recent proposals [22, 95] that the security protocols standardized by organizations should be accompanied by specifications and machine-checked proofs. In this book, we show how this can be accomplished and also highlight some standards where formal modeling and analysis led to their improvement.

1.3 Application domain

TAMARIN is a general purpose model checker and is not restricted to analyzing security protocols. However this is where its strength lies, given its built-in support for solving constraints that capture possible adversary deductions about cryptographic messages.

TAMARIN has been applied to a wide range of security protocols by users in both academia and industry. Table 1.1 provides an overview of some of the previous applications explored by the TAMARIN community. These include traditional security protocols where Alice and Bob authenticate each other or exchange a session key. But they also go far beyond traditional security protocols and come from diverse problem domains including distance-bounding, e-voting, and secure routing.

Key Exchange	Authentication	Large Case Studies
Naxos [102]	WS-Security [74]	TLS 1.3 [45, 46]
Signed Diffie-Hellman [102]	ACME (Let's Encrypt) [74]	IEEE 802.11 WPA2
Station-to-Station [102]	**Industrial**	(WiFi) [50]
KEA+ [102]	DNP3-SAv5 (Grid) [43]	5G-AKA [23]
IKEv2 [65, 94]	MODBUS [59]	5G handover [96]
Wireguard [56, 67]	OPC-UA [59]	SPDM 1.2 [40, 41]
PQ-Wireguard [71]	**Distance Bounding**	Apple iMessage PQ3 [83]
Noise protocol family [67]	Brands and Chaum [86, 87]	**Non-monotonic global state**
Group protocols	Meadows et al. [86, 87]	Keyserver [88]
GDH [103]	Hancke and Kuhn [86, 87]	Envelope [88]
TAK [103]	Swiss-Knife [86, 87]	Exclusive secrets [88]
(Sig)Joux [103]	Kim and Avoine [86, 87]	Contract signing [79]
STR [103]	**Payment**	TESLA1 [88]
Identity-based KE	EMV (Chip-and-PIN,	PKCS#11 [51, 79]
RYY [103]	contactless) [18, 24, 100]	YubiKey [80]
Scott [103]	**Vehicular**	YubiHSM [80]
Chen-Kudla [103]	V2X revocation [112]	Anonymous Attestation [113]
E-voting (Hyperproperties)	**Secure routing**	TPM 2.0 [111]
Alethea [17]	DRKey (SCION) [47]	**Transparency**
Belenios [9]	**PKI**	KUD/DECIM (incl. global
Bulletin boards [70]	ARPKI (incl. global	state) [115]
Selene [30]	state) [13, 20]	

Table 1.1: Examples of protocols modeled and analyzed using TAMARIN

We will give examples of protocols throughout this book. In Chapter 18 we will also highlight three success stories, describing larger, impactful applications of TAMARIN. These three examples, TLS 1.3, 5G-AKA, and EMV were each developed by some subset of this book's authors together with other colleagues. We emphasize though that there are many other impactful examples, not covered here, by other users who have independently applied TAMARIN to ambitious, large-scale protocols.

These include payment systems [100], e-voting systems [9], and distance-bounding protocols [86].

Chapter 2
An Example

To further motivate TAMARIN's use and to illustrate some of the pitfalls of informal reasoning, let us look at an actual security protocol. We chose a relatively simple protocol for entity authentication where two parties, with the help of a trusted third party, authenticate each other's identity and also establish a shared session key.

Many such protocols have been proposed in the past and the one we selected was proposed as part of an existing standard: ISO/IEC 9798 [21, 72]. This standard was put forth by ISO (the International Organization for Standardization) and IEC (the International Electrotechnical Commission), who jointly provide standards for Information Technology. This standard describes a family of protocols for entity authentication, which are widely used and are even mandated by numerous other standards that require entity authentication as a building block. Examples include the Guidelines on Algorithms Usage and Key Management [64] by the European Committee for Banking Standards and the ITU-T multimedia standard H.235 [73].

Although the protocol we present is relatively simple compared to other modern protocols, it involves numerous options and its correctness is not obvious. Hence we start first with a simplified version of the protocol as a warm up. We also use it to introduce basic notions and syntactic conventions needed for more complex examples.

2.1 A simplified version

Consider a protocol where two agents, call them A and B, who wish to authenticate each other and establish a shared key sesk with the help of a trusted third party called T. In practice T will be a key server who generates session keys for the authenticating parties. We assume that A and B each share a symmetric key with T prior to the protocol's start so they can securely communicate with T. In contrast, we do not assume that A and B share any secrets with each other and the point of the protocol is to establish a session key between them.

As notation, we denote a symmetric key shared between agents A and B by k(A,B). We use the binary function symbol senc to denote symmetric encryption, writing senc(m,k) for the symmetric encryption of the message m with the key k. We use angled brackets to indicate the tupling of messages, e.g, <m1,m2>. However, in some cases, as in the protocol that follows, we will simplify notation by omitting some brackets and just using commas to indicate tupling.

With the above conventions, our simplified protocol can be written in an informal "Alice-and-Bob" notation as follows.

```
1. A -> T: A,B
2. T -> A: senc(<sesk,B>,k(A,T)),
           senc(<sesk,A>,k(B,T))
3. A -> B: senc(<sesk,A>,k(B,T))
```

Before describing what the protocol does, we expand on the notation and associated conventions used. The protocol above is presented in what is often called "Alice-and-Bob" notation as, in the cryptographic folklore, the two parties wishing to establish a key are often named Alice and Bob. However, protocol descriptions generally are intended to describe steps that can be taken by any agents, not just those specifically named Alice and Bob. Hence the protocol description constitutes a template where A and B are variables, effectively denoting *protocol roles*, rather than hard-coded *agent names*. Namely, A is the initiator role, B is the responder role, and T is the trusted third-party role. In reality, agents like Alice, Bob, and Charlie may execute the protocol in multiple sessions, instantiating these variables with their own identities and the identity of their intended partners. Nevertheless, when describing the protocol's steps, we might gloss over these distinctions and write things such as "A sends a message that B receives", whereas what is actually meant is that "the agent playing in the role A sends a message received by the agent playing in the role B."

The above distinction between agents and roles is a potential source of confusion for protocol newcomers. Unfortunately the use of A and B to name both agents (shorthand for Alice and Bob) and roles is now long established in the security protocol literature. It would have been clearer to give the roles more descriptive names like the *initiator role* I, the *responder role* R, the *server role* S, etc. and use different terms, such as alice or a to name the agents, thereby making this distinction readily apparent. We will (for the most part) stick with standard Alice-and-Bob notation, using context to disambiguate whether the role or the agent is intended. Where we wish to make this completely explicit we will use lower-case strings for agent names, like a.

Keeping the above conventions in mind, we now turn to how the protocol is intended to work. We can describe the three steps as follows.

Step 1: A sends T its name and the name of the intended recipient B.

Step 2: T generates a fresh session key sesk. In practice, T would use a pseudorandom number generator to generate this. The details associated with such auxiliary

2.1 A simplified version

steps are, however, often omitted in Alice-and-Bob protocol descriptions. T pairs sesk with B's name in a first message and A's name in a second message and then encrypts these messages with K(A,T) and K(B,T), respectively. T then sends the paired result to A. Upon receiving the pair, A decrypts the first half of the message to check that its communication partner is the same B that A named in Step 1. This check is left implicit in Alice-and-Bob notation: parties generally check the messages they receive against their expectations. No checks can be performed on the second message, as it is ciphertext that A cannot decrypt.

Step 3: A forwards the second message, the ciphertext, to B. B can decrypt this and thereby sees that its communication partner is A. Moreover, B learns the session key sesk, which A learned in the previous step. Hence both parties can use this key to secure future communications.

The above steps are fairly typical for a protocol that uses a trusted third party to set up a session key. A tells T who the two communication partners are (A and B), and T generates messages for both parties containing a session key and protected by encryption using pre-distributed keys (set up prior to the protocol's execution) that A and B share with T. Different variants of this protocol are also possible. For example, T could send the first message to A and the second directly to B. But, as is common practice, both messages are sent to A, who then forwards the second message to B. This second message, which is "opaque" from A's perspective (A cannot decrypt the message, but can forward it) is sometimes called a "ticket" in protocols such as Kerberos. In the end, both parties share the session key sesk. Moreover, the messages that A and B receive each name the intended communication partner with whom sesk should be used.

This protocol appears to be quite straightforward. It is a mutual authentication protocol as both parties, A and B, receive assurances about their communication partner. Moreover, it also sets up a shared session key. We might informally reason about its correctness as follows. Since the messages sent in Step 2 are encrypted using the pre-distributed keys, the session key will only be known by A, B, and T (who is trusted). Of course, an active adversary could change A or B in the message sent at Step 1 since these names are sent in the clear, however A would notice such mischief. If A's name were changed, then T would use the wrong symmetric key in Step 2 and A would be unable to decrypt this message. Moreover, if B's name were changed, then A would see this, as it is contained in the message that A decrypts. Finally, the message B receives, encrypted by the trusted party T, names A, with whom the key is shared. Hence, after the protocol's completion, A and B share a session key and both of them know who their partner is.

Closer examination reveals that the protocol actually has some problems. Neither party has any guarantees that the other party actually has the session key after the protocol has ended. For example, the adversary could hamper availability by intercepting and dropping the third message, preventing B from receiving the session key. Or the adversary could block the second message, preventing A from receiving the key, but sending the second part of it onto B. Moreover, A can be fooled in various ways. For example, the adversary can replay a message from a previous protocol run between A and B in Step 1. As for B, it can be fooled by any party C that runs the protocol with T, claiming to be A; C can just forward the second message in Step 2 to B. B would then end up believing that it shares a key with A, even though A was never involved.

It is unlikely that anyone would use this protocol as it stands in practice. It is too simple and its flaws are open to abuse. The protocol we present next addresses the problems identified above. It introduces mechanisms such as counters and nonces to prevent messages from being replayed. Moreover, both A and B must demonstrate to the other agent that they possess the newly generated session key. Finally, to make the protocol more generally usable, agents may include additional text fields in the messages they send, which can be leveraged in different application-specific contexts.

2.2 The real deal

2.2.1 The ISO-IEC four pass authentication protocol

We now turn to the actual protocol of interest, the *ISO-IEC 9798-1 four pass authentication protocol*. This protocol both improves upon and generalizes the previous protocol. Namely, it adds both replay protection and key confirmation, where each party provides evidence that it possesses the session key. The protocol is also flexible, like a Swiss Army knife with numerous blades. The protocol supports three different mechanisms to provide replay protection. It also includes eight optional text fields that can be used to include application-relevant data in the protocol messages exchanged. We have chosen this protocol as it provides a realistic example of a protocol that might be (and was) proposed by a standardization committee and used in practice. Moreover, it is sufficiently complex so that its analysis is non-obvious, despite being relatively simple for a security protocol.

Figure 2.1 depicts this protocol pictorially as a Message Sequence Chart (MSC) to improve readability. The translation between this notation and Alice-and-Bob notation is straightforward and which notation one prefers is a question of taste. As with Alice-and-Bob notation, keep in mind, when reading it, that this should be understood as a template describing, at a high-level, what steps should be taken by the agents executing in the three protocol roles, named T, A, and B. Indeed, we can think of each role as corresponding to a *state machine*.

The protocol consists of four steps, also called *passes*, where messages are exchanged. These correspond to the arrows in the MSC. Some specialized notation is used to allow for different implementation options. Namely, TVP denotes a time-variant parameter, which may be a sequence number, a random number, or a timestamp. TN denotes either a time stamp or a sequence number. Text refers to a text field, which

2.2 The real deal

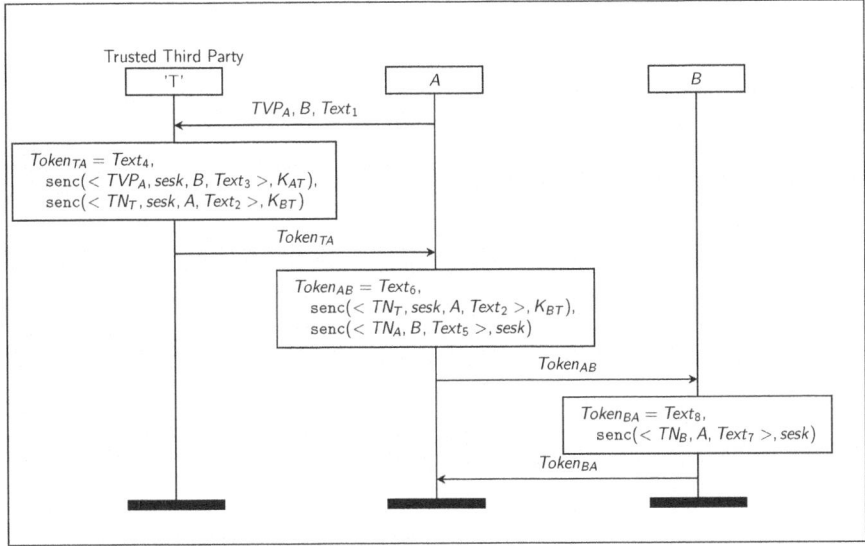

Fig. 2.1: ISO/IEC Four Pass Authentication Protocol

is always optional. The use of text fields is not further specified in the standard. Note too that all of these may be subscripted.

As with the simplified protocol, T generates a shared session key that A and B each receive along with the names of their partner. There are four main differences.

1. In the first step, it is assumed that T gets the initiator A's name from the protocol context. In contrast, we made this explicit in the simplified version. We also make it explicit that the protocol executes with a *single* key server by naming this key server 'T' in the rules, rather than leaving it as a variable, which would allow for arbitrarily many key servers. Note that the quotes around 'T' make it a constant, as we will explain in Section 3.1.2. (Note that the standard does not state whether there can be multiple key servers acting as trusted third parties.)

2. The protocol now includes replay protection. TVP_A is intended to prevent a replay in Step 2 as A can check that the term containing it was recently generated by T. For example, if TVP_A were the nonce sent in Step 1, then A would get its nonce back. Similarly, B has replay protection, as the first message (the ticket) it receives from A in Step 3 contains TN_T. This is either a timestamp or a sequence number; hence B can determine whether it was recently generated (in the former case) or not replayed (in the latter case).

3. The protocol builds in key confirmation whereby each party can confirm that its partner possesses the session key. This is because the last two messages are encrypted with the session key, which necessitates possessing this key to compute the encryption. Hence, when B receives the message in Step 3, it knows that A has

the session key sesk and analogously for A when it receives the message in Step 4. Note that these messages also contain a timestamp or sequence number to prevent their replay.

4. The protocol includes eight optional text fields. Some of these are cryptographically protected. This provides confidentiality and optionally integrity protection, depending on the properties of the encryption function used, in particular whether authenticated encryption is used.

Even to the well-trained eye, the steps taken and the rationale for them appear sensible. However, even for a modestly sized protocol such as this one, considerable care is needed to understand (and even more so to prove) what properties the protocol actually provides and in what contexts it can be safely used. Part of the complexity, which is standard for all security protocols, comes from the difficulty in envisioning all the ways that an adversary can interact with the protocol. Another part comes from the sheer number of variants that arise from different choices of nonces, timestamps, and counters for the TVPs and TNs.

Note that these three mechanisms differ, both in how they work and in their underlying assumptions. For example, nonces require a good random value generator, whereas counters require initialization and resynchronization; in both cases, further details on the mechanism and its requirements are not given in the protocol and can be a source of problems in practice. The mechanisms also differ in the properties they achieve. For example, timestamps can ensure *recentness*: the timestamp can be checked against a clock to determine that the message containing it was recently sent. In contrast, counters and nonces provide no guarantee of recentness as there are no requirements on when messages must be sent. Moreover, nonces are unpredictable, whereas counters and timestamps can be guessed. The standard does not provide a rationale for choosing among these options. Other variants come from the optional text fields, whose use is not prescribed and whose properties are not described.

2.2.2 Properties and adversary model

So what properties does this protocol actually have? The ISO/IEC standard does contain some statements about the intended properties of all protocols in the standard. Namely, the standard states that the goal of an entity authentication protocol is to establish whether the claimant of an identity is in fact who it claims to be. So, in this protocol, the two parties, A and B, should establish each other's identity. Moreover, although it is not stated in the standard, one may also expect that any keys, such as sesk, established during the protocol's execution are intended to be a secret shared between A and B. We interpret these three properties as follows.

Key Secrecy: The session key sesk generated and sent by the key server T to the two parties, is not learned by the adversary.

2.2 The real deal

Authentication for A: the initiator A authenticates the responder B in that if A concludes its role of the protocol, believing that it was running it with B, then B was running the protocol in the responder role and agreed on the same session key sesk.

Authentication for B: this is dual to the last property, namely when the responder B completes its role with some A, then A was running the protocol as the initiator and again there is agreement on the session key.

The standard also states that the given protocols should be resilient to certain kinds of attacks, i.e., they should provide replay attack prevention and reflection attack prevention. We caution against this kind of security specification. There are many kinds of attacks, including those that are as yet unnamed, or not even conceived. Rather than specifying an incomplete list of attacks that should not happen, one should instead specify what constitutes secure behavior, e.g., what it means for one party to authenticate another party or for a key to be secret, formalizations of which are coming shortly. Together with an adversary model, this specifies what the protocol should achieve, no matter what the adversary does, within the specification of the adversary's capabilities.

As for the three properties, the ISO/IEC standard, like many others, leaves some details open to interpretation. So our interpretation of authentication and key secrecy, given above, may differ from what the standard's writers actual intent was. This is a common problem as even basic notions such as authentication are usually underspecified in standards and other protocol documents. In Section 5.9 we will explain, for example, that authentication actually has many different interpretations with varying degrees of strength. In the simplest case, authentication might simply mean that an agent was *alive*, i.e., it took part in the protocol. Alternatively, authentication might have a stronger meaning such as the agent was alive, operating in the intended role, and *agrees* with other agents on protocol-relevant data such as nonces and session keys.

Note that the interpretations that we have given above are more precise than the standard. But nevertheless they are still informal. We will formalize them shortly. Precision is a prerequisite to formality, and usually much of the work involved in formal modeling is in making all aspects of the protocol (the description of the roles, the intended properties, and the assumed adversary) precise.

There are other protocol properties that could be specified, for which the standard is silent. In particular, the specification makes no statements about the properties of the text fields, i.e., their confidentiality or authenticity. In general, when using Formal Methods, a central issue is to work out such details, especially when they are not given by the protocol's designer or, in this case, the standard itself.

A similar challenge is to work out the adversary model. The ISO/IEC standard is completely silent on this point. We will assume for our analysis that the adversary is an active network attacker. For other protocols, we may consider even more powerful adversaries; for example, those that can compromise some of the protocol participants, revealing their keys, or even choosing their keys. Of course, the standard's missing

```
1   theory ISO_IEC
2   begin
3   builtins: symmetric-encryption
4
5   rule Setup:         /* Setup shared keys between $X (variable) */
6     [Fr(~kXT)]        /* and 'T' (fixed trusted server)          */
7     --[]->
8     [!SharedKey($X,'T',~kXT)]
9
10  rule A1:            /* A initiates protocol with T */
11    [Fr(~tvpA), Fr(~text1) ]
12    --[]->
13    [Out(<~tvpA,$B,~text1>),StA1($B,~tvpA)]
14
15  rule T:    /* T receives message from A and responds to A */
16    let m1 = ~text4
17        m2 = senc(<tvpa,~sesK,B,~text3>,kat)
18        m3 = senc(<~tnT,~sesK,A,~text2>,kbt)
19        tokenTA = <m1,m2,m3>
20    in
21    [In(<tvpa,B,txt1>),
22     !SharedKey(A,T,kat),!SharedKey(B,T,kbt),
23     Fr(~text2),Fr(~text3),Fr(~text4),Fr(~sesK),Fr(~tnT)]
24    --[Sent(A,B,~sesK)]->
25    [Out(tokenTA)]
26
27  rule A2:   /* A receives message from T and responds to B */
28    let t2 = senc(<tvpA,sesk,B,text3>,kat)
29        tokenTA  = <t1,t2,t3>
30        m1 = ~text6
31        m2 = t3
32        m3 = senc(<~tnA,B,~text5>,sesk)
33        tokenAB = <m1,m2,m3>
34    in
35    [In(tokenTA),!SharedKey(A,T,kat),
36     StA1(B,tvpA),Fr(~text5),Fr(~text6),Fr(~tnA)]
37    --[ALearns(A,B,sesk)]->
38    [Out(tokenAB),StA2(A,B,~tnA,sesk)]
```

Fig. 2.2: ISO/IEC Protocol (Part 1)

explanation of the intended adversary's capabilities is problematic: if a developer uses this protocol as part of a system where there are stronger adversaries than the one we model, then the properties verified may no longer hold. In general, one should prove protocols secure under the strongest possible adversaries as then they will be secure against any weaker adversary and, hopefully, the real-world adversaries are no stronger.

2.2.3 Protocol formalization

In Figures 2.2 and 2.3, we include the complete specification of the protocol and the three properties we presented. The full specification is also given in **ISO_IEC.spthy**, in the book's supplementary material. We have numbered the lines consecutively over the two figures for ease of reference. When specifying protocols in TAMARIN, there are various options in how one formalizes cryptography and other operations, with

2.2 The real deal

```
39  rule B:  /* B receives message from A and responds to A */
40    let
41        t2 = senc(<tnt,sesk,A,text2>,kbt)
42        t3 = senc(<tna,B,text5>,sesk)
43        tokenAB = <t1,t2,t3>
44        m1 = ~text8
45        m2 = senc(<~tnB,A,~text7>,sesk)
46        tokenBA = <m1,m2>
47    in
48        [In(tokenAB),!SharedKey(B,'T',kbt),
49         Fr(~text7),Fr(~text8),Fr(~tnB)]
50        --[BLearns(A,B,sesk)]->
51        [Out(tokenBA)]
52
53  rule A3:  /* A receives response from B */
54    let
55        t2 = senc(<tnb,A,text7>,sesk)
56        tokenBA = <t1,t2>
57    in
58        [In(tokenBA),StA2(A,B,tna,sesk)]
59        --[Done(A,B,sesk)]->
60        []
61
62  lemma secrecy:
63    "All a b k #i. Sent(a,b,k)@i ==> not (Ex #j. K(k)@j)"
64
65  lemma AauthenticatesB:
66    "All a b k #i. Done(a,b,k)@i ==> Ex #j. BLearns(a,b,k)@j"
67
68  lemma BauthenticatesA:
69    "All a b k #i. BLearns(a,b,k)@i ==> Ex #j. ALearns(a,b,k)@j"
70  end
```

Fig. 2.3: ISO/IEC Protocol (Part 2)

each option leveraging different language features. Here we select one set of options and provide just high-level intuition on how we formalize the protocol steps depicted in Figure 2.1. Other options in formalizing protocols and other TAMARIN features will be described in due time.

In the specification's first three lines, we name our model ISO_IEC. We also state that it uses TAMARIN's built-in modeling support for symmetric encryption, where the encryption of the message m with the key k is written senc(m,k).

Lines 5-60 contain multiset rewriting rules formalizing how the protocol's global system state can evolve during execution. Recall that the system states are represented by multisets, which generalize sets by allowing elements to occur multiple times. For system states, the multisets' elements are *facts*, where a fact is a predicate symbol applied to zero or more terms. A fact represents part of the (global) system state. For example, the fact Out(token) models that the message token is output that has been sent to the network by some agent, whereas the fact In(token) models that token is available on the network as input to be read by some agent.

The Setup rule models the protocol's setup assumptions. Namely, symmetric keys have been set up (out-of-band) between parties X and a (fixed) key server 'T'. Specifically the left-hand side on Line 6 formalizes what conditions must hold for the rule to fire. Here kXT must be a freshly generated key, recorded in the system state.[1] The rule's right-hand side (Line 8) formalizes the effect of firing the rule. Namely, the fact SharedKey(A,'T',kXT) is added to the state, thereby recording that kXT is a key shared between X and 'T'.

To help understand TAMARIN's rules, we make a brief diversion on how rules are applied; see Chapter 3 for the full story. First, a rule's left-hand side is a multiset of facts that represent the conditions that must hold for the rule to fire. Namely, this multiset must match some subset of facts in the system state. When the rule fires, each fact on the left-hand side is removed from the multiset (unless the fact is prefaced by the ! symbol, indicating that it persists after rule application), and the instances of the facts on the rule's right-hand side are added to the system state. This leads to a transition that updates the system state.

Second, the two sides of the rule are separated by an arrow, which itself is labeled with a multiset of *actions*. In this rule, the arrow on Line 7 is labeled with the empty multiset of actions. Actions are like facts in that they are built from predicates applied to terms. However, rather than representing parts of the global state, they instead model actions taken by agents or taken during the protocol's set up. Actions thereby play a role analogous to labels in labeled transition systems and, as we see in section 2.2.4, they are used for property specification.

A final point is that fresh facts are handled specially in TAMARIN. Namely, TAMARIN has a built-in rule that can always fire (there are no conditions on its left-hand side) and generates new, fresh terms, adding them to the global state. This means that there is an unbounded supply of different values that can be used by protocol participants when they require them, e.g., for nonces or keys. Hence the Setup rule can always fire and set up symmetric keys between arbitrarily many agents $X (including the agents A and B) and the fixed keyserver 'T'.

We now turn to the remaining five rules. These directly describe the actions taken in the Message Sequence Chart in Figure 2.1. They are named to specify the sequences of actions taken by each of the three agents in their role. The first of these rules, A1, formulates the first step that A takes: for a fresh time-value parameter tvpA and some arbitrary text message text1, a message is sent out to the network containing the 3-tuple <tvpA,B,text1>, intended for the communication partner B. The rule also models that the agent taking this step records in its local state that tvpA was generated for B, with the fact StA1(B,tvpA).

Note in the above rule that we model the text message text1 as being freshly generated, reflecting that it is an arbitrary message. As the standard does not describe how this (or any other) text field is used, we simply make it an arbitrary term. As no tests are performed on it, by either party, we do not even bother to save it in the agent's state. This is a modeling decision, providing an interpretation of the standard's

---

[1] We gloss over annotations on terms and predicates such as ~, $, and !, which indicate that a value is freshly generated, a constant is publicly known (i.e., known to all parties), and that a fact persists after rule application. These annotations will be explained in detail later.

2.2 The real deal

underspecification on how text fields are to be handled. The text fields could be modeled in other ways, e.g., as known strings that serve as labels and are checked by the messages' recipients. However, this interpretation would change the protocol's semantics and would go beyond what is described by the standard and what might be found in some standards-conform implementations.

The rule T models the step taken by the trusted third party 'T'. Namely, 'T' receives as input the 3-tuple of messages sent by A (or the adversary). Afterwards, 'T' builds two encrypted messages, the first for A and the second, which is the ticket (see the explanation in Section 2.2.1), for B. To construct these messages, 'T' uses the keys associated with these agents by sharedKey facts. 'T' finally constructs, and sends, an output message, which is again a 3-tuple: a text text4 and the two encrypted messages, matched with m1, m2, and m3, respectively.

In this rule, we use pattern matching, In(<tvpa,B,txt1>), to decompose messages and let bindings to make local definitions. This simplifies our specification of the constructed messages. It is important to note that all variables occurring in the constructed messages are bound on the left-hand side of the rule, when checking the conditions for the rule to fire. For example, the appropriate keys for the parties A and B are fixed by the two SharedKey facts in the left-hand side of the rule, when they are applied to the system state. This rule has an action fact Sent(A,B,sesk) that records (in the system trace) that, when this rule is fired, a session key sesK was generated by the key server intended to be used between the protocol initiator A and the responder B.

The rule A2 describes A's second step. A receives the 3-tuple of messages from 'T' (or the adversary). A then decrypts the 2nd message from this 3-tuple, extracting its contents, which includes the session key sesk. Note that we use pattern matching in TAMARIN to perform this decryption: t2 must match an encrypted term of form senc(<tvpA,sesK,B,text3>,kat), where the fact SharedKey(A,T,kat) is required for the rule to fire. This models that A shares the key kat with 'T', and A can therefore decrypt this message. Afterwards, A builds the response message, which includes the ticket and a message encrypted with the session key sesk that contains tnA (which is a timestamp or nonce) and the name of the intended partner B. A records in the state that its partner B should learn both tnA and sesk. The rule's action records that the initiator A learns a session key sesk intended to be shared with the responder B.

The rule named B in Figure 2.3 describes B's one and only step. Namely B receives the 3-tuple of messages from A (or the adversary), decomposes it into its three parts, and crafts a response, which is a pair of a text text8 and a message that contains a new timestamp or nonce tnB. The rule's action records that the responder B learns a session key, sesk, that should (already) be shared with the initiator A.

The final rule, A3, formalizes A's receipt of this last message. A decrypts this with the session key, thereby completing its role of the protocol. The rule's action records the protocol's completion.

2.2.4 Property formalization

The final part of the theory file, given in Lines 62–70 in Figure 2.3, formalizes the properties that we expect the protocol to satisfy, namely the three properties informally described in Section 2.2.2. These properties state that each agent authenticates its intended partner and that the session key is secret. Each property is given as a *lemma*, reflecting that TAMARIN should be used to prove it.

Recall that properties are given as formulas that are interpreted over the model's traces. These traces are incrementally constructed, where each rule's application extends the trace with an instance of the actions that label the applied rule. For example, when the multiset rewriting rule T is applied, the trace is extended with the action Sent(a,b,k), for some a, b, and k, indicating that the trusted server 'T' generated the key k, intended to be shared by the initiator a and the responder b.[2] Moreover, the trace also contains actions recording those terms t that the adversary *knows*, which is modeled by the fact K(t). TAMARIN has built-in support for reasoning about the adversaries' knowledge: the adversary knows some term t either because it was sent by some agent over the network (i.e., Out(t)), or it can be constructed by the adversary from other messages that were previously sent. Section 6.8 contains more details on this point.

With the above at hand, we turn to our first property, key secrecy. It is formalized as whenever we have Sent(a,b,k) at some position i in a trace, then we do not have K(k) at some position j. Here the values a, b, and k are arbitrary and they can therefore match the terms contained in any Sent-action occurring in the trace. Said less technically, the lemma secrecy states that whenever the key server generates a key k intended to be shared between the initiator and the responder, the adversary does not learn this key.

The second and third properties proven are examples of *correspondence properties*, which formulate a correspondence between events in the trace. Namely, they state that when one party has completed its role in the protocol, then the other party was also executing its role, and the two parties agree on relevant data. The relevant data here is the partner's identity and the session key.

In more detail, the second property, AauthenticatesB states that when an initiator a finishes its role (corresponding to the rule A3, which generates the Done event) believing that it shares the key k with the communication partner b, then b was executing its step of the protocol (producing the BLearns event), believing it was talking with a and sharing the same session key k. Intuitively, this states that the protocol's initiator a, upon completing its role, draws the right conclusions about its communication partner and their shared secret. Analogously BauthenticatesA states that, for the agent b in the protocol's responder role, the conclusions that b

---

[2] Here we use lower-case variables, like a, to emphasize that these are agent names, not roles. As they are universally quantified, they may be instantiated by any agent. Recall the discussion about roles versus names, and naming conventions in Section 2.1

2.2 The real deal

draws about the agent a in the initiator role are correct. That is, if b concludes its role (generating the event Blearns) believing that it is speaking with a and sharing the key k, then a is executing its role, believing it is speaking with b and sharing the same key k.

2.2.5 Analysis

We use TAMARIN to analyze all three lemmas, either proving them or finding counterexamples.

TAMARIN proves the secrecy lemma automatically. The proof of this lemma requires first stating and proving an auxiliary lemma, which can be done automatically using TAMARIN's autoprove strategy with auto-sources. The use of auxiliary lemmas and the automated construction of a useful class of lemmas (called sources lemmas) is explained in Section 8.3.

In contrast to secrecy, the two authentication lemmas AauthenticatesB and BAuthenticatesA are false and for each of these lemmas TAMARIN automatically discovers attacks. In Figure 2.4 we illustrate the attack TAMARIN found on the property AauthenticatesB, depicting it as a Message Sequence Chart. The translation from TAMARIN's output, which is given as a *dependency graph*, to a Message Sequence Chart, will be described in Section 6.5; we have included the dependency graph for this attack in Chapter 19 but suggest the reader consults it only after reading Section 6.5.

The attack TAMARIN finds on AauthenticatesB is sometimes called an "Alice talks to Alice attack." It represents the case where an agent, say a, plays in multiple protocol roles: here the initiator role and the responder role. (Recall the distinction between agent names and roles, discussed in Section 2.1.) The attack arises as part of a's message from its second step (Rule A2) is directly reflected back to a in its third step (Rule A3) without any party, including a, having executed in the B-role (Rule B). Hence there is a Done event without a corresponding BLearns event. This can be seen in the corresponding dependency graph produced by TAMARIN, depicted in Figure 19.1 in Chapter 19.

Whether an agent can actually play in multiple roles will depend on both the protocol and how it is used in practice. For many protocols, this flexibility is possible and desirable. For example, in an authentication protocol, an agent a may authenticate other agents, i.e., agent a may play in the initiator role and also be authenticated by other agents, i.e., play in the responder role. Moreover, whereas a human agent is unlikely to want to authenticate herself, the agents performing authentication are often software components implementing some services. One can envision use cases where an agent may use different services with the same identity and these services wish to authenticate each other, whereby instances of Alice will talk to other instances of Alice. In any case, security protocols such as those for entity authentication are designed to be general so they can be used in many contexts. If contexts like those where Alice talks to Alice are not intended to be supported, then this restriction should be explicitly part of the protocol specification. This was not the case for the ISO/IEC protocol. If it were, we would then include this restriction in the model (we will see in Section 5.10.2 how we could prevent such scenarios using trace restrictions) that we would subject to analysis.

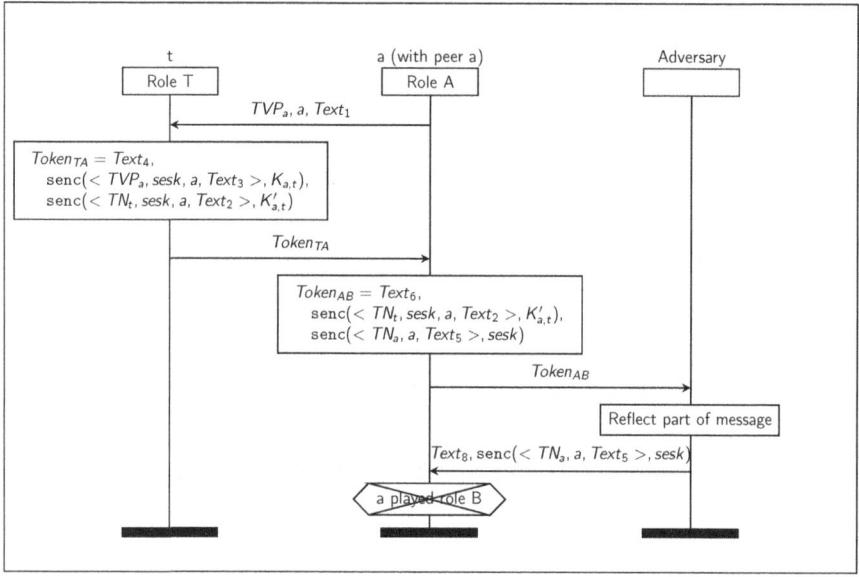

Fig. 2.4: Attack on Property AauthenticatesB. The crossed-out hexagon denotes that an expected property is not met. After a completes the A role with its assumed partner a, one would expect that there was an instance of a performing the B role, but this is not the case.

In Figure 2.5 we illustrate the attack on the second authenticity property BauthenticatesA. This attack is more subtle than the previous one and exemplifies the kind of attack that designers often overlook. Although it is not an Alice talks to Alice attack, it does exploit that an agent can be an initiator in one protocol run and a responder in another. The essence of the attack is the responder is fooled about the identity of the initiator. Namely, there are two different agents, named d and c, and c starts the protocol as the initiator with d in the responder role. In the last message in the MSC, c receives a message that tricks it into believing that it is involved in a (separate) protocol run, playing in the responder role, where d is the initiator. The agent c has been fooled, as d never initiated a protocol run with him.

This attack works because the message that agent c received is of the correct form to be received in the responder role. It is constructed (here, by the adversary) from two previous messages (one from t's response and the other from d's response) and

2.3 Summary

contains a ticket encrypted for c together with a message encrypted with the session key contained in the ticket. Hence, after receiving this message and responding to it, c concludes that it has just played in the responder role (which is just this one protocol step) with the agent d. However, the correspondence property fails as d had not played in the initiator role. Figure 19.2 shows TAMARIN's dependency graph, witnessing this attack.

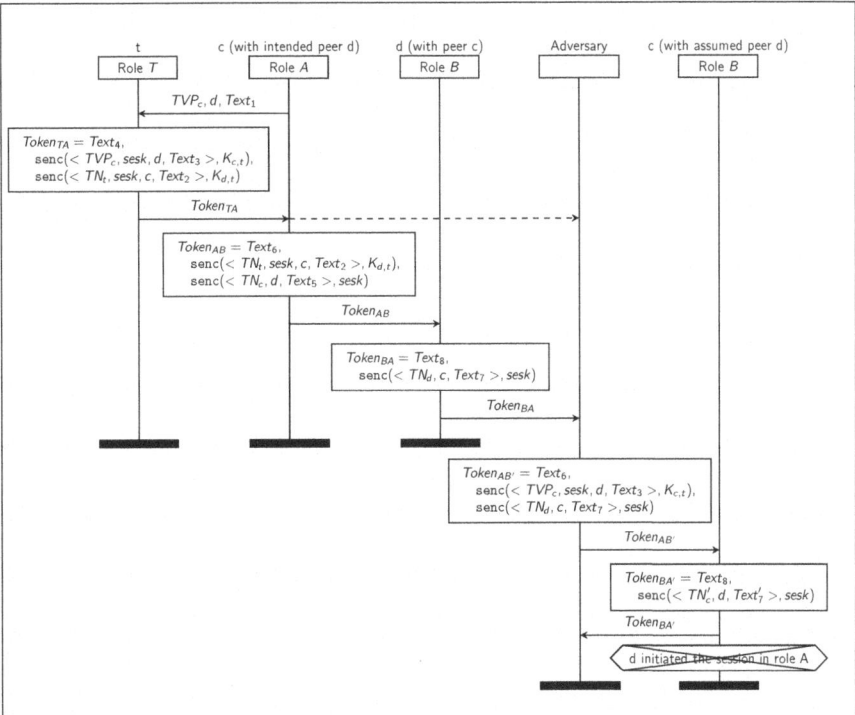

Fig. 2.5: Attack on Property BauthenticatesA. The crossed-out hexagon denotes, as before, the violated property, and the dashed line denotes the adversary eavesdropping on the token.

2.3 Summary

We have used the ISO-IEC four pass authentication protocol to give a first impression of how TAMARIN is used. Although the protocol itself is relatively simple, the possible behaviors it gives rise to in the presence of a network adversary are exceedingly subtle. And finding subtle corner cases representing attacks is precisely where TAMARIN excels. Moreover, when the intended property does hold, one gets a proof of that.

Our explanations were at a high level. In subsequent chapters, we will delve into the details. We will also later present more significant examples.

Part II
Modeling Foundations

Chapter 3
Foundations of Protocol Modeling in TAMARIN

TAMARIN's language and algorithms for constructing proofs build on research in both term rewriting and order-sorted equational logic. Our focus in this book is however practically oriented: using TAMARIN to reason about security protocols rather than explaining this underlying theory. Nevertheless, some knowledge of these foundations is helpful for specifying protocols and understanding how to interact with TAMARIN. General background on these topics may be found in the book on term rewriting by [6] and the survey on order-sorted logic and computation by [104].

3.1 Protocol modeling with multi-set rewriting

In the appendix, Chapter 20, we provide the syntax of security protocol theories in TAMARIN. Here we start with a high-level overview, before explaining the individual parts in this chapter and subsequent ones.

As we saw in the introduction, to model a protocol in TAMARIN's input language, we specify the state machines for the protocol's different roles as well as for the adversary. These specifications (along with some additional transition rules we will meet shortly) together define a single global transition system. The state of this system models, for example, the "local" states of the parties executing runs of the protocol's role state machines, the adversary's state, and the state of the communication network. The system's transitions correspond, for example, to a party performing a step in a role's state machine or to the adversary constructing a message.

In reality, the parties that run a protocol like TLS do not run a single instance of a state machine for their role: they can run multiple instances of these machines concurrently, and we refer to each such state machine run as a *thread*. For example, when Alice uses a web browser in the Internet, her browser may use the TLS protocol to connect on her behalf to multiple servers concurrently for multiple services and tabs. Moreover, even when communicating with a single server, multiple threads of the "client" role may be running concurrently. Similarly, the server can be running many threads corresponding to instances of the "server" role concurrently, with any number of parties. To reflect these real-world situations, we typically model that each party can be running an arbitrary number of instances of the protocol's roles. In order to keep track of the state of each of these threads, we typically assign a unique thread identifier to each of them.

We specify the system's transitions using *multiset rewriting rules*. Consider, for example, the following rule.

```
[ State(~threadID, $A, 'Waiting'), In(msg) ]
--[ ReceivedMessage($A, msg) ]->
[ State(~threadID, $A, 'Done') ]
```

This rule models the situation where there is a protocol thread, identified by ~threadID, for some party $A, that is in a Waiting state. Upon receiving a message msg from the network, the thread can transition to the Done state, logging the transition as ReceivedMessage($A, msg).

TAMARIN has a set of built-in rules. These rules specify an adversary who controls the network and they also include a rule for generating fresh values. TAMARIN's users additionally provide their own rules to specify the protocol under consideration and, optionally, additional adversary capabilities.

More formally, TAMARIN uses three kinds of syntactic categories to specify the transition system:

- **Terms** that represent protocol messages, bitstrings, or variables.
- **Facts** that are used for two purposes.
  1. Facts are used to record information in the transition system's current state and to perform checks against such information. Examples include State(...) for active threads and In(...) and Out(...) for input and output to the adversary-controlled network, modeling asynchronous communication (see also Section 3.1.8).
  2. Facts can log performed actions, such as ReceivedMessage(...), that are relevant for property specification.
- **Rules** that model the transition system's possible transitions.

We discuss each of these categories in turn below.

3.1.1 Symbolic modeling

A central question is how to represent the messages manipulated by and communicated in protocols. Although, in reality, the messages are bitstrings in a computer's memory or transmitted over a network, we work with a term-based representation of these strings where the terms represent how the bitstrings are constructed by applying cryptographic functions to data. This is in the tradition of early work on building

3.1 Multi-set rewriting

methods and tools for security protocol analysis [54, 92]. Working with terms rather than bitstrings provides a higher-level of abstraction for the messages that protocols manipulate, which allows analysis methods to scale. Moreover, it means that we can directly leverage results from the domains of term-rewriting, equational reasoning, and unification.

For example, we represent the application of a hash function H to a constant string not as the concrete bitstring that would result from applying a given hash function to the string, but rather as a term like H('Hello World'). Similarly, we represent the symmetric encryption of a message m with some key k as the term senc(m, k).

This use of terms to represent cryptographic messages is often called the *symbolic model* of cryptography [2] as it represents the bitstrings that are manipulated in cryptography by terms in a term algebra. Additionally, since terms may contain variables, we can reason symbolically about classes of messages rather than considering each concrete instantiation. Note that an alternative to the symbolic model is to use a cryptographic model, where messages are represented as bitstrings and the adversary is modeled as a probabilistic polynomial time Turing machine [2, 10]. Such models are substantially lower-level than their symbolic counterparts, which enables one to reason about details like message and key length, but at the cost of significantly increased complexity in both formalization and proofs.

Note that security protocols often work with randomly generated values. These values play a crucial role in many security protocols and are used to generate keys, challenges, and nonces ("Numbers Used Once"). In the symbolic model, we do not reason *probabilistically* about such values and the adversary's knowledge of them but rather *possibilistically*. Namely, bitstrings are either known to the adversary (or it is possible for the adversary to efficiently learn them from other messages that the adversary has seen) or else they are randomly drawn from a large space such that the adversary cannot efficiently guess or brute-force their value.[1]

3.1.2 Terms

TAMARIN allows users to define their own language of terms that are manipulated by the protocols they define. The set of function symbols and constants that are used to construct terms are determined by a *signature*. TAMARIN also employs a very simple typing discipline using *sorts*, which are a simple kind of types, to distinguish between different kinds of data. We describe this below.

Messages are modeled as terms in an *order-sorted term algebra* [104]. Sorts denote sets of terms, whereby every term has a sort. Order-sorted refers to an ordering on

---

[1] For cryptographers: negligible events, such as guessing a random value from a large space, are modeled as being impossible in symbolic models. Moreover, any non-negligible event becomes a possibility, independent of the concrete probability.

sorts corresponding to a subsort ordering, where sort B is a subsort of sort A means that every term of sort B is also of sort A.

TAMARIN's sorting discipline for terms is very simple: we have a top sort *msg* and two incomparable subsorts *fr* and *pub* of the top sort. For the two subsorts, we assume there are two countably infinite sets of values. The first set is the set of **fresh values**, which model freshly generated random values, keys, or nonces, which we consider to be unguessable by the adversary. The second set is the set of **public constants**, which model known or guessable constants such as agent identities, which the adversary can know. Public constants are written as text strings enclosed in single quotes, such as 'Hello World' or 'label1'. For more details about how public constants are used in practice see Section 10.1.3.

We also assume the existence of a countably infinite set of **Variables** for each sort. Variables have names that are unquoted text strings, like myVar3, and are optionally preceded by a type declaration. Note that variables do not have a global scope: the variables in a multiset rewriting rule are local to that rule. Hence when a variable is instantiated during a rule's application, as explained shortly, this instantiation has no effect on variables in other rules that happen to have the same name or on other instantiations of the same rule.

There are two basic declarations that fix a variable's sort. Variables without an explicit type declaration are of the generic top sort *msg*, and can therefore be instantiated with any term. **Public variables** are variables prefixed with a dollar sign ($). These variables are of sort *pub* and they can only be instantiated with elements of the set of public constants, which are known to the adversary. We use this, for example, for variables that are always instantiated with agent identities, like $C or $S, which respectively represent arbitrary client or server names. In contrast, **fresh variables** are variables prefixed with a tilde (~). These variables are of sort *fr*, and they can only be instantiated with elements from the set of fresh values, representing randomly generated values, nonces, or keys; e.g., ~v, ~clientNonce, or ~sessionKey.

Function symbols model the application of publicly known functions or algorithms. Functions have a name and an arity, which is the expected number of arguments. Note that all function symbols work on the top-level sort of *msg*, i.e., all their arguments are of top sort, as is their result. Thus, when declaring functions, simply specifying their arity suffices; in particular an explicit sort for the function's arguments or result is not needed. For example, a hash function H of arity 1 can be declared as follows.

```
functions: H/1
```

The set of such declarations constitutes the signature that TAMARIN uses to determine which terms are well-formed. Note that functions, so declared, are *abstract functions*. They are simply given a name, an arity, and some of their properties may be subsequently specified via equations and reasoned about using those equations. However, we do not specify a concrete realization of them, for example, a specific cryptographic hash like SHA-1 for the above declaration H.

3.1 Multi-set rewriting

Some frequently used function symbols such as (nested) `pair` have abbreviations: `<a,b,c>` is a shorthand for `pair(a,pair(b,c))`. Another example of a function is symmetric encryption: to encrypt a message `<m, ~n>` with a key k, we define the function symbol senc of arity 2 and write `senc( <m, ~n>, k )`.

Note that by default, function symbols are considered to be bijective and one-way: if the adversary knows `f(X)`, this does not mean it can infer X. We will see in section 3.1.4 how to define function symbols with other properties. Note too that public variables and fresh variables can only be instantiated with elements from their corresponding base sets, and therefore do not contain any function symbols.

By default, the adversary can use all functions to construct new terms. It is possible to introduce so-called *private* function symbols. Such functions can be used in rules, but the adversary cannot use them to construct terms. Private function symbols are declared with their arity, and the `[private]` annotation. For example

```
functions: secret/1 [private]
```

creates a function symbol named `secret` taking one argument, and which the adversary cannot use to construct terms.

Terms are built from fresh values, public constants, variables, and function symbols.

Example 1 (Term) Consider the following term:

`senc( < $C, ~nC, 'hello' >, ~k )`

This term contains the following basic terms:

- `$C`: a public variable that can be instantiated with any public constant.
- `~nC`: a fresh variable that can be instantiated with any fresh value.
- `'hello'`: a public constant.
- `~k`: a fresh variable that can be instantiated with any fresh value.

From these basic terms, a nested pair is constructed by pairing three terms to get `pair($C, pair(~nC, 'hello'))`, which is equivalent to `<$C, ~nC, 'hello'>`. The function symbol senc models symmetric encryption, and has arity two. Its first argument is the message and its second argument is the key. In the above term, the nested pair is used as the message and `~k` is used as the key.

Messages are terms that are *ground*, meaning that they do not contain any variables.

3.1.3 Substitutions

Substitutions are functions from variables to terms that are homomorphically extended to functions on terms. We write $t\sigma$ to denote applying the substitution σ to the term t. This application replaces each variable x in t by the term $x\sigma$.

Example 2 (Term substitution) Consider the variables v and w, the term t = <v,H(<w,v>)>, and the substitution

$$\sigma = \{v \mapsto \text{<x,\$B>}, w \mapsto \text{H(\textasciitilde nA)}\}.$$

We then have

$$w\sigma = \text{H(\textasciitilde nA)}$$

and

$$t\sigma = <\ \text{<x,\$B>},\ \text{H(\ <H(\textasciitilde nA)},\ \text{<x,\$B>}\ >\ )\ >.$$

3.1.4 Term equality and equational theories

A TAMARIN specification typically contains a set of equations that define an *equational theory* [6, 91], which specifies when two terms may be considered equal.[2] By default, the equal sign (=) in TAMARIN denotes equality with respect to the given equational theory. Note that this use of equality should not be confused with assignment as found in imperative programming languages.

Without equational theories, we are simply specifying a free term algebra, which is where two terms are equal if and only if they are syntactically identical. For example, without an equational theory, H(x) is never equal to G(y), no matter how we instantiate the variables x and y. Intuitively, unless the specified equations say otherwise, function symbols behave like "one-way" or "non-invertible" functions: F(G(x)) cannot be equal to x since these two terms are syntactically different. Moreover, function symbols behave as if they were injective: if x is not equal to y, then G(x) cannot be equal to G(y).

This interpretation is too strict for some functions and for a more accurate model equational theories are needed. For example, when modeling encryption we would specify an encryption algorithm with function symbols for the encryption and the corresponding decryption algorithm. We would then use equations to specify the relationship between these algorithms: the decryption of an encrypted ciphertext using the appropriate decryption key yields the original plaintext (see equations below). This relationship between decryption, encryption, and the encryption key is not captured by the free term algebra.

Example 3 (Built-in equational theory for symmetric encryption) To model symmetric encryption, we use two function symbols of arity two, senc and sdec, to respectively

---

[2] Formally, a set of equation $\mathcal{E}$, together with a set of terms $\mathcal{T}$, defines an equational theory as the set of equations that can be derived from rules formalizing that equality is a congruence relation (reflexive, symmetric, transitive, and a congruence) as well as closing up under all substitution instances of equations, replacing variables by terms in $\mathcal{T}$ [78]. When no confusion can arise, we will use the term *equational theory* both to refer the set of equations $\mathcal{E}$ and the equational theory it defines.

3.1 Multi-set rewriting

model encryption and decryption. We then use the following equation to express that decrypting an encryption with the same key yields the original plaintext:

$$\text{sdec(senc(m, k), k)} = \text{m}.$$

The next example presents TAMARIN's built-in modeling of Diffie-Hellman style exponentiation.

Example 4 (Built-in equational theory for Diffie-Hellman) To model Diffie-Hellman exponentiation in a prime order group, we use five reserved symbols: ^ for modular exponentiation, * for the multiplication of exponents, 1 for the identity with respect to multiplication, DH_neutral for the identity as base with respect to exponentiation, and inv for the inverse. The equational theory for these symbols is defined as follows.

$$
\begin{aligned}
(x\hat{\ }y)\hat{\ }z &= x\hat{\ }(y\hat{\ }z) \\
\text{DH\_neutral}\hat{\ }x &= \text{DH\_neutral} \\
x*(y*z) &= (x*y)*z \\
x\hat{\ }1 &= x \\
x*1 &= x \\
x*y &= y*x \\
x*\text{inv}(x) &= 1
\end{aligned}
$$

For more details on TAMARIN's built-in equational theories, see Chapter 7. For specifying your own equational theories, please see Chapter 14.

3.1.5 Facts

The terms from the previous section are used to model messages. We turn next to the syntactic we use to model system transitions.

We define the state of the global transition system as a multiset of **facts**. A multiset (sometimes also called a "bag") is simply a set whose members may occur multiple times. Each fact in the multiset is built from a fact symbol applied to zero or more terms. Except for a few built-in fact symbols, explained next, facts are user-defined and their meaning is given by their use in the protocol specification.

Informally, we can consider facts as playing a role analogous to sticky notes posted on a refrigerator. Namely, they keep track of the current state of our transition system, where the note's title is the fact name, and the note's content is a sequence of terms.

For example, consider modeling an initiator process that consists of several steps, like sending a message, receiving a message, and sending a follow-up message. We could use a fact Initiator(ThreadID, 'state_2', AgentID, m) to represent that there exists a thread with identifier ThreadID of an agent AgentID that performs the initiator role (encoded as the fact name), and whose thread is at state_2 after receiving a message m. As a second example, we may want to define a fact KeyPair(AgentID,privateKey,publicKey) to represent that an asymmetric key pair has been generated for the agent AgentID.

TAMARIN has several built-in fact symbols:

- K/1: K(t) is used to check whether the adversary can derive the term t,
- In/1: In(t) represents that t was received from the (adversary controlled) network,
- Out/1: Out(t) represents that t was sent to the network, and
- Fr/1: Fr(t) represents that t was freshly generated.

Additionally there are the reserved facts KU/1 and KD/1 that are used internally by TAMARIN (both are refinements of K, and are used in TAMARIN's search algorithm). We will return to them in Section 6.8.

3.1.6 Linear and persistent facts

As we will see in the next section, system transitions consume facts from the state and produce (other) facts.

We differentiate between two types of facts.

- **Linear facts** are those facts whose names do not start with an exclamation mark (!). These facts can be removed from the state by transitions, e.g., Initiator(ThreadID,...).
- **Persistent facts** are those facts whose names start with an exclamation mark (!), e.g., !LongTermKey($A,...). These facts are never removed from the state, but are only "read" in the sense that they can occur on the left-hand side of a multiset rewriting rules and are not consumed when the rule fires.

In practice, we will mostly use linear facts. We will use persistent facts for the long-term storage of data, such as long-term keys in a public key infrastructure.

3.1.7 Rules

A transition system in TAMARIN is specified by a set of *multiset rewriting rules*, provided in a TAMARIN input file. These rules have the form

[L]--[A]->[R],

where L stands for "left-hand side", R stands for "right-hand side", and A stands for "observable logged actions". Here, L, A, and R are each multisets of facts. Note that we omit the surrounding multiset brackets because the rule notation already includes

3.1 Multi-set rewriting

square brackets. Note that multiset rewrite rules have a single premise and conclusion, each of which are a multiset of facts. For simplicity, however, we will often call the premise facts simply premises and the same for the conclusion facts.

We will ignore the actions A for now: the main purpose for these facts is to serve as the "glue" between the transition system and the property specification language. We will return to them in Chapter 5 when we introduce the property specification language.

Note that when A is the empty multiset, we omit the middle square brackets and simply write

[L]-->[R].

Intuitively, rules specify transitions as follows: if there exists an instantiation of the facts in L in the current state of the system, we can make a transition, and replace the L facts in the state by the R facts with the same instantiation. Consider the following small example of this.

Example 5 (Rewrite rules) Consider the following rules.

- [ ]-->[C('1')]
- [C(x)]-->[D(x)]
- [C(x)]-->[C(f(x))]

If the transition system's initial state is the empty multiset, only the first rule applies in that state. Its application leads to a transition to the state [C('1')]. Afterwards, we can make a transition using the second rule, and end up in the state [D('1')]. Alternatively, we can make an arbitrary number of transitions using the third rule, to end up with [C(f(f(...f('1'))))], after which we can still make a single transition using the second rule. The first rule can also be used repeatedly, each time enabling the use of the other two rules on the new copy of C('1') in the state, as explained before.

Next, consider an example using persistent facts.

Example 6 (Rewrite rules and persistent facts) Consider the following rules.

- [ ]-->[!E('hello')]
- [!E(x)]-->[F(f(x))]

Recall that !E(...) is a persistent fact, meaning that it is never consumed by a rule's application. Starting in the initial state, we cannot yet apply the second rule. However, once we have applied the first rule, the second rule can be applied arbitrarily many times because !E(...) is never removed from the state.

For each rule, we require that all variables that occur in the actions A or in the right-hand side R also occur in the left-hand side L. The only exception is for public variables, namely those prefixed with a dollar sign $, which may occur in A or R only. This requirement ensures that the transition system is well-defined. In particular, as we will see shortly, this requirement ensures that all executions and traces of the transition system can be trivially ground.

Besides the user-specified rules in a TAMARIN input file, TAMARIN also has a set of built-in rules that, for example, encode a network adversary, or specific cryptographic schemes.

Fresh rule

TAMARIN always includes one special rule that produces fresh values. In protocol specifications, this allows us to refer to unique, unpredictable values in rules by putting a *Fr* fact on the left-hand side. In practice, we use this to model the generation of random values from a sufficiently large space, private keys, etc. The corresponding built-in rule is

```
Fresh: []--[]->[ Fr(~x)],
```

where *x* must be of type fresh. By itself, this rule might appear ill-defined as the variable ~x does not occur on the rule's left-hand side. However, this special rule gets its meaning through a restriction on the semantics, as we will see in the next section.

3.1.8 Default network model and message deduction rules

TAMARIN's default built-in network model uses Out(x) and In(x) facts to represent, respectively, messages sent and received over a network that is fully controlled by the adversary. Hence sending a message directly adds the message to the adversary's knowledge; this is represented by the collection of persistent !K facts in the state. Similarly, receiving messages from the network is possible only when the adversary knows that message. This is modeled by the following two rules.

```
[ Out(x) ]-->[ !K(x) ]
[ !K(x) ]--[ K(x) ]->[ In(x) ]
```

Additionally, the adversary can produce fresh values, it initially knows the set of public messages, and it can apply any function to the messages it already knows. This is captured by the following three rules.

```
[ Fr(~x)]-->[ !K(~x)]
[ ]-->[ !K($x)]
[ !K(x1)...!K(xn)]-->[!K(f(x1,....,xn))]
```
, for all function symbols f

Intuitively speaking, these rules allow the adversary to manipulate messages as desired. For example, the adversary can generate new messages and keys, decrypt messages that it received for which it knows the decryption key, perform Diffie-Hellman exponentiation, hash, and sign messages.

3.2 The semantics of TAMARIN's rules

Now that we have the core syntactic ingredients in place to specify systems in TAMARIN, we explain how they define a transition system with an associated set of traces.

We define a single "global" transition system that models a distributed algorithm in the presence of an active network adversary, where the algorithm and adversary are specified using rules. The state of the transition system is a multiset of facts, and the initial state of our system is the empty multiset, i.e.,

$$S_0 = [\,] \,.$$

3.2.1 Transitions

We extend the notion of substitution to facts and (multi)sets of facts in the expected way, i.e., a substitution is applied recursively to its components.

Let R be a set of rules constructed over a given signature and let S be a state of the system, i.e., a multiset of facts. The rules typically consist of the user-specified rules in a TAMARIN input file, TAMARIN's default built-in rules (including the Fresh rule), and user-requested built-in optional rules.

We write $set(M)$ to denote the set of elements in the multiset M. For example, $set([x, y, y]) = \{x, y\}$. We use the $\sharp$ superscript to denote multiset variants of standard set operations. For example, we write $S \subset^\sharp T$ to denote that S is a sub-multiset of T.

Let $G^\sharp$ denote the multiset of all *ground* facts, which are all facts built from the signature that do not contain variables. For example, Init('hello','Alice') is in $G^\sharp$, but Resp(H(~x),'test') is not in $G^\sharp$ because ~x is a variable.

Let *gri* be the function that, given a set of rules, yields the set of all ground instances of those rules.

Example 7 (Ground rule instances) Consider the rule

```
ExampleRule : [ Fr(~n) ]-->[ S($A, H(~n)) ] ,
```

where S is a fact symbol of arity 2 and H is a function symbol of arity 1. Then *gri*(ExampleRule) is

$\{$ `[Fr(x)]-->[S(y, H(x))]` $\mid$ x is a fresh value and y is a public constant$\}$.

We specify a labeled operational semantics for R (including the Fresh rule) using a labeled transition relation *steps* of the following type:

$$steps(R) \subseteq G^\sharp \times \bigl(gri(R \cup \{\text{Fresh}\})\bigr) \times G^\sharp.$$

For a multiset of facts l, we denote by $lfacts(l)$ the multiset of linear facts in l, and we denote by $pfacts(l)$ the multiset of persistent facts in l.

We define *steps* below using inference rule notation. This states that for each instance for which the premises (above the line) hold, the conclusion (below the line) can be drawn:

$$\frac{\texttt{[l]--[a]->[r]} \in gri(R \cup \{\text{Fresh}\}) \quad S' = \bigl(S \setminus^\sharp lfacts(1)\bigr) \cup^\sharp r \quad lfacts(1) \subseteq^\sharp S \quad set(pfacts(1)) \subseteq set(S)}{(S,\ \texttt{[l]--[a]->[r]}\ , S') \in steps(R)}$$

Informally, this rule states that we can make a step from S to S' using a ground rule instance `l--[a]->r`, if

1. `l--[a]->r` is a ground instance of a rule in R or the Fresh rule,

2. S' is the result of removing the linear facts in l from S, and adding the facts in r,

3. the multiset of linear facts in l occurs in S, and

4. the set of persistent facts in l occurs in S.

The first clause effectively adds the Fresh rule and ensures that only ground rule instances can be used for a step. The second clause defines the new state S' after taking the step from S. The third and fourth clauses state the requirements for taking the step: sufficiently many linear facts must be present to be consumed, and for persistent facts, which are not consumed, we simply require at least one instance of each to be present in S.

3.2.2 Executions and traces

An execution of R with respect to an equational theory E is an alternating sequence of states and ground rule instances

$$[S_0,\ \texttt{l1--[a1]->r1},\ S_1,\ \texttt{l2--[a2]->r2},\ S_2, \ldots, S_{k-1},\ \texttt{lk--[ak]->rk},\ S_k]$$

such that the following three conditions hold:

(E1) $S_0 = [\,]$,
(E2) For all $i \in \{1, \ldots, k\}$, we have $\bigl(S_{i-1}, (\ \texttt{li--[ai]->ri}), S_i\bigr) \in steps(R)$, and

3.2 Semantics of rules

(E3) for all $i, j \in \{1, \ldots, k\}$:
```
li--[ai]->ri = []--[]->[ Fr(n) ] and
lj--[aj]->rj = []--[]->[ Fr(n) ],
```
then $i = j$.

Condition (E1) ensures that we start from the initial state with an empty multiset. Condition (E2) ensures that the transition is valid according to the rules. Finally, Condition (E3) is a semantic restriction that ensures the main property of fresh values, namely that they are unique. Note that equality here is modulo the equational theory E, as usual.

We denote the set of executions of a set of rules R by $execs(R)$. Note that when we specify properties of transition systems, we specify them not over the system's executions, but rather over the sequences of multisets of action facts that arise in the executions. These sequences constitute the system's *traces*. By specifying properties over the action facts, we give the modeler the freedom to formalize what aspects of system execution (given by the actions associated with transition rules) are relevant for specifying the properties of interest.

More formally, for each execution

$$[S_0, \text{l1--[a1]->r1}, S_1, \text{l2--[a2]->r2}, S_2, \ldots, S_{k-1}, \text{lk--[ak]->rk}, S_k],$$

we define the corresponding *trace* as the sequence

$$[set(\text{a1}), set(\text{a2}), \ldots, set(\text{ak})]$$

and denote the set of all traces of a set of rules R by $traces(R)$. We write $idx(tr)$ for the set of all indices of the trace tr, and tr_i for the i-th entry of the trace tr.

Example 8 (Executions) Consider the following three rules R:

```
[ Fr(~x)    ]--[]->[ S(~x,$A), !T(~x) ]
[ S(x, $A)  ]--[]->[]
[ !T(x)     ]--[]->[ S(H(x), 'chain') ]
```

The following sequence $EX1$ is a possible execution of R:
```
[
  [                        ], [           ]--[]->[Fr(n1)                       ],
  [Fr(n1)                  ], [Fr(n1)]--[]->[S(n1,'Alex'),!T(n1)],
  [S(n1,'Alex'),!T(n1)], [!T(n1)]--[]->[S(H(n1),'chain')    ],
  [S(n1,'Alex'),!T(n1),S(H(n1),'chain')]
]
```
where n1 is a fresh value.

A possible alternative execution, $EX2$, is the following:
```
[
  [              ], [      ]--[]->[Fr(n4)             ],
  [Fr(n4)        ], [      ]--[]->[Fr(n5)             ],
```

```
    [Fr(n4),Fr(n5)], [Fr(n5)]--[]->[S(n5,'Blake'),!T(n5)],
    [Fr(n4),S(n5,'Blake'),!T(n5)]
]
```

where n4 and n5 are fresh values.

Example 9 (Actions and traces) Consider the following rules R:

```
[ Fr(~x),Fr(~y) ]--[ Gen(~x),Gen(~y) ]->[ S(~x,~y) ]
[ S(k,1)        ]--[ Flag(k)         ]->[ S(1,'')  ]
```

The set of executions of these rules includes the following:

```
[ Fr(n9),Fr(n7) ]--[ Gen(n9),Gen(n7) ]->[ S(n9,n7) ],
[ S(n9,n7)      ]--[ Flag(n9)        ]->[ S(n7,'') ],
[ S(n7,'')      ]--[ Flag(n7)        ]->[ S('','') ],
[ S('','')      ]--[ Flag('')        ]->[ S('','') ]
```

where n9 and n7 are fresh values. The trace t corresponding to this execution is:

```
[ { Gen(n9),Gen(n7) },
  { Flag(n9)        },
  { Flag(n7)        },
  { Flag('')        } ]
```

We have $idx(tr) = \{1, 2, 3, 4\}$ and, for example, $tr_1 = \text{Gen(n9)},\text{Gen(n7)}$ and $tr_2 = \text{Flag(n9)}$. We will show in Section 5.10.2 how we can use restrictions on traces to provide even more fine-grained control over the set of traces modeled by a set of rules.

Chapter 4
Modeling State Machines

Now that we have seen TAMARIN's modeling language and its semantics, we turn to its practical usage, which is to model protocols. We have already given an example of formalizing a security protocol in Chapter 2. In this chapter, we describe protocol modeling more systematically, focusing on modeling the state machines associated with a protocol's roles.

Multiset rewriting is a general modeling formalism and offers many ways to model a security protocol and the adversary. This flexibility is analogous to programming languages where one may implement a function in many different ways. For TAMARIN, there is no one modeling paradigm that must be followed. However, there are standard approaches that generally work well.

As we have previously observed, a protocol can be decomposed into different roles, each with an associated state machine. Examples of such roles include the client, server, initiator, responder, or a trusted third party such as a key server. We model each of the relevant state machines separately within the global transition system that we defined in Chapter 3. Namely, for each transition in a state machine, corresponding to a step of an agent playing in the associated role, we specify a multiset rewriting rule that can create or change the local state of the role's state machine. For example, for a protocol with an initiator and a responder role, we might have a multiset rewriting rule for our global transition system that models an initiator constructing and sending the protocol's first message over the network. We would also have a rule for the responder role stating that the agent playing in this role receives that first message and sends a response.

To help visualize how this works in practice, in Figure 4.1 we show a simplified version of the client state machine for TLS 1.3, where each transition corresponds to a multiset rewriting rule in TAMARIN. In this state machine, the client starts in the state c_0, and chooses one of three main modes to communicate with a server. Afterwards, the client sends a corresponding "ClientHello" message, and waits to receive the server's "ServerHello" response in the corresponding mode. After processing the response, it sends "ClientFinished" and transitions to the state c_{2a}. Next the client

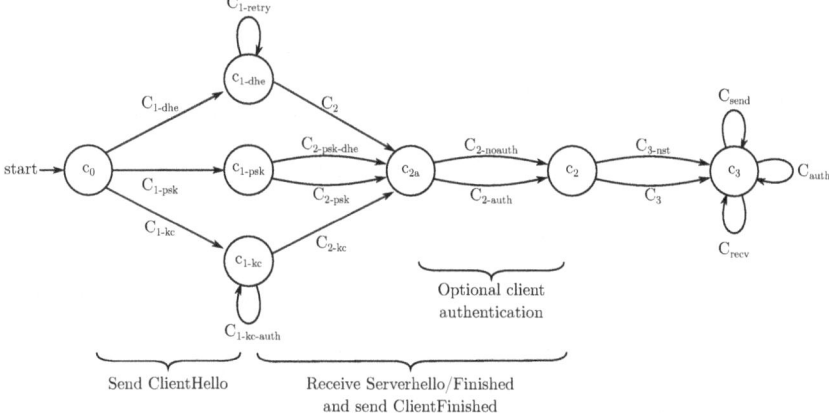

Fig. 4.1: Simplified state machine for TLS 1.3 clients.

optionally authenticates itself and carries out key confirmation after which the client is ready to send and receive messages. In TAMARIN, we model each transition in such a state machine by a rule. See [101] for full details on this. Moreover, for the complete TLS model we would also include the rules for the server and the associated set up rules.

In reality, not only does each protocol role correspond to a state machine, but agents can run any number of instances of such state machines concurrently, with each state machine maintaining its own local state. As a result, in the overall, global transition system, there can be infinitely many global states. Hence, when TAMARIN proves theorems, it is proving them about an infinite state system. In fact, one may have infinitely many states even without concurrency since a single role automaton may have a loop where an agent generates fresh messages and sends them to the network.

As remarked in Section 3.1, we refer to each such state machine run as a thread. After a thread computes and sends the first message of its associated role, the thread will remain dormant until a follow-up message with the expected format is received. In TAMARIN, we typically model a thread's state using facts that we informally call "state facts"; these often take as an argument an explicit thread identifier.

Note that a model must be self-contained in that it specifies everything needed to set up the protocol and for its subsequent execution. For the setup, any data that should be shared must be explicitly modeled using "set up" or "initialization" steps, which themselves can be modeled by a state machine. For example, TAMARIN has no built-in notion of a public key infrastructure or any other kind of key distribution. Hence, if a protocol makes use of pre-distributed keys, then their distribution must be explicitly modeled. We will illustrate these points below.

4.1 A simple challenge-response protocol

Let us start with a small example: a simple challenge-response protocol that is run between a client (C) role and a server (S) role. When a client runs the protocol, it generates a fresh symmetric key k and encrypts this together with a tag[1] '1' using the server's public key pk(S). It then sends the ciphertext to the server. When the server receives this message, it decrypts the ciphertext using its private key to obtain k, and responds with the key's hash h(k).

We can write this protocol in Alice-and-Bob notation as follows.

```
C -> S: aenc{'1',k}pk(S)
S -> C: h(k)
```

To model this protocol, we will specify a role state machine for each of the two protocol roles. In addition, we will specify a third state machine that predistributes keys as part of the key infrastructure. We explain these in turn, starting with the key infrastructure.

4.1.1 Key infrastructure

Security protocols typically have setup assumptions. For the above protocol, one assumes that, prior to its execution, servers have generated public/private key pairs and that clients know the public keys of the servers they wish to communicate with.

For asymmetric encryption schemes, we would model this setup assumption in the following way. We assume that private keys are freshly generated (unguessable) values and that there is an abstract function pk that, given a private key, can compute the corresponding public key. We register the generated key pairs as part of the state of the global transition system using persistent facts !Pk(.) and !Ltk(.), which stand for *public key* and *long-term key*, respectively. We model these facts as being persistent because each time that parties execute the protocol they should use these registered keys, and the keys will not be removed or updated. (In reality, keys may expire or be revoked, but for this basic example we assume that this does not happen.) Combined with the fact that all TAMARIN theories start with a theory name and a begin command, this results in the following:

```
1   theory SimpleChallengeResponse
2   begin
3
4   functions: pk/1
5
6   rule Register_pk:
7       [ Fr(~ltk) ]
```

---

[1] The server checks that the tag is present in the decrypted text to prevent the adversary from inserting random messages as ciphertexts. Note that it is good design practice to differentiate protocol messages by including explicit tags.

```
8     -->
9     [ !Ltk($A, ~ltk), !Pk($A, pk(~ltk)), Out(pk(~ltk)) ]
```

In the above, Lines 1 and 2 are required for all models and name the theory. Line 4 states that there is a function pk of arity 1. Lines 6–9 define the rule Register_pk: each time this rule is instantiated with any public constant for $A, a new private key of type fresh ~ltk is randomly generated for this party. Further rules, lemmas, etc. may be given, which we omit here and the theory must end with an end command, also omitted.

As we can see in the right-hand side of the rule on Line 9, the rule's application produces three facts:

- !Ltk($A, ~ltk) stores the private key ~ltk so that its owner (here a server $A) can use it in multiple threads.

- !Pk ($A, pk(~ltk)) stores the public key pk(~ltk) so that clients know which key to use to encrypt messages for the server $A.

- Out(pk(~ltk)) captures that public keys are actually public by sending them out to the network. Hence the adversary learns all public keys. Note that the adversary can invoke rules as long as the premises are met, but it does not learn any of the involved terms unless they are sent on the network.

We have now modeled the generation of key pairs. However, we have not yet defined how they are used for encryption and decryption. We therefore introduce two function symbols, aenc and adec, both of arity two. The first is the encryption function aenc, which takes a message and a public key as arguments, and represents the resulting ciphertext. The second is the decryption function adec, whose arguments are a ciphertext and a key, and represents the decrypted plaintext.

```
11    functions: aenc/2, adec/2
12    equations: adec(aenc(m, pk(k)), k) = m
```

We also provide the above equation formalizing that the adec function allows agents, including the adversary, to decrypt messages when they know the appropriate private key. Note that this equation only specifies what decryption returns when the right private key is used. Otherwise the equation is not applicable and the plaintext cannot be computed.

As we will see later, we can choose to model decryption by honest participants in two ways: either by having them explicitly apply adec to incoming messages, or by pattern matching against the encryptions. In this example we will use the latter, as we also did in Chapter 2. However, for more complex protocols that explicitly handle decryption failures, one might want to use the decryption function in the rules for honest agents. We discuss the tradeoffs involved in Section 10.1.6.

4.1.2 Servers

We next model the state machine for the server's role. The server uses a hash function, which is non-invertible, which we model by defining a function symbol h without an associated equational theory.

```
13    functions: h/1
```

When a server receives a message, it decrypts the message with its private key. Here we model this using pattern matching: the server's rule can only be instantiated for incoming messages that match the given pattern. This corresponds to all messages that it could decrypt using its private key.

We give the rule below. We have written the rule on several lines, although we could have alternatively written it on a single line. It contains the rule keyword, the rule's name (Server), and the rule's body, of the form [l]-[a]->[r]. Note that comments are prefixed by // or wrapped, e.g., /* possibly multi-line comment */.

```
15    rule Server:
16        [ !Ltk($S, ~ltkS)              // look up the private-key
17        , In( aenc{'1', k}pk(~ltkS) )  // receive a request
18        ]
19      --[ AnswerRequest($S, k)
20        ]->
21        [ Out( h(k) ) ]    // return the hash of the key
```

For each instance of this rule, $S will be instantiated with a concrete public constant. On Line 16, the rule's premise retrieves a registered private key for $S. Because !Ltk is a persistent fact, it is not removed from the state of the global transition system after the rule is applied; hence it can still be used by later instances of the rule.

Line 17 uses the predefined In fact to model receiving a message from the network that matches the given pattern, i.e., for any value of k. We will see the purpose for the action on Line 19 in the next sections. Line 21 is the rule's conclusion and sends the response message h(k) on the network using the predefined Out fact.

4.1.3 Clients

We next model the state machine for the client's role. In contrast to the server role, the client carries out two steps: sending the initial challenge message, and then waiting until the response is returned to check that it is indeed as expected. We model each of these steps with a separate rule.

```
23    rule Client_Step_1:
24        [ Fr(~k)            // choose fresh key
25        , !Pk($S, pkS)      // lookup public-key of server
26        ]
27      -->
```

```
28        [ Client_State_1( $S, ~k ) // store server and key for thread
29        , Out( aenc{'1', ~k}pkS )  // send encrypted key to server
30        ]
```

In the above rule, the client first implicitly uses the Fr rule in the premise to obtain a freshly generated value for the key k. The variable $S has the *public* type (denoted by the $), and thus it can be instantiated with any public constant, denoting the name of the specific server that the client wants to communicate with. Using the !Pk fact, a public key of that server is retrieved.

The rule's conclusion consists of two facts. The first fact Client_State_1 stores the internal state of this specific thread of the client while it awaits the server's response. This thread's internal state stores the specific server that is the intended communication partner and the freshly generated key ~k.

Note that because ~k is freshly generated, each time this rule is instantiated, it will produce a unique instance of the Client_State_1 fact, modeling a uniquely identifiable thread. If the protocol's first client step were not to produce a fresh value, we would typically introduce an explicit internal thread identifier, modeled as a fresh value, and put it in the state fact to distinguish between threads.

The second fact in the rule's conclusion is the Out fact, which represents sending the encrypted key on the network.

The second rule of the client role, shown below, models receiving the response message in a thread that previously performed the first step.

```
32    rule Client_Step_2:
33        [ Client_State_1(S, k) // retrieve thread state
34        , In( h(k) ) // receive hashed session key from network
35        ]
36      --[ SessKeyC( S, k ) ]-> // state that the session key 'k'
37        []                      // was setup with server 'S'
```

In the premise, we can see that this rule can only be instantiated when there are Client_State_1 facts in the global state. Then, the concrete instance is removed from the multiset after the rule is instantiated. This is because it is not a persistent fact and does not occur in the conclusion.

Using pattern matching, we write In(h(k)) to denote that the rule can additionally only be triggered if there is an incoming message that matches the hash of the key we generated in the first step. Note that the full input file is available at **SimpleChallengeResponse-P2.spthy**.

4.2 Further concepts

4.2.1 Threads and sessions

In the security protocol literature, the notion of a *session* is interpreted at least two ways. In the first interpretation, a session refers to a *local* session (thread), i.e., an execution of a single role of the protocol by a particular agent. In the second interpretation, a session refers to a synchronized execution of an instance of a protocol involving multiple agents that each perform one of the protocol's roles. For example, this could be a shared session where a server and a client communicate together and compute a shared session key. In this book, we will mainly use "thread" and "session" to denote local sessions performed by a single agent, as in the first interpretation.

We model threads by instances of rules, which under TAMARIN's semantics can be instantiated any number of times within an execution. Concretely, this means that the possible executions of the previously given model of the simple challenge-response protocol include executions with arbitrarily many threads. Moreover, for this protocol, the traces of the global transition system also include traces that have an arbitrary number of agents, each of them executing an arbitrary number of instances of the client or server role.

Thus, by default, protocols in TAMARIN model an unbounded number of threads and sessions. As a consequence, TAMARIN's analysis is not restricted to only consider a small finite number of sessions. The analysis also considers scenarios where the adversary combines information from an arbitrary number of sessions to try and violate some of the protocol's goals.

We will see later how this can be restricted, for example by using trace restrictions (Section 5.10.2).

4.2.2 Loops

The state machines corresponding to a protocol's roles may contain loops. For example, loops arise when parties wish to continuously transmit messages, or compute a new session key at regular intervals. In a role state machine, this is manifested as a transition that ends in a state that was previously visited. Because we model the role's state machines using rewrite rules in TAMARIN's models, such a transition is modeled by setting the state machine's local state to a prior one. Concretely, loops can be directly modeled in TAMARIN by producing facts on the right-hand side of rules that enable the firing of the same or earlier rules.

For example, the following two rules model the looping state machine from Figure 4.2. In particular, the second rule outputs an A(x) fact that matches with the fact on the left-hand side, enabling looping.

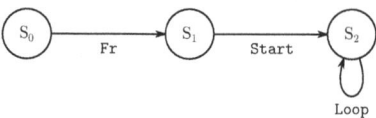

Fig. 4.2: A role state machine with a loop. Circles denote states and edges denotes transitions annotated by the rule name.

```
rule Start: [ Fr(x) ]  --[ Start(x) ]-> [ A(x) ]

rule Loop:  [ A(x) ]   --[ Loop(x)  ]-> [ A(x) ]
```

Note that we could change the right-hand side of the second rule to A(h(x)) to model that the function h can be applied any number of times. For this modified rule, there are traces with actions that contain h(h(h(h(·)))), etc. The full input file is available at **Minimal_Loop_induction.spthy**.

In practice, loops are easy to model, but can be challenging for TAMARIN's automatic reasoning during its backwards search. This is explained in Section 6.2 and we will present some ways for dealing with this challenge in Section 9.1.

4.2.3 Basic branching

With the components discussed so far, we can model non-deterministic choice and branching based on pattern matching, by modeling a rule for each possible choice and branch, respectively.

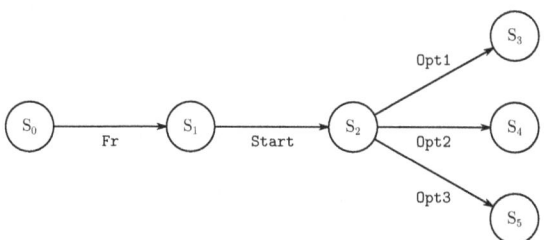

Fig. 4.3: A role state machine with branching.

```
rule Start: [ Fr(x) ]  --[ Start(x) ]-> [ A(x) ]

rule Opt1:  [ A(x) ]   --[ Option1(x) ]-> [ B(x) ]
rule Opt2:  [ A(x) ]   --[ Option2(x) ]-> [ C(x) ]
rule Opt3:  [ A(x) ]   --[ Option3(x) ]-> [ D(x) ]
```

By modifying the left-hand sides of the rules, we can also introduce further branching conditions such as requirements on received messages. For example, by including

4.2 Further concepts

In(h(x)) in the left-hand side of rule Opt3, the branch can only be taken if h(x) can be received from the network. As another example, one could add a second argument $T to the A fact, which could be used to pattern match on particular constants as in the following example.

```
rule Start: [ Fr(x), In($T) ] --[ Start(x) ]-> [ A(x,$T) ]

rule Opt1:  [ A(x,'1') ]            --[ Option1(x) ]-> [ B(x) ]
rule Opt2:  [ A(x,'2') ]            --[ Option2(x) ]-> [ C(x) ]
rule Opt3:  [ A(x,'3'), In(h(x)) ] --[ Option3(x) ]-> [ D(x) ]
```

We will return to more expressive forms of branching, which can involve predicates and "else"-like negated clauses, in Section 5.10.4. Both examples are available in input files **Minimal_branch.spthy** and **Minimal_branch_alt.spthy**

Chapter 5
Specifying Trace Properties in TAMARIN

Now that we have seen how a protocol model is specified using multiset rewriting, we turn to the question of how to specify protocols' intended security properties. Among the usual properties that we are interested in are (key) secrecy and different kinds of agreement properties. These are expressible as so-called *trace properties*, which we examine in this chapter. We will address other kinds of properties, in particular privacy-style properties, which are usually represented as equivalence properties, in Chapter 13.

We have seen that a multiset rewriting system gives rise to a set of *traces* representing the executions of the system modeled, also interacting with the adversary. Each trace is a finite sequence of the labels on the transition arrows of the rules used. These labels are called synonymously *observable logged actions*, *action facts*, or simply just *actions*. A *trace property* then specifies a set of traces and it represents a set of desired protocol behaviors in terms of its sequences of observable actions. If the protocol state machine, describing how the protocol actually executes in the adversary's presence, has behaviors that are not included in the specified property, then we have a violation. This constitutes an attack on the protocol.

In TAMARIN, trace properties are specified as formulas in first-order logic, built from actions and quantifying over message terms and timepoints. The timepoints are associated with occurrences of actions and are simply used to order events, as opposed to specifying real-time requirements on precisely when events occur. They therefore enable the specification of properties that depend on the events' relative ordering.

To explain this further, consider the following small example consisting of two rules.

```
rule Send:
  [State(~tid, 'ready'), Fr(~n)]
  --[Sent(~n)]->
  [State(~tid, ~n), Out(~n)]

rule Receive:
  [State(~tid, ~n), In(~n)]
```

```
--[Received(~n)]->
  [State(~tid, 'done')]
```

These rules contain two unary action facts, `Sent(·)` and `Received(·)`. We will use these facts to specify a trace property for this protocol stating that any instance of `Received(x)` requires that an instance of `Sent(x)`, with the same parameter x, appears earlier in the trace. We specify this in TAMARIN using the keyword `lemma` and writing the following formula:

```
lemma SentBeforeReceived:
  "All x #i. Received(x)@#i ==> Ex #j. Sent(x)@#j & #j < #i"
```

Note that whenever it is clear that a variable must be of timepoint sort, we can (and often do) omit the # prefix identifying the type of the variable. Hence, in the above formula, we would usually write `Received(x)@i`, `Sent(x)@j`, and `j < i`.

Note too that the timepoint ordering `j < i` is not even needed in the above lemma, as it is implicitly included already. Specifically, observe that the property specified must hold for all traces of our transition system and we can thus consider the prefix of any execution up to the timepoint i where `Received(x)` appears. This prefix is itself a valid trace and there must therefore be an instance of `Sent(x)`, as otherwise the formula would be violated on that trace. Hence if the formula is never violated on any trace, then for all traces every appearance of `Received(x)` must be preceded by `Sent(x)`. As an aside, note that without the explicitly given `j < i`, the formula is also satisfied when these two events both occur at the same timepoint. This may not be desirable for all models and thus one adds the ordering. However, the simultaneous occurrence of these events is impossible for the given transition system.

All lemmas are implicitly considered to be "all-traces" lemmas unless stated otherwise. This means that they formalize that the given formula holds for all traces of the protocol model and their proof entails checking that there is no trace violating the formula. The alternative is "exists-trace" lemmas, for which the keyword `exists-trace` must be explicitly added after the `rule NAME:` before the actual formula to be proven. An exists-trace lemma is used to check that at least one trace exists. In essence, the proof of such a lemma attempts to find (and show) a trace. Thus, if a trace is found, its interpretation is different: for an all-traces lemma, the trace represents a violation, while for an exists-trace lemma, it represents a success. See the lemma `executable` in Section 5.3 for an example.

5.1 Syntax

Formulas in TAMARIN are written in a guarded fragment[1] of many-sorted first-order logic with a dedicated sort *time* for timepoints. Quantification is supported over both timepoints and messages, using the standard quantifiers. Formulas are then built with

---

[1] In this chapter we will give examples of guarded formulas. We will later formally define guarded formulas in Section 11.5.

5.1 Syntax

standard logical connectives. Timepoint variables must be prefixed with # whenever it is not guaranteed by the context that they are timepoints as opposed to variables of type message. We recommend using the timepoint prefix # for all timepoint variables (except in the case of @#i), but note that this timepoint prefix symbol # may be omitted in other places as well (see below). The actual syntax is:

- All for universal quantification
- Ex for existential quantification
- ==> for implication
- & for conjunction
- | for disjunction
- not for negation
- f @ i for an action (that includes parameters) f and a timepoint #i (as only timepoints are possible in that position, the # is optional, and we generally omit it)
- #i < #j for timepoint #i happening prior to #j (also here both # are optional, but we keep them for clarity)
- #i = #j for timepoint equality (here the # is mandatory)
- x = y for message variable equality
- Pred(t1,...,tn) for the predicate Pred applied to the terms t1 to tn.

Any defined action fact name can be used in formulas, while the terms that are the arguments of the action facts are limited as follows. They can be constructed from the quantified variables, single-quote wrapped strings (interpreted as public constants as explained), and any of the defined free function symbols, i.e., function symbols that do not appear on the left-hand side of an equation.

Function symbols appearing on the left-hand side of an equation are called *reducible* as instances of them in terms may be replaced by (instances of) the equation's right-hand side. Reducible function symbols are forbidden in formulas for technical reasons.[2] For example, a hash function h for which no equations are defined is irreducible and can be used in formulas. For the usual asymmetric encryption with adec and aenc and the equation adec(aenc(m, pk(k)), k) = m, the function symbol adec is reducible and thus may not be used in formulas, while aenc is irreducible and can be used.

All of the variables must be guarded, for example, universally quantified variables must appear in an action or an equation after the quantifier, and the outermost logical operator inside the quantifier must be an implication. Essentially, *guardedness* requires one to immediately bind quantified variables to actions in the traces. For the formal definition and recommendations on how to make lemmas guarded, see Section 11.5. The full input file is available at **SentBeforeReceived.spthy**. The previous example lemma named SentBeforeReceived is a guarded formula as the quantified variable x is immediately used in the Received action, which we show here again:

---

[2] The normalization of reducible functions is performed by pre-computing so-called variants and this cannot be done in the logical formulas without creating case-splits, resulting in many formulas that would need to be analyzed. Fortunately, there are ways to work around this limitation, which we show in Section 15.1.2 for advanced signature models.

```
lemma SentBeforeReceived:
  "All x #i. Received(x)@#i ==> Ex #j. Sent(x)@#j & #j < #i"
```

If we modify it as follows it would be unguarded:

```
lemma SentBeforeReceivedUnguarded:
  "All x y #i. Received(x)@i ==> Ex #j. Sent(y)@j"
```

The problem here is that the variable y is quantified in the antecedent of the implication, but only bound to an action in the consequent, violating our guardedness requirement.

5.2 Semantics of trace formulas

We now give the precise semantics of trace formulas. This section is technical and may be skipped on first reading. In the following section, Section 5.3, we illustrate the semantics on a concrete example.

We associate a domain $\mathbb{D}_s$ with each sort s (namely *msg*, *pub*, *fr*, and *time*). The domains for message, fresh, and public variables are ground terms, fresh values, and public constants respectively (see Section 3.1.2). The domain for temporal variables $\mathbb{D}_{time}$ is $\mathbb{Q}$. We call a valuation θ a function from the set of all variables to terms and $\mathbb{Q}$ that respects sorts (e.g., a variable of sort public cannot be mapped to a fresh value). We homomorphically extend the application of a valuation θ from variables to terms, i.e., the application $t\theta$ applies θ to all variables inside t.

Given an equational theory E, the satisfaction relation $(tr, \theta) \models_E \mathtt{f}$ between traces tr (see Section 3.2.2), valuations θ, and trace formulas $\mathtt{f}$ (see Section 5.1) is defined inductively as follows:

$(tr, \theta) \models_E$ `fa @ i`	iff $\theta(i) \in idx(tr)$ and $\mathtt{fa}\theta \in_E tr_{\theta(i)}$
$(tr, \theta) \models_E$ `All x.g`	iff for all $u \in \mathbb{D}_s : (tr, \theta[x \mapsto u]) \models_E g$, where x is of sort s
$(tr, \theta) \models_E$ `Ex x.g`	iff there exists $u \in \mathbb{D}_s : (tr, \theta[x \mapsto u]) \models_E g$, where x is of sort s
$(tr, \theta) \models_E$ `g ==> h`	iff $(tr, \theta) \models_E g$ implies $(tr, \theta) \models_E h$
$(tr, \theta) \models_E$ `g & h`	iff $(tr, \theta) \models_E g$ and $(tr, \theta) \models_E h$
$(tr, \theta) \models_E$ `g	h`	iff $(tr, \theta) \models_E g$ or $(tr, \theta) \models_E h$
$(tr, \theta) \models_E$ `not g`	iff not $(tr, \theta) \models_E g$
$(tr, \theta) \models_E$ `#i < #j`	iff $\theta(i) < \theta(j)$
$(tr, \theta) \models_E$ `#i = #j`	iff $\theta(i) = \theta(j)$
$(tr, \theta) \models_E$ `x = y`	iff $x\theta = y\theta$
$(tr, \theta) \models_E$ `Pred(t1,...,tn)`	iff $(tr, \theta) \models_E g$ and Pred is defined as Pred(t1,...,tn) <=> g

5.3 Secrecy on a toy example

Overloading notation, we write $tr \models_E f$ if $(tr, \theta) \models_E f$ for all θ, and for a set of traces TR we write $TR \models_E f$ if $tr \models_E f$ for all $tr \in TR$. Finally, we say that a set of rules R satisfies a formula f if $traces(R) \models_E f$.

5.3 Secrecy on a toy example

To illustrate the semantics of formulas just given, we present an example of how to formulate a simple version of secrecy. The full input file is available at **ToySecrecyAuthentication.spthy**. We do this using a toy protocol that uses a shared symmetric key, stored in the persistent fact SharedKey and generated by the following rule.

```
rule GenerateSharedKey:
  [Fr(~k)]
--[]->
  [!SharedKey(~k)]
```

We also have two rules that model sending and receiving a fresh value (representing an arbitrary message) encrypted under a shared key. We use the standard way to model symmetric encryption in TAMARIN, introduced in Section 3.1.4.

```
rule SendEncrypted:
  [!SharedKey(~k), Fr(~n)]
--[Sent(~n,~k)]->
  [Out(senc(~n,~k))]

rule ReceiveEncrypted:
  [!SharedKey(~k), In(senc(~n,~k))]
--[Received(~n,~k)]->
  []
```

To rule out careless errors during modeling, we recommend checking that the protocol, as modeled, is actually executable. This is done by using TAMARIN to find a completed protocol trace where the steps are the expected ones taken by honest agents. Namely, all received messages should be exactly as they were sent and the execution does not involve adversary interference, i.e., the adversary does not help participants finish their roles. Furthermore, one should inspect manually that the rule instances in the trace are ordered as expected and that no steps are missing.

To ask TAMARIN to find such an execution, we use a lemma prefixed using the exists-trace keyword, which means that a completed trace respecting the property is considered a success. This keyword is necessary as, by default, TAMARIN tries to prove the property for all traces.[3]

Our first lemma, named executable, is as follows.

```
lemma executable:
  exists-trace
  "Ex n k #i #j. Received(n,k)@i & Sent(n,k)@j"
```

---

[3] The all-traces keyword can be given, but is usually left implicit. For a lemma with all-traces the existence of a trace contradicting the property represents an attack.

This lemma can be proven by TAMARIN, as there are protocol traces satisfying the formula. For example, consider the following trace, which corresponds to the three rules defining the protocol being executing in their normal order:

$$[\emptyset, \{\texttt{Sent(~n1, ~k1)}\}, \{\texttt{Received(~n1,~k1)}\}].$$

Note that the first step is the empty set as the rule `GenerateSharedKey` has no actions. Given this trace, we see that our lemma holds as there exist values n (~n1 in this example), k (~k1 in this example), #j (2 in this example), and #i (3 in this example), such that at timepoint 2 we have the action `Sent(~n1,~k1)` and at timepoint 3 we have the action `Received(~n1,~k1)`.

Note that there are also protocol traces where the formula given in the lemma statement is not satisfied. An example is the following trace corresponding to a key generation and two messages being sent, but without any being received:

$$[\emptyset, \{\texttt{Sent(~n1, ~k1)}\}, \{\texttt{Sent(~n2, ~k1)}\}].$$

The lemma however still holds, as it is prefixed with the `exists-trace` keyword. Hence it suffices that it is satisfied for at least one protocol trace.

Continuing this example, there are also more complicated protocol traces that satisfy the formula. As an illustration, consider the following trace:

$$[\emptyset, \{\texttt{Sent(~n1, ~k1)}\}, \{\texttt{Sent(~n2, ~k1)}\}, \{\texttt{Received(~n1,~k1)}\},$$
$$\{\texttt{Received(~n1,~k1)}\}].$$

So what trace will TAMARIN return? In general, there is no guarantee that TAMARIN returns the shortest or otherwise "simplest" trace. Note that TAMARIN does not return a trace, but rather a graph representing potentially a set of traces (see Section 6.1 for details on how to run TAMARIN and Section 6.5 on how to read the graphs).

We next formulate the secrecy of the sent term n. Namely, we state that whenever the value n is sent encrypted with the key k, then the adversary does not know the value n. To this end, we make use of action facts of the form K(m), which represent the adversary's knowledge of some message m.

```
lemma secrecy:
    "All n k #i. Sent(n,k)@i ==> not (Ex #j. K(n)@j)"
```

When verifying this lemma, TAMARIN proves that for all traces, if there is a `Sent(n,k)` action on the trace, there cannot be a `K(n)` action on the trace. Note that there is no constraint on the events' ordering. Hence, both a trace where the `K(n)` happens before the `Sent(n,k)` event or a trace where `K(n)` happens afterward constitute counterexamples. For example, both of the traces

$$[\ldots, \{\texttt{Sent(~n1,~k1)}\}, \ldots, \{\texttt{K(~n1)}\}, \ldots]$$

and

$$[\ldots, \{\texttt{K(\~{}n1)}\}, \ldots, \{\texttt{Sent(\~{}n1,\~{}k1)}\}, \ldots]$$

are counterexamples.

As further examples, the following two traces satisfy the formula and are not counterexamples.

$$[\emptyset, \{\texttt{K(\~{}n1)}\}, \{\texttt{Sent(\~{}n2,\~{}k1)}\}, \{\texttt{Received(\~{}n2,\~{}k1)}\}]$$

$$[\emptyset, \{\texttt{K(\~{}n1)}\}, \{\texttt{Sent(\~{}n2,\~{}k1)}\}, \{\texttt{Received(\~{}n1,\~{}k1)}\}]$$

The first trace is a normal protocol execution, with the adversary additionally generating a fresh value, which is however unrelated to the values used by the protocol; hence the formula is satisfied even though a K action occurs. The second trace satisfies the formula, but it cannot be generated by the given protocol rules: it is impossible to receive a message that was not sent because of the symmetric encryption using the shared key, which prevents the adversary from producing a valid message. Here, because the protocol's rules use the built-in In(·) and Out(·) facts for sending and receiving messages, the threat model that is considered is TAMARIN's default adversary that controls the network. In this model, the adversary cannot access the shared keys as long as they are not explicitly revealed, and therefore cannot act as a malicious agent. We will return to modeling malicious or compromised agents in Section 5.7.

For the given protocol, this lemma will be verified automatically by TAMARIN. It holds because the adversary has no way to decrypt the message enc(n,k) as it lacks knowledge of the shared key k. This is because there is no rule revealing this shared key to the adversary, and there is no way for the adversary to deduce it from what is sent, since encryption is assumed to work perfectly, as is usual in the symbolic model.

5.4 Authentication on the toy example

To continue the previous example, we illustrate a simple authentication property:

```
lemma authentication:
  "All n k #i. Received(n,k)@i ==> Ex #j. Sent(n,k)@j"
```

This lemma states that whenever a party with the secret key k has received n, then n was actually (previously) sent by someone with access to that secret key. TAMARIN easily verifies this lemma.

Note that in our specification of this property, we did not refer to the names of agents or exclude the case that an agent may be talking to itself. Augmenting the specification to explicitly exclude such cases will be explained later.

5.5 Modeling a public key infrastructure

In the remaining sections of this chapter we will model a public key infrastructure (PKI) in which all agents have a public/private key pair, and each agent knows the public keys of all other agents. To model this, we assume the existence of a function pk/1 that, given a private key, returns the corresponding public key. This function is already predefined when using one of the two built-in models asymmetric-encryption and signing. Otherwise, the function can be explicitly defined using:

```
functions: pk/1
```

To model the PKI, we introduce a rule for key registration, with the full file available at **PKIdef.spthy**.

```
rule Register_pk:
  [ Fr(~ltk) ]
    -->
  [ !Ltk($A, ~ltk), !Pk($A, pk(~ltk)), Out(pk(~ltk)) ]
```

The rule Register_pk creates a new fresh key ~ltk and assigns this to the agent $A as A's private key. This rule creates persistent facts !Ltk(A, ltk) and !Pk(A, pubk) for the private and public key. Additionally, the public key is given to the adversary using the Out(·) fact, effectively making the key public. To model that any agent X accesses its private key, a protocol rule that is executed by X can look up the persistent fact !Ltk(X, ltk) and use ltk. The fact !Pk(X, pubk) can be used to get the public key pubk of any agent X. We will see concrete examples of how such facts are used in protocol rules in the next sections.

This basic PKI model can be extended to model various forms of compromise and corruption, i.e., the fact that the adversary might learn the private keys of some agents, or is a malicious agent. We will return to this in Section 5.7.

5.6 Simplified Signed Diffie-Hellman Example

We next consider an example of slightly greater complexity that provides a more realistic example of formalizing secrecy. Namely we formalize a simplified version of the Signed Diffie-Hellman protocol with the same threat model of an adversary that actively controls the network.

In this protocol, we have two rules for the initiator, who sends a message and subsequently receives a response, and a single rule for the responder, who receives a message and immediately responds. The second rule of the initiator and the one responder rule have the action SessionKey with the key as a parameter. The secrecy lemma, called Secrecy, asserts that the adversary never learns the claimed key. We explain this step-by-step.

5.6 Simplified Signed Diffie-Hellman Example

The theory name is `SignedDH_simple`, and we include the two built-in theories `diffie-hellman` and `signing`. The former was explained previously in Example 4 and the latter will be given in Section 7.1.4 and explained there. In short, the `signing` built-in adds an operator pk/1 (just like asymmetric encryption) and a constant true/0, as well as a sign/2 and verify/3 operator. The idea is that signing takes a message and a private key, while verifying takes a message, a signature, and a public key. Signature verification then returns the result true only when a correctly built signature is verified against the right message. The full input file is available at **SignedDH_simple.spthy**.

```
theory SignedDH_simple begin

builtins: diffie-hellman, signing
```

Next, we create the public key infrastructure as described in Section 5.5.

```
rule Register_pk:
  [ Fr(~ltk) ]
  -->
  [ !Ltk($A, ~ltk), !Pk($A, pk(~ltk)), Out(pk(~ltk)) ]
```

The initiator's first rule picks a fresh thread-id ~tid for identification, picks a fresh ephemeral DH public key ~ekI, looks up its private signing key, and sends out its name $I, its expected partner's name $R, the DH exponentiation 'g'^~ekI, and a signature with its private key on a tag '1' and the previously mentioned three values. The tag is used to ensure that a responder's message is not mistaken for an initiator's message. A state fact Init_1(·) stores all the required information.

```
rule Init_1:
  [ Fr(~tid), Fr(~ekI), !Ltk($I, ltkI) ]
  -->
  [ Init_1( ~tid, $I, $R, ~ekI )
  , Out( <$I, $R, 'g' ^ ~ekI, sign(<'1', $I, $R,'g'^~ekI>,ltkI) > ) ]
```

The initiator's second rule looks up the state in Init_1(·), looks up the partner's public key, and receives the response message from the responder. It checks the signature's validity with the retrieved public key, and expects the tag '2' to be included. This signature verification is encoded using the built-in _restrict action fact, which we will explain in detail in Section 5.10.3. The received message consists of the responder and initiator names, a DH share from the responder that is received and stored as Y, and the signature on all this. The rule also emits the action fact SessionKey(·) with the DH shared value Y^~ekI, i.e., the exponentiation of the received Y with the initiator's own private share.

```
rule Init_2:
  [ Init_1( ~tid, $I, $R, ~ekI )
  , !Pk($R, pkR)
  , In( <$R, $I, Y, m2> )
  ]
--[ _restrict( verify(m2, <'2', $R, $I, Y>, pkR) = true )
  , SessionKey($I,$R, Y^~ekI) ]->
  []
```

The responder uses a single rule to receive the message from the initiator and then to respond. For this, it looks up its own secret key in order to produce a signature, and the partner's public key to verify their signature on the received message. The DH share from the responder's partner is received as X and the resulting shared secret is X^~ekR, emitted in the action SessionKey(·). No thread-id is used here as no state is kept.

```
rule Resp:
  [ !Pk($I, pkI)
  , !Ltk($R, ltkR)
  , Fr(~ekR)
  , In( <$I, $R, X, m1> )
  ]
--[ _restrict( verify(m1, <'1', $I, $R, X>, pkI) = true )
  , SessionKey($I,$R, X^~ekR) ]->
  [ Out( <$R, $I, 'g'^~ekR, sign(<'2', $R, $I, 'g'^~ekR >, ltkR)> ) ]
```

The secrecy lemma states that for all SessionKey(·) actions in the trace, the adversary will not know the claimed session key sessKey.

```
lemma Secrecy:
  "All I R sessKey #i.
    SessionKey(I,R,sessKey)@i
    ==> not (Ex #j. K(sessKey)@j) "
```

This lemma is verified by TAMARIN as the adversary cannot get the ephemeral secret of either of the participants and cannot compute the shared key without at least one of the two ephemerals.

5.7 Modeling malicious or compromised agents

In the previous examples, we considered a threat model with an adversary that actively controls the network, but is otherwise an outsider to the system. In many cases, we want to prove much stronger security guarantees, for example with respect to threat models in which some of the agents are malicious, or where the adversary can compromise data from some agents at some point in time.

The standard way of modeling malicious agents is to allow the adversary to obtain the long-term secrets of parties, often modeled in a Reveal (or Corrupt) rule. For protocols whose outputs are strictly computed by applying public functions to the agent's long-term secrets, received inputs, and fresh values, an active network adversary can emulate the agent's honest behavior by using the agent's long-term keys.

We can specify a threat model that includes malicious agents by including a rule that reveals their long-term keys to the adversary. This rule is annotated with an action Reveal(·), whose argument denotes the party whose long-term keys are revealed. Messages constructed using those long-term keys might therefore be maliciously

5.7 Modeling malicious or compromised agents

generated. So, for a long-term key stored in an Ltk(·) fact, we can model a reveal rule as follows, with the full input file available at **ToyRevealHonest.spthy**.

```
rule Reveal_ltk:
  [ !Ltk(A, k) ]
--[ Reveal(A) ]->
  [ Out(k) ]
```

Here, the private key k is output to the network, and we record in the trace that the agent named A has been compromised, by a Reveal(A) action. Thus, if Reveal(X) occurs in a trace for some X, we consider X to be a potentially malicious or compromised agent. If a Reveal(X) does not occur, we say that X is *honest*.

In a given execution of a protocol, there are typically multiple concurrent sessions between many pairs of agents. For a threat model with malicious agents, standard properties that we would like to express are often of the form "if the participants of my session are honest, then the key should be secret", or "if my partner is honest, then authentication should hold".

To formulate such properties, we need to record for each session who the participants are in a particular instance of the protocol. There are different ways of doing this, and which one is best depends on the property we want to specify.

For example, in the rule below, the agent A is in its final state and believes that it shares a key t with the agent B, as formalized by the Completed(A,B,t) action. To make it easier to specify specific threat models later, we additionally record other actions: The CompletedKey(t) action independently records the key, the Actor(A) action records that *A* is the identity of the party executing the rule, and Peer(B)[4] records that *B* is the intended communication partner. For some properties, we want to refer to all parties assumed to be involved, for which we record the actions Participant(A) and Participant(B). Note that all properties that can be specified using these five action facts can also be specified using only the first action fact (Completed(A,B,t)), and we will show some examples below. However, using meaningful action fact names can make property specifications clearer and can prevent modeling errors.

```
rule Finish:
  [ FinalState(A, t, B) ]
--[ Completed(A,B,t)
  , CompletedKey(t)
  , Actor(A), Peer(B)
  , Participant(A), Participant(B) ]->
  [ ]
```

Properties can then be made conditional on the fact that some parties should be honest (e.g., the actor, the peer, or both participants). For example, if we only want to specify that a key is secret if both parties are honest, we can use one of the three formulations below, which are equivalent and all of them are verified successfully.

---

[4] In the literature, the intended communication partner is often referred to as the *peer*. In this book, we use the terms peer and partner interchangeably.

```
lemma SecrecyByState:
  "All A B t #i. Completed(A,B,t) @i
                 & not (Ex #k. Reveal(A)@k)
                 & not (Ex #k. Reveal(B)@k)
             ==> not (Ex #j. K(t)@j)"

lemma SecrecyActorPeer:
  "All A B t #i. CompletedKey(t) @i
                 & Actor(A)@i & not (Ex #k. Reveal(A)@k)
                 & Peer(B)@i & not (Ex #k. Reveal(B)@k)
             ==> not (Ex #j. K(t)@j)"

lemma SecrecyHonestParticipants:
  "All A B t #i. Completed(A,B,t) @i
                 & not(Ex C #k. Participant(C)@i & Reveal(C)@k)
             ==> not (Ex #j. K(t)@j)"
```

If we want to strengthen our threat model to also include key-compromise impersonation style attacks [19, 27, 76], we should also consider the security of sessions whose actor was compromised, i.e., where only the peer is honest. Intuitively, the idea is that in the presence of an active network adversary, the security of an agent's protocol thread need not depend on the security of that agent's long-term keys – the agent knows who it is – but still crucially relies of the security of the peer's long-term keys.

The preceding SecrecyHonestParticipants lemma is not suitable to specify such a stronger property where only the peer is required to be honest because we cannot identify the peer. However, the first two lemmas, SecrecyByState and SecrecyActorPeer, can be directly adapted, leading to the following two properties.

```
lemma SecrecyByStateOnlyPeer:
  "All A B t #i. Completed(A,B,t) @i
                 & not (Ex #k. Reveal(B)@k)
             ==> not (Ex #j. K(t)@j)"

lemma SecrecyActorPeerOnlyPeer:
  "All t #i B. CompletedKey(t) @i
                 & Peer(B)@i & not (Ex #k. Reveal(B)@k)
             ==> not (Ex #j. K(t)@j)"
```

In this example protocol, both lemmas are successfully verified. However, for other protocols, the results could be different for the preceding three lemmas. For example, the Needham-Schroeder-Lowe protocol [84] serves as a differentiating example, as all sessions with honest participants are secure, but sessions whose actor can be compromised are insecure. More examples are given in [19, 27]. We will also expand on this further in the next sections with different flavors of secrecy, and a hierarchy of authentication properties.

5.8 Flavors of secrecy

Some initial intuition on how to specify secrecy is given in Section 5.3. However, there are many different flavors of secrecy. For all of them, in the rule where an agent believes that a value is secret, we use a Secret(·) or SessionKey(·) or Property(·) action and then formulate the actual notion of secrecy using a lemma. Note that you can use any other name for these action facts in your models instead.

First, there is secrecy in the case where there is no adversary corruption, yielding the standard lemma seen before in Section 5.3 or Section 5.6 and called Secrecy there. In the following, we use the Signed Diffie-Hellman protocol from **SignedDH_PFS.spthy** for which we have seen a simpler version in Section 5.6. The first lemma we recall is the one given there, where the adversary is essentially passive and not a participant. Note the name of the action pointing to the completion of the protocol is now SessionKey and takes three arguments: two agent names followed by the key.

```
lemma Secrecy:
  "All I R sessKey #i.
    SessionKey(I,R,sessKey)@i
    ==> not (Ex #j. K(sessKey)@j) "
```

TAMARIN proves this lemma in the simple previous version. However it triggers a violation in an extended model of the protocol where the following reveal rule (see Section 5.7) is included.

```
rule Reveal_ltk:
    [ !Ltk(A, ltk) ]
  --[ LtkReveal(A) ]->
    [ Out(ltk) ]
```

This rule models a long-term key reveal and its application compromises the long-term key of an agent. As explained in Section 5.7, this also models malicious agents. Other kinds of reveals are also possible, such as partial or full session state reveal, all of which can be modeled, see Section 10.3.

Then, secrecy with an active adversary that can compromise the long-term keys of participants and that can be a malicious participant itself, can be checked with the following lemma. This property is only of interest when neither of the two parties in the current protocol run have been compromised, as otherwise the property will be trivially violated, hence these cases are excluded in the lemma. Note that an adversary can compromise all other parties. Here, this does not give the adversary any advantage as every other party also running a version of this protocol is irrelevant for this property.

```
lemma Secrecy_nopartners_revealed:
  "All I R sessKey #i.
    SessionKey(I,R,sessKey)@i
    & not (Ex #k. LtkReveal(I) @k)
    & not (Ex #k. LtkReveal(R) @k)
    ==> not (Ex #j. K(sessKey)@j) "
```

We can also define forward secrecy (sometimes called perfect forward secrecy) where even the possible compromise of a long-term key after a session does not allow the adversary to recover session keys. This is an even stronger version of the previous lemma. In this scenario, everyone else can always be compromised, and the parties involved in the protocol can be compromised afterwards.

```
lemma Secrecy_Forward:
  "All I R sessKey #i.
    SessionKey(I,R,sessKey)@i
    & not (Ex #k. LtkReveal(I) @k & #k < #i)
    & not (Ex #k. LtkReveal(R) @k & #k < #i)
    ==> not (Ex #j. K(sessKey)@j) "
```

TAMARIN verifies that the `SignedDH_PFS` protocol satisfies the last two properties. TAMARIN also finds a counterexample that shows a violation of the simple `Secrecy` lemma, as before.

Alternative versions of secrecy can be specified that account for the compromise of the participating agents' ephemeral keys. Those versions of secrecy also allow the combination of the reveal of the participating agents' long-term and ephemeral keys. Furthermore, extended Canetti-Krawczyk (eCK) secrecy with a notion of matching session can be modeled. Examples for all this can be found in the TAMARIN GitHub repository.

5.9 A hierarchy of authentication properties

There are many different notions of authentication considered in the literature. They often have subtle, but important, differences in the guarantees they provide as each captures different aspects of authentication and, depending on the context, different authentication properties are relevant. TAMARIN's property language is very flexible and can be used to state a wide range of properties, as the modeler desires.

A fairly standard set of properties, used in many case studies, is based on Lowe's hierarchy of authentication properties [85]. We use this hierarchy to introduce the reader to different ways to formalize standard authentication properties in two party protocols. The hierarchy contains four properties, listed in increasing strength, i.e., each property entails those preceding it.

- aliveness
- weak agreement
- non-injective agreement
- injective agreement

Furthermore, note that each of these properties applies from either party's viewpoint, and possibly for different terms that one wants to agree upon. Moreover, our convention for action facts is that their first argument given is always the name of the party in whose rule the action appears.

5.9 A hierarchy of authentication properties

Now, these protocols have agents named A and B (public variables) executing the roles 'A' and 'B' (constants) respectively. The authentication property is for an agent in the role 'A' to authenticate an agent in the role 'B'. The actions are as follows: Commit(A,B,<'A','B',t>) appears in the rule where the agent A in the role 'A' has all the information it needs to conclude that the protocol execution was a success, which is usually at the end of a run.

Specifically, the action contains the party's name A as the first argument, their partner's name B as the second argument, and a triple as the third argument. The triple in turn consists of the role constant 'A' of the role for which this Commit will be used in a property, the role constant 'B' for the partner role, and the actual data t.

For the agent B in the role 'B', there is then the related action Running(B,A,<'A','B',t>) added to a rule appearing after this agent has all the relevant information, in particular knowing its partner's name and the term t on which agreement is sought. Note that the agent in whose rule this appears is named first following our convention, i.e., B is the first argument. The partner A is given as the second argument. Importantly, the triple still starts with 'A', followed by 'B', as this Running fact is used for the property from the point of view of role 'A'.

Additionally, when using these actions in lemmas, we sometimes shorten the triple <'A','B',t>, which we write in the rules, to just a variable params in the lemmas. Of course, the variable params can pattern-match <'A','B',t>, so it is appropriately instantiated. See also the following (non-)injective agreement formulations for examples of this use.

In the formulas for (non-)injective agreement below, we will have that for all Commit claims there exists a matching Running claim. This of course means that such a Running claim happened before the Commit, as discussed in the initial part of Chapter 5. Therefore, for a protocol to possibly satisfy such a property, the rule in which the Running claim is an action must causally precede the rule where the Commit happens. This notion of "causally preceding" is commonly achieved by the rules being linked with a message flow from the former to the latter rule.

We have formulated the arguments for Commit and Running in a way that avoids a possible confusion where a Commit and Running are matched when executed by the same role. We achieve this through the ordering of the fixed role constants 'A' and 'B' in the arguments. When used in the order 'A','B' then the property is for the agent in the role 'A'. Otherwise, when the constants are ordered 'B','A' it is for the agent in the role 'B'. These are set when the action is given in a rule. In the lemma, they just need to be the same for the two actions to match.[5] The resulting lemmas for each level are then as follows.

---

[5] An alternative modeling approach could rename the actions with, e.g., a postfix label naming the viewpoint. So Commit(·) would become Commit_A(·). The drawback with this alternative is that lemmas must now be written twice, once for each viewpoint, and even more often for protocols with more parties. (We do not show this alternative version here, but note that it is an easy exercise to write them down.)

We explain next the main authentication properties and formally specify them as well. For their formal specifications, we fix a basic threat model, specifying that the property must hold for all sessions whose participants are not compromised, but other agents may be compromised. The properties can be similarly specified with respect to other threat models, for example, where the adversary is an outsider that cannot compromise or impersonate agents, or where the adversary can even corrupt the actor but not the peer of the session.

Aliveness is the weakest property. It only requires that the partner has previously run the protocol, possibly in a different role and with someone else as the perceived partner. Here, A is the party for which the lemma is expressed and B is the partner. Note that this lemma uses a new kind of actions called Create, which is logged whenever the agent name of the expected B is instantiated with an additional thread identifier, and the role it is created in, e.g., Create(B, id, 'A'). This must have happened at a prior timepoint. For the example threat model, we specify that the property is required to hold if the session's participants are not compromised (indicated by the Reveal(·) action.)

```
lemma aliveness:
  "All A B t #i.
    Commit(A,B,t)@i
  & not (Ex #r. Reveal(A) @ r)
  & not (Ex #r. Reveal(B) @ r)
    ==>  (Ex id rl #j. Create(B,id,rl) @ j & j < i)"
```

Weak agreement is next in the hierarchy and the agreement here is only on the partner's name, not on the actual roles or on any term. Hence the Commit and Running actions used for this property usually do not include roles.

```
lemma weakagree:
 " /* Whenever somebody commits to running a session, then*/
    All A B t1 #i.
      Commit(A, B, t1) @ i
      /* and adversary did not reveal the participants' long-term keys */
         & not (Ex #r. Reveal(A)@r)
         & not (Ex #r. Reveal(B)@r)
    ==>
         /* there is somebody running a session with matching participants */
      (Ex t2 #j. Running(B, A, t2) @j & j < i)"
```

Non-injective agreement ensures that the correct partner matches, the partner is in the right role, and the partner has the same view on the agreed upon term. So the agents really talked to each other with the right values. However, it is possible to replay messages so that a party would accept this again.

```
lemma noninjective_agree:
 " /* Whenever somebody commits to running a session, then*/
    All actor peer params #i.
        Commit(actor, peer, params) @ i
    /* and adversary did not reveal the participants' long-term keys */
      & not (Ex #r. Reveal(actor)@r)
      & not (Ex #r. Reveal(peer)@r)
       ==>
```

5.9 A hierarchy of authentication properties

```
                /* there is somebody running a session with the same parameters */
                    (Ex #j. Running(peer, actor, params) @ j & j < i)"
```

Injective agreement is the strongest property in the hierarchy presented. It is like non-injective agreement but with an added uniqueness property, ensuring that replays are prevented. Essentially, no second Commit instance is possible for the same term t.

```
lemma injective_agree:
  " /* Whenever somebody commits to running a session, then*/
    All actor peer params #i.
      Commit(actor, peer, params) @ i
    /* and the adversary did not reveal the participants' long-term keys */
    & not (Ex #r. Reveal(actor)@r)
    & not (Ex #r. Reveal(peer)@r)
    ==>
      /* there is somebody running a session with the same parameters */
        (Ex #j. Running(peer, actor, params) @ j & j < i
            /* and there is no other commit on the same parameters */
          & not(Ex actor2 peer2 #i2.
                Commit(actor2, peer2, params) @ i2 & not(#i = #i2)
             )
        )"
```

In general, the respective timepoint ordering in these four lemmas for the Commit happening before the Running, usually expressed as j < i, can be omitted, yielding equivalent lemmas. This is because the adversary can just stop the run at the point when the Commit is emitted, and then either there is a Running that comes before, or the lemma is violated. However, as we will later see, there is an exception to this. Namely, users can specify so-called trace restrictions (Section 5.10.2) to ensure progress of some kind and, in this case, the equivalence may no longer hold. It is therefore prudent to explicitly specify the timepoint ordering.

Separating examples

We now exemplify the different properties on a number of simple examples, highlighting the difference between them. In all these examples, we use the previously described public key infrastructure, with a long-term key reveal, that we recall first:

```
rule Register_pk:
  [ Fr(~ltkA) ]
--[ Register($A) ]->
  [ !Ltk($A, ~ltkA), !Pk($A, pk(~ltkA)), Out(pk(~ltkA))]

rule Reveal_ltk:
  [ !Ltk(A, ltkA) ] --[ Reveal(A) ]-> [ Out(ltkA) ]
```

Example 10 (Weak Agreement) First, we present the example protocol where the initiator sends its name and its desired partner's name, signed under its private key, to the partner. The expected response is the same content, signed by the partner's private key:

```
1. A -> B: sign(<A,B>,sk(A))
2. A <- B: sign(<A,B>,sk(B))
```

The initiator rules are

```
rule Init_A:
  [ Fr(~id)
  , !Ltk(I, ltkI), !Pk(R,pkR)
  ]
--[ Create(I, ~id, 'A') ]->
  [ St_A_1(I, ~id, ltkI, pkR, R)
  ]

rule A_1_send:
  [ St_A_1(I, ~id, ltkI, pkR, R)
  ]
--[ Running(I, R, 'anyroles')  // relevant for weak agreement only,
                                // as the roles are not taken into account
  ]->
  [ St_A_2(I, ~id, ltkI, pkR, R)
  , Out(sign(<I,R>,ltkI))
  ]

rule A_2_receive:
  [ St_A_2(I, ~id, ltkI, pkR, R)
  , In(mA2)
  ]
--[ _restrict( verify(mA2, <I,R>, pkR) = true )
  , Commit(I, R, <'Init', 'Resp'>)
  , Finish(I, R)
  ]->
  [
  ]
```

and the responder rules are

```
rule Init_B:
  [ Fr(~id)
  , !Ltk(R, ltkR), !Pk(I, pkI)
  ]
--[ Create(R, ~id, 'B') ]->
  [ St_B_1(R, ~id, ltkR, pkI, I)
  ]

rule B_receive_send:
  [ St_B_1(R, ~id, ltkR, pkI, I)
  , In(mB1)
  ]
--[ _restrict( verify(mB1, <I,R>, pkI) = true )
  , Running(R, I, <'Init', 'Resp'>)
  ]->
  [ Out(sign(<I,R>,ltkR))
  ]
```

with the executability specified by this lemma (whose proof succeeds and results in an example graph in interactive mode).

```
      /* and the adversary did not reveal the participants' long-term keys */
      & not (Ex #r. Reveal(actor)@r)
      & not (Ex #r. Reveal(peer)@r)
        ==>
          /* there is somebody running a session with the same parameters */
          (Ex #j. Running(peer, actor, params) @ j & j < i
```

5.9 A hierarchy of authentication properties

```
                /* and there is no other commit on the same parameters */
                & not(Ex actor2 peer2 #i2.
```

Note that in this example, we modeled signature verification using embedded restrictions using the _restrict(·) action fact, which we will explain in detail in Section 5.10.3.

This protocol provides weak agreement as the parties indeed have the same (correct) view that they are talking to each other. Hence TAMARIN verifies this lemma. Note, however, that there is no replay protection and that an initiator message can be seen as a responder message from that agent. Thus, this example does not provide non-injective or injective agreement, and the file **AuthHierarchy1WA.spthy** gives further details for this example. This protocol provides aliveness of course, which is also verified by TAMARIN in the file, while the stronger (non-)injective agreement property lemmas are violated.

Example 11 (Non-injective agreement) The next protocol provides non-injective agreement, but not injective agreement. Thus it is susceptible to replay attacks. Its first message is the same as in the previous protocol, but the second message contains only the initiator's name, signed by the responder. This way, the message of an initiator (respectively responder) cannot be mistaken as one coming from that agent but in the responder (respectively initiator) role. The protocol is:

```
1. A -> B: sign(<A,B>,sk(A))
2. A <- B: sign(A, sk(B))
```

See the file **AuthHierarchy2NIA.spthy** for the TAMARIN code for this example, which provides non-injective agreement but not injective agreement. The injective agreement lemma shows a violation, while both the non-injective agreement and weak agreement lemmas are verified.

Example 12 (Injective Agreement) Our last example provides all the illustrated authentication properties including injective agreement. The example includes a fresh nonce to distinguish different runs, thereby preventing replay. The protocol is:

```
1. A -> B: Na, sign(<A,B>,sk(A))
2. A <- B: sign(<A, Na>,sk(B))
```

See the file **AuthHierarchy3IA.spthy** for the TAMARIN code for the example providing injective agreement. All the lemmas are successfully verified in this theory.

Note that all of the properties we presented above are from the point of view of the initiator, while the responder is ignored. Also note that as TAMARIN's property specification is general purpose, one can formulate other authentication properties as required. For example, one could capture a notion like anonymous agreement where a party knows that they agree on data with another party, without knowing who that party is.

5.10 Additional features for specifying properties

TAMARIN provides several additional mechanisms to help users specify properties and to use them for fine-grained system modeling: predicates, restrictions, and embedded restrictions.

5.10.1 Predicates

It is common to re-use formulas, or parts thereof, across models. To reduce duplication, users can define predicates as formula shorthands. A predicate is written as

```
predicates: Formula1 <=> Formula2
```

which is syntactic sugar for inlining `Formula2` everywhere `Formula1` is written. This applies in both lemmas and restrictions.

For example, one could define:

```
builtins: multiset
predicates: Smaller(x,y) <=> Ex z. x + z = y

[...]

lemma one_smaller_two:
    "All x y #i. B(x,y)@i ==> Smaller(x,y)"
```

Similar to `builtins`, one may use `predicates` to define multiple predicates by separating them with commas and optional whitespace, including newlines.

5.10.2 Restrictions

Restrictions are also trace properties and they have the same format as lemmas, although their semantics and usage are rather different. Like lemmas, restrictions are guarded first-order logic formulas, introduced with the keyword `restriction`. In contrast to lemmas, a restriction limits the set of traces TAMARIN considers. A restriction is thus never proven. Instead, it constitutes an assumption about the system, and any property proven for a system with restrictions is only guaranteed to hold with respect to the stated restrictions. The following restrictions are collected and available at **Restrictions.spthy**.

As a simple example, consider a restriction stating the **equality** of two terms occurring in a specific action.

```
restriction Equality:
  "All x y #i. Eq(x,y) @#i ==> x = y"
```

5.10 Additional features for specifying properties

This restriction will ensure that in any rule with the Eq(x,y) action, the terms matched by the variables x and y are the same (considered modulo the equational theory, as usual). The modeler can then add an Eq action to any rule where such an equality is desired. This can, for example, be used to check whether a signature verification succeeds, whether a message decrypts correctly and yields the challenge sent by the agent, etc. For example, using the signature built-in (See Section 7.1), the following rule uses the restriction for the Eq action fact to model signature verification:

```
builtins: signing

rule R_Recv_Verify_Signature:
  [ In(m)
  , S_R_1(~tid, $I, $R, ~nonce, pkI )
  ]
--[ Eq( verify(m, <$R,~nonce>, pkI ), true)
  ]->
  [ S_R_2(~tid, $I, $R, ~nonce, pkI )
  ]
```

For this rule with the Equality restriction above, properties would only be evaluated for traces where the received messages in all instances of this rule are successfully verified to be signatures of the corresponding instances of $R and ~nonce with respect to the key pkI.

There are other common restrictions that are used frequently, which capture relations such as inequality, comparison, and the number of occurrences of rule instances. As usual, the actions used in these restrictions must be added appropriately to the system's rules. We give examples of such restrictions next.

We can specify an **Inequality** restriction using a similar annotation, Neq(x,y), but stating that it is not the case that the two values are the same:

```
restriction Inequality:
  "All x #i. Neq(x,x) @ #i ==> F"
```

OnlyOnce is a restriction specifying that certain actions, possibly with specific parameters, occur at most once in a trace. We specify two different versions of it:

```
restriction OnlyOnce:
  "All #i #j. OnlyOnce()@#i & OnlyOnce()@#j ==> #i = #j"
restriction OnlyOnceV:
  "All #i #j x. OnlyOnceV(x)@#i & OnlyOnceV(x)@#j ==> #i = #j"
```

The version OnlyOnce() without a parameter can occur at most once in any rule instance. For example, with the above restrictions, if OnlyOnce() is an action in the rules R1 and R2, then each trace can have at most one instance of either of R1 or R2.

The generalized version OnlyOnceV(x) is sometimes also called Unique(x), and enables more fine-grained specification. This restriction states that OnlyOnceV(x) can occur at most once in each trace for a specific value of x.

In practice, we can use this to restrict specific rules to at most one instance, but still allow multiple different rules to occur in the same trace, by putting an action OnlyOnceV('R1') in rule R1, and OnlyOnceV('R2') in rule R2.

Moreover, we can also use it to restrict specific uses of a rule. For example, we can ensure that each agent registers only one key in a PKI, for example by modifying the key registration in Section 5.6 in the following way:

```
rule Register_pk:
  [ Fr(~ltk) ]
    --[ OnlyOnceV(<'key',$A>) ]->
  [ !Ltk($A, ~ltk), !Pk($A, pk(~ltk)), Out(pk(~ltk)) ]
```

The resulting model, available at **SignedDH_simple_OnlyOnceV.spthy** still allows any number of agents to register public keys, but each agent can register at most one key.

The **SubMultiset** and **SuperMultiset** restrictions can be used to specify orderings using the built-in `multiset`. We can then add a restriction to enforce the subset or superset orderings. The action goes on a rule as usual, and the restriction to add is as follows.

```
builtins: multiset
restriction SubMultiset:
  "All x y #i. SubMultiset(x,y)@#i ==> Ex z. x + z = y"
restriction SuperMultiset:
  "All x y #i. SuperMultiset(x,y)@#i ==> Ex z. x = y + z"
```

Some example uses for restrictions are:

- accepting only particular values for certain inputs, using the equality restriction above; for example, checking that the verification of a signature succeeds; and
- limiting the number of sessions to show a smaller, nicer-looking attack, if there is one.

As mentioned earlier, restrictions are assumptions. They must therefore be carefully considered and justified by the modeler outside of TAMARIN.

5.10.3 Embedded restrictions

Using the special `_restrict` keyword as an action, which takes a formula as an argument, we can specify restrictions directly within rules, with the full file available at **CombinedRestrictions.spthy**.

```
rule MakeChoice:
  [In($X)]
--[Choice($X), _restrict(($X='string1') | ($X='string2'))]->
  [Chosen($X)]
```

Informally, the restriction specifies that the rule can only fire if $X is equal to either 'string1' or 'string2'. Such restrictions can also be useful when modeling branching or case distinctions, where each case has its own rule with a corresponding embedded restriction, or to model that a protocol step performs specific checks, such as verifying a signature or comparing multiple values.

5.10 Additional features for specifying properties

When TAMARIN encounters rules with embedded restrictions, it automatically replaces the embedded restriction by an action that stores the relevant variables, and generates a restriction as in Section 5.10.2. For example, the above rule MakeChoice is internally translated into the following:

```
[ In( $X ) ]
--[ Choice( $X ), Restr_MakeChoice_1( $X, $X ) ]->
[ Chosen( $X ) ]
```

Note the automatically generated Restr_MakeChoice_1 fact[6], which records the local variables of the rule instance relevant for the restriction. The corresponding restriction is generated as:

```
"∀ x #NOW x.1.
  (Restr_MakeChoice_1( x, x.1 ) @ #NOW) ⇒
  ((x = 'string1') ∨ (x.1 = 'string2'))"
```

The automatically generated restrictions identify the timepoint of the rule instance by the variable #NOW. The full expanded file is available at **CombinedRestrictions-expanded.spthy**.

For this model, we can prove the following expected lemma, which states that the only choices that can ever occur in a trace must be either string1 or string2:

```
lemma ChoiceInvariant:
  "All x #i. Choice(x)@i ==> (x='string1')|(x='string2')"
```

Embedded restrictions can also be used to formulate more complex constraints. For example, we can specify that a rule can only be instantiated in traces where another action fact occurs:

```
rule AfterChoice:
  [Chosen('string1')]
--[ AfterString1(), _restrict(Ex #i. Choice('string2')@i) ]->
  []
```

When we add this rule with its embedded restriction, TAMARIN internally automatically translates AfterChoice into the rule

```
[ Chosen( 'string1' ) ]
--[ AfterString1( ), Restr_AfterChoice_1( ) ]->
[ ]
```

and the restriction

```
"∀ #NOW.
  (Restr_AfterChoice_1( ) @ #NOW) ⇒ (∃ #i. Choice( 'string2' ) @ #i)"
```

Intuitively, the AfterChoice rule can only be instantiated when the left-hand side is contained in the global state, and the restriction holds. This implies that both 'string1' and 'string2' must both occur as choices in the trace. Indeed, TAMARIN can prove the following lemma.

---

[6] The name of this fact, which is automatically generated, is irrelevant and simply must be unique.

```
lemma CombinedRestrictions:
  "All #i. AfterString1()@i ==> (
    (Ex #j. Choice('string1')@j )
    &
    (Ex #j. Choice('string2')@j )
  )"
end
```

Another example of the use of embedded restrictions can be found in Example 10, where we used them to model signature verification.

5.10.4 Combining predicates and restrictions for branching

In real-world systems, the formulas that specify case or branch conditions can be complex and often include "else" branches. To avoid duplication and increase readability, we can combine embedded restrictions with predicates.

In the following example, our goal is to have a case distinction on an adversary-provided value:

Case A: its top-level operator is f;

Case B: its top-level operator is g with the specific first argument '1'; or

Case C: the value is something else.

The following model captures these options using predicates and embedded restrictions, both to improve readability and to encode the else-clause for case C, with the full file at **RestrictionsPredicatesElse.spthy**.

```
functions: f/1, g/2

predicates: ConditionA(x) <=> ( Ex z. x = f(z) ),
            ConditionB(x) <=> ( Ex z. x = g('1',z) )

rule AttackerProvides:
  [ In(X) ]-->[ CaseInput(X) ]

rule RuleA:      // Case A
  [ CaseInput(X) ]
--[ Choice('A',X), _restrict(ConditionA(X)) ]->
  []

rule RuleB:      // Case B
  [ CaseInput(X) ]
--[ Choice('B',X), _restrict(ConditionB(X)) ]->
  []

rule RuleC:      // Case C "else"
  [ CaseInput(X) ]
--[ Choice('C',X)
  , _restrict(not ( ConditionA(X) | ConditionB(X) ))
  ]->
```

5.10 Additional features for specifying properties

[]

For this model, TAMARIN can prove that the cases are mutually exclusive, using the following lemma.

```
lemma RulesPartition:
  "All case1 case2 x #i #j.
    Choice(case1,x)@i & Choice(case2,x)@j
      ==> (case1 = case2)"
```

Part III
The Tamarin System

Chapter 6
A First Glimpse Under the Hood

In this chapter we explain how to start TAMARIN, how it works internally, and how to interpret its output. For TAMARIN to work, two tools it depends on must be installed. One tool needed is Maude [106], which is used for variant computation and unification modulo associativity-commutativity. The other tool needed is GraphViz [69], which is used for visualizing graphs.

6.1 Running TAMARIN

TAMARIN supports two interfaces, each offering users a different way to interact with the tool.

The first interface is a graphical user interface that is accessed from a web browser. This is the interface that most users will use most of the time as it supports an `interactive mode` of usage where users interact with the prover. For example, they can have TAMARIN display (incomplete) protocol executions as graphs and use these graphs to visualize attacks or debug models. Moreover, they can try different proof strategies to extend these graphs and explore different proof alternatives.

The second interface is a simple `command-line` interface. It can be used to re-run existing files, to simply check protocol descriptions for syntax errors, or to measure the time needed for proof construction.

6.1.1 Web interface

To run TAMARIN in its interactive mode on the file named `theory.spthy`, run the command: `tamarin-prover interactive theory.spthy`. This will start TAMARIN and invite the user to connect to the web interface.

```
The server is starting up on port 3001.
Browse to http://127.0.0.1:3001 once the server is ready.

Loading the security protocol theories './*.spthy' ...

[Some messages about the different theories being loaded]

Finished loading theories ... server ready at

  http://127.0.0.1:3001
```

After connecting to http://127.0.0.1:3001, the user is presented with TAMARIN's welcome page (see Figure 6.1).

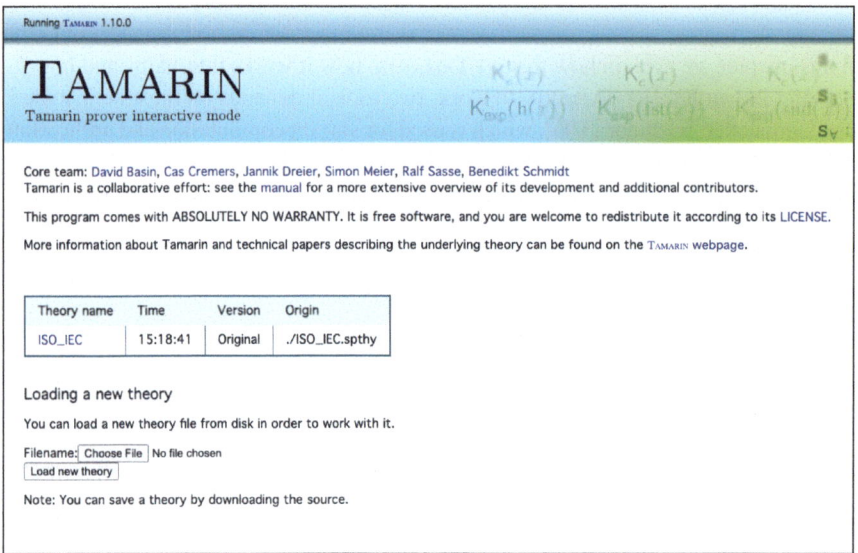

Fig. 6.1: TAMARIN's welcome page in interactive mode

On the welcome page, TAMARIN lists all theory files it has loaded. Note that even when given just a single file name, in interactive mode TAMARIN will automatically load all files in the same directory. One can also upload additional files using the form in the "Loading a new Theory" section at the bottom of the page, specifically the "Choose File" and "Load new theory" buttons.

When clicking on a theory, TAMARIN shows the following screen (see Figure 6.2). On the left, there are links to the Message theory (i.e., the function signature, equations, and adversary rules), to the Multiset rewrite rules (the protocol and network rules), and to the Raw and Refined sources (the result of TAMARIN's precomputations explained in Chapter 8). On the right, TAMARIN shows the keyboard shortcuts that can be used for quick navigation. On the top right, there are links to

6.1 Running TAMARIN

navigate back to the main menu, to download the current proof state or the source file, and to adjust the level of details shown in the graphs.

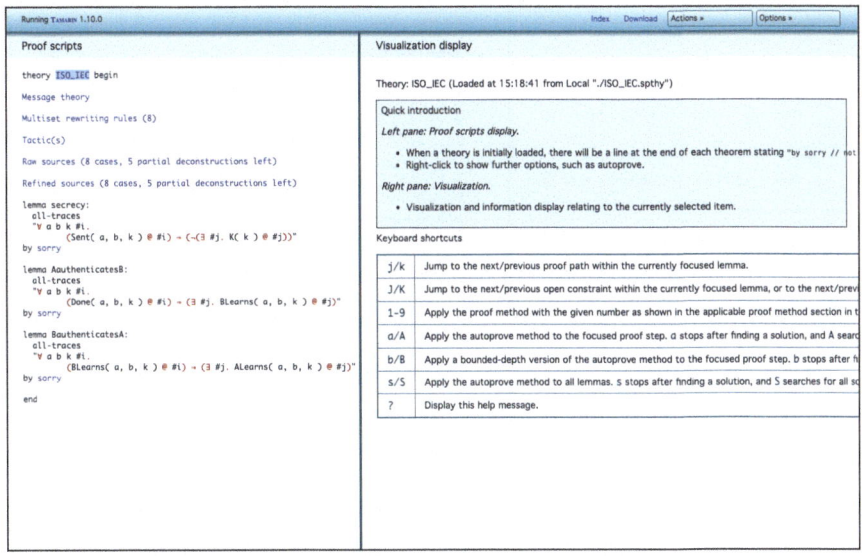

Fig. 6.2: The theory `ISO_IEC` loaded in TAMARIN

When clicking on `Message theory`, TAMARIN shows the theory's signature. Namely, it displays the (built-in or user-defined) functions and equations, as well as the adversary rules that it deduced from the equations (see 6.3).

The link `Multiset rewrite rules` can be used to inspect the protocol and network rules (together with the variants TAMARIN computed, see Section 6.7), as well as protocol restrictions, if they exist (see 6.4).

The next link can be used to inspect the tactics (see Section 16.3 for more information on tactics). Finally the last two links can be used to inspect the results of TAMARIN's internal precomputations. We will elaborate on all these options in this chapter.

6.1.2 Command line

To run TAMARIN in command-line mode on the file `theory.spthy`, simply call TAMARIN as follows.

```
tamarin-prover theory.spthy
```

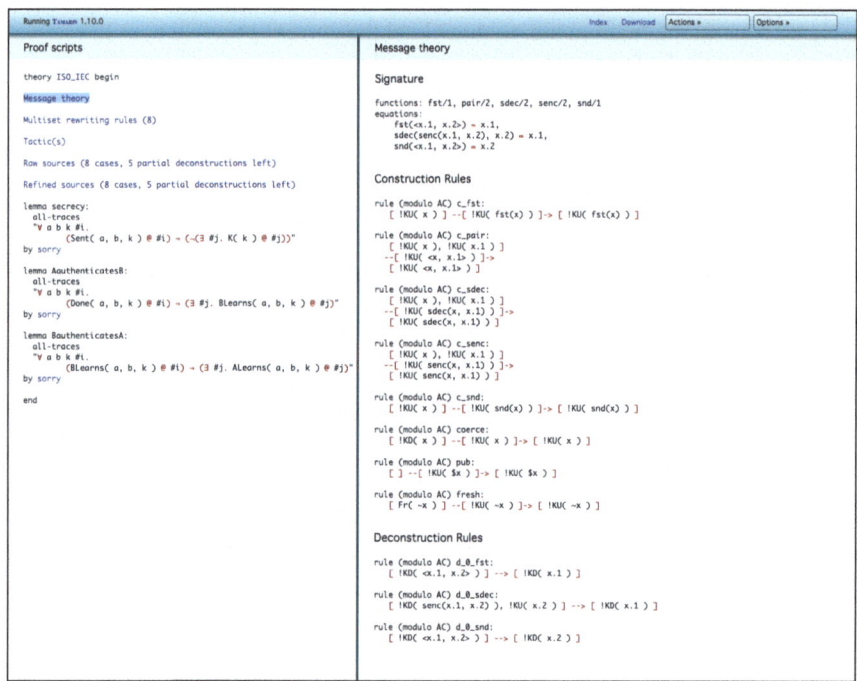

Fig. 6.3: The message theory

TAMARIN will load the file, check wellformedness, and output a pretty-printed and cleaned-up version with comments removed, but again without proving any of the lemmas. To actually prove the lemmas, add the flag --prove.

```
tamarin-prover theory.spthy --prove
```

TAMARIN will now try to prove all lemmas in the theory using its autoprover. Afterwards, it will output a summary of all the results. Namely, TAMARIN prints a line for each lemma stating whether the lemma was proven or disproven, and how many proof steps were required. It also prints the total processing time.

```
==============================================================================
summary of summaries:

analyzed: ../tamarin-book/latex/theories/Minimal_Loop_induction.spthy

  processing time: 0.22s

  Start_before_Loop (all-traces): verified (8 steps)
  Satisfied_by_empty_trace_only (exists-trace): verified (3 steps)

==============================================================================
```

6.1 Running Tamarin

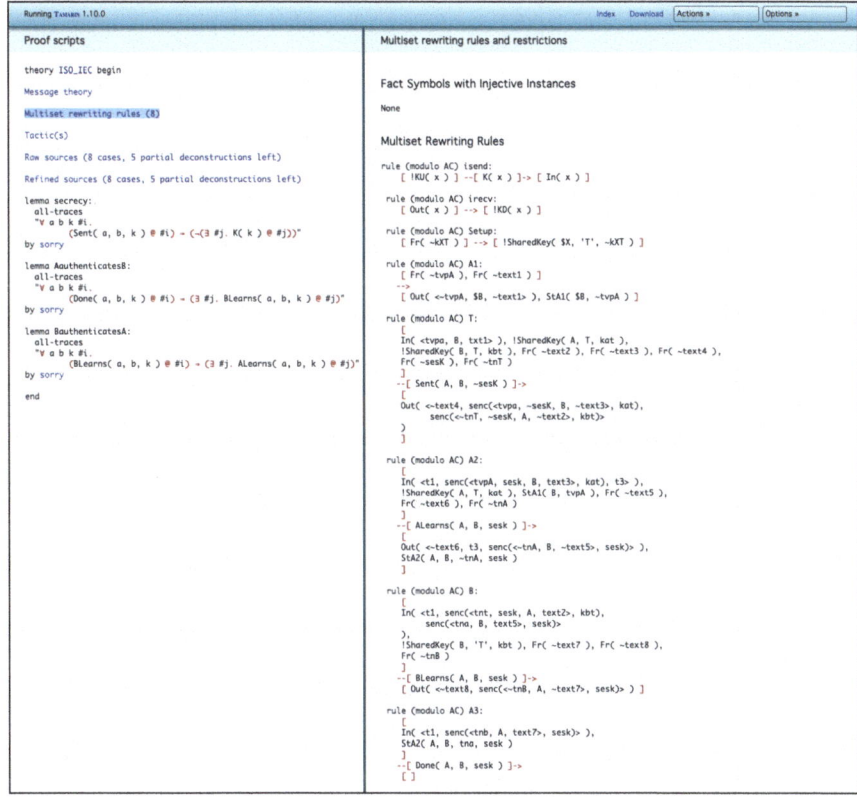

Fig. 6.4: The multiset rewrite rules

Note that Tamarin's output can be stored in a file and reloaded later. This also includes the proof(s). When loading a file containing a (partial) proof, Tamarin will verify all proof steps, and report when it fails to check any of the steps.

To see all options, run `tamarin-prover --help`. The most important options, and their corresponding flags, are:

- `--prove[=LEMMAPREFIX*|LEMMANAME]`: Prove all lemmas that start with LEMMAPREFIX or the lemma whose name is LEMMANAME.
- `--heuristic[=(C|I|O|P|S|c|i|o|p|s)+]`: Specify heuristic to use (the default is 's'). See Section 6.6 for more details on heuristics.
- `--stop-on-trace[=DFS|BFS|SEQDFS|NONE]`: Specify how to search for traces. The default is DFS (depth-first search). However BFS (breadth-first search) may help, in particular for `exists-trace` lemmas, or when one expects to find a counterexample. SEQDFS forces a sequential search, thus deactivating Tamarin's built-in parallelization. NONE tells Tamarin to continue its search even after a (counter-)example has been found.

- `--bound[=INT]`: Fix the depth bound for the bounded autoprover in interactive mode.
- `--quit-on-warning`: Run in strict mode, which means quitting when any warning is emitted.
- `--auto-sources`: Try to auto-generate sources lemmas. See Chapter 8 for more details.
- `--parse-only`: Just parse the input file and pretty print it as is. This can be useful to quickly check if a file parses without performing any further checks, or to pretty-print an input file.
- `--output[=FILE]` and `--Output[=DIR]`: Specify an output file or output directory.
- `--defines[=STRING]`: Define flags for TAMARIN's internal preprocessor. See Section 10.2.3 for more details.
- `--diff`: Turn on observational equivalence mode, as explained in Chapter 13.
- `--oraclename[=FILE]`: Set the path to the external oracle heuristic (default './oracle'), as explained in Section 16.4.
- `--open-chains[=PositiveInteger]`: Limit the number of deconstruction chain constraints to be resolved during precomputations (the default is 10). See Section 8.1 for more details.
- `--saturation[=PositiveInteger]`: Limit the number of saturations during precomputations (the default is 5), as explained in Section 8.1.
- `--precompute-only`: Only run precomputations and show case numbers, as well as partial deconstructions. See Section 8.1 for more details.
- `--quiet`: Do not display oracle or tactic calls. See Section 16.3 and Section 16.4 for an explanation of oracles and tactics.
- `--verbose`: Display debug information during proof construction.
- `--derivcheck-timeout[=INT]`: Set the timeout for message derivation checks in seconds (default 5). The value 0 deactivates checks. See Section 10.1.6 for more details.
- `--debug`: Show server debugging output (only in interactive mode).
- `--no-logging`: Do not show web server logs (only in interactive mode).
- `--version`: Print version information.

6.2 How TAMARIN works

Here we provide an overview of how TAMARIN works when proving trace properties. Equivalence properties are handled differently and are described in Chapter 13.

TAMARIN takes as input the protocol model (the rules, equational theories, and restrictions), as well as the specification of the security properties to prove (the lemmas). It then tries to construct a proof or a counterexample for each property.

Internally, after parsing the input file, TAMARIN first performs some wellformedness checks to ensure that the input file is syntactically correct, and to detect potential

6.2 How TAMARIN works

modeling errors. It then converts both the protocol model and the security properties into constraints. Moreover, it precomputes some larger "composite" constraint reduction steps that it uses to speed up reasoning later.

To verify whether a protocol satisfies a given security property, TAMARIN checks whether the union of the constraints for the protocol model and the constraints for the *negation* of the security property, taken together, have a solution. This proceeds by a sequence of constraint reduction steps.

Constraint reduction can (and ideally will) lead to a set of constraints where it is clear whether there is a solution. But this reduction might not terminate. Moreover, each reduction step can lead to branching in the search space, resulting in multiple independent sets of constraints that all must be considered, for example due to a case distinction.

If no constraint reduction rule is applicable and the constraints are consistent, this means a solution to the constraints exists. In TAMARIN, this corresponds to a non-empty set of traces coherent with the protocol model (as they satisfy the protocol's constraints) that violate the security property (as they also satisfy the constraints for the property's *negation*). This solution thus constitutes a set of attacks.

If no solution exists because the constraints are contradictory, then there is no trace coherent with both the protocol model and the property's negation. Hence the property is proven. See Section 1.2 and Figure 1.2 for an illustration of the general approach.

The constraints TAMARIN uses represent the minimal requirements for a valid solution, e.g., the required rule instances and their ordering, and they are of two types: formulas which must hold (for example, initially the negation of the property to prove, or restrictions), and graph constraints. Graphs are used abstractly to represent constraints on (partial) traces. In these graphs, which are called *dependency graphs* in TAMARIN, each node is an instance of a rule. The edges connect the facts consumed by a rule to their origins, i.e., the rule instance that created each fact. This also describes a partial order on the rule instances. Overall, there can be three different types of graph constraints: node constraints (assigning a rule instance to a node), premise constraints (requiring the presence of a certain premise), and edge constraints (linking two nodes).

Consider the following toy example, with the full file available at **Dependency-Graph.spthy**.

Example 13 (Example from [88]) We have three rules:

```
rule Init:
  [ Fr(~a), Fr(~k) ]
  --[ ]->
  [ K(~k), St(~a, ~k), Out( enc(~a,~k) ) ]

rule End:
  [ St(a, k), In(<a,a>) ]
  --[ Fin(a) ]->
```

[]

```
rule Reveal:
  [ K(x) ]
  --[ Rev(x) ]->
  [ Out(x) ]
```

The `Init` rule creates a fresh message a and a fresh key k, encrypts the message with the key, and outputs the result. It also stores the key in one fact, and the message and key in another fact.

The `End` rule recovers the stored message and key, and matches an input consisting of a pair containing two copies of the stored message.

The `Reveal` rule allows the adversary to reveal a stored key.

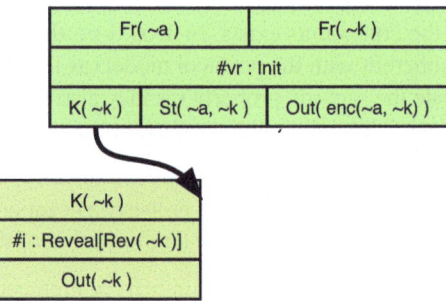

Fig. 6.5: Dependency graph for lemma `CannotReveal` after second step

Now consider Figure 6.5. This graph consists of five constraints:

- two node constraints, which are the instances of rules `Init` and `Reveal`;
- an edge constraint linking the K(~k) conclusion of the `Init` rule to the K(~k) premise of the `Reveal` rule; and
- two premise constraints for the premises Fr(~a) and Fr(~k), which still must be resolved to have a complete execution.

Note that the dependency graph only represents the *minimal* requirements for a certain event (here the `Reveal` rule instance) to occur, and it actually covers many possible ground traces. In this example, it simply states that `Init` must take place *before* `Reveal` (because of the edge). However there can be arbitrary other rule instances before, between, or after these two rule instances. Moreover, the variables must be instantiated with ground values, etc. Section 6.3 explains this in more detail.

To illustrate how TAMARIN's constraint solving works, consider the following lemma.

6.2 How TAMARIN works

```
lemma CannotReveal:
  "not( Ex y #i. Rev(y)@#i )"
```

In a first step, TAMARIN creates an empty constraint system and adds the formula's negation to it. Thus we obtain a constraint system with no graph constraints, but with the formula `Ex y #i. Rev(y)@#i`.

There is only one rule in the model that has a `Rev` fact as an action: the `Reveal` rule. TAMARIN can therefore refine the model by converting the formula into a node constraint with a rule instance of the `Reveal` rule. Moreover, as the variables are existentially quantified, TAMARIN can treat them as free variables. TAMARIN also adds a new premise constraint: the origin of the premise `K(~k)` must be found. The current state of the constraint system is shown in Figure 6.6.

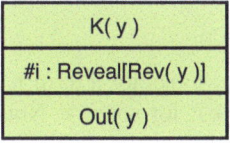

Fig. 6.6: Constraint system for lemma `CannotReveal` after first step

Again, as there is only one rule producing the K fact, namely the `Init` rule, TAMARIN can refine the system by adding an instance of the `Init` rule as a node constraint (with the same `~k`) and an edge constraint linking the `Init` rule's conclusion with the `Reveal` rule's premise. Moreover, there are two premise constraints: `Fr(~a)` and `Fr(~k)`. The system's state is shown in Figure 6.5.

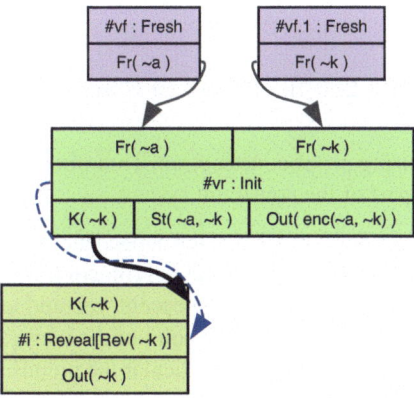

Fig. 6.7: Final solved constraint system

TAMARIN can then solve the remaining two premise constraints using instances of the fresh rule, which again is the only rule producing Fr facts. We thereby end up with the solved system shown in Figure 6.7.[1]

Each of these steps actually corresponds to the application of one *constraint reduction rule*. TAMARIN has numerous such rules, which refine the formulas or graph constraints. Each constraint reduction rule is guaranteed to preserve the set of solutions, which ensures the correctness of TAMARIN's reasoning. As previously observed, a constraint reduction step can result in multiple cases, for example when performing a case distinction on the possible rules that produce a specific fact. In general, the constraint reduction rules transform a constraint system into a set of constraint systems.

While solving constraints, TAMARIN also takes the equational theory into account. In this example, we have the following functions and equation:

```
functions: enc/2, dec/2
equations: dec(enc(m, k), k) = m
```

This means that when TAMARIN looks for a term t, it must actually consider two cases: t or dec(enc(t, k), k), for some k. Note that, to speed up reasoning, TAMARIN computes the normal forms of terms. This way it does not need to consider all possibilities at each step. See Section 6.7 for a more detailed explanation of this approach.

As previously mentioned, TAMARIN precomputes *sources* for all facts used in the protocol model. Given a fact, each source corresponds to a unique way of producing that fact by performing multiple constraint solving steps in one go. In the above example, TAMARIN will precompute one source for the K fact, which consists of an instance of the Init rule plus two instances of the Fresh rule (see Figure 6.8). The same dependency graph is actually also the only source for the St fact (see Figure 6.9).

6.3 How dependency graphs relate to traces

As explained above, during proof construction, TAMARIN incrementally constructs dependency graphs as part of the constraint system.

Consider the example from Section 6.2, and the dependency graph shown in Figure 6.5. This dependency graph constrains the possible protocol traces to those that contain at least one instance of the rule Init at timepoint #vr and an instance of the rule Reveal at some later timepoint #i. At this point of the constraint solving, since not all dependencies have been solved yet (in particular the premises of the rule Init), it might still be the case that the protocol has no such traces, in which case there is no solution.

---

[1] To simplify the graph visualization and speed up reasoning, fresh premises are automatically resolved and the corresponding rule instances are by default not shown in the graph visualization.

6.3 How dependency graphs relate to traces

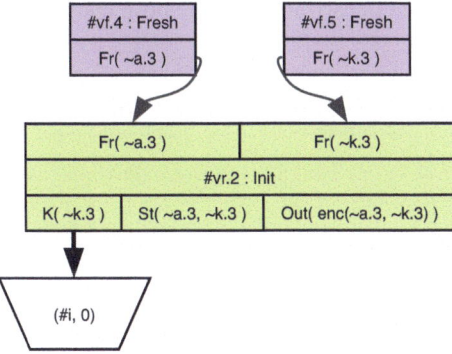

Fig. 6.8: Source of the fact K

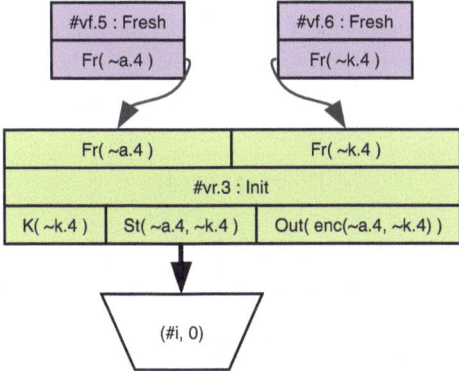

Fig. 6.9: Source of the fact St

Solved constraint systems: Once TAMARIN can determine that there exists at least one trace that instantiates the dependency graph and meets all its constraints, the constraint system is considered to be "SOLVED" and a trace can be constructed.

For example, consider the graph in Figure 6.7 from the same example. This constraint system is solved and hence we can construct a trace that satisfies it. We can do this as follows.

1. Pick any linearization of the partially ordered rule instances in the dependency graph.
2. Instantiate each variable in the constraint system with a ground term that does not already occur in the constraint system in a sort-respecting way. Namely, for each fresh variable, the ground term must be chosen from the set of fresh values; for each public variable, the ground term must be chosen from the set of public constants.

For example, one possible linearization of the above constraint system is:

1. Fresh @ #vf
2. Fresh @ #vf.1
3. Init @ #vr
4. Reveal @ #i

Another possible linearization is:

1. Fresh @ #vf.1
2. Fresh @ #vf
3. Init @ #vr
4. Reveal @ #i

The actual trace only contains the action facts of the rules (hence the instances of the Fresh and Init rules become "invisible" here), in the linearized order, where additionally all variables have been replaced by ground terms. A possible trace corresponding to the above linearization(s) is thus

$$[\text{Rev}(kA) @ 4],$$

where kA is a fresh value and 4 is a timepoint.

Note that for a solved constraint system, there are usually infinitely many traces that satisfy it. The traces are determined by each linearization of the partial order, and each possible variable instantiation. Moreover, the dependency graph only indicates which actions must necessarily be in the trace, but it does not exclude the occurrence of other actions.

For the above example, the following traces are also solutions to the same constraint system and dependency graph:

- [Rev(kB) @ 4], which is a trace with a different variable instantiation.
- [Rev(kA) @ 4, Rev(kB) @ 8], which is a trace with the graph duplicated, and with a different variable instantiation.
- [Rev(kA) @ 4, Fin(kA) @ 10], or even
  [Rev(kA) @ 4, Rev(kB) @ 8, Fin(kA) @ 17],
  which are traces with other rule instances added, possibly in an interleaved fashion.

6.4 The constraint-solving algorithm

As previously explained, TAMARIN uses constraint solving to prove or disprove lemmas, where each constraint reduction step generates one or more new constraint

6.4 The constraint-solving algorithm

```
lemma Client_auth_injective:
  all-traces
  "∀ S k #i.
        (SessKeyC( S, k ) @ #i) ⇒
        (∃ #a.
          (AnswerRequest( S, k ) @ #a) ∧
          (∀ #j. (SessKeyC( S, k ) @ #j) ⇒ (#i = #j)))"
simplify
solve( Client_1( S, k ) ▶₀ #i )
  case Client_1
  solve( !KU( h(~k) ) @ #vk )
    case Serv_1
    solve( !KU( aenc(<'1', ~k>, pk(~ltkS)) ) @ #vk.1 )
      case Client_1
      solve( (#i < #j) ∥ (#j < #i) )
        case case_1
        solve( Client_1( $S, ~k ) ▶₀ #j )
          case Client_1
          by contradiction /* cyclic */
        qed
      next
        case case_2
        solve( Client_1( $S, ~k ) ▶₀ #j )
          case Client_1
          by contradiction /* cyclic */
        qed
      qed
    next
      case c_aenc
      by sorry
    qed
  next
    case c_h
    by sorry
  qed
qed
```

Fig. 6.10: Partial proof tree of lemma `Client_auth_injective`

systems. This leads to a proof tree, which is visible in the GUI, or output when TAMARIN is run on the command line.

Figure 6.10 presents a TAMARIN proof tree, visible on the left-hand side in the GUI. All blue lines correspond to an application of a constraint reduction rule, with the resulting set of refined constraint systems listed below. There can be any number of these "cases" (including zero), which again must be resolved, and so on. The qed symbol marks the end of a list of cases.

6.4.1 Proof methods

TAMARIN uses different types of *proof methods* to solve different types of constraints:

- The proof method for *premise constraints* is typically used to find the origin of facts from the protocol rules. It is shown as solve(Fact(terms) ▶ #timepoint) in the proof tree. For example, the second proof step in Figure 6.10, solve(Client_1(S, k) ▶ #i) solves the premise Client_1(S, k) in the rule instance #i.

- The proof method for *action constraints* is used to solve formula constraints, for example, when a formula requires a certain action to be present in the trace, or to solve intruder deduction constraints as described in Section 6.8. The application of this proof method is shown as solve(Fact(terms) @ #timepoint) in the proof tree. For example, the third proof step in Figure 6.10, solve(!KU(h(~k)) @ #vk) solves the intruder deduction constraint !KU(h(~k)) in the rule instance #vk. In essence, it computes whether (and if so, how) the intruder can obtain h(~k).

- The proof method for *disjunctions* turns a disjunction inside a formula into a case distinction at the level of the constraint system. The application of this proof method is shown as solve(f1 ∥ f2) in the proof tree, where f1 and f2 are formulas. For example, the fifth goal in Figure 6.10, solve((#i < #j) ∥ (#j < #i)), is a disjunction goal.

- *Contradiction* is a proof method used when TAMARIN can show that the current constraint system is contradictory. Examples of this are dependency graphs with a circular dependency, or a formula evaluating to false given the current dependency graph. Contradictions are displayed as contradiction in the proof tree, together with a brief comment describing the type of contradiction (e.g., /* cyclic */ or /* from formulas */). As a contradictory constraint system has no solutions, TAMARIN stops solving further constraints for these systems, effectively "closing" a branch of the proof tree. In Figure 6.10, there are two contradictions.

- *Simplify* is a proof method used to simplify a formula from the formula constraints and also to translate it into other constraints. Typically this is the first step in the proof tree (as in Figure 6.10), and it translates the negation of the lemma into a set of graph constraints and potentially other formulas. This is shown as simplify in the proof tree.

- The *induction* proof method allows TAMARIN to prove a lemma using induction on the length of the trace. It is shown as induction and is only available as the first proof step. For more details, see Section 9.1.

- The proof method for *deconstruction chain* constraints is used to compute whether the adversary can extract a given term from some message. This proof method's application is shown in the proof tree as solve((#timepoint1, i1) ~~> (#timepoint2, i2)), where i1 and i2 are integers. See Section 6.8 and Chapter 8 for more details.

- Applications of the proof method for *equation split* constraints are written in the proof tree as solve(splitEqs(i)), where i is an integer. This proof method is used to perform a case split on different possible substitutions, for example when considering rule variants. See Section 6.7 for details.

6.4 The constraint-solving algorithm

- `sorry` is a special proof method that does not prove anything. It simply serves as a placeholder in the proof tree for a proof that still needs to be completed.
- SOLVED in the proof tree means that TAMARIN has reached a *solved* constraint system, where no proof methods are applicable. The dependency graph then corresponds to a protocol execution that respects all constraints. Typically, this will be a counterexample constituting an attack on the security property being reasoned about. The exception is `exists-trace` lemmas, where this execution corresponds to a proof that the trace exists.

6.4.2 An example

Example 14 (Simple Challenge Response Protocol)

Consider again the following example from Chapter 4, where the full file is available at **SimpleChallengeResponse.spthy**:

```
rule Register_pk:
  [ Fr(~ltk) ]
  -->
  [ !Ltk($A, ~ltk), !Pk($A, pk(~ltk)), Out(pk(~ltk)) ]

rule Client_1:
    [ Fr(~k), !Pk($S, pkS) ]
  -->
    [ Client_1( $S, ~k ), Out( aenc{'1', ~k}pkS ) ]

rule Client_2:
    [ Client_1(S, k), In( h(k) ) ]
  --[ SessKeyC( S, k ) ]->
    []

rule Serv_1:
    [ !Ltk($S, ~ltkS), In( aenc{'1', k}pk(~ltkS) ) ]
  --[ AnswerRequest($S, k)
    ]->
    [ Out( h(k) ) ]
```

Consider the following lemma specifying injective agreement:

```
lemma Client_auth_injective:
  " /* for all session keys 'k' setup by clients with a server 'S' */
  ( All S k #i.  SessKeyC(S, k) @ #i
      ==>
        /* there is a server that answered the request */
        (Ex #a. AnswerRequest(S, k) @ a
            /* and there is no other client that had the same request. */
            & (All #j. SessKeyC(S, k) @ #j ==> #i = #j)
        )
  ) "
```

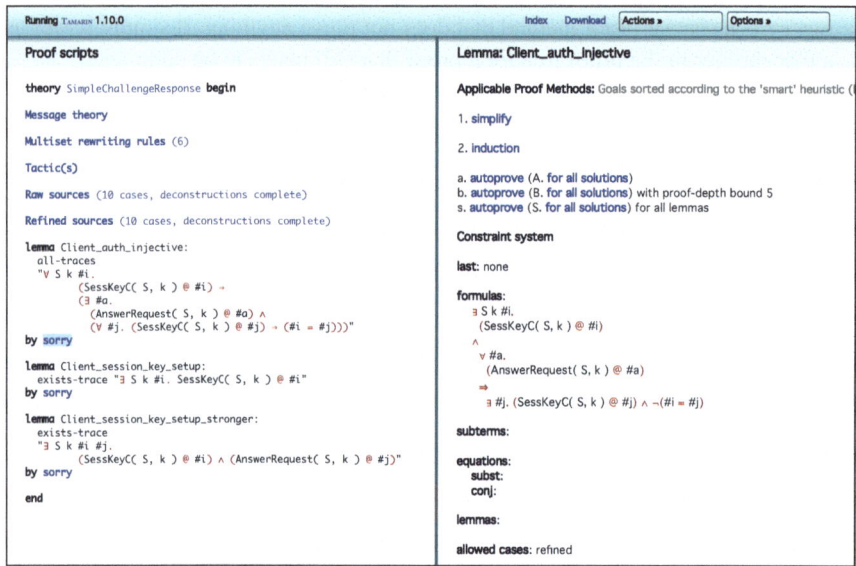

Fig. 6.11: Initial proof state

To illustrate how TAMARIN reasons, consider the first steps in the proof tree given in Figure 6.10. Initially, TAMARIN shows the constraint system given in Figure 6.11. There are two applicable proof methods: `simplify` and `induction`. TAMARIN also shows six variants of the "autoprover", a normal version a that tries to automatically prove the current lemma, and a bounded version b that stops at a given proof depth, thereby ensuring termination. The third version A (for all solutions) tries to fully explore the reachable constraint systems from the current state and continues working even after a counterexample has been found, at which point the first two versions would have stopped. Analogously, B applies a bounded "autoprover", but continues after a counterexample has been found. Finally there is a version s (and S, analogous to A and B) that tries to prove all lemmas at the same time. These "autoprovers" always apply the first possible proof method. Which proof method is ranked first depends on the heuristic used, see Section 6.6.

Below the applicable proof methods, TAMARIN shows the current state of the constraint system. Here, the system is initialized only with one formula: the negation of the property to be proven. The lemma states that for all `SessKeyC(S, k)` actions (i.e., session keys 'k' set up by clients with a server 'S'), there is an `AnswerRequest(S, k)` action (i.e., a server that answered the request), and all other `SessKeyC(S, k)` actions are actually identical to the initial one. Hence, the negation states that there exists a `SessKeyC(S, k)` action and for all `AnswerRequest(S, k)` actions there exists a different `SessKeyC(S, k)` action.

6.4 The constraint-solving algorithm

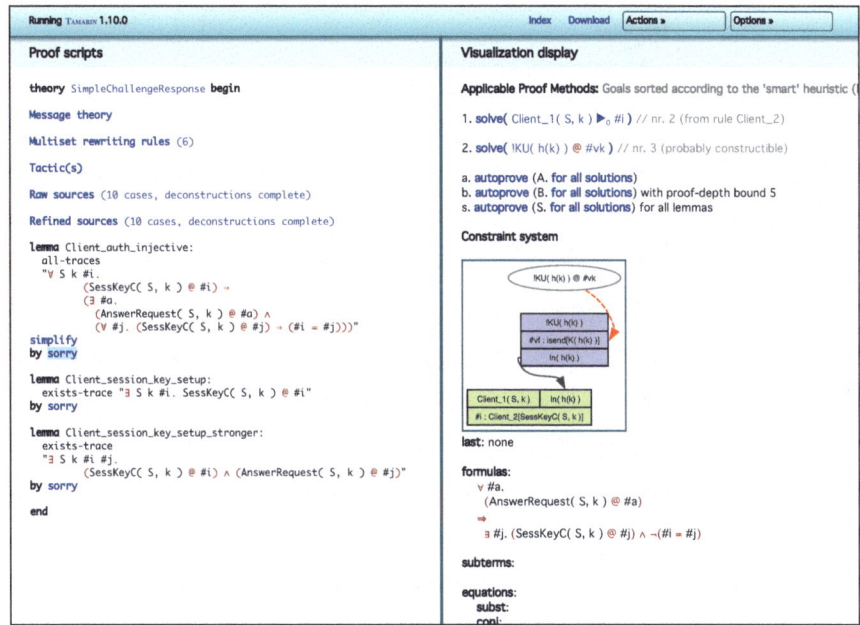

Fig. 6.12: Proof state after the first step

After applying `simplify`, one obtains the state shown in Figure 6.12. The proof tree on the left now contains the `simplify` step, and the constraint system on the right-hand side has been refined:

- A partial dependency graph is shown. It contains an instance of the `Client_2` rule, since this is the only rule containing a `SessKeyC(S, k)` action.

- The formula has been simplified. Given that the graph already contains a `SessKeyC(S, k)` action, it now only remains to show that for all `AnswerRequest(S, k)` there exists a different `SessKeyC(S, k)` action, as this would constitute a valid counterexample to the lemma.

- TAMARIN also lists the solved formulas from the previous steps as well as all unsolved and solved constraints (see Figure 6.13). In this case, the solved constraint corresponds to the `SessKeyC(S, k)` action constraint, which was solved using the instance of the `Client_2` rule in the dependency graph. The two unsolved constraints are the two open premises from the graph: the `Client_1(S, k)` fact and the input of `h(k)`.

After applying `solve( Client_1( S, k ) ▶ #i )`, one obtains the state shown in Figure 6.14. Here TAMARIN has solved the `Client_1( S, k )` premise constraint by adding an instance of the `Client_1` rule (thus the name of the case in the proof tree) to the dependency graph. The formulas are unmodified, and the solved constraints are updated. Note that TAMARIN directly solved the `!Pk( $S, pk(~ltk) )` premise

```
formulas:
  ∀ #a.
   (AnswerRequest( S, k ) @ #a)
  ⇒
   ∃ #j. (SessKeyC( S, k ) @ #j) ∧ ¬(#i = #j)

equations:
  subst:
  conj:

lemmas:

allowed cases: refined

solved formulas:
  ∃ S k #i.
   (SessKeyC( S, k ) @ #i)
  ∧
  ∀ #a.
   (AnswerRequest( S, k ) @ #a)
  ⇒
   ∃ #j. (SessKeyC( S, k ) @ #j) ∧ ¬(#i = #j)

unsolved goals:
  !KU( h(k) ) @ #vk // nr: 3" (probably constructible)"

  Client_1( S, k
  ) ▶₀ #i // nr: 2 (from rule Client_2)" (useful2)"

solved goals:
  SessKeyC( S, k
  ) @ #i // nr: 0 (from rule Client_2)" (useful2)"
```

Fig. 6.13: Details of the constraint system at Step 2

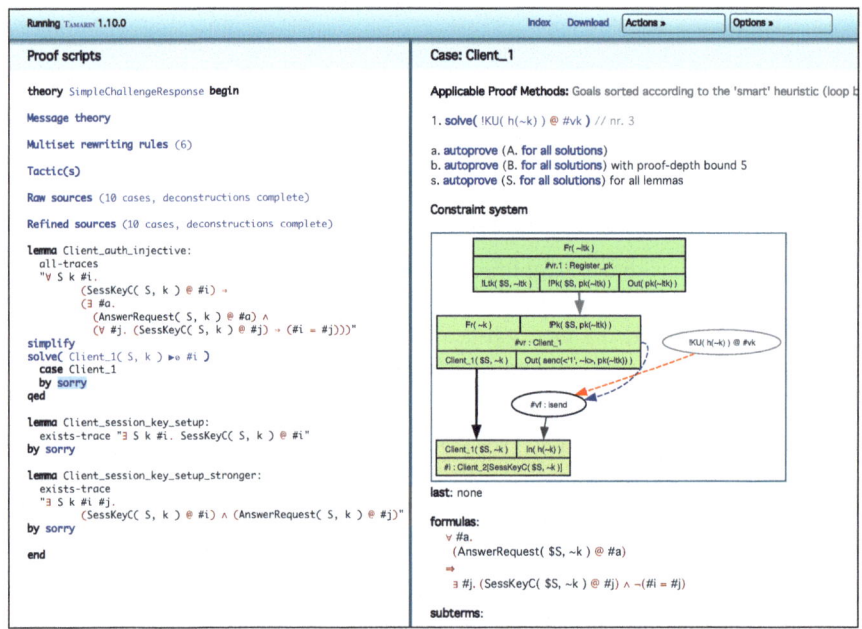

Fig. 6.14: Proof state after the second step

6.4 The constraint-solving algorithm

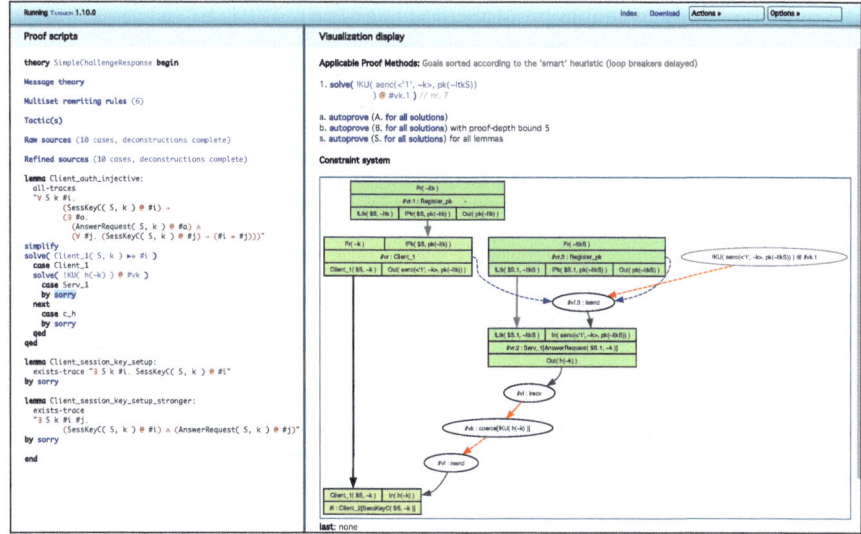

Fig. 6.15: Proof state after the third step, first case

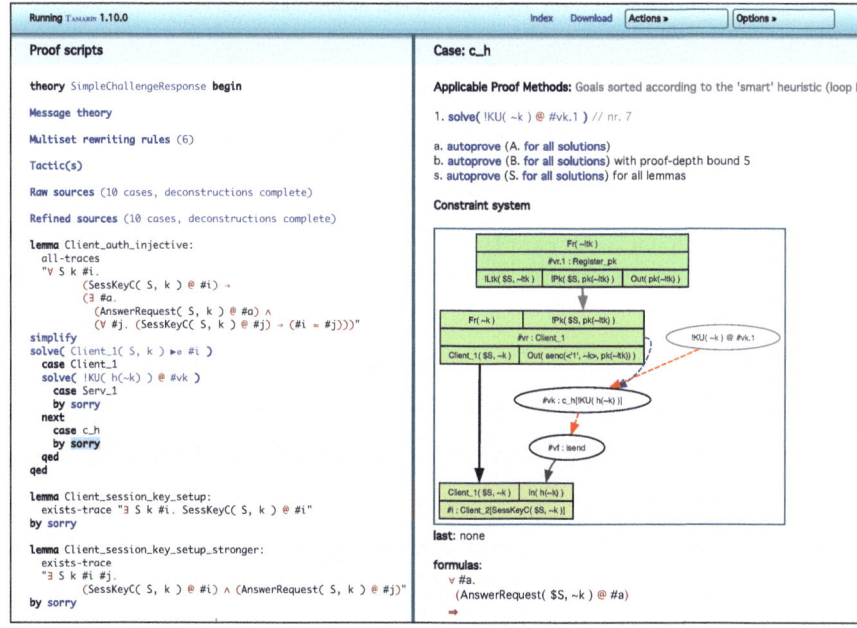

Fig. 6.16: Proof state after the third step, second case

of the added `Client_1` rule instance; this is due to TAMARIN's precomputations as explained in Chapter 8.

The only remaining available proof method is `solve( !KU( h(~k) ) @ #vk )`. When applying this method, one obtains the state shown in Figure 6.15. There are now two cases, displayed in the proof tree on the left: either the message corresponds to the output of a `Serv_1` rule instance shown on the right, or the adversary constructed the message by applying the hash function h (case `c_h`) to ~k (as in Figure 6.16). TAMARIN then must proceed in both branches of the proof tree to check whether either of them leads to a solved constraint system.

6.4.3 Proof method annotations

> **Applicable Proof Methods: Goals sorted according to 'smart' heuristic (loop breakers delayed)**
>
> 1. **solve(** Client_1(S, k) ▶₀ #i **)** // nr. 2 (from rule Client_2)
>
> 2. **solve(** !KU(h(k)) @ #vk **)** // nr. 3 (probably constructible)
>
> a. **autoprove** (A. **for all solutions**)
> b. **autoprove** (B. **for all solutions**) with proof-depth bound 5
> s. **autoprove** (S. **for all solutions**) for all lemmas

Fig. 6.17: Example list of available proof methods

When TAMARIN lists the currently available proof methods in its graphical user interface (see, e.g., Figure 6.17), the methods may also have annotations:

- An action constraint is `currently deducible` either when it is composed only from public constants and does not contain private function symbols, or when it can be extracted from a sent message using just unpairing or inversion.

- An action constraint is `probably constructible` when it concerns a message that does not contain a fresh name or a fresh variable, and therefore can likely be constructed by the adversary.

- An action constraint is `useful` when it appears in specific ways in the formulas of the constraint system.

- To avoid loops when solving premise constraints, TAMARIN computes a set of premises, called `loop breakers`, that are sufficient to break all possible loops (similar to a vertex feedback set used in graph theory). The idea is to consider a graph containing a node for each rule, and an edge between rule 1 and rule 2 if 2 has a premise fact that is part of the conclusion facts of rule 1. This graph over-approximates possible sequences of rules and, in particular, any potential looping sequence of rule instances will show up as a cycle in this graph. The goal is then to remove a minimal set of premises (the `loop breakers`) so that the remaining graph has no cycles. Note that this set is not, in general, unique,

6.5 Dependency graph visualizations

and TAMARIN might not compute the "optimal" solution. One can influence this computation using the [no_precomp] fact annotation, see Section 8.1.

All these annotations are used by TAMARIN to prioritize the available proof methods: a constraint that is currently deducible or probably constructible has a low priority. The same holds for loop breakers.

6.5 Dependency graph visualizations

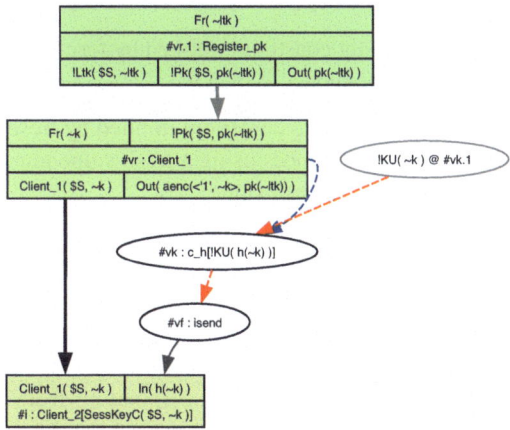

Fig. 6.18: A dependency graph with the default level of detail

As shown above, TAMARIN uses dependency graphs to abstractly represent protocol traces. The different symbols and colors in the graph have specific meanings. Consider, for example Figure 6.18. Their meanings are:

- Protocol rule instances are represented as rectangular boxes with a green background, where different shades of green distinguish different rules. The top part contains the premise facts and the bottom part the conclusion facts. In the middle, TAMARIN shows the timepoint, the rule's name, and the action facts.

In practice, the different shades of green can be quite similar. If desired, a rule can be annotated with a custom color (in RGB notation) to help reading the graph, as in the following example where the rule test will be shown in a red box:

```
rule test [color=FF0000]
...
```

- Round white boxes with a black border represent the actions taken by the adversary or the network.

- Round white boxes with a gray border represent open action constraints concerning the intruder deduction.
- Black or gray solid arrows show the origins of In and Fr facts as well as protocol facts (i.e., facts introduced by the users in the rules modeling the protocol, in contrast to built-in facts such as K, KU, KD, Out etc.). Grey is used for persistent (reusable) facts, and black for linear (consumed) facts (in particular also for Fr and In facts).
- Dashed arrows link network and adversary actions. They can also represent additional "precedence" constraints, even on protocol rule instances. For example, a restriction may require that a certain rule instance happens before another one. The color(s) of the arrow indicate(s) the reason for precedence constraint:
  - Black represents an ordering constraint implied by formulas, for example by a restriction or the current lemma.
  - Dark blue represents an ordering constraint implied by fresh values. As fresh values are unique, all rule instances using a fresh value must appear after the rule instance that created that fresh value.
  - Red represents steps in which the adversary composes terms to create other terms.
  - Dark orange represents a constraint implied by TAMARIN's normal form conditions, see Section 6.8.3.
  - Purple represents an ordering constraint originating from an injective fact instance, see Section 10.1.7.

  Note that an arrow can have multiple colors if there are multiple reasons for its existence. For example, an arrow can be black and blue if it is implied by formulas and a fresh value.
- Orange and green arrows, which are not shown in this example, help visualize the deconstruction part of the adversary deduction. Orange arrows represent solved deconstruction chains and green arrows represent open (unsolved) deconstruction chains. Deconstruction chains are explained in Section 6.8.

The level of details shown in the graphs can be configured in the GUI. By default, network and intruder actions are compressed into round white boxes. By clicking on "Options" and "Graph simplification off", one can display these parts of the graph in full detail (see Figure 6.19 for an example). In particular, TAMARIN then shows the instances of the Fresh rule in purple, which are otherwise hidden by default, as well as the precise rule instances for the network and adversary rules in various tones of blue. Round white boxes with a gray border can still appear and represent open constraints.

Three other graph simplification levels, L1–L3, are available,

- L1: the fresh and adversary rules are hidden, but all arrows are shown;

6.5 Dependency graph visualizations

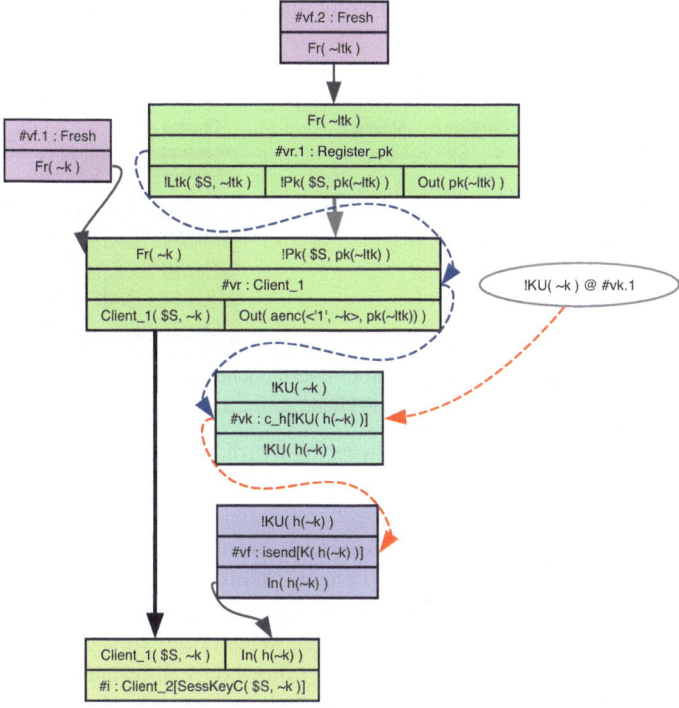

Fig. 6.19: Graph simplification turned off

- L2 (default): same as L1, but TAMARIN only shows a transitive reduction of the arrows, i.e., arrows implied by other arrows are hidden (except for black ones); and
- L3: same as L2, but TAMARIN only shows a full transitive reduction of the arrows (including the black arrows).

When placing the different nodes of the graph, GraphViz (the graph rendering tool used by TAMARIN) tries to minimize the number of edge crossings. This can result in situations where rules of different agents are "mixed", or two rules belonging to the same agent and the same session are placed far away, with other rules "in between". To avoid this and improve the readability of the graphs, TAMARIN can cluster rule instances based on rule annotations or their names.

Rules can be annotated using role names as follows:

```
rule test[role="Initiator"]:
    [...]
    -->
    [...]
```

TAMARIN will then group together all rules that are annotated with the same role name. These grouped rule instances are split into different sessions using the following heuristic: all rules instances connected using linear facts are considered to be part of the same session.

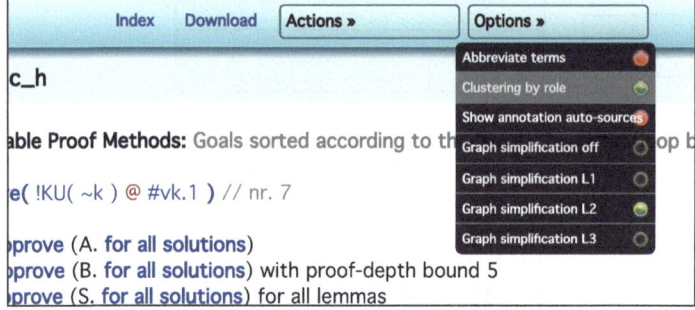

Fig. 6.20: The "Clustering by role" option

Instead of explicitly defining the roles, TAMARIN can also cluster rules based on their names. To enable this option, one must enable "Clustering by role" in the options menu at the top right corner in TAMARIN GUI (see Figure 6.20). When enabled, TAMARIN will group rules based on their names, i.e., all rules whose names start with the same prefix and end with an underscore followed by different number, will be considered as part of the same role. For example, in Example 14, the rules Client_1 and Client_2 will be grouped together into the cluster Client (see Figure 6.21).

Note that the role names and the clustering has no effect on the semantics of the rules; they only influence the graph visualization.

6.6 Heuristics

As we have seen, at any given proof step there may be multiple proof methods available. To decide which proof method to apply first, TAMARIN uses *heuristics*.

Heuristics play an important role in whether TAMARIN terminates and how quickly it terminates, i.e., its efficiency. For many examples, choosing the "right" proof method to apply first allows TAMARIN to terminate quickly, and a different choice may lead to a much larger proof or even non-termination. However, the heuristics applied have no influence on the result's correctness: as the constraint reduction steps are sound and complete by construction, any conclusion obtained by TAMARIN is always correct, no matter which proof methods were used to arrive there and the order in which they were applied.

The heuristic(s) that TAMARIN uses are specified in three ways:

1. using a command-line flag `--heuristic=`...;

6.6 Heuristics

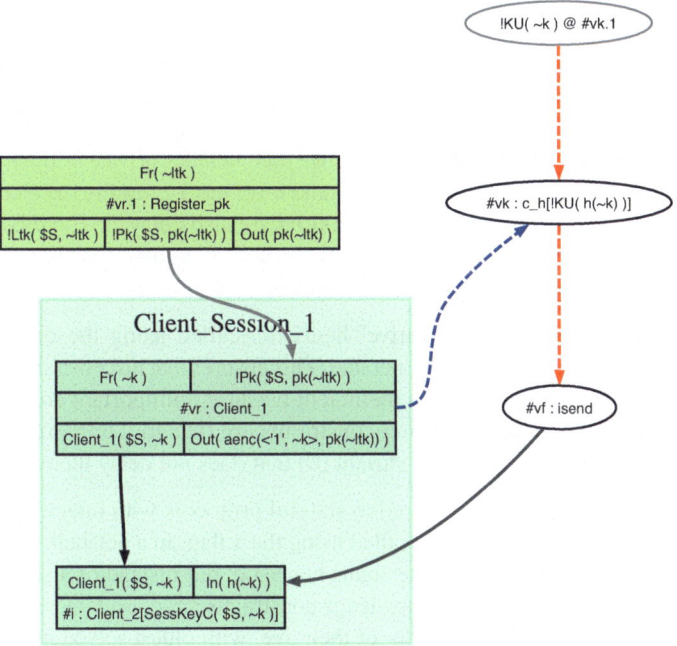

Fig. 6.21: The `Client` cluster. Additional session will be shown in different boxes.

2. using the `heuristic:...` instruction in an input file; and
3. using a *lemma annotation*.

Lemma annotations are specified after the lemma name in square brackets, for example, `lemma Example [heuristic=...]`. They can be used to specify how the lemma is to be proven (e.g., by defining the heuristic), or used within the file (e.g., if it should be reused to prove a subsequent lemma, etc.).

The priority of the different heuristic choices is as follows:

1. The command-line option (`--heuristic=...`) has the highest priority, followed by
2. the lemma attribute (`heuristic=...`), and
3. the global choice per input file (`heuristic:...`).
4. If none of the above is given, TAMARIN uses the default heuristic (`s`).

In the GUI, TAMARIN shows at each proof step which heuristic it currently applies. See, for example, Figure 6.17: "Proof methods sorted according to the 'smart' heuristic".

There are various built-in heuristics:

- The default heuristic is called the 'smart' heuristic and can be called using the s flag (i.e., `heuristic: s` for example). As the name suggests, this heuristic works well on many examples. It prioritizes chain constraints, disjunctions, premise constraints, action constraints, and adversary knowledge that includes private or fresh terms, in this order. `Probably constructible` and `currently deducible` constraints are assigned lower priority. `Loop breakers` are also delayed. There is a variant of this heuristic, which can be called using the S flag, that does not delay loop breakers.
- The 'consecutive' or 'conservative' heuristic, called using the c flag, solves constraints in the order they are generated. This ensures that no constraint is delayed indefinitely. However, it is often inefficient because unimportant constraints are solved before the more interesting constraints are treated. `Loop breakers` are still delayed and there is again a variant (C) that does not delay them.
- There is a special heuristic tailored to stateful protocols with injective facts (see Section 10.1.7 for more details), called using the i flag. In a nutshell, the heuristic applies the same priorities as the smart heuristic, but instead of a strict priority hierarchy, the fact, action, and knowledge constraints are considered to have equal priority and are solved in the order of their age, with oldest solved first.

  The rationale behind this heuristic is as follows. For stateful protocols with an unbounded number of runs, solving a fact constraint may create a new fact constraint for the previous protocol run. It then makes sense to prioritize existing fact, action, and knowledge constraints before solving the fact constraints of that previous run, as solving those constraints will likely create other earlier fact constraints and so on, resulting in a loop. Again, there is a variant (I) that does not delay loop breakers.
- Tactics (see Section 16.3) can be used to specify custom heuristics inside the TAMARIN input file based on a small tactic language. They can be used to tailor a heuristic to a protocol when the standard heuristics are too inefficient or fail.
- The oracle rankings (o and O) allow the user to provide an arbitrary external program that ranks the available proof methods, which is used to modify the underlying heuristic. These rankings use the consecutive ranking C as starting point of the external program when o is selected (respectively they use the smart heuristic s as starting point when O is selected) heuristic as baseline, which is modified by the external program. See Section 16.4 for more details on how oracles work.

It is possible to provide several heuristic flags. In that case, they are employed in a round-robin fashion depending on the proof-depth. For example, calling TAMARIN with the flag `--heuristic=Css` tells the tool to use the 'Consecutive' heuristic first, followed by the smart heuristic twice, followed by the 'Consecutive' heuristic, and so on.

6.7 Handling equations

As explained in the previous chapters, TAMARIN uses *terms* to represent messages, and *equations* to model the algebraic properties of the (cryptographic) functions used to compute messages. For example, the following equation can be used to model symmetric encryption:

```
equations: sdec(senc(m, k),k) = m
```

For TAMARIN, given a set of equations, *all* reasoning is modulo the set of equations (also called *equational theory*). For example, when checking whether a given value can be input to a rule, TAMARIN must check whether the value matches the input, modulo the equational theory.

Reasoning modulo the equational theory can be computationally expensive. Hence, TAMARIN uses a number of techniques and restrictions to handle equations efficiently. We explain these in the remainder of this section.

Orienting equations

The first technique is to *orient* equations from the left side of the equation to the right side of the equation. This turns the equations into rewrite rules, where terms can be rewritten using the oriented equations. For example, the term sdec(senc(h(n), k), k) can be rewritten to h(n) when orienting the equation just defined. Without this orientation, one could also apply the equation in the other direction, for example, rewriting h(n) to sdec(senc(h(n), k), k), which is undesired.

Convergent equations

TAMARIN only works with *convergent* equations. A rewrite system is called convergent if it is both *terminating* and *confluent*. Terminating means that for any term there is only a finite number of possible rewrite steps that can be applied. Confluent means that independently of the order in which one applies the rewrite steps, one always obtains the same term at the end. In the case of a convergent rewrite system, all terms have a unique normal form, which can be computed by simply applying all rewrite rules until none of them are applicable any more. We say that a term is *normalized* if it is in normal form. Moreover, two terms are equal modulo the equational theory if and only if their normal forms are syntactically equal.

To exemplify these ideas, we present two small toy equational theories that violate termination and confluence, respectively. An equational theory violating termination is one with a single constant a and the equation a=a. From the term a, arbitrarily many rewrite steps are possible; thus rewriting does not terminate. For confluence, consider a simple example with the three constants, a, b, and c, and the two equations a=b and a=c. Starting from a, we can reach both b and c, neither of which can be further rewritten. But the resulting terms are different. For more involved examples and more details on the theory, we refer the reader to [6].

Internally, TAMARIN always first normalizes terms, which allows it to compare the resulting normal forms syntactically (and not modulo the equational theory). Ideally, we would only have to perform this normalization during the pre-computation. However, as we show next, instantiating a rule with normalized terms can lead to non-normal terms.

Consider the following rule, which receives a message and decrypts it using a fixed key, for which the full file is available at **Variants.spthy**.

```
rule decrypt:
  [ !Key(k), In(msg) ]
--[ ]->
  [ Out(sdec(msg,k)) ]
```

Consider too an instance of this rule where the argument of the In fact is senc(m1, k). This rule instance would have as an argument of Out the term sdec(senc(m1, k), k), which is not in normal form. To avoid normalizing terms every time a rule is instantiated, TAMARIN computes so-called *variants*, which intuitively correspond to computing the possible normalizations in advance. The variants are shown in interactive mode when clicking on Multiset Rewriting Rules, or when exporting a file. A variant of a rule is a substitution that can be applied to the rule to obtain a possible normalized instantiation of the initial rule.

For our example rule, TAMARIN shows the following variants, shown in the full file available at **Variants_Export.spthy**:

```
rule (modulo AC) decrypt:
   [ !Key( k ), In( msg ) ] --> [ Out( z ) ]
  variants (modulo AC)
  1. k     = k.4
     msg   = msg.4
     z     = sdec(msg.4, k.4)

  2. k     = x.4
     msg   = senc(x.5, x.4)
     z     = x.5
```

First, note that TAMARIN slightly modified the initial rule: it replaced the term sdec(msg, k)) with a new variable z. It then computed two variants, as there are two cases, depending on the input.

- In general, for an input msg.4 and a key k.4, the output z is sdec(msg.4, k.4) (variant 1).

- If the input is an encryption of the form senc(x.5, x.4), where x.4 is used as the decryption key, then the decryption in the output z will normalize to x.5 (variant 2).

6.8 Adversary deductions

This way, TAMARIN does not need to constantly normalize terms: if it encounters an encryption and the corresponding key, then the second variant is used, otherwise the first[2]. TAMARIN computes a complete[3] set of variants for all rules when loading a theory, and then reasons using these variants rather than the initial rules. Note that for this to work out, TAMARIN requires that the equational theory yields only a finite number of variants. For some equational theories, the set of variants is infinite, and in that case it is impossible to compute all of them. Having only a finite number of variants is called the *Finite Variant Property (FVP)* [36] of an equational theory. Note that convergence is a necessary condition for the FVP, but it is not sufficient.

Equation store

TAMARIN also employs another optimization based on variants, called an *equation store*. The idea is that for complex equational theories, a rule can have numerous variants. For example, when using Diffie-Hellman exponentiation, some rules have more than 40 variants. However, when inserting such a rule into the dependency graph, TAMARIN would immediately generate all 40+ subcases, one for each variant, all of which must be resolved separately. In practice, it is often more efficient to not immediately split on all these cases, and continue with the modified rule without substituting variables. To remember which substitutions still must be applied, TAMARIN stores the substitutions corresponding to the variants in an equation store. It also adds an equation split constraint `splitEqs(i)`, for some `i`, to the list of unsolved constraints. When this constraint is solved, TAMARIN generates a subcase for each variant by applying one of the equations from the store. In the above example, there would be two subcases: one for variant 1 (an input that is not a correct encryption), and one for variant 2 (the input is an encryption with the right key).

6.8 Adversary deductions

TAMARIN implements an active network adversary, often called the Dolev-Yao adversary, due to the seminal work on symbolic reasoning for cryptographic protocols by Dolev and Yao [54]. This adversary is in complete control of the network, i.e., it can intercept, read, modify, or delete all messages sent over the network. It can also inject messages it constructed itself, by applying functions to terms it already knows. Essentially, this adversary is only limited by the cryptography: for example, to decrypt a value, it must know the right key.

---

[2] In fact, using the first variant with an encryption and the corresponding key yields non-normal terms. As TAMARIN ignores cases with non-normal terms, these cases are, in fact, exclusive.

[3] The set of variants is complete if for any substitution instantiating the terms of a rule, there exists a variant and a substitution that together are syntactically equal to the normalized version of the instantiated rule.

6.8.1 Why the naive Dolev-Yao implementation fails

In theory, such an adversary could be easily modeled using only a few multiset rewrite rules, as shown in Section 3.1.8. However, reasoning with these rules cannot be effectively automated.

Recall that Out and In model sending and receiving messages. Using a new persistent fact K (for *knows* or *knowledge*), the following rules allow the adversary to learn all messages output by the protocol, and to choose the messages input by the protocol.

```
rule irecv:
    [ Out( x ) ] --> [ !K( x ) ]

rule isend:
    [ !K( x ) ] --[ K( x ) ]-> [ In( x ) ]
```

Similarly, the following rules model that the adversary can learn all public values, and generate its own fresh values.

```
rule pub:
    [ ] --> [ !K( $x ) ]

rule fresh:
    [ Fr( ~x ) ] --> [ !K( ~x ) ]
```

Finally, the adversary can also apply functions to terms. So for any function f of arity n, the following rule models its application to n terms by the adversary.

```
rule f:
    [ !K( x.1 ), ..., !K( x.n ) ] --> [ !K( f( x.1, ..., x.n ) ) ]
```

In TAMARIN, all rules are considered modulo the equational theory. For example, applying the decryption function to a message encrypted with the same key will yield the plaintext message through normalization.

The above adversary rules give a concise and precise description of the adversary's capabilities. The problem with this approach can be seen with a small example. Consider a simple equational theory with a function $<\cdot,\cdot>$ for pairing, and two functions fst and snd with the following equations.

```
fst( < x.1, x.2 > ) = x.1,
snd( < x.1, x.2 > ) = x.2
```

For each of these three functions, we would then model the corresponding rule that allows the adversary to apply them.

```
rule pair:
    [ !K( x.1 ), !K( x.2 ) ] --> [ !K( < x.1, x.2 > ) ]

rule fst:
    [ !K( x ) ] --> [ !K( fst( x ) ) ]

rule snd:
    [ !K( x ) ] --> [ !K( snd( x ) ) ]
```

6.8 Adversary deductions

In this example, the adversary could, for example, generate two public values $A and $B, compute the pair <$A, $B> by applying the rule pair, then extract $A and $B again, then recompute the pair <$A, $B>, and so on.

To avoid these loops when constructing proofs, TAMARIN uses a different approach to model the adversary's deduction. First, we explain how TAMARIN splits the adversary deduction rules into deconstruction and construction rules. Second, we look at normal form conditions that limit what deductions the adversary will consider. Third, we will look at how exactly TAMARIN solves deconstruction constraints.

6.8.2 Splitting the adversary deduction rules

TAMARIN splits adversary deduction rules into two sets: *deconstruction* and *construction* rules. The deconstruction rules decompose terms, extracting smaller subterms. Once the terms are decomposed, the adversary can then use these terms to construct larger terms, but it cannot return to decomposing the created terms. If the right-hand sides of all equations are strict subterms of the left-hand sides, this yields a terminating procedure. Thus, if we want to know whether a given term t can be deduced from a set of terms S, we first decompose the terms in S, which will terminate as the terms only get smaller. Afterwards, the construction rules can compose the resulting terms into larger terms, but only up to the size of the specific term t being investigated, which again terminates. In TAMARIN, this division is enforced by splitting the K fact into two facts: KD (read: K *down*) for the deconstruction part, and KU (read: K *up*) for the construction part.

Concretely, TAMARIN uses the following construction rules for the applications of the fst, snd, and pairing functions. Note that all these rules now operate on KU facts, instead of K facts.

```
rule c_fst:
    [ !KU( x ) ] --[ !KU( fst(x) ) ]-> [ !KU( fst(x) ) ]

rule c_snd:
    [ !KU( x ) ] --[ !KU( snd(x) ) ]-> [ !KU( snd(x) ) ]

rule c_pair:
    [ !KU( x ), !KU( x.1 ) ]
  --[ !KU( <x, x.1> ) ]->
    [ !KU( <x, x.1> ) ]
```

The next two rules allow the adversary to generate fresh and public values.

```
rule pub:
    [ ] --[ !KU( $x ) ]-> [ !KU( $x ) ]

rule fresh:
    [ Fr( ~x ) ] --[ !KU( ~x ) ]-> [ !KU( ~x ) ]
```

Moreover, TAMARIN uses the following deconstruction rules.

```
rule d_0_fst:
  [ !KD( <x.1, x.2> ) ] --> [ !KD( x.1 ) ]

rule d_0_snd:
  [ !KD( <x.1, x.2> ) ] --> [ !KD( x.2 ) ]
```

These rules correspond to the application of the fst and snd functions on a pair. They can be seen as a variant of the c_fst and c_snd rule, respectively, for the case where the equation applies. Note that they only operate on KD facts.

We need to slightly adapt the send and receive rules: the adversary sends messages that it can construct, and messages that it receives are first considered for deconstruction.

```
rule isend:
[ !KU( x ) ] --[ K( x ) ]-> [ In( x ) ]
rule irecv:
[ Out( x ) ] --> [ !KD( x ) ]
```

The receive rule now creates a KD fact instead of a K fact, so that deconstruction rules can be applied. The send rule uses a KU fact, so that the adversary can construct arbitrary terms as protocol inputs.

Finally, there is a new rule called coerce that allows the transition from term deconstruction to construction.

```
rule coerce:
  [ !KD( x ) ] --[ !KU( x ) ]-> [ !KU( x ) ]
```

The coerce rule converts a KD into a KU fact. This stops further deconstruction and allows TAMARIN to move to the construction part of the proof.

Together, these rules prevent the adversary from looping rule applications as in the above example: once it has constructed a pair, the pair is stored inside a KU fact, but the deconstruction rules for fst and snd need a KD fact. Still, this decomposition into two parts does not limit the adversary: one can show that the adversary can still deduce the same terms that it could deduce using the initial rules.

Note that there is a subtlety when it comes to deconstruction rules for more complicated equations. Consider the following equation that models symmetric encryption.

```
sdec(senc(m, k),k) = m
```

The deconstruction rule TAMARIN computes for this equation is as follows.

```
rule d_0_sdec:
  [ !KD( senc(m, k) ), !KU( k ) ] --> [ !KD( m ) ]
```

As expected, the senc(m, k) term is inside a KD fact. However, the key k used to decrypt is inside a KU fact. This is important, as it allows the adversary to compose terms to generate more complicated keys. Note that terms inside KD facts can still be used via the coerce rule. The exact procedure used to generate the deconstruction rules is described in [57].

6.8 Adversary deductions

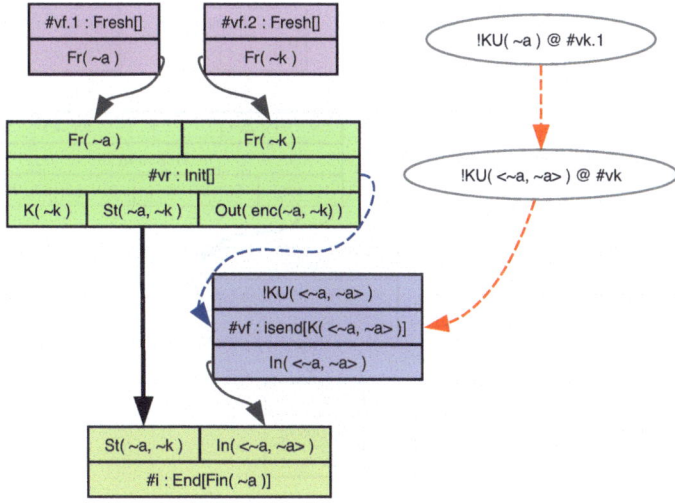

Fig. 6.22: An open input, from Example 13

6.8.3 Normal form conditions for adversary deductions

TAMARIN also uses *normal form conditions* to normalize the adversary deduction in a given dependency graph. There are multiple such conditions, and any deduction not respecting these conditions is ignored by TAMARIN. One can regard this as only considering one representative from a class of equivalent deductions: if the adversary could derive a term t from a set of terms in multiple different ways, it suffices to consider only one possible such derivation. Naturally, these conditions have been proven sound. Examples of these conditions include:

- Terms must always be in normal form.
- The adversary is not allowed to deduce the same value twice.
- The adversary cannot apply the coerce rule on pairs; any pair must be fully deconstructed first.

There are other such conditions, some of which are tailored for special equational theories such as Diffie-Hellman exponentiation.

6.8.4 Backwards reasoning for deduction constraints

As explained in Section 6.2, TAMARIN reasons backwards: starting for example from a protocol input. So how can the adversary compute such a valid input?

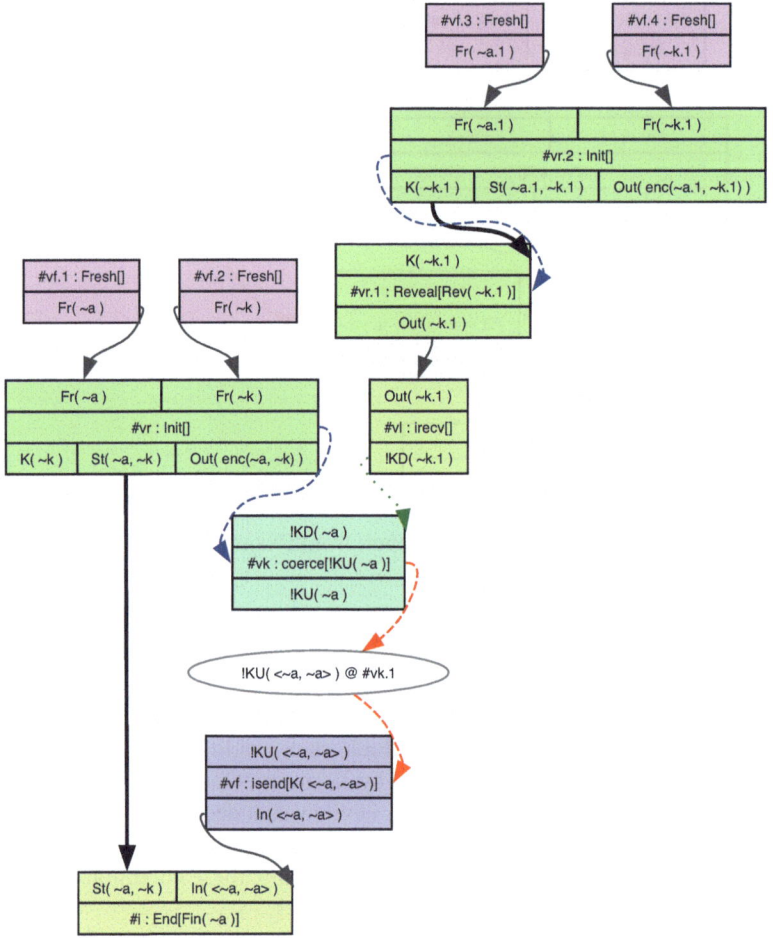

Fig. 6.23: A deconstruction chain from the Reveal rule.

To solve such adversary deduction constraints, TAMARIN proceeds as follows. An input must stem from the isend rule. This in turn implies that there must be a KU fact with the corresponding term. This fact can either be created using a construction rule, or is the result of the coerce rule. If it is the result of the coerce rule, we now need a KD fact with the term in question. To solve KD premises, TAMARIN uses a special type of constraint, called a *deconstruction chain* constraint. It initially links the open KD premise to an instance of the irecv rule. It is resolved either using a direct edge or using one or more deconstruction rules in between.

Consider Example 13 from Section 6.2, and the following lemma[4].

---

[4] Note that normally TAMARIN does not show all the steps described in the following, as much of this reasoning is precomputed (see Chapter 8) and the precomputed sources are used instead to speed

6.8 Adversary deductions

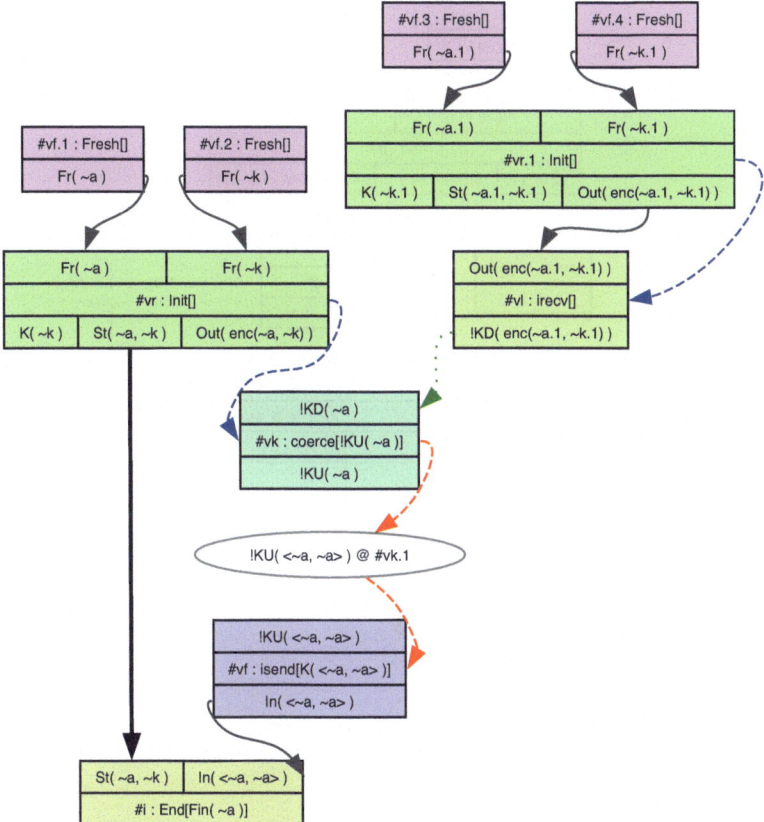

Fig. 6.24: A deconstruction chain from the Init rule.

```
lemma Execute:
  exists-trace
  "Ex a #i. Fin(a)@#i"
```

During the proof of this lemma, TAMARIN encounters the following situation, pictured in the dependency graph given in Figure 6.22: the End rule has a premise constraint <~a, ~a>. TAMARIN has already reduced this to the unsolved constraint !KU(~a) @ #vk.1, i.e., the adversary only needs to learn ~a to generate the pair required as the input. Since the fresh value was generated by a protocol rule, the adversary cannot generate the same value. Hence, when considering the possible sources for this value, TAMARIN generates two subcases, one for each protocol rule

---

up the reasoning. Most of the time, deconstruction chains are only visible in the form of *partial deconstructions*, i.e., incomplete deconstruction chains remaining at the end of the precomputations (see Chapter 8). The images shown here were generated by preventing TAMARIN from solving deconstruction chains during precomputation using the argument -c=0 (see Section 8.1).

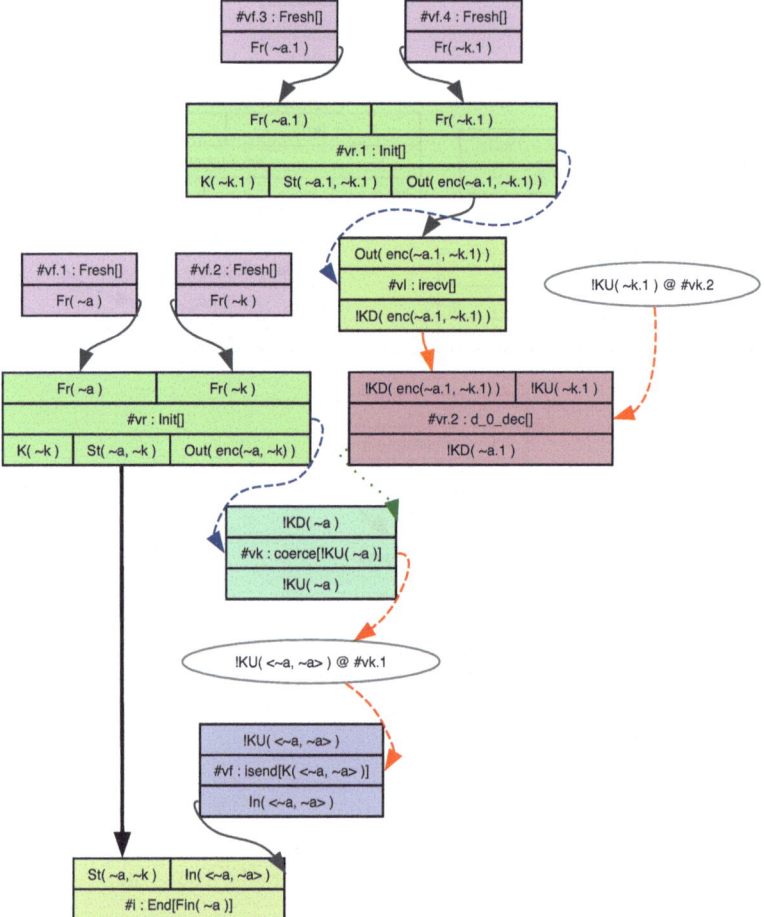

Fig. 6.25: A deconstruction chain from the Init rule, now with a deconstruction rule added for decryption.

that has an Out fact in the conclusion: the Reveal and Init rules. The two subcases are given in Figures 6.23 and 6.24.

One can see that, in both cases, TAMARIN added a coerce rule and an isend rule, and that both are linked using a green dotted arrow. This arrow corresponds to a *deconstruction chain*, and a corresponding chain constraint has also been added to the list of unsolved constraints: solve((#vl, 0) ~~> (#vk, 0)). When solving such a chain constraint, TAMARIN considers multiple possible solutions: either the chain can be replaced with a direct edge (i.e., one can unify the conclusion and the premise and add an edge), or a deconstruction rule can be added if the terms do not match and cannot be unified.

6.8 Adversary deductions

In the first case, where the output comes from a Reveal rule, the output and the "target" are both fresh variables, so TAMARIN adds a direct edge by unifying ~k.1 and ~a. This then leads to a contradiction, as the same fresh value would be created by two different instances of the fresh rule (#vf.1 and #vf4). Thus TAMARIN immediately closes this case.

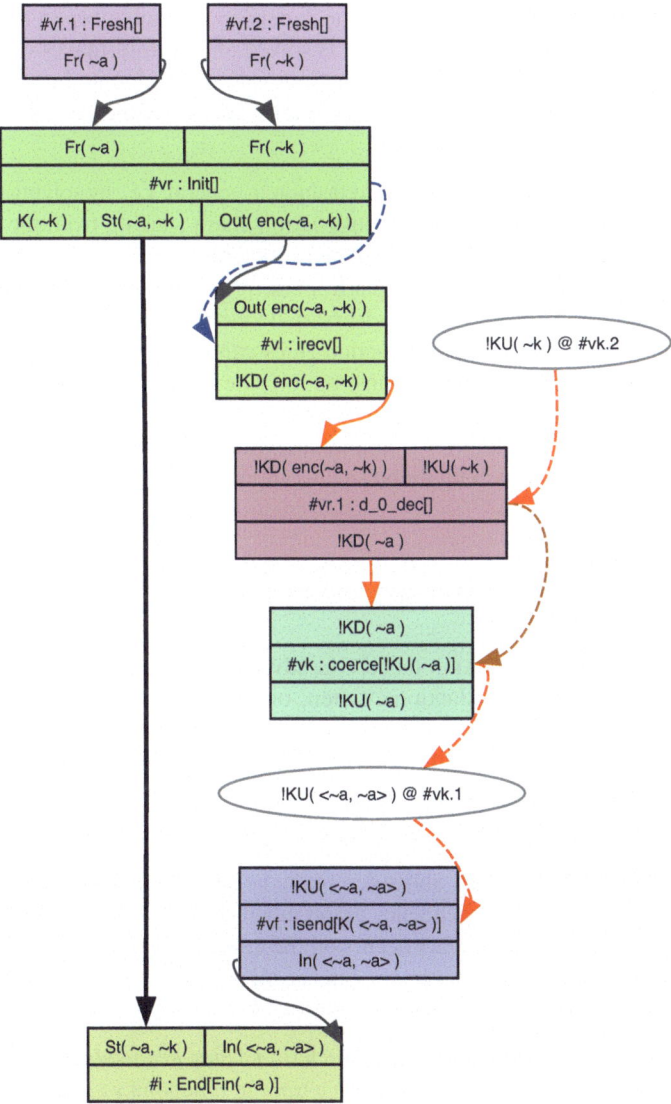

Fig. 6.26: The solved deconstruction chain.

In the second case, where the output comes from the Init rule, TAMARIN knows that a direct edge does not work as an encryption (enc(~a.1, ~k.1)) and a fresh variable (~a) cannot be unified. Thus it adds a decryption deconstruction rule, which leads to the dependency graph given in Figure 6.25.

Note that there is still an unsolved chain constraint as, in general, one might need to apply other deconstruction rules. However, in this case, TAMARIN can only solve it using a direct edge, and we end up with the dependency graph given in Figure 6.26. Here the deconstruction chain constraint is solved and both instances of the Init rule have been merged as they use the same fresh values, which must be unique. Note that one open constraint is still left: TAMARIN must check whether the adversary can obtain the key required for decryption.

Note that TAMARIN reasons in a backward fashion in general, i.e., by solving premises. In this case, TAMARIN solved the deconstruction chain starting from the protocol output, a conclusion fact, and produced the needed messages in a forward fashion, i.e., building the message needed as input from the previous output. This is necessary to use the decomposition part of the adversary deduction efficiently, as the form of the term determines which deconstruction rules can be applied. For example, on an encryption, the only relevant deconstruction rule is the decryption rule. When starting from the premise, i.e., the desired term, TAMARIN would not know whether a certain deconstruction rule (for example decryption) makes sense until it finally encounters the output (which might be an encryption, or not).

6.8.5 Reasoning about adversary knowledge

So far we discussed how TAMARIN models the adversary and how it reasons efficiently about possible adversary deductions. Often, one also needs to reason about the adversary in lemmas. For example, we might state that a term t is secret if the adversary cannot deduce it. For this, one can use the K action fact on the isend rule inside a lemma to check that a term cannot be derived by the adversary.

```
"All t #j . A(t)@#j ==> not( Ex #i. K(t)@#i )"
```

During TAMARIN's search, the above lemma is negated to find a counterexample. TAMARIN thus constructs a dependency graph in which both A(t)@#j and K(t)@#i occur. Recall that the K action fact occurs on the isend rule, whose premise is any KU fact. This ensures that the adversary can use all construction and deconstruction rules on all outputs to try to deduce t.

Note that there is subtle difference between a term t being *deducible* by the adversary at a step #i, and having the action K(t) on a trace at timepoint #i. The action K(t) at timepoint #i means that the adversary deduced t in *this* precise step, so clearly t was deducible at this point. However, any term t.1 that was deduced before is obviously still deducible at this point, but there is no such action, as timepoints are unique in TAMARIN and we cannot execute multiple rules at the same time. Moreover,

6.8 Adversary deductions

as TAMARIN computes the trace in a lazy backwards fashion, there can be other terms that are deducible, but for which no K action exists (yet), simply as it was not necessary to deduce them so far.

When looking carefully at the rules, we can see that the construction rules and the coerce rule are annotated with a KU action containing the term constructed or "coerced" in that rule. These special annotations are used for sources lemmas, where one must reason about the intermediate terms that were used during the construction of a message, as explained in Section 8.2.

Note that for these and other intermediate lemmas, one can use both KU and K actions. However, for the final lemmas defining the desired properties, one should generally only use the K actions as they are the ones defined by TAMARIN's semantics.

Finally, even when using K and KU actions together, it is not possible to reason about all the terms that TAMARIN has deduced, as the deconstruction rules have no actions. We will return to this in Section 11.8.2.

Chapter 7
Built-in Equational Theories for Common Operators

TAMARIN's expressiveness and its usefulness stems, in part, from the wide range of operators that it supports. TAMARIN has built-in support for common operators and users may additionally define their own operators. We describe the built-in operators in this section

By default, TAMARIN always includes the definitions of several basic operators for constructing and decomposing tuples of terms. Namely it includes the pairing function pair/2 with the shorthand <·,·>, as well as the first tuple projection operator fst/1 and the second tuple projection operator snd/1. Moreover, it adds to every equational theory the equations fst(pair(x,y))=x and snd(pair(x,y))=y. The pairing function may be nested, creating ordered lists in a right-associative manner. That is, TAMARIN allows the user to write tuples like <x,y,z> without explicit parenthesization, with the interpretation being <x,<y,z>>.

TAMARIN additionally has default built-in models for a range of cryptographic primitives, such as hashing and encryption, that can be turned on by adding the line

```
builtins: NAME
```

with NAME the name of the desired equational theory. In the following, for each built-in, we give the respective function declarations and equations that are included when the built-in is added. In Chapter 14 we will explain how the user can define such equational theories themselves. Not only can all of the built-ins be freely combined with each other, their combination with other user-defined theories is possible, although there are some limitations in the latter case as explained in Chapter 14. We present an overview of the available equational theories in Table 7.1.

We start with the subset of built-in equational theories that are just syntactic sugar, called *syntactic built-ins*. Giving their name as a built-in is just shorthand for adding a set of operators and equations, as they are shown below. The operators and equation sets contained therein can be written by users themselves and specifying these directly in the theory is equivalent to adding the syntactic built-in. We include the built-in names, with their resulting expansion, in **EquationalTheoriesBuiltinSyntacticSugar.spthy**. They

Built-in name	Description	Section
hashing	Defines a hash function h	7.1.1
asymmetric-encryption	Asymmetric encryption	7.1.2
symmetric-encryption	Symmetric encryption	7.1.3
signing	Basic signatures	7.1.4
revealing-signing	Signatures allowing plaintext extraction	7.1.5
multiset	Multisets (bags) in messages	7.2.1
xor	Exclusive-or	7.2.2
diffie-hellman	Diffie-Hellman style exponentiation	7.2.3
bilinear-pairing	Bilinear pairing	7.2.4
natural-numbers	Natural numbers and counters	7.2.5

Table 7.1: Overview of built-in equational theory names, with a short description, and section reference for details.

include hashing, asymmetric-encryption, symmetric-encryption, signing, and revealing-signing.

7.1 Syntactic built-ins

Syntactic built-ins constitute shorthands: they are simply replaced by predefined functions and equational theories. Hence the user could alternatively just include this replacement directly in their input file, or arbitrarily rename the functions.

7.1.1 Hashing

The built-in hashing declares the function name h/1, i.e., a function named h of arity 1 for which no equations are given:

```
builtins: hashing
```

is equivalent to

```
functions: h/1
```

This is intended to model a perfect one-way and collision resistant hash function, for which there is no way to recover the pre-image or find a collision. For more advanced models of imperfect hash functions, see Section 15.2.2.

7.1.2 Asymmetric encryption

The built-in `asymmetric-encryption` declares a `pk/1` function that takes a private key as an argument and represents the associated public key. The encryption function `aenc/2` takes the message and the public key as arguments and represents the resulting ciphertext, while the decryption function `adec/2` takes the ciphertext and private key to extract the message. Thus,

```
builtins: asymmetric-encryption
```

is equivalent to

```
functions: pk/1, adec/2, aenc/2
equations:
    adec(aenc(m, pk(k)), k) = m
```

Note that this corresponds to a deterministic encryption scheme as there is no randomness used in the encryption function.

To model a non-deterministic encryption scheme, one can simply add a third argument to the encryption function as follows:

```
functions: penc/3, pdec/2, pk/1
```

```
equations: pdec(penc(m,pk(k),r), k) = m
```

Here `penc` stands for *probabilistic* encryption and `pdec` stands for *probabilistic* decryption. Note that these equations model a very strong, non-malleable, encryption scheme, as there is no way to modify a ciphertext. This is in contrast, for example, to textbook RSA (without padding) or ElGamal encryption.

7.1.3 Symmetric encryption

For `symmetric-encryption`, the built-in declares two functions. The function `senc/2` represents the symmetric encryption of a message with a key, resulting in a ciphertext. The decryption function `sdec/2` takes a ciphertext, the key, and extracts the message. Thus,

```
builtins: symmetric-encryption
```

is equivalent to

```
functions: sdec/2, senc/2
equations:
    sdec(senc(m, k), k) = m
```

This models a deterministic scheme without an initialization vector. Similarly to asymmetric encryption above, one can add a third argument to the encryption function to model a non-deterministic scheme with an initialization vector.

Note that this model formalizes an encryption scheme that is again much stronger than many schemes used in practice. In general, one cannot detect during decryption whether the ciphertext was created using a given key; consider, for example, a one-time pad. But here, the equation only applies when this is the case. Note that one can still have rules that apply independently of the key; for details see the discussion in Section 10.1.6. In practice, symmetric encryption schemes can have a range of different properties. See, for example, Section 15.2.3 on how to model authenticated symmetric encryption.

7.1.4 Signing

Signing adds a function pk/1, as in `asymmetric-encryption`. We also declare the function true/0, which takes no arguments, and is used as the output in case of successful signature verification. The function sign/2 takes a message and a private key representing the signature, while the function verify/3 takes a signature, the message, and the public key, and is equal to true if and only if a signature can be verified:

```
builtins: signing
```

is thus equivalent to

```
functions: true/0, pk/1, sign/2, verify/3
equations:
    verify(sign(m, k), m, pk(k)) = true
```

Note that this corresponds to a deterministic signature scheme as there is no randomness used in the signature creation function. For more details and for more precise models of signatures see Section 15.1 and also [74].

7.1.5 Signatures that reveal the plaintext

Revealing-signing is a version of signing that additionally declares the getMessage/1 function. This function can extract the message inside a signature, and is otherwise (except for minor renaming) just like the signing case above:

```
builtins: revealing-signing
functions: true/0, pk/1, getMessage/1,revealSign/2, revealVerify/3
equations:
    getMessage(revealSign(m, k)) = m,
    revealVerify(revealSign(m, k), m, pk(k)) = true
```

7.2 Algorithmic built-ins

Unlike the previous built-ins, the built-ins given in this section are not syntactic sugar for a user-definable equational theory. This is mostly due to their use of underlying equational axioms, such as associativity-commutativity (AC), which TAMARIN does not allow the user to define. The reason for this is that most equational theories using AC symbols directly lead to the non-termination of TAMARIN's reasoning algorithms, if no special optimizations are present. In practice, this means that a user cannot just simply include such equational theories in their model (or under renaming), and should instead always use builtins: NAME in their model.

7.2.1 Multisets (bags)

The simplest such built-in is that of multisets (of terms), using builtins: multiset, which was introduced in [103]. This built-in defines a function symbol +, which takes two arguments and is associative-commutative. Hence one can write x + y + z without explicit parenthesization instead of functional prefix notation like +(x,+(y,z)).

7.2.2 Exclusive-or

The exclusive-or theory is available with builtins: xor and was added in [58]. It declares the function symbol XOR/2, which can also be written as ⊕, and the neutral element constant zero/0. The XOR function is associative-commutative and can be written without parentheses (like multisets). XOR satisfies that zero is the neutral element, and that terms self-cancel, as shown here.

```
x XOR zero = x
x XOR x = zero
```

Note that constructing terms from XOR as the outermost (top-level) operator, and having them sent out on the network, creates a very large search space for TAMARIN and often leads to non-termination. We suggest, where possible, "hiding" the XOR term underneath an encryption or a hash function, e.g., h(x XOR y). This yields much better termination results than sending x XOR y directly.

7.2.3 Diffie-Hellman exponentiation

The builtins: diffie-hellman provides exponentiation ^/2 (which can also be written as exp/2 using prefix notation) and multiplication */2, limited to the exponents. The multiplication is associative-commutative. Moreover, repeated exponentiation is equal to the multiplication of the exponents, as expected.

```
(x^y)^z = x^(y*z)
```

The constant ONE/0 (also written as 1) is neutral both for exponentiation and multiplication, and the inverse function inv/1 gives the inverse and cancels multiplicatively.

```
x^1       = x
x*1       = x
x*inv(x) = 1
```

The constant DH_neutral/0 is the neutral element as the base of exponentiation.

```
DH_neutral^x = DH_neutral
```

The general Diffie-Hellman theory was introduced in [102]. The neutral element was introduced later in [47] and represents the fixed point under exponentiation. Every group contains such a neutral element, but whether it can occur in protocol executions depends on the implementation. For example, some implementations use a coordinate system where the neutral element cannot be expressed, whereas other implementations explicitly check whether received values correspond to the neutral element and reject them when this is the case.

By default, the Diffie-Hellman theory assumes the worst case, i.e., that there is no explicit check for the neutral element and that it can be expressed in the implementation. For example, the following rule could be instantiated with the neutral element.

```
builtins: diffie-hellman

rule any_element:
  let key = v^~s
  in
  [ In(v), Fr(~s) ]
  --[ UncheckedNeutralKey(key) ]->
  [ ]
```

When instantiated with the neutral element, the adversary can in fact derive the value of key despite not knowing ~s. Thus the following lemma is false and TAMARIN finds a counterexample.

```
// Lemma is false: if adversary sends the neutral element,
// it can infer the key
lemma secret_key:
  "All #i x. UncheckedNeutralKey(x)@i ==> not Ex #j. K(x)@j"
```

In the counterexample, the adversary inserts the neutral element for v, and by the equation above, the key key is also equal to the neutral element.

As mentioned above, whether this attack is possible in reality depends on the coordinate system, or whether neutral elements are checked and rejected. If we know that for a given protocol or its implementation, the neutral element is rejected or cannot be represented, we can explicitly model the rejection check by pattern matching the received values to 'g'^x, for some new variable x. The variable only

7.2 Algorithmic built-ins

serves to check the structure of the term, but should not be used outside of the pattern matching, since the recipient cannot derive this term.

Thus, we can model the rule from above with the pattern matching check.

```
rule no_neutral_element:
  let v = 'g'^x // pattern matching structure of v to exclude neutral element
      key = v^~s
  in
  [ In(v), Fr(~s) ]
  --[ CheckedNonNeutralKey(key) ]->
  [ ]
```

For the above rule, the derived key is secret since ~s is secret. Hence TAMARIN can prove the following lemma.

```
// Lemma holds: if received v is of the form 'g'^x,
// it is not the neutral element
lemma secret_key_with_check:
  "All #i k. CheckedNonNeutralKey(k)@i ==> not Ex #j. K(k)@j"
```

The full file for this is available at **Neutral_element_check.spthy**.

In practice, Diffie-Hellman constructions have many other subtle side cases based on, e.g., small subgroups and invalid curve elements. We will return to this topic in Section 15.2.1 and full details are provided in [47].

7.2.4 Bilinear pairing

The builtins: bilinear-pairing models bilinear pairings and was introduced in [103] and includes all of the previous diffie-hellman theory. Their combination also works, as DH is just a subset of bilinear-pairing, and including both is no different from including just bilinear pairing. The new functions are pmult/2 for point multiplication, where pmult(x,p) denotes multiplying the scalar x with the point p, and em/2 for the bilinear map with two points, where em is commutative. The equations state that 1 as a scalar is neutral for point multiplication, that repeated point multiplication with scalars is the same as multiplying the scalars first, and that scalar multiplication can be pulled outside the bilinear pairing of points as exponentiation.

```
pmult(1,p) = p
pmult(x,(pmult(y,p)) = pmult(x*y,p)
em(pmult(x,p),q) = em(p,q)^x
```

7.2.5 Numbers and counters

TAMARIN provides basic support for reasoning about natural numbers, which can be used to model counters and other such mechanisms. The support is enabled through a natural-numbers built-in, by including in the input file:

```
builtins: natural-numbers
```

Recall that TAMARIN has a top-level type Msg with two incomparable sub-types, Fresh and Pub. The `natural-numbers` built-in defines the Nat type as another sub-type of Msg, which is again incomparable with both of Fresh and Pub. We can indicate that a variable is of type Nat by adding a % prefix (or :nat suffix) to the variable's name.

The built-in provides support for

- the constant 1, denoted by %1 or 1:nat,
- an addition operator %+,
- the equality relation =, and
- a less-than relation denoted by << or the Unicode symbol ⊏.

For technical reasons, TAMARIN does not support full arithmetic. Notably, there is no neutral element 0, division, or multiplication of two variables. While these would also be useful for modeling, their addition would lead to undecidable problems associated with the case distinctions in TAMARIN's proof search and we lack tractable procedures even for the special cases that typically arise. The full theoretical details for this built-in are described in [48].

Consider the following simple example of a protocol, available in the file **naturals.spthy**, where the state fact S(tid,n) contains a thread identifier and a counter value. We have two rules: init and step, where the first rule creates an S fact with a fresh tid and counter value one, and the second rule increments the counter. Both rules have actions A(tid,n) that log the updated parameters of the S fact.

```
rule init:
    [ Fr(~tid) ]
    --[ A(~tid, %1) ]->
    [ S(~tid, %1) ]

rule step:
    [ S(~tid, %n) ]
    --[ A(~tid, %n %+ %1) ]->
    [ S(~tid, %n %+ %1) ]
```

We can then prove the following lemma.

```
lemma increasing:
  "All tid n1 n2 #i1 #i2.
    A(tid,n1)@i1 & A(tid,n2)@i2 & #i1 < #i2
      ==> n1 << n2"
```

This lemma states that for two A actions with the same tid at timepoints #i1 < #i2, the number n1 at #i1 must be smaller than the number n2 at #i2.

An important design choice in TAMARIN's modeling of natural numbers is that any term of the Nat type can be directly derived by the adversary. In this sense, the Nat type behaves like the Pub type: Nat terms are never secret. Thus, one could consider elements of the Nat type to represent "small" numbers that an adversary might guess.

7.2 Algorithmic built-ins

If one wants to model large unguessable numbers instead, we recommend using the fresh type. However, that type neither supports addition nor an ordering relation.

Chapter 8
Pre-computations and Partial Deconstructions

TAMARIN performs various optimizations to accelerate proof construction, and we discuss one such optimization in this chapter. Namely, when loading an input theory, TAMARIN performs pre-computations to speed up constraint solving later on. The idea is to pre-compute larger constraint solving steps for common parts of the search, which TAMARIN is likely to encounter multiple times.

8.1 Pre-computations and sources

For all protocol facts, TAMARIN performs a backwards search for their sources, using the constraint solving algorithm described in Section 6.2. The sources of a protocol fact are those partial executions that yield that fact. These executions are usually incomplete, as trying to compute the complete executions could cause non-termination of the precomputations. For example, adversary deduction steps are not fully explored as this might not terminate. Similarly, protocol facts that can appear in loops are also not explored fully.

Additionally, TAMARIN pre-computes the sources of KU facts, where it considers different subcases depending on the form of the term inside the fact. In particular, it computes the sources of:

1. KU(~x), i.e., fresh values; and

2. KU(f(x.1, ..., x.n)) for all functions f defined in the equational theory.

In a nutshell, these pre-computation steps yield sources as follows. For each protocol fact and instance of the KU facts, TAMARIN generates an empty constraint system with a constraint that requires the presence of the fact in question. It then applies its normal constraint solving procedure. However, to avoid non-termination of the pre-computations, TAMARIN stops the constraint solving when it encounters a case distinction with more than one subcase. This means that a source can (and typically does) contain one or more open constraints.

Example 15 Consider the following simple challenge-response protocol, available at **sourcesWithoutLemma.spthy**.

```
1. I -> R: {'req',I, n}pk(R)
2. I <- R: {'resp',n}pk(I)
```

In the first step, the initiator sends out a request (identified using the constant 'req') together with his name and a fresh nonce, encrypted using the responder's public key. The responder answers with a response message (identified using the constant 'resp') together with the nonce, encrypted using the initiator's public key.

Using the model of a public key infrastructure first shown in Section 5.6 and discussed in Section 5.5, we can model this protocol using the following three rules.

```
// Initiator
rule Rule_I_1:
  let m1 = aenc{'req', $I, ~n}pkR
  in
    [ Fr(~n), !Pk(R, pkR), !Ltk($I, ltkI) ]
  --[ SecretI($I,R,~n) ]->
    [ Out(m1), State_I($I, R, ~n, pkR, ltkI) ]

rule Rule_I_2:
  let m2 = aenc{'resp', ~n}pk(ltkI)
  in
    [ State_I($I, R, ~n, pkR, ltkI), In(m2) ]
  --[ ]->
    [ ]

// Responder
rule Rule_R:
  let m1 = aenc{'req', I, x}pk(ltkR)
      m2 = aenc{'resp', x}pkI
  in
    [ !Ltk(R, ltkR), In(m1), !Pk(I, pkI)]
  --[ ]->
    [ Out(m2) ]
```

The sources contain 9 cases, including all three protocol facts, and six subcases for the KU facts, including fresh values and all functions defined:

- !Ltk(t.1, t.2)
- !Pk(t.1, t.2)
- State_I(t.1, t.2, t.3, t.4, t.5)
- !KU(~t.1)
- !KU(adec(t.1, t.2))
- !KU(aenc(t.1, t.2))
- !KU(fst(t.1))

8.1 Pre-computations and sources

- !KU(pk(t.1))
- !KU(snd(t.1))

For example, the fact `State_I` has only one source, which is given in Figure 8.1. Note that here all premises have been solved as there is only one source for the `!Ltk` and `!Pk` facts, which is the rule `Register_pk`.

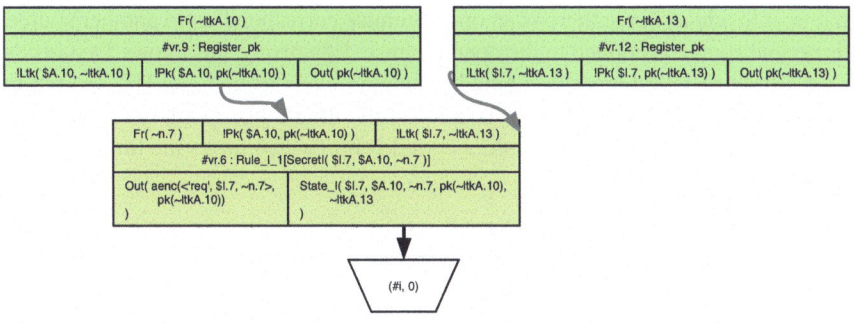

Fig. 8.1: Only source of the fact `State_I`. All constraints have been solved.

The fact `!KU( ~t.1 )` has 4 sources and one example is given in Figure 8.2. Note that this source contains open constraints as the origin of the key used for decryption (constraint `!KU( ~ltkA.20 )`) remains to be solved.

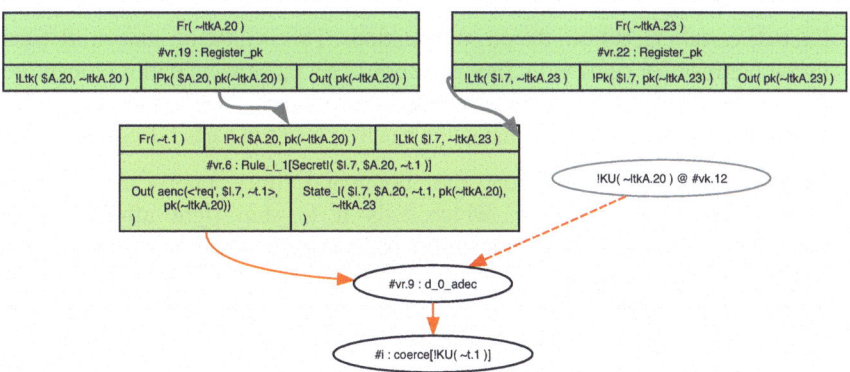

Fig. 8.2: One of the four sources of fact `!KU( ~t.1 )`. The constraint `!KU( ~ltkA.20 )` still needs to be solved.

If TAMARIN encounters a chain constraint (see Section 6.8) that it cannot entirely resolve, for example as it contains variables, this constraint remains unsolved. A source that contains such an open chain constraint is called a *partial deconstruction*. Partial deconstructions are often problematic as they can cause non-termination later on during proof search. Intuitively, this happens as these partial deconstructions can be applied in all cases where the intruder needs a term, because the unresolved variable(s) can potentially match anything. Section 8.2 explains how partial deconstructions can be solved using *sources lemmas*.

Once TAMARIN has finished pre-computing the sources, it applies a saturation process. That is, if inside a source there is an open premise corresponding to another source, this second source is applied to the open premise. Effectively, this allows TAMARIN's proof search to take bigger combined reasoning steps in one go. The saturation process is applied repeatedly to all sources until either a fixedpoint is reached, i.e., there are no further changes, or until a bound is hit (which limits the time spent on the process).

Although care has been taken to limit TAMARIN's pre-computation time, in some examples the pre-computation might appear to not terminate as the time required can still be substantial. In such cases, the pre-computations can be fine-tuned using different (command-line) parameters and annotations. In particular, the following options are available.

- Set the maximal number of saturation steps to the value N using the command-line parameter `--saturation=N`.
- Limit the number of chain constraints to solve to a maximum of N using the command-line parameter `--open-chains=N`. This is useful when using complicated equational theories leading to numerous cases. However, too small a number can result in partial deconstructions.
- Exclude certain facts from the precomputations. This is done by annotating facts in the premises of rules with `[no_precomp]`. As those facts will no longer be precomputed, solving them will only happen at runtime, which can increase proof construction time. Moreover, this option can also result in partial deconstructions.
- When running TAMARIN on the command line, one can use the `--precompute-only` option, which tells it to stop right after the pre-computation. TAMARIN will then simply print a digest of the pre-computations, e.g.:

```
Multiset rewriting rules: 7
Raw sources: 9 cases, 6 partial deconstructions left
Refined sources: 9 cases, deconstructions complete
```

This can be used to check how much time the pre-computation takes, to check whether there are partial deconstructions, and whether they are resolved.

In practice, if TAMARIN seems to be looping on startup, one can try to limit the first two parameters to enable loading the theory. Once the theory is loaded, the interactive mode can be used to analyze the problem's causes and then relax the parameters slowly.

8.2 Sources lemmas

One can inspect the result of TAMARIN's initial pre-computations for a theory using the link `Raw sources` in the interactive mode. This link appears in the left-hand pane as can be seen, for example, in Figure 6.12. TAMARIN then shows if there are any partial deconstructions left, and when this is the case, one can analyze them.

To solve partial deconstructions, one must provide extra action fact annotations and state a specific type of lemma allowing TAMARIN to solve the open chains. Such lemmas are called `sources` lemmas and are annotated as `lemma name [sources]: ....`

The entire process works in two steps. First, TAMARIN computes the `Raw sources`. Next, it applies all `sources` lemmas. Sources lemmas are used to restrict sources in such a way that partial deconstructions are prevented, but no attacks are missed, and we will show an example in Section 8.4. After applying the sources lemmas, TAMARIN shows either `deconstructions complete` or a number of `partial deconstructions left` in the GUI. This second step results in the `Refined sources`. Sources lemmas are proven on the raw sources using induction (see Section 9.1). The refined sources are then used to prove the remaining non-source lemmas.

Note that source lemmas are always applied before proving non-source lemmas, independently of the order in which they appear in the input file. Moreover, as non-source lemmas are proven using the refined sources (i.e., after applying the sources lemmas), the non-sources lemmas are not valid if a sources lemma cannot be proven; however, any attacks found are still valid. For strategies on how to write and use sources lemmas see Section 8.4. In many cases, TAMARIN can also try to generate a suitable sources lemma itself, as explained in the next section.

8.3 Auto-sources

TAMARIN can be run using the `--auto-sources` flag. When run using this option, if there are partial deconstructions left in a theory, TAMARIN will try to automatically generate a suitable sources lemma. This lemma, called `AUTO_typing`, will be added at the end of the theory, and it must be proven like a normal sources lemma.

Intuitively, to generate this lemma, TAMARIN applies an approach similar to the one described in Section 8.4. TAMARIN will try to find matching outputs for all inputs that cause partial deconstructions, and similarly matching conclusion facts for the premise facts causing partial deconstructions. It then adds the necessary action facts to the rules (starting with `AUTO_IN_` or `AUTO_OUT_`), and generates the lemma using these actions. If there are rules that have multiple variants with respect to the equational theory, TAMARIN will replace the rule with all its variants before computing and adding the action facts. This is necessary as only some of the variants might actually be relevant for the sources lemma, and it might be impossible to correctly annotate the rules without computing the variants first.

In practice, when encountering partial deconstructions, one can simply try running TAMARIN using the --auto-sources flag. Although there is neither a guarantee that the generated lemma resolves all partial deconstructions nor that it is correct, this works in many cases in practice. One simply needs to verify the automatically generated sources lemma just as a normal sources lemma. If this succeeds, one can safely continue.

The automatic lemma generation may fail to identify all sources correctly in some cases, in particular when using non-subterm-convergent equational theories or AC symbols. In such cases, there can be partial deconstructions left, or one will not be able to prove the generated lemma. In either case, one must write a lemma manually.

When exporting a theory containing an automatically generated lemma, this lemma (and its proof if it exists) is exported like any other lemma. Since TAMARIN will have modified some rules by adding actions, the modified rules are also exported instead of the original rules. Moreover, if TAMARIN had to replace a rule by its variants to add the actions, then these variants together with the added actions are also exported explicitly (whereas normally, variants are not explicitly exported by TAMARIN; however that is not sufficient here as the added actions would be dropped). Afterwards, everything can be loaded again as usual.

The annotations generated by TAMARIN are hidden by default in the graphs in interactive mode (except when proving the auto-generated sources lemma). One can make them visible again using the Show annotation auto-sources button in the Options menu in the top right corner.

8.4 Using sources lemmas

To see how to write a sources lemma, consider Example 15 from before. A simple property to verify about this protocol is the secrecy of the nonce. The following lemma expresses this property.

```
" not(
    Ex A B s #i. SecretI(A, B, s) @ i  & (Ex #j. K(s) @ j)
       & not (Ex #r. RevLtk(A) @ r)
       & not (Ex #r. RevLtk(B) @ r)
  )"
```

Unfortunately, when trying to prove this lemma directly, TAMARIN fails to complete the proof. The reason for this is the presence of partial deconstructions. One partial deconstruction (also called an *open chain*), out of the six found by TAMARIN, is given in Figure 8.3. In this graph, TAMARIN tried to find the sources of encryptions and found a partial deconstruction where the adversary extracts from the response the value at the position of the nonce. At this stage, this value is only a variable (x.10),

8.4 Using sources lemmas

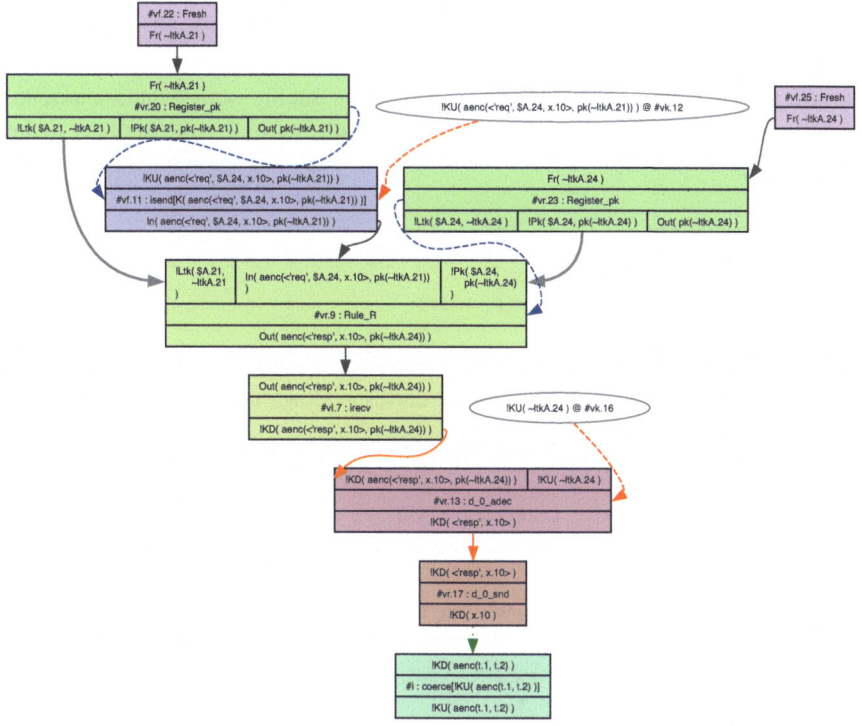

Fig. 8.3: Partial deconstruction (with graph simplification turned off) caused by the variable x.10 from the input of rule `Rule_R`

as TAMARIN had not yet solved the input of the rule. So potentially, the value could be an encryption, for example, if the adversary crafted the request message.

Unfortunately, at this point, TAMARIN cannot further resolve the deconstruction chain as currently there only is a variable, so it cannot decide whether the variable actually is an encryption or not. TAMARIN also cannot resolve the situation by solving the input (to get more information about the real value), because doing this in general might cause non-termination of the precomputations.

At this point we can step in and help TAMARIN eliminate the partial deconstruction. To do this, we write a sources lemma that specifies the different possible inputs, giving TAMARIN sufficient information to completely resolve the open chain. In this concrete example, there are actually not many possible cases:

- Either the input was the expected protocol message coming from the initiator, in which case we have a fresh value, or
- the adversary crafted a message of the right format. In this case, however, it is of no interest for the adversary to extract x.10 again because the adversary already

knew it before (as it created the ciphertext itself). So TAMARIN can eliminate this case, independently of the concrete value for x.10.

We now need to express this as a lemma, given in the full file **sourcesWithLemma.spthy**. We start by adding an action In_R(m1, x) to the rule Rule_R so we can refer to the input message m1 and the variable x causing the partial deconstruction.

```
rule Rule_R:
  let m1 = aenc{'req', I, x}pk(ltkR)
      m2 = aenc{'resp', x}pkI
  in
    [ !Ltk(R, ltkR), In(m1), !Pk(I, pkI)]
  --[ In_R(m1, x) ]->
    [ Out(m2) ]
```

We also need an action Out_I(m1) for the corresponding output of m1 in Rule_I_1.

```
rule Rule_I_1:
  let m1 = aenc{'req', $I, ~n}pkR
  in
    [ Fr(~n), !Pk(R, pkR), !Ltk($I, ltkI) ]
  --[ SecretI($I,R,~n), Out_I(m1) ]->
    [ Out(m1), State_I($I, R, ~n, pkR, ltkI) ]
```

Using these two actions we can now write the sources lemma as follows.

```
lemma sources [sources]:
  "All #i m x. In_R(m, x)@#i ==> (
    (Ex #j. Out_I(m)@#j & #j < #i)
    |
    (Ex #k. KU(x)@#k & #k < #i)
  )
  "
```

This expresses what we intuitively formulated above: when receiving a message m with variable x in rule Rule_R, then either this was the output of an initiator in rule Rule_I_1, or the adversary knew x before.

Note that in this lemma we use KU and not K to reason about the values previously known by the adversary. The reason for this is that the K annotation is only present on the isend rule. In the above example (see Figure 8.3), even if the adversary constructed the input aenc(<'req', $A.24, x.10>, pk(ltkA.21)) to rule Rule_R by itself, i.e., it knows $A.24 and x.10 individually, there will be no K($A.24) and K(x.10) actions, but only a K(aenc(<'req', $A.24, x.10>, pk(~ltkA.21))) action. However, there will be KU($A.24) and KU(x.10) actions, as all construction rules have KU annotations. Note that there will also be a KU(aenc(<'req', $A.24, x.10>, pk(~ltkA.21))) action, as the aenc constructor also has a KU annotation. For more details on the adversary deduction, see Section 6.8, and for recommendations on when to use KU, see Section 11.8.2.

When adding this lemma to the theory, TAMARIN can solve all partial deconstructions, and verify the secrecy of the nonce as stated above. The added sources lemma itself must also be proven, and TAMARIN can successfully discharge that as well.

8.4 Using sources lemmas

If there are multiple rules or inputs causing partial deconstructions, one must write a lemma for each of them. In this case, it is advisable to merge all lemmas into one large lemma at the end, by simply connecting the formulas using a logical AND (&). This large lemma is usually easier for TAMARIN to prove as the induction hypothesis becomes stronger (it can use the formula for all other rules when proving one of them), and it prevents the partial deconstructions from one input to interfere with the proofs of source lemmas for other inputs.

Overall, the approach is as follows:

1. Identify the rules, messages and variables causing the partial deconstructions, by inspecting the raw sources
2. For each message input, look for matching outputs
3. Add the necessary actions to the rules (for inputs and outputs)
4. Add the sources lemma to the theory

TAMARIN's auto-sources feature (see Section 8.3) implements the same approach, but might fail in some cases, in particular in the presence of complex equational theories. Then, one can try to manually write a suitable sources lemma.

When manually writing a sources lemma it can sometimes be helpful to write it incrementally: look at a first partial deconstruction, write a lemma for it, re-run TAMARIN to check which partial deconstructions remain, extend the lemma to cover the next partial deconstruction, and so on.

For the theory behind partial deconstructions and sources lemmas in TAMARIN, see Chapter 8.4.4 in [88]. For details on the algorithm that automatically generates sources lemmas, see [37, 38].

Chapter 9
Lemma Annotations

Annotations can be associated with a lemma declaration using square brackets after the lemma name, for example, `lemma example [use_induction]`. Adding annotations can change how a lemma is proven, e.g., by using induction as in the example just given. Annotations can also specify that a lemma is an auxiliary lemma, intended to be reused in the proof of other lemmas. Moreover, as we have seen in Chapter 8, a `sources` annotated lemma is proven using induction and the `sources` lemma additionally changes the sources used for all other proofs.

In this chapter, we explain the use of the lemma annotations `use_induction`, `reuse`, and `hide_lemma`. There is a further lemma annotation `heuristic` to specify lemma-specific heuristics, which we will return to in Section 16.4. In equivalence mode, lemmas can also be annotated with `left`, `right`, or `both`, as explained in Section 13.1.

9.1 Induction

For all the examples seen so far, with the exception of `sources` lemmas, the proofs constructed have not required any form of induction. We now turn to TAMARIN's support for this important reasoning principle. Induction is often needed, for example, to prove properties of protocol models whose rules can be linked together in a looping fashion. For such models, an attempted proof without induction will typically not terminate.

To prove a given property with induction, one adds the `use_induction` annotation to the lemma name. Alternatively, using the GUI, one can manually select `use_induction` as the first step without annotating the lemma.

Abstractly, one can think of TAMARIN's induction as a form of induction on the length of the trace, where the induction hypothesis is assumed for all time points except for the last one, which must be proven. When using induction, an associated constraint system is generated that results in an initial case split with two subcases: (i) the empty trace and (ii) any other trace.

In subcase (i), TAMARIN must establish the property for the base case, i.e., the empty constraint system. In subcase (ii), the induction distinguishes the last timepoint, so that all other time points happen earlier. The induction hypothesis then states that the property can be assumed for all other (earlier) non-last timepoints. TAMARIN then needs to prove that the property also holds for the last timepoint, via the constraint system. If the constraint system can be solved, then we have proven the property for the last timepoint and TAMARIN can conclude subcase (ii). If both subcases are established then, by the soundness of the induction rule, the property holds in general. For details of the correctness of this proof method, see [88], which also contains the detailed constraint reduction rules for induction.

Let us consider an example, abbreviated from [88], which showcases some lemmas that TAMARIN requires induction to prove, with the file available at **Minimal_Loop_induction.spthy**.

```
theory Minimal_Loop_Example begin

rule Start:  [ Fr(x) ]  --[ Start(x) ]-> [ A(x) ]

rule Loop:   [ A(x) ]   --[ Loop(x)  ]-> [ A(x) ]

lemma Start_before_Loop [reuse, use_induction]:
  "All x #j. Loop(x) @ j ==> (Ex #i. Start(x) @ i & i < j)"

lemma Satisfied_by_empty_trace_only [use_induction]:
  exists-trace
  "All x #j. Loop(x) @ j ==> F"

end
```

Induction is needed to prove the lemma Start_before_Loop (hence it is annotated with use_induction) in this example as each Loop instance has a predecessor that is either the Start (and we are done, as that satisfies the formula), or another Loop instance. Using the previously described proof steps without induction, TAMARIN will unroll an infinitely long chain of Loop instances without terminating, as we explain below.

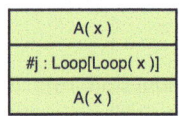

Fig. 9.1: Starting point

When TAMARIN analyzes the lemma Start_before_Loop, it starts the constraint solving with the formula representing that we are done once a Start with the right

9.1 Induction

parameter is found, as well as the formula that there is a Loop with the parameter. That second formula is resolved into the first system in Figure 9.1.

Afterwards, two steps are possible. First, if the A comes from an instance of the Start rule, see Figure 9.2, we are immediately done, having found a Start. The other possibility is that it comes from an instance of the Loop rule, see Figure 9.3.

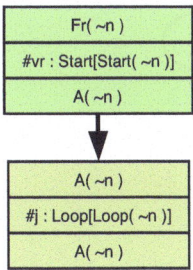

Fig. 9.2: Closed with a Start

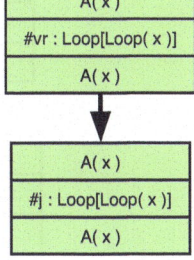

Fig. 9.3: Continued with a Loop

From this second state, we have the same two steps again, closing in Figure 9.4, and looping in Figure 9.5. This illustrates that the example lemma will not be provable with the normal constraint solving, and induction is therefore needed.

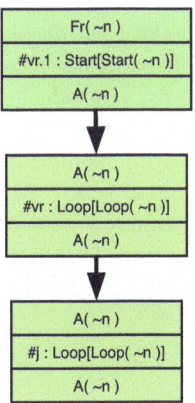

Fig. 9.4: Closed with a Start

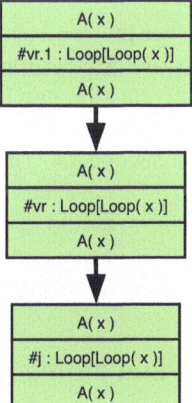

Fig. 9.5: Continued with a Loop again

Using the induction proof method, TAMARIN's approach is different from what we have just described. Most cases are still treated and resolved as before. However, the cases have additional information about the induction hypothesis that can be applied to all non-last timepoints. In particular, this happens in the previous non-terminating loop. Once there are two instances of Loop connected to each other, the first of the two is non-last, so the induction hypothesis applies. Hence, for this Loop instance, a Start exists, and thus the proof is completed, as only one Start is required overall, see Figure 9.6. Note that the addition of the Start with the dotted line comes from the application of the induction hypothesis.

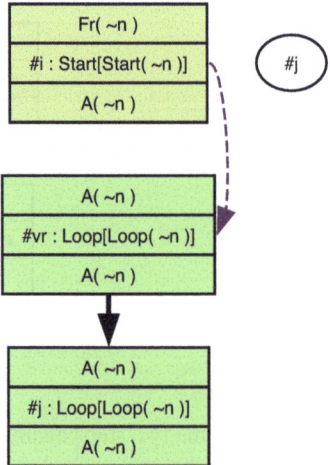

Fig. 9.6: Inductive step

In general, when proving a lemma with induction, one must take care that the induction hypothesis is sufficiently strong for the proof to succeed. In particular, it can be useful to merge different sources lemmas (or other lemmas proven by induction, see also the next section) into one, so that the induction hypothesis becomes stronger; see the discussion in Section 8.4. The same can be true when proving multiple implications. Namely, it may be advantageous to prove a lemma stating (A | B | C) ==> D for some formulas A, B, and C, rather than proving three lemmas A ==> D, B ==> D, and C ==> D, as this strengthens the induction hypothesis; see [49] for an example.

9.2 Reuse and hiding

The reuse annotation does not influence how the annotated lemma is proven. Instead, lemmas with this annotation are used as hypotheses in proof steps when proving subsequent lemmas. For reuse, the order that lemmas occur in the input file matters, and any lemma name annotated with reuse is used in all subsequently occurring lemmas (except for sources lemmas, which do not use reuse lemmas to avoid possible circularity). This behavior is different from sources lemmas, which affect the precomputations and thus indirectly the analysis of all lemmas, independent of their location in the input file.

Lemmas annotated with reuse can be used to prove properties about a protocol, often invariants, that subsequently help to prove the main properties of interest. For a larger example combining reuse and induction see Section 9.3.

A reuse lemma is applied in the subsequent proofs, regardless of whether it has already been successfully verified or not. This makes it convenient for the user, who can then verify lemmas independently from each other. This is especially useful when the reuse lemma has been proven in a prior TAMARIN run and one then adds additional lemmas. This way, one need not re-prove the reuse lemma (which may be time consuming) with each addition.

Of course, with the above approach, one risks that a reuse lemma is never proven or, even worse, that the lemma is incorrect. In this case, all subsequent proofs may be incorrect. Hence, when proving a lemma, it is the user's obligation to ensure that all prior reuse lemmas have also been proven (or are provable). Without checking this, no guarantees result from TAMARIN proving a lemma that may be reusing prior, unprovable, reuse lemmas.

Reuse lemmas do not always reduce proof search and their use may sometimes lead the proof of other lemmas astray by creating unneeded loops. It is therefore possible to disable the use of a given reuse lemma. For example, to disable the reuse lemma called NAME when proving some other lemma, one can add the annotation hide_lemma=NAME to the other lemma. All previous reuse lemmas not hidden in this way will be used in the proof.

Naturally, one can combine the different annotations. For example, one may prove a reuse lemma using induction, while hiding another previous reuse lemma. All the annotations are given as a comma-separated list inside square brackets.

9.3 An example: a simple hash chain

In this example, the property we want to show is not immediately verifiable by TAMARIN. We must first state an auxiliary reuse lemma and prove this lemma using induction.

Our example, given in **Minimal_HashChain.spthy**, models a simple hash chain. It can be seen as a precursor to protocols like TESLA [97]. The idea of the TESLA protocol is to authenticate broadcast messages, which are sent to multiple recipients simultaneously. The sender starts by computing a chain of hash values by repeatedly applying a hash function to an initial value, say up to n times. The sender then uses the resulting values in reverse order, essentially as keys for a MAC. This means the sender starts by releasing the result of hashing the value n times. Then it releases the result of hashing the value $n - 1$ times, etc. This allows the recipient to easily check that hashing the latest received value results in the previously received value, linking the two values. However, an adversary cannot inject packets easily, as it would have to be able to compute the pre-image of a hash, which is assumed to be hard, as usual. Note that protocols like this are intended for use with low-power devices. Thus, it uses symmetric encryption rather than signatures or other more complex mechanisms.

The protocol model we present now models repeated hashing by repeated application of a function f(·) to an argument. There are three rules to start, step, and stop a chain of applications of the hash function to a fresh seed value. The seed value is also output to the adversary. In the step rule, the current value is hashed and stored, while a ChainKey action is produced for the current value. In the stop rule, a last ChainKey action is logged, and a persistent end fact, called !Final(·) is added to the state. The intermediate values are henceforth referred to as keys.

```
// Hash chain generation
rule Gen_Start:
  [ Fr(seed) ] -->
  [ Gen(seed, seed)
  , Out(seed) ]

// The ChainKey-facts are used by the sender rules to store the
// link between the keys in the chain.
rule Gen_Step:
    [ Gen(seed, chain) ]
  --[ ChainKey(chain) ]->
    [ Gen(seed, f(chain) ) ]

// At some point the sender decides to stop the hash-chain
// precomputation.
rule Gen_Stop:
    [ Gen(seed, kZero) ]
  --[ ChainKey(kZero) ]->
    [ !Final(kZero) ]
```

Then, for any arbitrary key, TAMARIN can check whether it was part of such a previously computed chain. This is the case when one can start with the Check0 rule, take steps by applying the hash function in the rule Check, and finish with rule Success if the reached value is the one stored in a !Final(·) state fact.

```
// Start checking an arbitrary key. Use a loop-id to allow
// connecting different statements about the same loop.
rule Check0:
    [ In(kOrig)
    , Fr(loopId) ]
  --[ Start(loopId, kOrig) ]->
    [ Loop(loopId, kOrig, kOrig) ]

rule Check:
    [ Loop(loopId, k,    kOrig) ]
  --[ Loop(loopId, k,    kOrig) ]->
    [ Loop(loopId, f(k), kOrig) ]

rule Success:
    [ Loop(loopId, kZero, kOrig), !Final(kZero) ]
  --[ Success(loopId, kOrig)
```

9.3 An example: a simple hash chain

```
]-> []
```

We would now like to prove the following lemma. It states that if there is Success for some loop id and associated starting key value, then that starting key value has a ChainKey action in the trace, meaning it was actually part of a previously generated hash chain (the ChainKey actions are emitted by the generation rules).

```
lemma Success_chain:
  "All lid k #i. Success(lid, k) @ i ==>
    Ex #j. ChainKey(k) @ j"
```

Unfortunately, a direct proof of this lemma fails, as TAMARIN would end up in a loop when trying to unroll the hash chain, which can be arbitrary long (this is analogous to the small example from Section 9.1). Attempting to prove this lemma with induction also fails because the Success action for this loop id will only ever appear once per hash chain and only at the end. Thus, the induction hypothesis is never applicable, as there is no Success action.

A solution is to prove an auxiliary lemma. To be able to prove something about the hash chain, we must reason about the looping actions used in this part of the model, i.e., Loop and ChainKey. When looking at the rule Success, we can see that the Success(lid, k) action from lemma Success_chain directly requires the premises Loop(lid, kZero, k) and !Final(kZero) to exist. From there, the lemma must show that a ChainKey(k) action exists in the trace. We can try to simply state this as an auxiliary lemma, using actions Loop (there is one for each created Loop fact) and ChainKey (which is created when producing the !Final(kZero) fact in rule Gen_Stop).

```
lemma Auxiliary_Success_chain [use_induction,reuse]:
  "All lid kZero k #x #y.
     Loop(lid, kZero, k) @ #x & ChainKey(kZero) @ #y
   ==> Ex #z. ChainKey(k) @ #z"
```

We declare this lemma to be a reuse lemma and insert it before the lemma Success_chain so that it can be used to prove that lemma. Moreover, the auxiliary lemma must be proven using induction as we have an arbitrarily long hash chain and TAMARIN will enter a loop otherwise; hence we add the option use_induction.

TAMARIN now succeeds in proving this lemma, as we talk about the actions actually appearing on each step of the hash chain, and the induction hypothesis can be applied. Moreover, this additional hypothesis is sufficient to prove our main lemma (and without induction).

Part IV
Using Tamarin in Practice

Chapter 10
Basic Modeling

In previous sections, we examined the foundations of modeling security protocols and how TAMARIN reasons about these models. We now turn to tradeoffs in modeling, that is choosing between different options when modeling protocols or formalizing their properties. We also consider some pitfalls that newcomers to TAMARIN should avoid. We note in this regard that there is often no one, specific, best modeling approach. However, there are certain standard patterns that have proven useful in practice, which we present in this section.

10.1 Modeling with state facts

We have previously explained state facts, which store the state of each agent's runs. We also use state facts to store the information available to the parties executing the protocol, for example information on the public key Infrastructure that they use to look up keys. Note that TAMARIN internally uses state facts to model the adversary's knowledge and to augment this knowledge using built-in rules that describe the kinds of knowledge deductions the adversary can make, as described in Section 6.8. In what follows, we give concrete recommendations to the modeler on how to use state facts when modeling protocols, for each individual agent.

10.1.1 Standard modeling conventions

Usually a protocol requires agents to take multiple steps during their execution. An agent's state stores all values that the agent has access to, and the progress that it has made so far. For an agent whose role consists of a linear sequence of steps, i.e., one without branching into or out of the sequence, the standard way to represent this is as follows.

Calling the role abstractly *Role*, we can write `Role('n', ...)` for the *n*-th state of this agent, or alternatively and more simply `Role_n(...)`. In the former case, the modeler should ensure that the number *n*, given as an argument, is incremented in each transition involving this state fact. In the latter case, the modeler should transform `Role_n(...)` to `Role_n+1(...)`. In both cases, the actual data available to the agent is stored as the fact's arguments, elided above.

10.1.2 Variables and their scope

Variable names are local: their scope is limited to the rule in which they appear. Hence the same variable name can be reused in multiple rules, and variable instantiations in one rule have no effect on the other rules. This is in contrast, for example, to how variables are used in imperative programs where a variable is assigned a value and keeps that value until the variable is subsequently reassigned. The full example file is available at **VariableNamesAndLet.spthy**.

To exemplify the use of variables, consider the following two rules.

```
rule CreateVarA:
  [ Fr(~tid), In(<X,Y>) ]
--[]->
  [ State(~tid, $A), S(<X,Y>) ]

rule UseVarA:
  [ State(id, B), S(<Y,X>) ]
--[]->
  [ ]
```

The first rule creates a `State` fact with two arguments, and the second rule consumes this fact, where `id` will be unified with `~tid` and `B` will be unified with `$A`. For ease of readability, one often uses the same variable names, but that is neither necessary nor does it connect them a priori. In fact, internally TAMARIN will name apart variables from different rules prior to attempting to unify the rules.

In this example, the `S` fact also has two arguments. These are named `X` and `Y` in the first rule, and `Y` and `X` in the second rule. This could lead to the perception that this is specifying a swap, but we see that this is not the case. Looking at the rules in detail, we see that the second rule is applied to the state resulting from the first rule. The result is that the value of `Y` of the second rule will be what was in `X` from the first rule. Similarly, the value of `X` from the second rule will be that of the value of `Y` from the first rule. The values are fixed by their argument position in `S`, rather than the variable names representing them. This example illustrates that using the same variable name in multiple rules has no effect, i.e., variables are indeed local. However, for readability, it is generally preferable to use the same names for the same terms whenever possible.

10.1.3 Using public variables and constants

Recall from Section 3.1.2 that public variables are those variables prefixed with a $. Any rule can create public variables as these variables can be used on the right-hand side of rules without having to appear on the left-hand side. Furthermore, two different public variables may or may not be the same, meaning that $A and $B can be the same agent or, respectively, different agents. However, public constants, written as quoted strings like 'name', are fixed. Note that a public variable can be instantiated with a public constant as explained in Section 3.1.2. Two syntactically different public constants like 'name' and 'name2' are always distinct.

A standard use of public constants in protocol descriptions is to tag protocol messages, so that the first message of a protocol is never mistaken for the second as they cannot be unified. Of course, this assumes that the adversary cannot change the tags, i.e., they are authenticated in some way to prevent this.

For public variables, the adversary knows all possible values they can take. Furthermore, the adversary also knows all public constants. There is no need for the adversary to learn them from any output first and the adversary can use them at any time.

10.1.4 Using fresh values

Fresh values are used to model keys, nonces, and other secrets or unique values. There is a single distinguished rule creating fresh values, the so-called Fresh rule, which embeds a new fresh value as argument in the conclusion fact Fr(·) it produces. TAMARIN ensures that each instance of the Fresh rule produces a different value, making all values unique, and unguessable for the adversary. All other rules can only use fresh values that they know and this can happen in one of three ways:

- Use a fresh value from a Fr(·) fact.
- Use a state fact that has one or more fresh values as arguments.
- Receive a fresh value from the network in an In(·) fact.

In the first case, the agent can now use the fresh value and be sure that no other agent knows the value, unless it sends out the value in some way. In the second case, all fresh values are either originally created by this agent, or received from the network (and thus potentially from the adversary). In the second and third case, the agent cannot be sure that the value is truly fresh. The adversary can of course also consume Fr(·) facts in its rules, thus learning fresh values that no one else knows.

The type annotation ~ can be used to indicate that a variable is of type fresh. In this case, it can only be instantiated using fresh values.

For rules that use a Fr(x) fact, TAMARIN automatically adds the fresh type to x, so it will be represented as ~x, irrespective of whether the modeler used the type annotation or not. In all other cases, the decision whether to add the annotation or not can influence the model's traces, as explained in the next section.

10.1.5 Effects of type annotations

Type annotations on the left-hand side of rules limit their applicability. Expecting a $A parameter in a state fact in the left-hand side of a rule means the rule can only be triggered if the state fact contains a public value in that position (thereby excluding compound terms, function applications, or fresh values). Similarly, if a public variable is used inside a pattern that is matching an input, the rule can only be triggered if the input contains a public value at that position. Thus, this type annotation can have an influence on a model's traces, and one should make sure that it is realistic for the agent receiving the input to be able to check whether the value in that position is actually a public value, or remove the type annotation to be sure not to miss attacks.

Similarly for a fresh ~x variable, if it occurs in a state fact on the left-hand side of a rule, then the rule can only be triggered with an instance of that state fact with a fresh value in that position.

In practice, for fresh values generated locally by an agent and stored inside a state fact, one can add the type annotation even for rules consuming this fact. This is without any risk of limiting the rules' applicability, as one can be sure that there will always be a fresh value in that position. When no annotation is given, TAMARIN may sometimes add it itself in the computed sources during pre-computation. It does so whenever it finds that all ways to create a fact actually have a fresh value in that position, thus ensuring no mistake.

Adding a ~ type annotation to a variable inside an input is more delicate, as this means that the agent receiving this input actually has a way of checking that this value is fresh, and not anything else. This may be reasonable when the agent already knows the value and knows that it is fresh, e.g., as it is stored in its state and is then also received and compared. However, when the agent learns a new value, it is a strong assumption on the overall setup to annotate this as fresh, as in practice it is typically not possible to check whether a value is really random. Adding this annotation in this case essentially assumes that the agent can distinguish fresh values from reused, or otherwise arbitrary, values.

Consider the following example.

Example 16 (Simple Challenge Response Protocol, again)

Consider the following example from Chapter 4:

```
rule Register_pk:
  [ Fr(~ltk) ]
  -->
  [ !Ltk($A, ~ltk), !Pk($A, pk(~ltk)), Out(pk(~ltk)) ]
```

10.1 Modeling with state facts

```
rule Client_1:
   [ Fr(~k), !Pk($S, pkS) ]
  -->
   [ Client_1( $S, ~k ), Out( aenc{'1', ~k}pkS ) ]

rule Client_2:
   [ Client_1(S, k), In( h(k) ) ]
  --[ SessKeyC( S, k ) ]->
   []

rule Serv_1:
   [ !Ltk($S, ~ltkS), In( aenc{'1', k}pk(~ltkS) ) ]
  --[ AnswerRequest($S, k)
   ]->
   [ Out( h(k) ) ]
```

In the rule `Client_2`, one could replace S by $S, and k by ~k without changing the model's traces as both values necessarily come from the fact `Client_1`. This fact is only produced by the rule `Client_1`. Hence we can be sure that the two values are of the respective types. In contrast, in `Serv_1`, replacing k by ~k would change the model's traces. This modification would entail that this rule could only be triggered if k is a fresh value, although in reality it would be impossible for the server to check whether the new key received is actually freshly generated. Hence, by making this change, one could potentially miss attacks where the adversary manages to trigger this rule using other, non-fresh, values.

Inside formulas the type annotations $ and ~ are forbidden, and if they are used TAMARIN will give an error. Formulas can only use untyped variables, and variables of type timepoint, prefixed with a #. Timepoint variables can only be used in formulas, and not in rules.

10.1.6 Pattern matching versus explicit deconstructors

There are two different ways to handle received messages in rules, where the receiving agent intends to perform some operation on them, such as decryption or checking a signature or a format with a tag. One can either use pattern matching, or an explicit deconstructor, combined with restrictions if necessary.

In principle, these two approaches have the same expressiveness, but there are some subtleties regarding their semantics. These subtleties consider both the applicability of the rules and the computations that can be modeled.

To illustrate the first point, consider decryption, with the full example file available at **PatternMatchingVSExplicitDeconstructor.spthy**. Recall the standard equational theory for symmetric encryption and decryption.

```
functions: senc/2, sdec/2
equations: sdec(senc(m,k),k)=m
```

A rule can either apply pattern matching (the first rule below) or explicitly use the deconstructor sdec (the second rule below). Pattern matching is the process of finding a substitution on variables such that the terms are equal, where equality here is defined modulo the equational theory.

```
rule decrypt_pattern_matching:
  [ !Key(k), In(senc(m,k)) ]
--[Received(m)]->
  []

rule decrypt_explicit_deconstructor:
  [ !Key(k), In(msg) ]
--[ Received(sdec(msg,k)) ]->
  []
```

The difference is that, in the first rule, the received term must be a correctly computed encryption under the known key k, while in the second rule anything is accepted and the decryption function with the known key is applied, even if this computation does not yield a meaningful result. Note that, in this use of the explicit deconstructor, the received message need not even be an encryption. Any message would be accepted. Hence, this modeling would be appropriate for those cases where the receiver cannot check whether the decryption is successful or not.

In contrast, for the pattern matching rule, the received message must have the right format. This means that, for the pattern-matching version, a decryption failure (say, due to a mismatch of the encryption and decryption key) is immediately visible to the agent, while the explicit deconstructor can always be applied. This modeling would thus be appropriate in case the receiver can (and does) check whether the decryption is successful or not.

This difference is clearly visible when looking at the variants (see Section 6.7) TAMARIN computes for both rules.

```
rule (modulo AC) decrypt_pattern_matching:
   [ !Key( k ), In( senc(m, k) ) ] --[ Received( m ) ]-> [ ]

rule (modulo AC) decrypt_explicit_deconstructor:
   [ !Key( k ), In( msg ) ] --[ Received( z ) ]-> [ ]
  variants (modulo AC)
  1. k = k.4
     msg = msg.4
     z = sdec(msg.4, k.4)

  2. k = x.4
     msg = senc(x.5, x.4)
     z = x.5
```

The pattern matching rule only has one variant, where the input is a correct encryption using the key k, whereas the explicit deconstructor version has a second variant (with number 1 here), corresponding to the case where the input is of a different form.

One can ensure that decryption was successful when using the explicit deconstructor, for example by having a tagged message of the form <'1', msg>. The receiver can

10.1 Modeling with state facts

then decrypt, unpair, and check that the resulting term is a '1' with the Equality restriction Eq given previously and used as follows.

```
rule decrypt_explicit_destructor_success:
  [ !Key(k), In(msg) ]
--[ Eq(fst(sdec(msg,k)),'1')
  , Received(snd(sdec(msg,k))) ]->
  []
```

This approach can become cumbersome though. Moreover, using pattern matching also typically results in better performance. However, for some scenarios the use of explicit deconstructors rather than pattern matching is required, see Chapter 15.

Another (semantic) difference between pattern matching and explicit deconstructors concerns the computable functions. Using pattern-matching, it is possible (on purpose or by accident) to give normal agents capabilities that are not given to the adversary by the equational theory, which can be problematic. For example, when receiving a value that is expected to be a hash, with pattern-matching the receiver's rule can match on In(h(X)), which thus learns and stores the value X. However, this is inappropriate for a cryptographic hash function as it specifically prevents (easy) computation of the pre-image of its result, and there is no explicit deconstructor and equation allowing this.

To help users use pattern matching correctly, i.e., to prevent mistakes like specifying unrealistic computations, TAMARIN reports warnings for this. To be precise, whenever the rules derive values that would not be derivable using the equational theory for the adversary with the same knowledge, then this is reported. For example, consider receiving a message from the network and pattern-matching it as h(X) in a protocol rule, when the agent acting does not know X already. Then this pattern matching gives the agent the power to invert the function h. The adversary cannot do that, unless an equation allows extraction of values under that function h. This check is activated by default. The flag to turn this feature off, respectively edit its time-out, is called -d (or --derivcheck-timeout). By default, the time-out is 5 seconds. Setting the value to 0 turns the feature off, and other values set the timeout.

Finally pattern matching can be used to implement certain checks which are difficult to model otherwise. When this can be justified, the warning can be ignored, or even deactivated. For example, a group element check in Diffie-Hellman protocols, which verifies whether a received value is actually an element of the current group, can be modeled using pattern matching.

```
rule group_element_check:
  [ In('g'^x) , ... ] --> [ ... ]
// here 'g' is the generator
```

In this rule, the input only matches values that are powers of the generator, i.e., group elements. Of course, TAMARIN will also raise a warning here, but that can be ignored, so long as a group element check is possible (and done) in practice for the used Diffie-Hellman implementation. To deactivate the warning, one can add the no_derivcheck annotation to the rule as follows.

```
rule group_element_check [no_derivcheck]:
  [ In('g'^x) , ... ] --> [ ... ]
// here 'g' is the generator
```

TAMARIN then no longer performs the check for this rule. All other rules will still be checked.

Apart from the above semantic differences, there is a more stylistic difference between pattern matching and explicit deconstructors. When using pattern matching, the equational theory is in some sense hard-coded into the rules, and any changes require updating all rules accordingly. In case of explicit deconstructors, changing an equation or a function does not necessarily require updating any of the rules.

10.1.7 Fact symbols with injective instances

TAMARIN has built-in support for reasoning about facts whose instances are always unique. At the end of this subsection we explain how to make use of these in practice. We call such facts *injective fact symbols* (or *injective facts* for short). In principle, such facts can appear in many different forms, but are then quite hard to detect, so TAMARIN limits itself to a specific subset. Namely, TAMARIN detects injective facts that have a fresh value at the first argument position of each instance, and are constructed and consumed in a way that ensures the uniqueness of their instances. Specifically, an injective fact is one where all instances of the fact F(~x, ...) come from either an initialization rule that creates this fact with an actual fresh fact Fr(~x) in its premise, or from a rule that has just consumed and again produced it. When this is the case, the uniqueness of the instances follows, i.e., there can only be at most one copy of this fact with this fresh identifier in the system at any time.

For example, consider the following two rules from the example file at **MinimalInjectiveFact.spthy**:

```
rule Init:
  [ Fr(~i) ]
--[ Initiated(~i) ]->
  [ Inj(~i, $Z ) ]

rule Reader:
  [ Inj(i, $Z) ]
--[ Read(i, $Z) ]->
  [ Inj(i, $Z ) ]
```

In this example, the Inj fact is injective because, for each i, there can be at most one Inj(i,_) fact in the system at any time. This might not be the case, for example, if there was a rule with two instances of Inj on its right-hand side, or if ~i was not freshly generated in the Init rule.

10.1 Modeling with state facts

Injective facts arise in various practical scenarios, for example, when modeling a database with mutable data. The data fields are represented by an injective fact, using a fresh value as index in the first argument, and data in other argument positions.

Note that identifying whether a fact symbol is injective is, in general, undecidable. This is why TAMARIN applies the above heuristic in a best-effort manner to detect them. When such facts are detected then specialized reasoning (described below) is applied. Note that this special reasoning is only needed when a fact is both consumed and produced in a rule. Facts that are only consumed are already handled by the standard heuristics.

You can check if TAMARIN detected that your theory contains injective facts by inspecting the loaded theory in the GUI. To do this, click on "Multiset rewriting rules" and look at the top of the right-hand pane. There you will see the names of all such detected facts underneath "Fact Symbols with Injective Instances", with "id" as their first argument, if there are any. For example, for the preceding two rules, this yields:

Proof scripts	Multiset rewriting rules and restrictions
theory MinimalInjectiveFact begin	
Message theory	Fact Symbols with Injective Instances
Multiset rewriting rules (4)	Inj(id,=)
Tactic(s)	

In the screenshot, TAMARIN displays that it detected that Inj is an injective fact and additionally that the second argument of this injective fact never changes, which is indicated by the equal sign in the second argument position.

We next consider the following simple lemma for the theory with the Init and Reader rules.

```
lemma injectivity: all-traces
  "All id #i #j Z1 Z2.
       Read(id, Z1) @ i & Read(id, Z2) @ j ==> Z1 = Z2 "
```

If we would try to prove this lemma automatically using the proof techniques presented thus far, the proof would not terminate. To construct a counterexample, TAMARIN would first consider two instances of the Reader rule with the same ~i but different $Z and then consider two parallel, ever-growing, backwards chains of Reader rule instances, without ever realizing that this cannot occur in this system. However, by detecting that Inj is an injective fact, TAMARIN can automatically prove this lemma, using the following reasoning.

For injective facts, TAMARIN can optimize its reasoning based on the following observation. Suppose one rule instance produced an injective fact with a fresh value at timepoint i, which is consumed in another rule instance at timepoint k. Then any rule at a timepoint in between, call it j, where $i < j < k$, cannot consume or produce this fact with this fresh value. This observation is helpful when TAMARIN's search has already connected two rules, by having the one at k consuming the fact produced at i, giving us the information that other instances of this fact with this value must be before or after, but not between these time points. In this case, TAMARIN can apply an additional constraint reduction rule, which marks this scenario as impossible. It turns out that this can reduce the overall search space and have a significant impact, also on TAMARIN's termination. Furthermore, the modeler does not have to do anything specific for this optimization to be applied when writing their theory file. The only condition is that the fact needs to have a fresh value at the top level in the first position (rather than inside a tuple or in later positions).

10.2 Macros and conditional blocks

10.2.1 Local macros

To help reduce modeling errors and also for the modeler's convenience, one may use *let bindings* in rules. A let binding maps variables to terms and is syntactic sugar for inlining all of the declared mappings into the rule. Let bindings are also local to each rule, like variable names. Syntactically, they start with the keyword `let`, followed by a comma-separated list of triples, each consisting of a variable name, an equal sign, and the term the variable is mapped to. This is followed by `in` and then the rule's remainder. The bindings are applied from left to right and they may be nested without needing to repeat the `let` boilerplate; see the second example below.

We first give a simple example, where we show a rule not using `let` and afterwards we give a second equivalent version using `let`, all available in the full file at **VariableNamesAndLet.spthy**.

```
rule WithoutLetBinding:
  [ State(id, A), Fr(~x), Fr(~k) ]
--[ Sent(senc(~x, ~k)) ]->
  [ State2(id, A, ~x, ~k), Out(senc(~x,~k)) ]

rule WithLetBinding:
  let msg = senc(~x, ~k)
  in
  [ State(id, A), Fr(~x), Fr(~k) ]
--[ Sent(msg) ]->
  [ State2(id, A, ~x, ~k), Out(msg) ]
```

When executing TAMARIN, the let bindings are inlined. If you examine the loaded theory associated with this example, you will see that the resulting rules `WithoutLetBinding` and `WithLetBinding` are identical, except for their names.

Our next example involves nested let bindings and it illustrates the order in which the bindings are applied, which is left to right. So, a variable mapping, once defined, is used in all subsequent bindings, but not vice versa.

```
rule ComplicatedLetBinding:
  let x = y
      y = z
```

10.2 Macros and conditional blocks

```
        w = y
    in
    [ F(x, y, w) ]
  --[ ]->
    [ ]
```

This example highlights that the order in which bindings are given is important. The bindings are applied to each other sequentially, in the order they are declared. Afterwards, the resulting mappings are applied simultaneously to the variables in the rule, as is standard for substitutions, yielding the resulting state fact F(y,z,z). In particular, x is mapped to y and this is not changed by the y=z following it. However, the last binding, w=y, is changed, so it maps w to z.

We present a final example that illustrates the use of let bindings to construct large terms and improve the readability of rules.

```
rule ConsecutiveLetBinding:
  let msg = senc(~x, ~k)
      triplemsg = <msg,msg,msg>
      toolarge = <triplemsg,triplemsg>
  in
  [ State(id, A), Fr(~x), Fr(~k) ]
--[ Sent(toolarge) ]->
  [ State2(id, A, ~x, ~k), Out(toolarge) ]
```

In this example, the term represented by toolarge amounts to a pair of triples of the original msg, which is thus repeated six times.

```
<<senc(~x,~k),senc(~x,~k),senc(~x,~k)>,
 senc(~x,~k),senc(~x,~k),senc(~x,~k)>
```

Note that internally this is represented by repeated use of the pairing operator, but for readability TAMARIN leaves out many of the pairing angle-brackets, as we have seen before. Recall that the pairing is right-associative, thus the pairings parenthesization is sufficient here.

10.2.2 Global macros for rules

TAMARIN also supports parameterized global macros, which apply to all rules in a theory. For large protocols, particularly those where large terms are used in multiple rules, using global macros makes the rules easier to read and write. For example, the following two rules

```
rule Client:
  [ !Ltk($S, ~ltkS), Fr(~m) ]
-->
  [ Out( <$S, aenc(~m, ~ltkS)> ) ]

rule Serv:
  [ !Ltk($S, ~ltkS), In( <$S, aenc(req, ~ltkS)> ) ]
-->
  [ Out( req ) ]
```

can be simplified by using a macro that defines the message format once, and is then used in both rules. This is available in **Macros.spthy**

```
macros: msg1(X, m, key) = <X, aenc(m, key)>
rule Client_1:
  [ !Ltk($S, ~ltkS), Fr(~m) ]
  -->
  [ Out( msg1($S, ~m, ~ltkS) ) ]
rule Serv_1:
  [ !Ltk($S, ~ltkS), In( msg1($S, req, ~ltkS) ) ]
  -->
  [ Out( req ) ]
```

Note that one can define multiple macros separated by commas, and that macros can have zero or more arguments. Moreover macros can use previously defined macros, as we illustrate here.

```
macros: macro1(x) = h(x), macro2(x, y) = senc(x, y), macro3() = $A,
        macro4(x, y) = macro2(macro1(x), y)
```

10.2.3 Conditional blocks and include statements

Sometimes one wants to model different variants of a protocol and ends up with several models in separate files. To avoid copying and repeating common code, TAMARIN's internal preprocessor can be used to dynamically activate and deactivate parts of the model, or to factor out and include common parts from external files.

TAMARIN's internal preprocessor uses cpp preprocessor style commands. We can use `#ifdef KEYWORD` followed by the part of the file that one wants to consider only some of the time, and ending that part with `#endif`. This part is then included when calling TAMARIN with the command-line argument `-DKEYWORD`. For example, one could have a part that is only about executability, given after `#ifdef executable`, and pass the argument `-Dexecutable` when one wants to consider this block. Else branches are also supported using the command `#else`, and the `#ifdef` can contain simple boolean formulas. Keywords can also be set to true using the command `#define KEYWORD` rather than using a command-line argument.

Other files can be included using `#include "path/to/file.spthy"`, where the path can be absolute or relative to the current file. Included files can again contain preprocessor commands, and recursively include other files.

The following snippet illustrates the possibilities, available in the file **Preprocessor.spthy**.

```
#define KEYWORD1

#ifdef (KEYWORD1 | KEYWORD2) & KEYWORD3

  ...
```

```
#else
...
#endif
#include "path/to/file.spthy"
```

10.3 Threat modeling

As explained in Section 1.1, when reasoning about security protocols it is essential to specify the associated threat model, which formalizes the adversary's capabilities. For this reason, this model is also called an *adversary model* in the literature and in this book. We explain next how such a model is built as a set of *adversary capabilities*, and how these capabilities are expressed using multiset rewriting rules, formalizing possible adversary actions.

10.3.1 Threat models as sets of capabilities

In many settings, protocols are run over an untrusted network like the Internet, which itself provides no security guarantees. Here it is natural that the adversary's capabilities include message eavesdropping (modeling a passive adversary) and message spoofing (modeling an active one).

Other capabilities arise from the adversary's ability to corrupt different parties. In principle, there are no bounds on the number of agents who can play in different roles, e.g., in the ISO/IEC protocol examined in Section 2.2, arbitrarily many agents could be the initiator or responder. In that example we did, however, model the trusted third party as being a single distinguished agent 'T'. Moreover, not all of these agents need be honest or have a secure system, e.g., they may intend to be honest but their systems are under the adversary's control. So an adversary capability here would be the ability to corrupt a party, thereby learning all the party's secrets. This corruption capability could be formalized as being static, i.e., the corruption occurs at the start of the protocol, or dynamic, whereby the adversary could compromise parties during protocol execution.

Working out the threat model is not always easy and it requires domain knowledge about all the intended contexts where the protocol will be used. If these contexts are not all known in advance, one may instead formalize a very strong threat model where the adversary is given many capabilities. If the protocol's security is provable with respect to this model, one has the attractive guarantee that the protocol is secure even when attacked by an adversary with all these capabilities. Moreover, it follows immediately that the protocol is secure against any weaker adversary too.[1] Conversely, if an attack is found, one can weaken the threat model by removing capabilities until one reaches a point where the desired properties are provable. In this way, one can work out the strongest adversary model (or models, see discussion below) under which the protocol is secure.

It turns out that there is a lattice ordering on threat models, where a threat model is a set of capabilities and the ordering is the subset ordering. Hence there may even be multiple, incomparable, strongest threat models, differing in the adversary's capabilities. [11] contains a detailed account of how one can classify protocols with respect to the strength of the adversaries that they resist. We also return to this topic in Section 17.1.

The threat model itself is formalized by:

1. providing rules that reflect the adversary's compromise capabilities and
2. conditioning the protocol's desired properties on the occurrence, or lack thereof, of different kinds of compromises.

For (1), the rules typically formalize which parts of the global state the adversary learns. Moreover, when such a rule fires, an appropriately named action is added to the trace. These actions are used for (2): they provide a way to speak about what compromises occur (e.g., who has been compromised, what has been compromised, and when the compromise occurred) in the statement of security lemmas.

We have already seen some examples of this. We gave examples of properties conditioned on long-term key corruption in Section 5.7. Furthermore, in Section 5.8, we saw examples of different secrecy properties in the presence of corruption. We will give a larger example in the next subsection.

Summarizing, the key to constructing the threat model is to formalize the different adversary capabilities. Common examples are compromising an agent's long-term secrets, their session keys, their entire state, or even the random number generator. This idea is also used in other settings, such as when using the computational model for cryptographic proofs. In that setting, the compromise of the entire state would be represented by an oracle, sometimes called *session state reveal*, that represents that an adversary might get control of a participant's computer during a protocol run and learn that agent's entire state. With this information, the adversary may thereafter impersonate the agent and learn the content of other transmitted messages.

---

[1] For properties such as secrecy and agreement, which are safety properties, if they hold for a protocol model, they will hold for any subset of its behaviors. They will therefore hold when the adversary has fewer capabilities and hence fewer behaviors.

10.3.2 An example

We provide an example here of the Naxos protocol from [81], originally modeled for TAMARIN in [102]. In this protocol, the agents combine long-term and ephemeral secrets into a final key, thereby providing protection against different elements being revealed.

The Naxos protocol provides strong security guarantees. To express this, it is necessary to formalize different compromise capabilities for the adversary. Naxos uses both long-term keys, which are per agent, and short-term keys, so called *ephemeral* keys, produced per session per agent. A compromise can then be of an agent's long-term keys, the ephemeral keys of certain sessions, or the resulting session keys.

The security property we consider is a notion of key secrecy. This property is formulated in terms of a distinguished *test session* and different combinations of ways that keys can be revealed. In more detail, the test session between two parties is secure even when both partners reveal the session key of all their other sessions. Moreover, they can additionally each either reveal the ephemeral key of the test session or their long-term key, and more. This is called eCK-security. For details on this example and its modeling in TAMARIN see [81, 102].

Here, we focus on how one can add different compromise scenarios to one's model, where different kinds of data are revealed. As we have seen, long-term key reveal is possible using the !Ltk fact created in the public key infrastructure generation rule. For session state reveal, we must consider the agent state during (or after) execution. We therefore store that in a way that we can add a reveal rule that can access that data, but without interfering with the normal protocol execution. For this purpose, additional state facts are added to the output of rules that contain the ephemeral key as well as the full resulting session key that was produced, called !Ephk($\cdot,\cdot$) and !Sessk($\cdot,\cdot$).

We now show the relevant rules of this model, with the full file available at **NAXOS.spthy**.

```
rule Init_1:
  let exI = h1(<~eskI, ~lkI >)
      hkI = 'g'^exI
  in
  [   Fr( ~eskI ), !Ltk( $I, ~lkI ) ]
  -->
  [   Init_1( ~eskI, $I, $R, ~lkI, hkI )
    , !Ephk(~eskI, ~eskI)
    , Out( hkI ) ]
rule Init_2:
  let pkR = 'g'^~lkR
      exI = h1(< ~eskI, ~lkI >)
      kI  = h2(< Y^~lkI, pkR^exI, Y^exI, $I, $R >)
  in
  [   Init_1( ~eskI, $I, $R, ~lkI , hkI), !Pk( $R, pkR ), In( Y ) ]
  --[ Accept( ~eskI, $I, $R, kI)
```

```
    , Sid( ~eskI, < 'Init', $I, $R, hkI, Y >)
    , Match( ~eskI, < 'Resp', $R, $I, hkI, Y >)
    ]->
  [   !Sessk( ~eskI, kI) ]
```

In the initiator rules, in the first rule we have the state fact !Ephk$(\cdot,\cdot)$ and in the second rule we have !Sessk$(\cdot,\cdot)$, while in the responder rule

```
rule Resp_1:
  let pkI = 'g'^~lkI
      exR = h1(< ~eskR, ~lkR >)
      hkr = 'g'^exR
      kR  = h2(< pkI^exR, X^~lkR, X^exR, $I, $R >)
  in
  [   Fr( ~eskR ), !Ltk($R, ~lkR), !Pk($I, pkI), In( X ) ]
  --[ Accept( ~eskR, $R, $I, kR )
    , Sid( ~eskR, <'Resp', $R, $I, X, hkr >)
    , Match( ~eskR, <'Init', $I, $R, X, hkr> )
    ]->
  [   Out( hkr ),
      !Ephk(~eskR, ~eskR),
      !Sessk( ~eskR, kR) ]
```

we have both of these facts. Using these facts, we can add the following two reveal rules.

```
rule Sessk_reveal:
   [ !Sessk(~tid, k) ] --[ SesskRev(~tid) ]-> [ Out(k) ]
rule Ephk_reveal:
   [ !Ephk(~s, ~ek) ] --[ EphkRev(~s) ]-> [ Out(~ek) ]
```

These are in addition to the usual reveal rule for the long-term key.

Using this, we can write a lemma that is conditioned on all relevant combinations of reveals under which the protocol stays secure, which TAMARIN proves for this protocol and lemma. In general, one could also consider a hierarchy of all possible combinations of reveals (see Chapter 17) and use TAMARIN to determine the strongest possible combinations of reveals where it is still secure. Here, we only show the one lemma with maximal reveals.

```
lemma eCK_key_secrecy:
  /*
   * If there exists a Test session whose key k is known to the
   * Adversary, then...
   */
  "(All #i1 #i2 Test A B k.
    Accept(Test, A, B, k) @ i1 & K( k ) @ i2
    ==> (
    /* ... the Test session must be "not clean".
     * Test is not clean if one of the following has happened:
     */
    /* 1a. session-key-reveal of test thread. */
      (Ex #i3. SesskRev( Test ) @ i3 )

    /* 1b. session-key-reveal of matching session */
    | (Ex MatchingSession #i3 #i4 ms.
```

10.4 Channel types

```
            /* ( MatchingSession's 'ms' info matches with Test ) */
               ( Sid ( MatchingSession, ms ) @ i3 & Match( Test, ms ) @ i4)
         & (
           (Ex #i5. SesskRev( MatchingSession ) @ i5 )
         )
          )
       /* 2. If matching session exists and ... */
       | (Ex MatchingSession #i3 #i4 ms.
              /* ( MatchingSession's 'ms' info matches with Test ) */
                 ( Sid ( MatchingSession, ms ) @ i3 & Match( Test, ms ) @ i4)
         & (
         /* 2a. reveal either both sk_A and esk_A, or */
           (Ex #i5 #i6. LtkRev   ( A ) @ i5  & EphkRev ( Test   ) @ i6 )
         /* 2b. both sk_B and esk_B */
         | (Ex #i5 #i6. LtkRev   ( B ) @ i5  & EphkRev ( MatchingSession ) @ i6 )
         )
          )
       /* 3. No matching session exists and ... */
       | ( ( not(Ex MatchingSession #i3 #i4 ms.
              /* ( MatchingSession's 'ms' info matches with Test ) */
                 Sid ( MatchingSession, ms ) @ i3 & Match( Test, ms ) @ i4 ) )
         & (
         /* 3a. reveal either sk_B, or */
           (Ex #i5    . LtkRev (B) @ i5 )
         /* 3b. both sk_A and esk_A */
         | (Ex #i5 #i6. LtkRev (A) @ i5 & EphkRev ( Test ) @ i6 )
         ) ) ) )"
```

10.4 Channel types

By default, when using In and Out in TAMARIN, we assume an insecure channel controlled by the adversary. Channels with different properties, i.e., built-in guarantees, can also be modeled, via state facts. Here, we simply assume that such channels exist and use them as building blocks for larger models; we do not care how these channels would be implemented or analyzed.

Possible properties for such channels include authenticity (an "authentic channel") or confidentiality (a "confidential channel"), as well as the combination of authenticity and confidentiality (a "secure channel"). These abstractions remove the need to use explicit cryptographic constructions (such as encryption and MACs) and key management for communication between parties in the model. These different kinds of channels can enable the faster analysis of larger protocols where such channels are just a building block. The channels and their properties have preferably been previously verified to actually be correct.

As an example, one can represent authentic channels using the following new facts (and the rules given below):

1. AuthSend(s,r,m) whose three arguments are the actual sender, the intended (but not guaranteed) receiver, and the message;

2. the persistent !Auth(s,m) fact whose two arguments are the authentic sender and the message;
3. AuthRecv(s,r,m) whose arguments are the actual authentic sender, the purported receiver, and the message.

For this type of channel, the adversary may select any desired receiver, as authenticity only guarantees the message sender's identity. The sender using this channel type can put the AuthSend fact with its own name, intended receiver name, and message on one of its rule's right-hand sides. A receiver uses the AuthRecv fact with the sender, receiver's name, and message in the left-hand side of one of its rules. Note that the message content is made available to the adversary as well, as the channel is not secret. This happens in the first of the two following rules modeling the internals (only defined once), which are translating from the send fact to the receive fact. The full file is available at **ChannelRules.spthy**.

```
rule authentic_channel_send:
  [ AuthSend(A,B,m) ]
--[ AuthChan_Out(A,B,m) ]->
  [ !Auth(A,m), Out(m) ]

rule authentic_channel_receive:
  [ !Auth(A, m), In(B) ]
--[ AuthChan_In(A,B,m) ]->
  [ AuthRecv(A,B,m) ]
```

The modeler will then only use the AuthSend and AuthRecv facts in all other rules of their model, while !Auth should only appear in these two standardized rules and nowhere else. Note that all of this is fully user-defined, and the above is just one possible version. None of the names shown are reserved in any way, so the modeler is required to take care.

Confidential channels work similarly, with a !Conf fact with the guaranteed receiver and the message. Confidential channels use a ConfSend fact with the agent's name as the first argument, the receiver who is the only one to receive the message as the second argument, and the message last. This is received with ConfRecv, which has the claimed sender, actual receiver, and message as arguments. For confidential channels, the adversary cannot extract the message. However, the adversary can create a confidential message for anyone, and can change the claimed sender of existing confidential messages (as they are not authentic). The three rules describing the internals are given next, noting that !Conf should not be used in any other rules.

```
rule confidential_channel_send:
  [ ConfSend(A,B,m) ]
--[ ConfChan_Out(A,B,m) ]->
  [ !Conf(B,m) ]

rule confidential_channel_receive:
  [ !Conf(B, m), In(A) ]
--[ ConfChan_In(A,B,m) ]->
  [ ConfRecv(A,B,m) ]
```

10.5 How do I know my model makes sense?

```
rule confidential_channel_send_adversary:
  [ In(<A,B,m>) ]
--[]->
  [ ConfSend(A,B,m) ]
```

Putting the properties of the two kinds of channel (authentic and confidential) together, we get a secure channel using `!Sec` with sender, receiver, and message arguments. We use `SecSend` and `SecRecv` in the agent rules and the internal rules similar to the above `ConfSend` and `ConfRecv`.

```
rule secure_channel_send:
  [ SecSend(A,B,m) ]
--[ SecChan_Out(A,B,m) ]->
  [ !Sec(A,B,m) ]

rule secure_channel_receive:
  [ !Sec(A,B,m) ]
--[ SecChan_In(A,B,m) ]->
  [ SecRecv(A,B,m) ]
```

In a secure channel, the adversary cannot learn the message or change either of the sender or receiver, as the name secure channel suggests. The presented version does not protect against replay though, as the `!Sec` fact is persistent, and can thus be reused. Removing the `!` and turning it into `Sec` would give a version where a message in a secure channel cannot be replayed.

Another advanced notion of channel provides the property of "eventual delivery" and uses restrictions to enforce progress, i.e., to only consider executions in which anything sent on such a channel is received at some later time. This requires annotating all rules carefully, but there is an automatic translation from SAPIC that takes care of this. For more on this, see [7].

The above channels have been used in many models successfully. Of course, there can also be other kinds channels with different properties, defined by the modeler as desired.

10.5 How do I know my model makes sense?

Given a protocol model, it is critically important to ensure that the model actually formalizes the intended protocol. Beyond careful manual inspection, there are various tool-assisted options that help catch mistakes made during modeling.

10.5.1 Executability of rules

The first approach to model validation is to check that the protocol model can be executed. By this we mean that the agents playing in the different roles can execute all the rules that constitute their role. One can check this, for each role, by writing a lemma with `exists-trace` that checks for the existence of an action in the trace that is emitted when the role's last rule is fired. To prove this lemma, TAMARIN must show that such a trace exists. If the lemma is not provable, then the emitted action is not reachable. This means that the protocol, as modeled, is not executable and any guarantees (e.g., for secrecy) that are provable, may hold simply because the protocol cannot run to completion.

If a trace terminating in a desired, final, action is found, one should then check it carefully. Does the trace have the expected form in the resulting dependency graph shown in TAMARIN's GUI? When this is the case, one has further evidence that the rules model the intended protocol steps. Note that this check should first be done for all agents separately. Afterwards, it should also be done for all agents at once as otherwise some uniquely created fact that two agents need for their different roles might have been consumed by one of them, so the protocol is not executable after all. Moreover, all the resulting executions should not involve help from the adversary, as the protocol modeled should be executable by the agents on their own. Finally, if the trace involves unnecessary steps, one can make the lemma more precise and require that each agent's rules are executed only once, and in the right order, to ensure that the expected protocol execution is possible.

In the early phases of model development, one can of course already look at traces up to the furthest point modeled to see how the model "works" and whether the traces match the modeler's expectations.

10.5.2 Sanity check: intentionally break the protocol

Additional sanity checks that one can perform are to either (1) add small weaknesses to the model or (2) specify unreasonably strong properties. In either case, one would expect TAMARIN to find attacks. An example of the former would be removing a check on a received value, e.g., that it is a nonce previously sent out. An example of the latter would be to strengthen a secrecy property by removing the part of a lemma formula saying "or a participant was corrupted." If this intentionally broken lemma is still verified, then something is likely modeled incorrectly.

Chapter 11
Common Workflows

For most protocols, the way TAMARIN is used follows similar patterns, and we describe here the most common workflows. This chapter brings together many concepts and techniques from previous chapters. In some cases, we will also point to additional, more advanced material from subsequent chapters.

11.1 TAMARIN's user interfaces

We start with an overview of the two user interfaces available when running TAMARIN. We start with the graphical user interface that allows interaction. Afterwards we describe the command-line interface, which is often used to reproduce results, or when analyzing many protocols or properties at once.

11.1.1 Analysis using TAMARIN's GUI

TAMARIN's most useful workflow uses its graphical user interface (GUI), as this supports the detailed inspection of attack traces and incomplete proofs. We already introduced the GUI in Section 6.1.1, but we will describe the complete workflow here. We provide a high-level overview of the workflow in Figure 11.2.

TAMARIN 1.10 does not include a text editor: users provide their own input file that describes their TAMARIN theory (named with the default extension .spthy) using any editor. There is also an "official" TAMARIN plugin for VSCode, available from the VSCode store or the TAMARIN website, providing syntax highlighting, syntax checking, and wellformedness checks similar to those provided by TAMARIN.

The user starts TAMARIN in interactive mode using the command

```
tamarin-prover interactive .
```

where '.' refers to the current directory, which we assume contains the .spthy file. This command starts a local web server with the graphical user interface.

Afterwards, the user can open a web browser and visit http://127.0.0.1:3001. This starts TAMARIN's graphical user interface, and presents the user a list of all .spthy files in the directory together with their theory names. The user can select any of these files, which in turn opens the main GUI view, and additionally shows any warnings or errors. We discuss how to handle warnings and errors in Section 11.4.

Note that the TAMARIN server does not reload new directory listings or file content: if the user edits the .spthy file, the server must be restarted.

In case there are no errors or warnings, one could next try to prove the specified lemmas. However, it is prudent to first check if there are any remaining partial deconstructions. In many (but not all) cases, partial deconstructions lead to non-termination, and it is recommended to first try to remove them using the techniques described in Chapter 8.

In practice, if there are any partial deconstructions, one would first re-run TAMARIN with the --auto-sources option, which automatically generates a new sources lemma. The user should now check both (i) that no more partial deconstructions remain, and (ii) that the generated sources lemma can actually be verified by TAMARIN. If either of these does not hold, the partial deconstructions can only be solved by a manually specified sources lemma. Chapter 8 explains how to approach this.

Next, the user can ask TAMARIN to verify the specified lemmas. One option is to press 'S', which causes TAMARIN to try to prove *all* lemmas in the file. Alternatively, the user can select 'sorry' for a specific lemma (in the left-bottom pane) and press 'a' to attempt to prove it. However, there is one catch here: TAMARIN's analysis of a specific lemma simply assumes (but does not attempt to prove) that all preceding reuse lemmas hold. It is up to the user to ensure that they also verify the preceding reuse lemmas, see also Section 9.2.

In the ideal case, TAMARIN's analysis terminates and TAMARIN reports that the lemma is either verified or falsified. By default, when a lemma is verified, the full proof tree is visible in the left pane (see 11.1 for an example with an exists-trace lemma). When a lemma is falsified, the counterexample dependency graph and formulas are shown in the right pane. For exists-trace lemmas, this is reversed: a verified exists-trace lemma shows the trace in the right pane.

Recall that the security of security protocols is, in general, undecidable. Hence, given a lemma to prove, TAMARIN may fail to terminate in a reasonable amount of time or even never terminate. In Section 11.6, we describe typical causes and solutions. In such cases, the analysis can be aborted or restarted, and the user interface can be used to inspect partial proofs. In practice, this amounts to not pressing 'a' or 'S', but rather using the proof-step methods to partially unfold the proof. The user can press a number (or click a proof step shown) to unfold exactly one proof step, where specifically pressing '1' uses the next proof step the automatic prover applies. The

11.1 TAMARIN's user interfaces

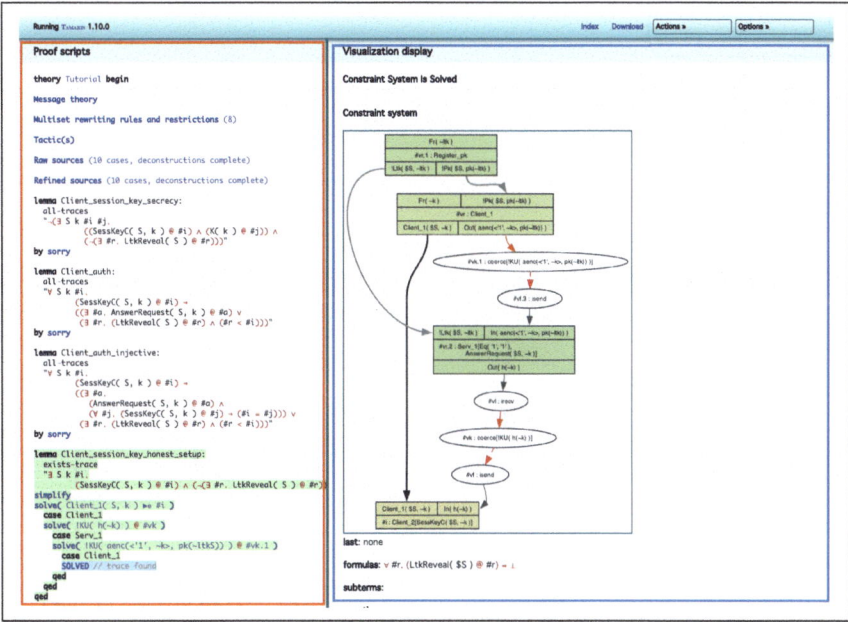

Fig. 11.1: The TAMARIN graphical user interface after selecting a theory. On the left (in the red box): the different elements of the loaded theory, in particular, the lemmas and their proofs. On the right (in the blue box): details for the selected proof step.

user can also press 'b' to unfold a set of proof steps (default depth 5), and repeat the process until the desired level of unfolding is reached. At this point, inspecting the case distinctions and dependency graphs will often yield insights into why TAMARIN fails to terminate or exhausts memory. These insights can help to formulate appropriate lemmas that can be added to the theory file, or influence the choices made by the heuristics.

In some cases, it can be convenient to modify the choices made by TAMARIN's heuristics. For example, a built-in heuristic might repeatedly select similar open constraints with slightly different parameters, rather than selecting those constraints that would lead to a completed trace or a contradiction. In this case, the user can try to manually guide TAMARIN to a proof by effectively acting as the human heuristic, and selecting different proof methods in some steps; see Section 11.2 for an example regarding a special class of lemmas. Note that the user can freely mix these methods: it is possible to unfold some steps in a proof branch by '1', then select some other proof methods in the next steps, and then ask TAMARIN to auto-complete the remainder of the proof branch by pressing 'a'. Once TAMARIN determines the proof is complete, the user can save the constructed proof, which we describe in Section 11.3.2.

For some complex proofs, and in particular when analyzing large sets of similar protocols for which manual proof method selection is infeasible (as is done in

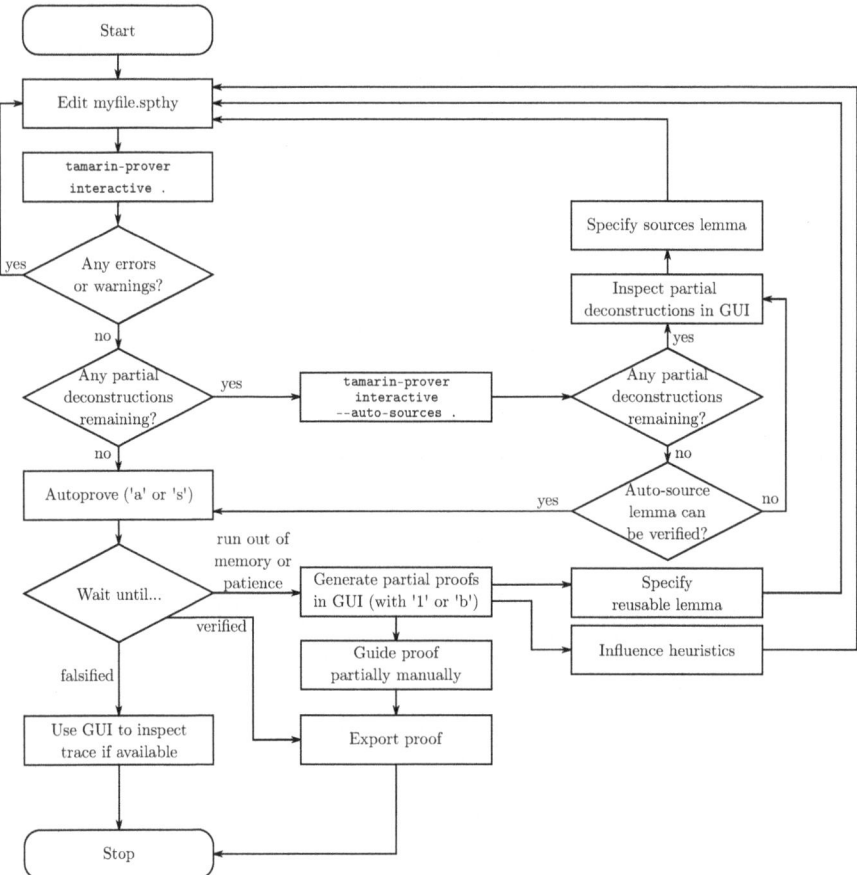

Fig. 11.2: The standard TAMARIN workflow using the graphical user interface. By default, the terminology in the picture corresponds to all-traces lemmas, whereby a proof establishes that no counterexample trace exists, and any trace found is a counterexample. In contrast, for exists-trace lemmas, the interpretation of counterexample and proof is swapped: a proof corresponds to finding a trace, and establishing that no trace exists is a counterexample.

Section 17.1), a tailored heuristic may help to automate proof construction. There are two main mechanisms to tailor TAMARIN's automatic proof heuristics:

1. Start the TAMARIN server with an option to select a different, built-in, general-purpose heuristic, see Section 6.6,

2. Encode the heuristic as fine-grained hints. In Chapter 16, we describe several such techniques, including fact annotation, using TAMARIN's tactic language, or writing an oracle program.

11.1.2 TAMARIN's command-line interface

We provide a high-level overview of typical command-line workflows in Figure 11.3. A notable difference from the graphical user interface is that less information is available: no information is provided about partial deconstructions, partial proof information, or details on any counterexamples. While the command-line mode is extremely useful for batch exploration of large sets of relatively simple models, the GUI is typically used for proving lemmas about complex models.

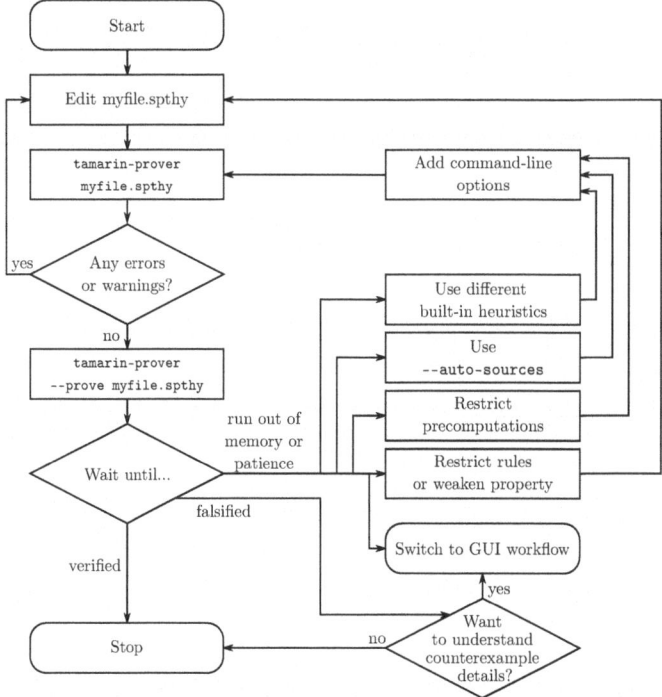

Fig. 11.3: Standard workflow for command-line TAMARIN usage.

11.2 Exists-trace lemmas

TAMARIN's heuristics are primarily optimized for finding proofs that a property holds for all traces, i.e., proving that certain traces do not exist. However, the heuristics are less effective for proving that at least one trace actually exists. This may lead to

> **Applicable Proof Methods:** Goals sorted according to the 'smart' heuristic (loop breakers delayed)
>
> 1. **solve(** Client_1(S, k) ▶$_0$ #i **)** // nr. 2 (from rule Client_2)
>
> 2. **solve(** !KU(h(k)) @ #vk **)** // nr. 3 (probably constructible)
>
> a. **autoprove** (A. **for all solutions**)
> b. **autoprove** (B. **for all solutions**) with proof-depth bound 5
> s. **autoprove** (S. **for all solutions**) for all lemmas

Fig. 11.4: Applicable constraint solving steps in the current state of the proof.

non-termination or memory exhaustion when proving an exists-trace lemma, even when the user has a strong intuition on why a simple trace exists.[1]

We will use the example of a simple challenge-response protocol, presented in Section 6.4, to show the situation for an exists-trace lemma in more detail. Consider the following lemma:

```
lemma Client_session_key_setup:
  exists-trace
  " Ex S k #i.
      SessKeyC(S, k) @ #i "
```

There are two main approaches to resolve non-terminating proof attempts. First, one can use the graphical user interface to incrementally build a proof that constructs, backwards, the envisioned trace. Assuming the user presses '1' when there is only one choice, two types of case distinction will appear in this process: (a) multiple applicable constraint solving rules to choose from in the right pane, and (b) case distinctions in the proof tree in the left pane. For type (a), the user can pick any of the listed options visible in Figure 11.4, which correspond to all possible instantiations of constraint solving rules that apply to the current constraint system. In some cases, TAMARIN's default heuristic will not order the applicable rules in an optimal way, and the user can choose to deviate from TAMARIN's recommended choice, which is the top one numbered 1.

For type (b) the user can pick the case that seems most promising in the left pane, shown in Figure 11.5. In that example, the case distinction shows the two possibilities that the h(k) is either produced by the Serv_1 protocol rule or constructed by the adversary (c_h) directly. As we are looking for a standard execution, we would choose the case of the protocol rule.

The second approach is to strengthen the exists-trace lemma by adding more information to it. For example, if we want to prove a lemma of the form $\exists P$ that expresses that there exists a trace in which an initiator role executes its final step, we may strengthen this lemma to $\exists Q = \exists (P \wedge P')$, where P' expresses that the initiator rule must have also executed its first step in the trace. While TAMARIN should, in principle, be able

---

[1] Note that all suggestions made in this section also apply to all-trace lemmas, and not just to exists-trace lemmas. Moreover, we will present more general methods to help termination and memory consumption in Section 11.6.

11.3 Further workflows

```
lemma Client_session_key_setup:
  exists-trace "∃ S k #i. SessKeyC( S, k ) @ #i"
simplify
solve( Client_1( S, k ) ▶₀ #i )
  case Client_1
  solve( !KU( h(~k) ) @ #vk )
    case Serv_1
    by sorry
  next
    case c_h
    by sorry
  qed
qed
```

Fig. 11.5: Proof tree of the current state of the proof with two incomplete branches, marked 'sorry'.

to establish this automatically, providing this information manually can sometimes speed up proofs substantially. Note that changing an all-traces lemma in a similar fashion may prove less than what was originally intended, so approach this with caution. Similarly, adding a restriction (that then applies to all lemmas of either kind) can help with termination, but changes the semantics, and one must check that it is still the intended meaning. In the previously given example, even though it is not necessary, we could strengthen the lemma to:

```
lemma Client_session_key_setup_stronger:
  exists-trace
  " Ex S k #i #j.
        SessKeyC(S, k) @ #i
      & AnswerRequest(S,k) @ #j"
```

11.3 Further workflows

We now explain how to run TAMARIN on a remote machine, how to import and export proofs, how to time proof construction, and different parallelization options.

11.3.1 Running TAMARIN remotely

Since TAMARIN uses a web browser for its GUI, you may run TAMARIN on a remote machine, for example using ssh, and connecting there from a local browser. If the server's port is not directly accessible (by default TAMARIN uses port 3001), for example, due to a firewall, you can use the following command to create a SSH tunnel from `localhost:3002` to SERVERNAME:3001.

```
ssh -L 3002:localhost:3001 SERVERNAME
```

Your browser can then connect to `localhost:3002`. Note that we are using a different port than usual just to make it easy to see which parameter is which.

To run multiple instances of TAMARIN on the same server, but on different ports, the flag `--port[=PORT]` can be used. Multiple SSH connections to different ports can then be combined with multiple TAMARIN runs at the respective ports. Moreover, the `screen` command runs TAMARIN in the background so that, for example, it continues running even after the ssh connection is closed.

11.3.2 Exporting and importing proofs

In command-line mode, TAMARIN's output can be redirected to a file using the `--output[=FILE]` flag. The output is again a valid TAMARIN file, and can be loaded again. This also includes any proof(s) done by TAMARIN.

In interactive mode, the link Download on the top right can be used to export the current state of the theory, including any (partial) proof(s) of the lemmas (see Figure 11.6).

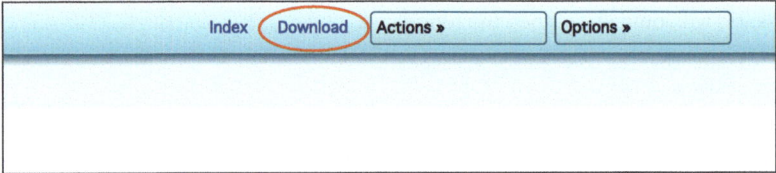

Fig. 11.6: Download link

When loading such a theory file, TAMARIN will parse the included (partial) proof(s), and verify all proof steps. If this fails at any point, this is shown in both interactive and command-line mode. In interactive mode, any invalid proof step appears in gray; in command line mode, the proof steps are annotated with `/* invalid proof step encountered */`. This can happen due to a version change of TAMARIN that might re-order some steps, or due to manual edits in the stored file.

11.3.3 Timing proof construction

To compute the time needed to prove a given lemma `Example`, one may call TAMARIN in the command-line mode using the parameter `--prove=Example`, e.g.,

```
time tamarin Example.spthy --prove=Example
```

TAMARIN will then only prove the lemma Example. Note that the duration of the pre-computation is included in this time. To get the time needed for the pre-computation, the user can time a run of TAMARIN on the input file without the --prove= flag.

To prove multiple lemmas, one may use --prove=Ex*, which will prove all lemmas that start with Ex.

TAMARIN's internal preprocessor (see Section 10.2.3) can also be used to control which parts of the input file should be treated.

11.3.4 Configuring parallelization

Internally TAMARIN's constraint solver is parallelized to exploit multi-core CPUs. The number of threads it uses can be configured using Haskell's runtime system (RTS), with the command-line parameter

```
+RTS -Nx -RTS
```

where x is the number of threads to use. Here is an example for four threads.

```
tamarin Example.spthy --prove +RTS -N4 -RTS
```

By default, Haskell will use as many threads as there are cores on the machine. In practice, when using servers with many CPUs and cores, it often makes sense to limit the number of threads as the synchronization overhead can rapidly exceed the speedup from the parallelized execution. A rough rule of thumb is to use 10 or fewer threads with TAMARIN 1.10.

If more cores are available, one can still fully use the server's computing power by proving multiple lemmas in parallel, e.g., using multiple TAMARIN instances and the parameter --prove=LEMMANAME to prove one lemma per instance.

11.4 Error messages and solutions

When loading a theory file, TAMARIN will report errors present or wellformedness warnings. Whereas an error prevents TAMARIN from loading a file, warnings do not stop TAMARIN from continuing. However, the warnings should also be taken seriously as they often indicate modeling errors or issues that endanger the correctness of the subsequent analysis.

All parser errors are reported in the terminal where TAMARIN was started, even in interactive mode. Only when loading theories from files explicitly in TAMARIN's GUI do parsing errors appear as a popup. All errors must be fixed before TAMARIN can load the file successfully. Note that TAMARIN may report that an error occurs after its real location in the file, for example if the error causes the parser to fail parsing the next construct.

Once a theory file is successfully parsed, TAMARIN will check wellformedness conditions to determine whether the file contains any obvious errors that could endanger the correctness of the analysis. If checks fail, TAMARIN will print a warning both in the user's terminal and in the interactive mode (on the first page after clicking on the Theory). If you want warnings to be treated as errors to prevent further TAMARIN interaction, you can use the command-line flag `--quit-on-warning`.

The following wellformedness conditions are checked by TAMARIN and their violation leads to warnings.

- No Out or K facts should appear in the premises of protocol rules and no Fr, In, or K facts should appear in the conclusions.
- All action facts used in lemmas or restrictions should appear somewhere in the rules.
- Facts must have the same arity everywhere, i.e., in all rules, lemmas, and restrictions.
- Fr, In, Out, and K facts must be of arity one.
- Fr facts must be used with a variable of type message or type fresh.
- All lemmas must be guarded formulas.
- All variables in the conclusions of a rule must appear in the premises, or be public variables.
- The premises of a rule must not contain reducible function symbols such as decryption, XOR, etc.
- The conclusions of a rule must not contain multiplication *.

If any of these conditions fails, TAMARIN gives a warning. We now discuss these warnings and how to fix them.

- Variable with mismatching sorts or capitalization

    This warning is triggered if a rule contains a variable that is either used with different sorts (e.g., once as a fresh variable and once without type annotation), or with different cases (e.g., a and A capitalized differently). Note that TAMARIN is sensitive to capitalization so a and A are different variables. However, in practice, having the same name with a different capitalization often corresponds to a typographical error, resulting in unwanted behavior.

    Solution: The warning is followed by a list of the problematic rules. Check whether variables have the same type annotations in all of these rules, and whether there is a variable that is both capitalized and lower case.

- Fresh public constants

    The warning

    ```
    rule X: fresh public constants are not allowed
    ```

11.4 Error messages and solutions

is triggered if the rule X contains a public constant (e.g., a string constant 'test'), but with a "fresh" type annotation (e.g., ~'test').

Solution: Ensure that no public constant is prefixed with the "fresh" type, by either removing the fresh annotation from rule X, or changing its type.

- Unbound variables

    The warning

    ```
    rule X has unbound variables
    ```

    is triggered if the rule X has an unbound variable, i.e., a variable that is used in the actions or the conclusions, but not in the premises.

    Solution: Ensure that all variables in the actions and conclusions are bound in the premises, or are of type public (e.g., $A).

- Special facts

    The warning

    ```
    Rule X uses disallowed facts on left/right-hand-side
    ```

    is triggered if special facts such as In, Out, Fr, and K are incorrectly used.

    Solution: Ensure that the rule X does not use any K facts, In and Fr facts only appear in the premises, and Out facts only appear in the conclusions.

- Fr facts must only use a fresh variable or a msg-variable

    Fr facts can only be used with variables of type fresh or message.

    Solution: Ensure that the Fr fact contains a variable of type fresh or message.

- Public constants with mismatching capitalization

    TAMARIN is sensitive to capitalization, i.e., 'test' and 'Test' are considered to be two different public constants. The situation here is similar to that with variables: having the same name, but different capitalization, often corresponds to a typographical error, resulting in unwanted behavior.

    Solution: Ensure that public constants have always the same capitalization. For example, avoid having 'test' and 'Test'.

- Inexistent lemma/restriction action

    TAMARIN checks whether all action facts used in lemmas or restrictions actually appear in some rule. When this is not the case, the following warning is triggered:

    ```
    Lemma/Restriction X references action Y but no rule has such
    an action.
    ```

    Solution: Ensure that the action Y used in lemma or restriction X actually appears in some rule. Note that lemmas and restrictions can only reason about action facts (i.e., facts "on the arrow"), but not about state facts (i.e., facts that appear in the premises or conclusions). Note too that sometimes this warning is triggered because a fact was inadvertently put into the conclusions or premises rather than the actions.

- Message Derivation Checks

  The warning

  ```
  The variables of the following rule(s) are not derivable
  from their premises, you may be performing unintended
  pattern matching.
  ```

  is shown if within a rule some variables on the right hand side cannot be deduced from the terms on the rule's left hand side using the functions and equations of the theory. This can be due to the use of pattern matching. See Section 10.1.6 for more details.

  Solution: In some cases the behavior is intended, in which case one can add the no_derivcheck annotation to the given rule. Otherwise, rewrite your rule to avoid the problematic pattern matching, or use function applications instead. See Section 10.1.6.

- Quantifier sorts

  The warning

  ```
  Lemma/Restriction uses quantifiers with wrong sort
  ```

  is triggered if a lemma or restriction quantifies over fresh or public variables. One can only quantify over message or timepoint variables.

  Solution: Ensure that variables quantified in the corresponding lemma or restriction are of sort message or timepoint.

- Lemma annotations

  The warning

  ```
  Lemma X: cannot reuse 'exists-trace' lemmas
  ```

  is triggered when an 'exists-trace' lemma is annotated with the reuse annotation.

  Solution: Remove the reuse annotation from lemma X.

- Formula guardedness

  In TAMARIN, all lemmas and restrictions must be guarded formulas. TAMARIN tries to convert all formulas into guarded formulas, but if this fails, the following warning is raised:

  ```
  Lemma/Restriction X cannot be converted to a guarded formula
  ```

11.4 Error messages and solutions

Solution: Rewrite lemma/restriction X so that it becomes guarded. This is mandatory as otherwise using the lemma or restriction will lead to errors. See Section 11.5 on how to write guarded formulas.

- `Reserved names`

  Protocol facts must not be called `Fr`, `In`, `Out`, `KU`, or `KD`. Otherwise, the following warning is triggered:

  `X contains facts with reserved names`

  Solution: Use different names for protocol facts.

- `Reserved prefixes`

  The warning

  `X contains facts with reserved prefixes ('DiffIntr', 'DiffProto') inside names`

  only occurs in equivalence mode. In this mode, facts starting with `'DiffIntr'` or `'DiffProto'` are automatically added by TAMARIN and have a special meaning, and therefore must not be used by the user.

  Solution: Rename any fact starting with `'DiffIntr'` or `'DiffProto'`.

- `Formula terms`

  The warning

  `Lemma/Restriction X uses terms of the wrong form`

  can be raised for different reasons. Within lemmas or restrictions, terms must be of a certain form. For instance, all variables must be bound, and either of type message, or timepoint. In particular, it is not possible to use variables of type fresh or public within lemmas or restrictions. Note that omitting the timepoint sort prefix # can also cause this error. Moreover, reducible function symbols (i.e., function symbols that can "disappear" when applying an equation, such as XOR, dec, etc.) also cannot be used.

  Solution: Ensure that there are no unbound variables, and no reducible function symbols. Check too whether timepoint variables are consistently prefixed using #, and that there are no fresh or public variables.

- `Multiplication restriction of rules`

  The warning

  `The following rule is not multiplication restricted`

  can be caused by two issues:

  1. A rule that uses a multiplication operator in its conclusion. In this case TAMARIN prints `Terms with multiplication: X` to show the problematic terms.

2. A rule that uses reducible function symbols in the premises, which can result in unbound variables in the actions or conclusions. In this case, TAMARIN prints the problematic variables after `Variables that occur only in rhs`.

Consider the following example.

```
The following rule is not multiplication restricted:
  rule (modulo E) Test:
    [ F( (a XOR b) ) ] --> [ G( (a*b) ) ]

After replacing reducible function symbols in the left hand side
with variables:
  rule (modulo E) Test:
    [ F( x.1 ) ] --> [ G( (a*b) ) ]

  Terms with multiplication:  (a*b)
  Variables that occur only in rhs:  a, b
```

The rule `Test` has two problems: it uses a multiplication in the conclusion (first issue) and it uses a reducible function symbol (XOR) in the premises. If a XOR b reduces to zero (for example because a = b), the variables a and b would not be well defined. Here TAMARIN tries to solve the problem by replacing a XOR b with a new variable x.1. However, in that case a and b would not be defined again. Note that if we had used a XOR b in the conclusion, TAMARIN would have replaced that by x.1 as well, and could have continued normally.

Solution: Avoid using reducible function symbols in the premises of a rule, and do not use multiplication * in the conclusions.

- Check presence of the --prove/--lemma arguments in theory

  When using the command-line parameter --prove=Y to specify which lemmas to prove, TAMARIN checks whether Y actually matches at least one lemma from the theory. If this is not the case, the following warning is triggered:

  ```
  Y from arguments do(es) not correspond to a specified lemma
  in the theory
  ```

  Solution: Check that Y actually matches a lemma.

- Variants

  When using the automatic source lemma generation (option --auto-sources), TAMARIN adds events, i.e., action facts, to individual variants of the rules. When exporting such a file, TAMARIN exports all variants explicitly to preserve these annotations. However, when loading a file with explicit variants, TAMARIN tries to recompute the variants and checks them against the loaded ones (modulo added action facts). If it detects a difference, the message

  ```
  rule X: cannot confirm manual variants
  ```

  is shown. Such a difference can be caused by manual edits, or, for example, by a different version of Maude.

11.4 Error messages and solutions

Solution: Check whether the variants are correct, i.e., the variants given in the file only have additional action facts compared to the automatically computed variants. If they are, you can ignore the warning, otherwise fix the variants in your input file or simply remove them. In that case, if you had used `auto-sources` before, you will probably also have to remove the sources lemma and generate a new one.

- `Left/Right rule`

  When using the automatic source lemma generation (option `--auto-sources`), TAMARIN adds events to individual variants of a rule. In equivalence mode, see Chapter 13, this must be done for both the left and right side of the system. Hence TAMARIN also exports both left and right side rules explicitly. When loading a file with explicit rules per side, TAMARIN will recompute rule instances for both sides and check that they match the initial rule (modulo added action facts). If it detects a difference, the message

  `Inconsistent left/right rule`

  is shown.

  Solution: As in the prior bullet titled `Variants`, check whether the left and right rule variants are correct, i.e., that the variants in the input file only have additional action facts compared to the automatically computed variants. You can also try to remove both rules and variants, and to generate a new sources lemma.

Other common error messages

The previously mentioned, error messages are generated by TAMARIN itself. In practice, it is possible to run into other types of errors that are caused by the user's operating system or the invocation of external dependencies such as Maude or oracle scripts. Because these depend on the user's specific operating system, library version, and general environment, we cannot give a full list. However, there are some commonly reported error messages that we describe below.

In the following, we use upper-case words as placeholders for parts of error messages that depend on the specific input file and command-line arguments. `ORACLE` is the name of the oracle script file.

- `tamarin-prover: ./ORACLE: readCreateProcess: posix_spawnp: does not exist (No such file or directory)`

  This error message can have two possible reasons.

  Potential cause 1: The first and most common cause is that the oracle script `ORACLE` cannot be found in the current directory.

  Solution 1: Ensure that the file exists and that you have specified the right (relative) path to the file.

Potential cause 2: Alternatively, the file is present, but it is a shell script whose first line (which starts with #!) is incorrectly specified for the system it is being executed on.

Solution 2: Inspect the ORACLE script to see which scripting language it uses, and adapt the first line of the script to specify the interpreter correctly for your system.[2]

For example, if the script requires python version 3, it may be sufficient to change the first line of your oracle script file to:

```
#!/usr/bin/env python3
```

Note that the details of the first line specification are system-dependent.

- ```
  FILE1: FILE2: No such file or directory
  tamarin-prover:readCreateProcess: ./ORACLE "TERM"
  (exit 127): failed
  ```

  This error likely indicates that the oracle file is a shell script that starts with the following line:

  ```
  #!FILE1 FILE2
  ```

  Solution: Modify the first line of the script (notably FILE2) to point to the correct interpreter as present on your system, similar to the second cause and solution of the previous error.

- ```
  tamarin-prover: ./ORACLE: readCreateProcess: posix_spawnp:
  permission denied (Permission denied)
  ```

  Solution: Ensure that the oracle file ORACLE (in the below, replace ORACLE by the filename of your oracle script) is readable and executable. On many systems this can be done by:

  ```
  chmod +rx ORACLE
  ```

- ```
  SHELL: ./ORACLE: Permission denied
  tamarin-prover: readCreateProcess: ./ORACLE "TERM"
  (exit 126): failed
  ```

  A likely cause is that the oracle script file ORACLE is not readable.

  Solution: The same as for the previous error.

- ```
  Server shutdown: 0 threads still running
  tamarin-prover: Starting the webserver on 127.0.0.1 failed:
  Network.Socket.bind: resource busy (Address already in use)
  Note that you can use '-interface="*4"' for binding to all
  interfaces.
  ```

---

[2] The details of shell scripting and configuring interpreters are beyond the scope of this book. Some information can be found at https://en.wikipedia.org/wiki/Shell_script.

This error occurs when starting TAMARIN in interactive mode and the port it wants to use for the webserver (3001 by default) is used by some other process. Often this is caused by another instance of TAMARIN running in parallel.

Solution: Terminate the other process/TAMARIN instance that is using the port, or choose a different port using the option `--port=X`.

11.5 Guardedness of lemmas

We refer the reader to Section 5.1 for the full syntax available to write lemmas. In TAMARIN, all lemmas must be guarded. A lemma is guarded if the following conditions are met:

- Variables that are universally quantified (i.e., quantified by All) must be directly used, either in a fact constraint f@#i, or in an equation s=t, and the following logical connector, i.e., the outermost connector inside the universal quantifier, must be an implication, i.e., ==>.

- Variables that are existentially quantified (i.e., quantified by Exists) must be directly used, either in a fact constraint f@#i, or in an equation s=t, and the following logical connector, i.e., the outermost connector inside the existential quantifier, must be a conjunction, i.e., &.

An example of a guarded lemma is as follows, with the full theory available at **Guardedness.spthy**.

```
lemma Guarded:
  "All x #i. Finished(x)@#i ==> Ex #j. Start(x)@#j"
```

The following lemma is not guarded as the variable y is quantified, but never used:

```
lemma NotGuardedUnusedVariable:
  "All x y #i. Finished(x)@#i ==> Ex #j. Start(x)@#j"
```

When loading a theory, TAMARIN checks whether each lemma is guarded, and tries to convert the formula into a guarded one, where possible. If this fails, TAMARIN will show an error message. For the above example, this looks as follows.

```
Guardedness:
  lemma `NotGuardedUnusedVariable' cannot be converted to a guarded formula:
    unguarded variable(s) 'y' in the subformula
      "∀ x y #i. (Finished( x ) @ #i) ⇒ (∃ #j. Start( x ) @ #j)"
    in the formula
      "∀ x y #i. (Finished( x ) @ #i) ⇒ (∃ #j. Start( x ) @ #j)"
```

In this case, it would be easy for TAMARIN to just eliminate the quantifier, $\forall y$, solving the problem. In general, this is not done as it is likely that the user has made an error that should be fixed, e.g., accidentally omitting y from some fact.

In practice, non-guarded formula errors are often caused by the following issues.

- Variables which are quantified, but never used, as in the above example.
- Variables which are quantified, but in the wrong location, as in the following example:

```
lemma NotGuardedQuantifiedInWrongPlace:
  "All x #i #j. Finished(x)@#i ==> Start(x)@#j"
```

Here #j is quantified at the beginning, but only used later, which violates our previously given syntactic definition of guardedness.

- Missing or misplaced parentheses.

In other cases, one can also try to find an equivalent formulation of the property, e.g., using logical transformations, that makes the formula guarded.

11.6 Termination and memory exhaustion

Section 8.1 already explained what to do if TAMARIN's precomputations take too long. Once TAMARIN can load the file, the user can then try to prove the given lemmas. Thus, in this section, we discuss common termination and performance problems when proving lemmas and how they can be solved. The first question is often how long to wait for a proof in TAMARIN, or for TAMARIN's precomputation, to terminate. Section 11.6.1 discusses how to get a rough idea of possible running times. We start with a high-level discussion here on both problems and solutions.

When a proof takes a long time to complete or fails to terminate, this can be caused by different underlying problems. We discuss these problems at a high-level here, along with possible solutions, and we delve deeper into this topic in the following subsections.

The main problems causing a runtime explosion or non-termination when proving lemmas are the following:

- Partial deconstructions (check in interactive mode whether there are any partial deconstructions left in the refined sources).
- A high number of variants (check the `Multiset rewriting rules` in interactive mode).
- Problematic patterns during proof construction (see Section 11.6.2 on how to identify and fix them).

Once the problems are identified, the user can try to fix them using different approaches, depending on the type of problem. Table 11.1 sums up the problems and possible solutions.

The following strategies can also help TAMARIN's proof construction:

11.6 Termination and memory exhaustion

- Adding type annotations inside rules whenever possible (see Section 10.1.5) helps TAMARIN by eliminating impossible executions earlier in the proof search based on the given types.
- Using pattern matching rather than explicit functions when this is appropriate, see Section 10.1.6. This leads to fewer rule variants and ultimately fewer cases.
- Fine-tuning the model can also help, for example by abstracting away or refining certain parts, or by making different choices in the model, where appropriate (Section 11.6.4).
- For certain datatypes or behaviors, such as counters or memory cells, special encodings or modeling strategies can help TAMARIN. See Section 7.2.5 for common examples.
- One can also try different heuristics. See Section 6.6 for a list of all built-in heuristics. Additionally, one can also define custom heuristics (see Chapter 16), which can help in the cases mentioned above.

Problem	Solution(s)
Partial deconstructions	Use --auto-sources (Section 8.3) or manually write a source lemma (Section 8.4)
High number of variants	Possible solutions: - Add type annotations whenever possible inside rules (Section 10.1.5) - Use pattern matching instead of explicit deconstructors, if possible (Section 10.1.6) - Simplify equational theory, if possible
Proof does not terminate	Try to recognize problematic patterns (see Section 11.6.2). Then, depending on the issue(s): - Add type annotations inside rules (Section 10.1.5) - Fine-tune model: try alternative formulations (Section 11.6.4) - Add auxiliary lemmas (Section 11.6.3) - Use induction (Section 9.1) if the model contains looping behavior - Use advanced encodings/modeling strategies for certain datatypes/behaviors (Section 7.2.5) - Try different heuristics (Section 6.6) - Develop custom heuristic (Chapter 16)

Table 11.1: Possible problems and solutions.

11.6.1 How long will my proof take?

In general, it is impossible to predict how much time is needed to prove a lemma. There are numerous factors that influence the complexity of proof construction, including the sheer number of rules in the theory, the presence of a complex equational theory (such as Diffie-Hellman exponentiation, XOR, or some user-defined theories), the complexity of the lemma's statement, the number of sources, etc. If some of these factors are present, verification times can increase, and non-termination becomes more likely.

In practice, most users start by analyzing their lemmas individually. If a lemma's proof takes substantial time, for example, more than a few minutes, then one should try to diagnose the reasons for this. Advice on this is given below in Section 11.6.2. If one anticipates that proof construction will be time consuming, for example, proving other lemmas for the same model was time consuming or the model is large and complex, an option is to let TAMARIN run overnight. There are also tools that can be used to run multiple lemmas in parallel, which are described in Section 11.7. This can help by applying "brute force" to prove lemmas when one has access to a powerful machine.

When the precomputations take too long, one can try to limit the saturation steps or the number of open chains to solve. Section 8.1 provides more information on this option.

11.6.2 Recognizing problematic patterns

When TAMARIN does not appear to terminate while trying to prove a lemma, one can look for certain patterns in the proof construction that are problematic as they can lead to non-termination, or at least substantial proof times.

The most common issue is repeating patterns in the proof. Consider the simple hash chain example from Section 9.3. When trying to prove the lemma Auxiliary_Success_chain without induction, one can immediately see a repeating pattern: TAMARIN adds an instance of the Loop rule, followed by an instance of the Gen rule, which triggers again an instance of the Loop rule, and so on (see Figure 11.7). In this case, it is simple to resolve this issue by proving the lemma using induction.

Sometimes, induction alone is insufficient, but the issue can be resolved using an auxiliary lemma. In this example, to prove the lemma Success_chain, one should prove the lemma Auxiliary_Success_chain first. See Section 9.3 for a detailed explanation of this example, and Section 11.6.3 on how to come up with such lemmas in general.

11.6 Termination and memory exhaustion

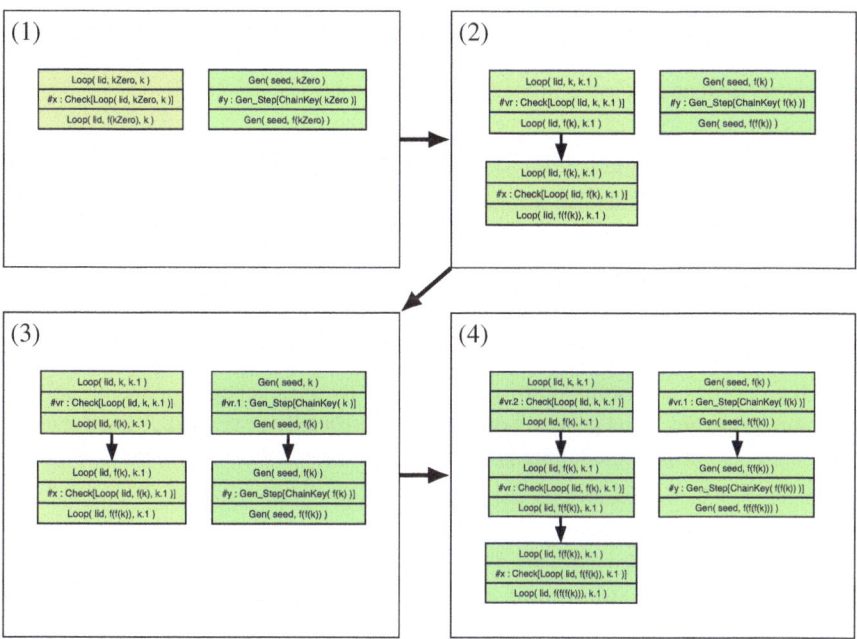

Fig. 11.7: Repeating pattern: alternating additions of Loop and Gen

A third possible solution is to avoid the problematic cases altogether by either manually avoiding the cases in an interactive proof, or by using a tailored heuristic (see Chapter 16). This is not always possible: in the simple hash chain example, all proof methods lead to the repeating pattern.

Another common issue is that sometimes solving some constraints causes large case distinctions in the proof, with dozens of subcases. Since all subcases must be eventually solved to conclude a proof (except if a counterexample is found earlier), it can help to avoid solving these constraints early. Often it is not necessary to solve all constraints to obtain the contradiction required to conclude a branch of the proof. In such cases, delaying the solving of such constraints can speed up the proof search enormously. To avoid solving such constraints, one can manually construct the proof in interactive mode, or define a tailored heuristic (Chapter 16).

11.6.3 Using auxiliary lemmas

When TAMARIN fails to prove a lemma, one can try to add auxiliary lemmas to prove helpful sub-properties. An example of this was given in Section 9.3.

There are different types of properties that can be useful to prove using auxiliary lemmas. For example, by inspecting the (failing) proof of the lemma, one can sometimes deduce a missing property, as in Section 9.3.

Another typical example concerns looping structures, where some fact is initialized once, and then continuously updated. In such cases, writing an auxiliary lemma stating that the use of this fact implies that it has been previously initialized is often helpful. Such lemmas must usually be proven by induction.

A third example is invariants, for example, stating that some data shared among different participants is always in sync, or that a certain value is only increasing, and so on.

Which properties are useful to prove as auxiliary lemmas depends on the model and the main properties being proven. Some trial and error may be needed. A good starting point here is to inspect the failing proof in interactive mode and try to understand the problematic cases.

11.6.4 Fine-tuning the model: finding the right abstraction

Making different modeling choices can have a large impact on TAMARIN's performance and termination. For example, leaving out untrusted parties in the model and giving the keys to the adversary instead can improve performance simply by reducing the number of rules and thus the model's size.

Moreover, abstracting details away can help TAMARIN. For example, instead of modeling counters explicitly, it can be advantageous to limit the model to the essential requirements (restrictions stating that a counter can only increase, etc.). For more on counters, see Section 7.2.5.

In particular, when it comes to modeling state, there are many ways to model the same behavior, but the solution chosen can affect how difficult it is for TAMARIN to prove lemmas. For example, for trace properties, it is often easier for TAMARIN to reason about state modeled using restrictions rather than using linear facts. Note the caveat that this is not necessarily true for equivalence proofs as restrictions often complicate TAMARIN's reasoning.

Finally, one may find inspiration on how to model certain constructs in past research papers that used TAMARIN to solve specialized problems. For example, [103] shows how to model parameterized systems, such as those occurring in group key agreement schemes.

11.7 Extensions and tools

There are several extensions that either work as a pre-processor for TAMARIN or that can be used to automate recurring tasks when handling large models with numerous lemmas.

The most widely used TAMARIN extension is SAPIC ("Stateful Applied Pi Calculus") [34, 79], which is now integrated into TAMARIN. In a nutshell, SAPIC takes as input a protocol specification in a variant of the applied pi calculus (similar to ProVerif), and compiles this to a TAMARIN specification. It can also generate ProVerif or DeepSec files, based on the same input. All translations are proven sound. This means that one can prove different lemmas using different tools, and the results hold for the initial model.

There is another, much simpler, tool that takes as input a subset of Alice & Bob style specifications and translates them to TAMARIN models [16].

The UT Tamarin [77] tool can be used to run TAMARIN in parallel on different lemmas, with different heuristics and timeouts, and to check the results against expected results. This can be useful when working with large models to try out different theorem proving options.

Finally, there are syntax highlighting modes for various editors, including Emacs, vim, and Visual Studio Code. For more details, see the installation section of the TAMARIN manual online [107].

11.8 Common questions

We conclude this section by addressing some additional questions that users have about TAMARIN and its workflows.

11.8.1 Why doesn't TAMARIN merge rule instances?

Users new to TAMARIN often wonder why TAMARIN does not merge multiple rule instantiations, which would simplify the attacks found by the tool. To ensure that no possible solution is missed, TAMARIN's constraint solver always tries to construct the most general possible solution. This has the side-effect that the counterexamples TAMARIN produces are not necessarily the simplest or shortest ones, but rather the most general ones. For example, sometimes it might be possible to merge two rule instances, or even two participants, and still have a valid counterexample. However, as long as the constraints do not oblige TAMARIN to merge the two rule instances, the tool will not do so, as such a merger could remove some possible solutions and hence affect correctness.

11.8.2 When should I use K, KU, or KD?

The meaning of K action facts is defined by TAMARIN's semantics; particularly relevant here is Section 3.1.8. In contrast, and as previously mentioned in Section 6.8.5, the action facts KU and KD are only defined in the *current* version of TAMARIN's algorithm, and their meaning might change in future updates of the tool. We therefore strongly recommend only using K when specifying properties, as KU and KD have no well-defined meaning in the semantics.

There are, however exceptions to the above. It can be useful in some cases to use KU when specifying sources lemmas or intermediate (reuse) lemmas. The reason for this is because, in TAMARIN's current algorithm, the KU action facts in a dependency graph under-approximate the terms that an adversary has derived. This is also the reason why KU is often used in sources lemmas, see Section 8.4. As long as the user specifies their intended protocol properties using K, but without KU and KD, these properties will be well-defined. KU and KD can be freely used in source lemmas or intermediate reuse lemmas that help to prove the target properties: if TAMARIN's algorithm verifies all properties in the file, the intended protocol properties hold, independent of the exact meaning of KU or KD.

11.8.3 Why does autoprove not terminate, but repeatedly pressing 1 or b does?

To explore the proof tree, TAMARIN uses *iterative deepening* search with a strategy where the bound is doubled at each iteration. An alternative strategy that sometimes terminates more quickly is to run TAMARIN using a breadth-first search strategy. This is accomplished using the command-line parameter `--stop-on-trace=BFS`; see Section 6.1.2 for more details. Thus, if an autoprove attempt does not terminate, but manual exploration does, try running TAMARIN with breadth-first-search or just export and store the manual proof.

Chapter 12
Case Study: 5G-AKA

We now present a large case study where we use many of the previously introduced features to model a complex real-world protocol. We chose the next generation mobile communication key agreement protocol 5G-AKA as our example.

The following account is based on our published paper [14], co-authored by Basin, Dreier, Hirschi, Radomirović, Sasse, and Stettler. Here we focus on the modeling decisions taken for the core of the protocol, and how we wrote the TAMARIN model for it. Along the way, we showcase this with TAMARIN code, exemplifying many of the features previously introduced in this book. For interested readers, we refer to the above paper for the presentation of the standard and how the core of the protocol was extracted from the standard, as well as a comprehensive account of the protocol's properties.

The first part of any analysis of a real-world standard is reading the standard's documents, which in the case of 5G are comprised of four separate documents, totaling 722 pages. From this, one extracts an overview of how the protocol is intended to work, what messages are sent, and how they are composed. We describe this in the next section, similar to [14], reusing diagrams from there.

Afterwards, we discuss how different parts of the protocol were modeled and analyzed in TAMARIN, and we draw conclusions.

12.1 Overview of 5G-AKA

5G is the name of the next generation, mobile communication network, which is used by billions of users and their devices worldwide. 5G standardizes how handheld mobile devices, such as cell phones and base stations, communicate with each other using radio waves. It also specifies how the base stations provide wider network access to the mobile devices. In particular, a user will usually only have a contract with one mobile phone provider in their home country (called the Home Network), paying for a subscription to use their network. However, when traveling abroad, there are usually no base stations operated by their provider. Instead, the user's device will connect to another provider's network (called the Serving Network), for so-called roaming access. Note that each Home Network provides a Serving Network for its own and other users. Furthermore, to ensure that phone calls and other kinds of communication stay secret, and that billing is authentic, there is a security protocol standardized as part of 5G, called 5G-AKA. This security protocol, which is used for key agreement, is what we modeled with TAMARIN.

The core protocol thus involves three entities: the Subscriber, the Serving Network, and the Home Network. Initially the Subscriber (in practice, their user equipment, i.e., the mobile phone, or possibly its SIM card) and the Home Network share a long-term symmetric key K, a user identifier SUPI, and each entity X maintains a counter called the sequence number SQN_X. Each entity has their own view of the sequence number and their views may be desynchronized, which necessitates a resynchronization protocol that we will describe later. We give an overview of main entities in Table 12.1.

Subscriber	User Equipment, e.g. phone or its SIM card, also called UE
SUPI	Subscriber Permanent Identifier
SUCI	Subscriber Concealed Identifier (the SUPI encrypted for the home network)
Serving Network	Local network that the Subscriber is currently connected to
SNname	Serving Network's name
Home Network	Network that the subscriber is subscribed to
idHN	Home Network Identifier
pkHN	Home Network's public key
K	Long-term symmetric key shared by the Subscriber and Home Network

Table 12.1: Main 5G-AKA entities and their meaning

We next provide an overview diagram of the protocol flow in Figure 12.1. The Subscriber will learn the SNname of the Serving Network from a prior unsecured message that is not depicted.

In the first message, the Subscriber (also called the User Equipment, UE) sends their concealed identifier (SUCI) together with a unique identifier for their home network idHN. The SUCI is built by taking the subscriber's permanent subscription identifier (SUPI) and asymmetrically (and randomized with some RS) encrypting the SUPI under their home network's public key pkHN. The resulting message is thus <aenc(<SUPI, RS>, pkHN), idHN>.

The Serving Network forwards this message, together with their name SNname, to the Home Network. The Home Network has the private key that is needed to decrypt the asymmetric encryption and extract the SUPI. Note that the SUPI itself consists of several fields, one of which is another identifier of the Home Network. The standard

12.1 Overview of 5G-AKA

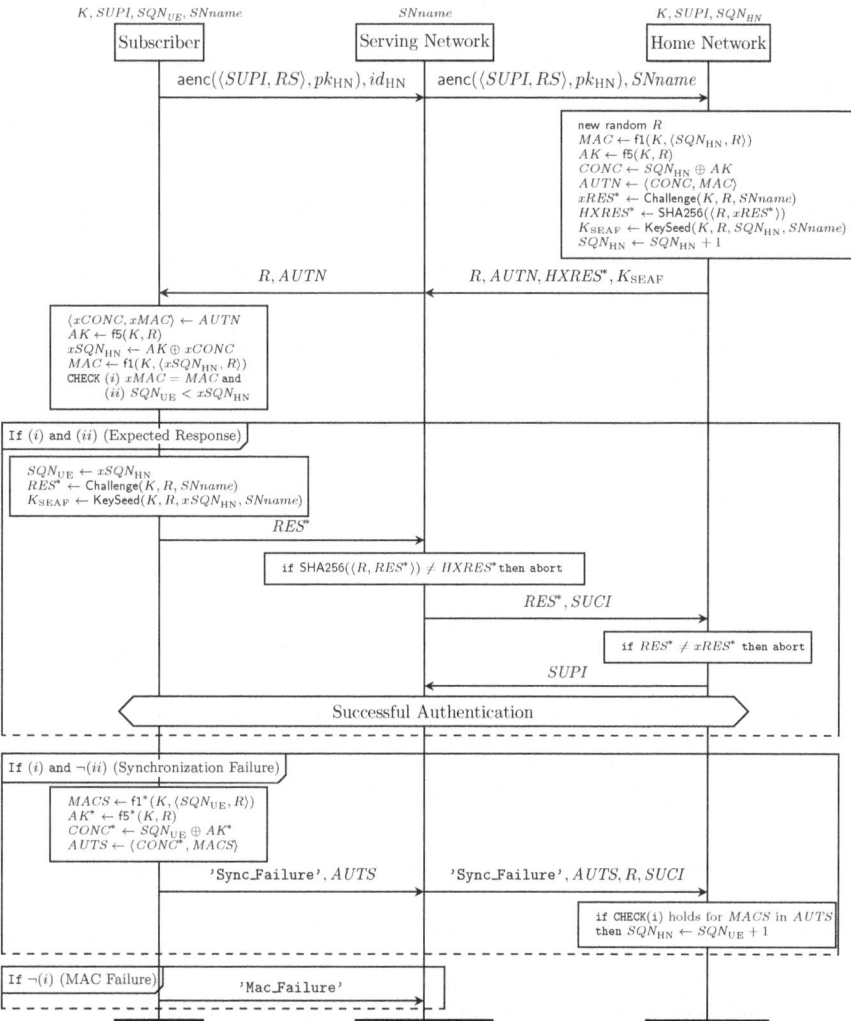

Fig. 12.1: The 5G-AKA protocol. The communication between the Subscriber and the Serving Network is over the air, and we assume the adversary has full access to this channel. The communication between the Serving Network and the Home Network is performed over a secure channel.

prescribes that the Home Network checks that the idHN matches the home network identifier in the SUPI, which also serves to detect forged encryptions. Based on the SUPI, the Home Network can now look up the shared long-term key K and the sequence number SQNHN for that SUPI.

At a high level, the Home Network now prepares a response for the Serving Network consisting of four parts: a random value R, an authenticated challenge AUTN, a hash of the expected response that the Subscriber must later send to the Serving Network HXRES*, and the seed for key material, KSEAF, to be used between Subscriber and Serving Network after authentication is successfully completed.

In more detail, the Home Network first samples a fresh random value R. The AUTN is built from a concealed sequence number CONC and a message authentication code, MAC, by pairing them. The concealed sequence number is the actual sequence number the HN has xor-ed with a one-way function f5 whose arguments are the key K and the random R, i.e., f5(K,R). The message authentication code is computed as f1(K, <SQNHN, R>). The intention behind the MAC is that the right Subscriber will be able to know this message came from their home network, check that the sequence number is correct, and then create the expected response, discussed next.

The Home Network computes the expected response called xRES, which is stored, but not shared with the Serving Network. This ensures that the Home Network gets guarantees as well, once the Serving Network forwards the actual response. Essentially, this prevents the Serving Network from claiming that a Subscriber of the Home Network is using their services, when they are not. The Serving Network still receives a hash of the expected response, called HXRES*, to be able to immediately abort when receiving incorrect Subscriber answers. The expected response xRES is computed as a function of the shared key K, the random value R, and the name of the Serving Network SNname, as Challenge(K, R, SNname) for an appropriate function Challenge. The key seed KSEAF is computed as KeySeed(K,R,SQNHN, SNname). Finally, the Home Network increments the sequence number.

The Serving Network receives the four parts of the message from the Home Network, and forwards R and AUTN to the Subscriber, storing HXRES* and KSEAF for later.

The Subscriber splits AUTN into the concealed sequence number xCONC and the MAC xMAC. Using the received R, it computes f5(K,R) and uses this to extract the unconcealed sequence number xSQNHN by XORing xCONC and f5(K,R). The Subscriber then computes the MAC it expects, MAC = f1(K, <xSQNHN, R>). Following this, the subscriber performs two checks: (i) that the received xMAC is the same as the computed MAC for authentication purposes, and (ii) that the received sequence number xSQNHN is strictly larger than the Subscriber's stored sequence number SQNUE.

If both checks (i) and (ii) succeed, the protocol then continues in the expected flow. We first describe this flow and return to the failed check cases afterwards. When both checks succeed, the Subscriber is then convinced that it has received a fresh and authentic challenge from its home network, and it computes the required response as well as the shared key for later use. To do this, the Subscriber first updates its view of the sequence number to the new, larger, number xSQNHN. It computes the response RES* with the function Challenge applied to the shared key K, received random value R, and the Serving Network name SNname. It computes the key seed

KSEAF for later communication as KeySeed(K, R, xSQNHN, SNname). Finally, the computed response RES* is sent to the Serving Network.

The Serving Network receives the Subscriber's RES* and checks that the hash of the previously received randomness R and the received RES* results in the previously stored HXRES*, as expected. Should this check fail, the Serving Network aborts. If the check succeeds, the Serving Network forwards the value RES* and (again) the concealed subscriber identity SUCI to the Home Network.

The Home Network just checks that the value RES* is the one it computed previously as xRES* for this SUCI. If not, it aborts. If successful, it responds with the unconcealed permanent identifier SUPI of the Subscriber. Note that this is not a protocol weakness, but generally mandated by law.

If the Subscriber's check (i) succeeded, but (ii) failed, the authentication was successful, but the Subscriber and Home Network are out of sync, and therefore have a different view of the sequence number. Thus, the re-synchronization protocol starts, which is not described further here.

If the Subscriber's check (i) failed, there is a MAC failure, triggering the Subscriber to abort and sending a last message with the constant 'MAC_FAILURE'.

12.2 Modeling 5G-AKA in TAMARIN

Note that we provide the full 5G model, as **5G_AKA.spthy**, in the accompanying collection of TAMARIN theories that come with this book [12]. You can use that file as a detailed reference, and you can run it yourself with TAMARIN directly.

Given the described 5G-AKA flows, one must still make several high-level choices and assumptions that lead to different models. The paper [14] analyzes a range of these models including, for example, different channel models and versions with and without fixes.

In this section, we present the version of 5G-AKA without our proposed fixes from [14], in what we call the binding channel version. This version makes the assumption that the channels internal to the home network actually work as one would expect, which is not explicitly specified in the standard.

At the highest level, as seen in Figure 12.1 and the protocol's description, the protocol involves three parties and more than ten message flows, including branching after checking the response. This results in a much larger model than those made for typical, small, two-party protocols. Moreover its traces, viewed in interactive mode, are also longer.

From the modeling perspective, the Serving Network is the easiest to model, because it has no long-term state beyond its identifier, and it communicates over secure channels to the Home Network. In contrast, the Subscriber and Home Network have permanent state, namely the shared key material, as well as mutable state, namely the sequence number. This sequence number and associated state is not just inside one session (or run) of the protocol, but across all runs for a Subscriber (respectively the Home Network for a fixed Subscriber). This means that the runs are interdependent, and this can cause looping behavior in TAMARIN's backwards search. Using auxiliary lemmas, as explained in Section 12.2.7, solves this problem.

To model the cryptographic primitives, we will use both built-in and user-defined operators. To model the secure communication between the Serving Network and the Home Network, we use secure channels. There are also rules to initialize all the entities, set them up with key material, and have bindings between Subscribers and their Home Networks. As part of the threat model, we consider various forms of compromise. Hence there are reveal rules that leak information to the adversary, which are marked in the trace by action facts. Additionally, counters are modeled for both the Subscriber and the Home Network. Finally, we have rules for each of the parties' send and receive steps.

12.2.1 Threat model for 5G-AKA

The Subscriber and Serving Network communicate over the air. Hence our threat model captures that the adversary can interfere with communication, which we model as a standard, active, Dolev-Yao adversary. Additionally, even for the wired connection between the Serving Network and the Home Network, one wants the protocol to provide some built-in security rather than only relying on the expected properties of the channel used (presumably TLS). Moreover, different parties could also be compromised. This includes a Subscriber's SIM card leaking its key under close inspection, a Serving Network base station being physically manipulated, or some attack inside the servers of a Home Network. In our threat model, we assume the adversary cannot guess sequence numbers, but it can manipulate any sequence numbers it learns, as it wishes.

Note that 5G-AKA's main security goals can only be obtained when communicating with a non-compromised party. The underlying idea of modeling compromised parties is that when in a specific run some non-compromised parties communicate, their security should not depend on the compromise of other parties. We typically formalize rules that model the compromise of *any* party, and then specify the goal for non-compromised parties as part of the security property.

12.2.2 Functions and equations

Prior to giving examples of rules, we first describe the equational theories and function symbols used. Namely, we use the built-in functions for asymmetric encryption,

12.2 Modeling 5G-AKA in TAMARIN

multisets, and exclusive-or. Note that in this model, natural numbers are represented by multisets of 1 added together. For newer models, we instead recommend modeling natural numbers using the approach described in Section 11.3.4, which was added to TAMARIN after this work was done.

The 5G-AKA protocols also make use of so-called Key Derivation Functions (KDF) that are used to derive a secret key from a secret and optionally another input, such as a label. We model these as function symbols without additional equations, reflecting that (i) one cannot infer the inputs to the KDF from its output, and (ii) KDF functions are collision-resistant. Finally, we declare additional functions, all of which are not invertible, and have different arities, i.e., different numbers of arguments.

```
builtins:
  asymmetric-encryption, multiset, xor

functions:
  // AKA functions (TS 33.102)
  f1/2,         // MAC-function    --> MAC
  f2/2,         // MAC-function    --> RES
  f3/2,         // KDF             --> CK
  f4/2,         // KDF             --> IK
  f5/2,         // KDF             --> AK (Hide Sqn)
  f1_star/2,    // MAC-function    --> MAC-S
  f5_star/2,    // KDF             --> AKS (Hide Sqn)

  // 3GPP KDFs (TS 33.501)
  KDF/2,        // KDF             --> K_ausf, K_seaf, XRES*
  SHA256/2      // KDF             --> HXRES*
```

Because we provide no equations for these user-defined functions, they will all be treated as one-way functions.

12.2.3 Channel model

Next, we present the model of the secure channels that are used between the Serving Network and the Home Network. The 5G standard expects them to use, e.g., TLS 1.3 [101], to establish and maintain a secure and replay-protected channel. The analysis of the full TLS 1.3 model [45] is already extremely challenging, and if we were to directly inline a detailed TLS model into our 5G-AKA model, the analysis would not be tractable. We therefore choose to abstract TLS as a black-box, secure channel. Additionally, this choice makes our result for 5G-AKA independent of the protocol-specific details of TLS, and also independent of the protocol that the Serving and Home Network actually use in practice. Essentially, this choice means that the wireless channel between the Subscriber and the Serving Network is controlled by the adversary, while the channel between a Serving Network and a Home Network has some level of protection.

We already presented generic secure channels in Section 10.4, but we use a variation in this work that includes replay protection. The SndS is a drop-in replacement for where one would put an Out for an unprotected channel, and RcvS replaces the In. We present the channels between two non-compromised parties first, and then discuss them.

```
rule send_secure:
  [ SndS(~cid,A,B,m) ] // ~cid denotes a channel identifier: should always
                       // be a fresh name (possibly attacker-created)
  -->
  [ Sec(~cid,A,B,m) ]
rule receive_secure:
  [ Sec(~cid,A,B,m) ]
  -->
  [ RcvS(~cid,A,B,m) ]
```

The two rules translate a secure send by a party to a secure receive by another party, using a shared fresh value as the channel id, and including sender, recipient and actual message. The rules for participants in a protocol will then use SndS as the replacement for Out and RcvS instead of In. The adversary learns nothing about these messages, senders, and recipients, and cannot replay messages because the Sec fact is not persistent.

Next, we introduce rules that model compromised parties that have access to the secure channels.

```
rule secureChannel_compromised_in:
  [ In(<~cid,A,B,x>) ] // attacker can learn cid with
                       // secureChannel_compromised_out
  --[ Rev(A,'secureChannel'),
      Injected(x)
  ]->
  [ Sec(~cid,A,B,x) ]
rule secureChannel_compromised_out:
  [ Sec(~cid,A,B,m) ]
  --[ Rev(B,'secureChannel') ]->
  [ Out(<~cid,m>) ]
```

The first rule models an adversary that compromised a sending endpoint A, and injects a message x into the channel between A and B for session cid. The second rule models an adversary that compromised an endpoint B, and receives a message m from such a channel. The respective compromised parties are reflected in the first argument of the Rev actions of the respective rules. We will show later how the properties are made conditional on the reveals to match the threat model. On the one hand, we can now evaluate whether this truly must be a secure channel, and learn which properties hold in this case. On the other hand, if the channel does not actually need to be secure, we will also learn that in our analysis.

12.2.4 Key generation and compromise

12.2.4.1 Key generation

The initial setup uses multiple rules. The first rule `init_servNet` creates the Serving Network; we do not show it in detail as it produces no key material.

The following rule initializes a Home Network.

```
rule init_homeNet:
  [Fr(~sk_HN),
   Fr(~idHN)]
  --[ HomeNet(~idHN) ]->
  [!HSS(~idHN, ~sk_HN),
   !Pk(~idHN, pk(~sk_HN)),
   Out(<~idHN, pk(~sk_HN)>)]
```

The rule's premises generate a unique name `idHN` and a private key `sk_HN` for this Home Network. An action fact `HomeNet(idHN)` is logged as well. The rule's conclusion creates the persistent facts `!HSS` and `!Pk`, each binding the Home Network name to its keys, the first to the private key and the second to the public key. Finally, the new Home Network's name and its public key are output to the adversary, as they are publicly known.

Next we look at how a Subscriber is initialized, and immediately bound to its assigned Home Network.

```
rule add_subscription:
  [Fr(~supi),
   Fr(~k),
   Fr(~sqn_root),
   !HSS(~idHN, ~sk_HN)]
  --[
    // Restriction
    Subscribe(~supi, ~idHN),

    // Auxiliary lemmas
    Sqn_Create(~supi, ~idHN, ~sqn_root),
    CreateUser(~supi, ~k, ~idHN)
  ]->
  [!Ltk_Sym(~supi, ~idHN, ~k, ~sqn_root),
   Sqn_UE(~supi, ~idHN, ~sqn_root+'1', ~sqn_root, '1'),
   Sqn_HSS(~supi, ~idHN, ~sqn_root+'1', ~sqn_root, '1')]
```

The rule creates a fresh identifier `supi`, a fresh shared key k with the Home Network, and a random starting value `sqn_root` for the sequence number. Starting the sequence number from a fresh value captures the threat model assumption that the adversary cannot guess sequence numbers. This rule also has three action facts. The first of them, `Subscribe` is used to bind this new Subscriber, identified by `supi` to a Home Network, identified by `idHN`. We define an additional restriction that enforces that each `supi` can only be initialized once, and is bound to a particular Home Network. The second and third action fact additionally bind the starting sequence number, respectively the shared key, to the Subscriber and Home Network combination and are used in different auxiliary lemmas.

In terms of state facts in the rule's conclusion, a persistent fact Ltk_Sym stores the identifiers for the Subscriber and the Home Network, together with their shared key, and for technical reasons the starting sequence number between them. Then a regular fact each for the Subscriber and the Home Network binds both their names, the current counter, which starts at the counter start variable plus one, then the counter start variable, and finally what has been added to it, namely one.

12.2.4.2 Key compromise

There are four key compromise rules. One rule is for the shared key k between the Home Network and the Subscriber, called reveal_Ltk_Sym, which we focus on below. There are two additional rules, which are similar, that reveal the initial sequence number counter and the Subscriber's identifier. Finally, there is also a rule to reveal the Home Network's private key.

```
rule reveal_Ltk_Sym:
  [!Ltk_Sym(~supi, ~idHN, ~k, ~sqn_root)]
  --[
    // Security properties
    Rev(~supi, <'k', ~k>),
    Rev(~idHN, <'k', ~k>)
  ]->
  [Out(~k)]
```

In this rule, the persistent fact contains the names of the Subscriber and the Home Network, as well as their shared key k and the sequence number's starting value. This rule reveals their shared key to the adversary by outputting it with Out. The rule's action facts record that this shared key was revealed from both the viewpoint of the Subscriber and the Home Network. Looking at the subscriber in more detail, Rev(supi, <'k', k>) identifies the subscriber named supi and reveals k of type key. This is shown by the constant 'k', paired with the actual value. This is helpful later for property specification.

12.2.5 Counters

To model the sequence numbers used in 5G-AKA we include them in our model. We have already seen how sequence numbers are initially set up. We now examine a rule that allows the Subscriber to increase its sequence number arbitrarily. This is used to get into a desynchronized state between the Subscriber and the Home Network, to check the functioning of the resynchronization protocol.

```
rule ue_sqn_increase:
  [Sqn_UE(~supi, ~idHN, Sqn, ~sqn_root, count),
```

12.2 Modeling 5G-AKA in Tamarin

```
  In(m)]
--[
   // Open chains
   Sqn_UE_Invariance(~supi, ~idHN, Sqn+m, ~sqn_root, count+m),

   // Auxiliary lemmas
   Sqn_UE_Change(~supi, ~idHN, Sqn+m),

   // Executability
   Sqn_UE_Desync()
  ]->
  [Sqn_UE(~supi, ~idHN, Sqn+m, ~sqn_root, count+m)]
```

In this rule, the premise fact Sqn_UE is simply modified in the conclusion, with the number m input from the network added to the current sequence number at the third position, and to the number of times the counter has been incremented, stored in the fifth position. The action facts are more interesting here. They include the first action fact Sqn_UE_Invariance used for a sources lemma (Section 8.4) that we need to give Tamarin to reason about the initial creation of sequence numbers and the number of times they have been incremented. The second action fact Sqn_UE_Change is used for an auxiliary lemma that checks that all sequence numbers only increase. The last action fact just states that there was a desynchronization, which we use in executability lemmas to check that the protocol can successfully re-synchronize after being in a desynchronized state.

12.2.6 Example protocol rules

We next consider how to model the Subscriber based on the protocol description shown in Figure 12.1, and we present the resulting rules. 5G *attach* is the initial procedure where the Subscriber connects to a 5G network. We focus on the scenario where this network attachment succeeds and we highlight some of the resulting rules. For the second rule we present, we explain, step by step, how we constructed it.

Looking at the protocol description, we expect the Subscriber to start attaching itself to a serving network by sending its first message. It also must remember its state, namely that it now waits for a response. To produce its message, it must first access its long-term storage for the shared key and its identifier. This is modeled in the following rule, which represents the Subscriber starting a new session with a Serving Network to attach itself and receive service.

```
rule ue_send_attachReq:
  let
    suci = < aenc{<~supi, ~R>}pk_HN, ~idHN>
    msg = suci
  in
  [!Ltk_Sym(~supi, ~idHN, ~k, ~sqn_root),
   !Pk(~idHN, pk_HN),
   Fr(~R),
   Fr(~tid)]
```

```
--[
  // Executability
  Start_UE_Session(~supi)
]->
[St_1_UE(~tid, ~supi, ~idHN, ~k, ~sqn_root),
 Out(msg)]
```

The first let binding captures the computation of the concealed subscription identifier `suci` as explained in the high-level overview. The message `msg` sent is then actually just the `suci`, as stated in the second let binding, but we use the extra name for consistency with other rules.

In the premises, this rule looks up the Subscriber's information in `!Ltk_Sym`, importantly its own identifier `supi` and its Home Network identifier `idHN`. From the state fact `!Pk`, the rule then gets the public key of the Subscriber's Home Network. As an alternative design option, this information could have instead been stored inside the Subscriber information. However, as it is in a persistent fact, this separate lookup makes no difference for this rule. Two fresh values are sampled as well. One value, `tid`, which is the thread identifier, is stored in the resulting state fact in the conclusion. The other value, R, is used to make the asymmetric encryption of `supi` non-deterministic, by including it in a pairing there. Thus, an adversary cannot compare two sent `suci` values and determine whether they come from the same Subscriber.

The rule's single action fact states that a new session was started. For the conclusions, in `St_1_UE` we store the state of the Subscriber (also called user equipment, thus the UE) after this first step. The Subscriber is now in the state where it can perform the next step in the protocol, modeled with the rule explained and shown below.

This next rule models that the Subscriber receives the response to the previously presented rule for it to attach to a Serving Network. This message comes from the Serving Network, which in the meantime should have exchanged messages with the Home Network. As per the protocol description, the Subscriber must receive such a message, perform some derivations and checks, and determine which of three cases applies. In our model, we chose to have separate rules for each of the three cases (success, synchronization failure, and MAC failure) formalized with precise conditions, so they apply whenever the input has the right form. We show next just the version of the second rule for the Subscriber, which performs these checks and covers the case where all the checks succeed. As seen in the protocol description, the Subscriber has its view of the shared sequence number. Thus, in this rule we use the state fact for the Subscriber's view of the sequence number, `Sqn_UE`, which is used across multiple sessions. This represents the UE's mutable state. This is something that is usually not part of smaller protocols and it leads to considerable proof complexity, which we will manage by proving auxiliary lemmas.

Given the rule's considerable complexity, we first present a simplified version of the rule showing only the left-hand and right-hand sides. We also omit the action facts and the let binding used to give an initial, high-level overview of the state transition.

12.2 Modeling 5G-AKA in TAMARIN

We also include line numbers (consistent between the presentation of the separate parts of the rule, so it is easier to follow), which are used for later reference.

```
1    rule ue_receive_authReq_freshness_success_send_authResp:

2

18       [St_1_UE(~tid, ~supi, ~idHN, ~k, ~sqn_root),
19        Sqn_UE(~supi, ~idHN, SqnUE, ~sqn_root, count),
20        In(msgIn)]

21

47       [St_2_UE(~tid, ~supi, ~idHN, ~k, ~sqn_root, idSN, K_seaf),
48        Out(msgOut),
49        Sqn_UE(~supi, ~idHN, SqnHSS, ~sqn_root, count+dif)]
```

For the left-hand side, in line 18, we see the lookup of the State St_1_UE that was produced in the first rule. In line 19, we see that the sequence number is stored by the UE in a state fact that is looked up as well. Lastly, in line 20 we see the input of a message, referred to as msgIn, which will be expanded in the let binding we later show.

On the right-hand side, in line 47 we see the next step of the UE's state for this attach, inside St_2_UE, which now additionally stores the identifier of the serving network, idSN, and the computed key K_seaf, which will be expanded in the let binding as well. The response is sent out as msgOut in line 48, which is expanded in the let binding that we will show soon. Finally, in line 49, the stored sequence number fact is updated by incrementing with the difference dif.

Let's look again at the left-hand side, now including the let bindings:

```
2    let
3       // Input, checks
4       SqnHSS = SqnUE + dif // check freshness
5       AK = f5(~k, RAND)
6       MAC = f1(~k, <SqnHSS, RAND>) // check on the MAC
7       AUTN = <SqnHSS XOR AK, MAC>
8       SNID = <'5G', idSN>
9       msgIn = < RAND, AUTN, SNID >

10

17    in
18       [St_1_UE(~tid, ~supi, ~idHN, ~k, ~sqn_root),
19        Sqn_UE(~supi, ~idHN, SqnUE, ~sqn_root, count),
20        In(msgIn)]
```

These let bindings are used to make the computations and checks in the "Expected Response" box in Figure 12.1. The msgIn that is received in line 20 is actually a triple, as expanded in line 9. Line 4 selects the sequence number value SqnHSS to use, which is larger than the one stored by the UE. Line 5 computes the key AK from the randomness RAND received in the message, and the stored long-term key k from the state fact in line 18. In line 6, the MAC is computed from the long-term key, sequence number, and randomness. The received AUTN is then implicitly, using pattern matching, checked to have the expected form in line 7. Namely, AUTN must be a pair consisting of the exclusive-or of the sequence number SqnHSS and the key AK, and the computed message authentication code MAC. To summarize, the let bindings ensure that the received message is of the right form, compared to Figure 12.1, and does all the necessary checks using pattern matching.

Now we look at the remaining part of the let binding, which is used for the right-hand side:

```
10      // Output
11      RES = f2(~k, RAND)
12      IK = f4(~k, RAND)
13      CK = f3(~k, RAND)
14      RES_star = KDF(<CK, IK>, <SNID, RES, RAND>)
15      K_seaf = KDF(KDF(<CK, IK>, <SNID, SqnHSS XOR AK>), SNID)
16      msgOut = RES_star
17
47      [St_2_UE(~tid, ~supi, ~idHN, ~k, ~sqn_root, idSN, K_seaf),
48      Out(msgOut),
49      Sqn_UE(~supi, ~idHN, SqnHSS, ~sqn_root, count+dif)]
```

Here we see that msgOut in line 16 is built in lines 11-14 from the known long-term key k, the received randomness RAND, and uses the serving network identifier from the let binding on the receiving side seen prior.

The final part that we have not yet shown contains the action facts, which are as follows:

```
21      --[
22          // Open chains
23          Sqn_UE_Invariance(~supi, ~idHN, SqnHSS, ~sqn_root, count+dif),
24
25          // Auxiliary lemmas
26          Sqn_UE_Change(~supi, ~idHN, SqnHSS),
27          Sqn_UE_Use(~supi, ~idHN, SqnHSS),
28          KSEAF(K_seaf),
29
30          // Security properties
31          Running(~supi, idSN,<'SEAF','UE',<'RES_star', RES_star>>),
32          Running(~supi, idSN,<'SEAF','UE',<'K_seaf', K_seaf>>),
33          Running(~supi, idSN,<'SEAF','UE',<'supi', ~supi>>),
34          Running(~supi, ~idHN, <'HSS','UE', <'K_seaf', K_seaf>>),
35          Running(~supi, ~idHN, <'HSS','UE', <'RAND', RAND>>),
36          Secret(<'UE', ~supi>, 'key', K_seaf),
37          Secret(<'UE', ~supi>, 'supi', ~supi),
38          Commit(~supi, ~idHN, <'UE','HSS',<'AUTN', AUTN>>),
39          Commit(~supi, ~idHN, <'UE','HSS',<'supi', ~supi>>),
40          Commit(~supi, ~idHN, <'UE','HSS', <'K_seaf', K_seaf>>),
41          Commit(~supi, idSN, <'UE','SEAF',<'K_seaf', K_seaf>>),
42          Commit(~supi, idSN, <'UE','SEAF',<'RAND', RAND>>),
43          Honest(~supi),
44          Honest(~idHN),
45          Honest(idSN)
46      ]->
```

12.2 Modeling 5G-AKA in TAMARIN

The action facts in general must be considered in the context of the lemmas where they are used, and we point out here which properties each of them belongs to. In line 23 we have the action fact that is used for removing partial deconstructions (also called open chains), i.e., in a sources lemma, as described in Section 8.2. The action facts in lines 26-28 are used in auxiliary lemmas that are reused for proof generation speedup; specifically the action KSEAF (Line 28) records the value of the derived key. The remaining action facts are used in different security properties. The Honest ones are used to ensure that the specifically named parties are not compromised when an agreement or secrecy property based on this rule is checked. The Secret ones are for secrecy lemmas, while the Commit ones are for agreement properties from the view of the UE. The Running ones are used by agreement properties from other parties' views.

We conclude by presenting the entire rule at once, and we will also comment on the protocol's continuation.

```
1   rule ue_receive_authReq_freshness_success_send_authResp:
2     let
3       // Input, checks
4       SqnHSS = SqnUE + dif // check freshness
5       AK = f5(~k, RAND)
6       MAC = f1(~k, <SqnHSS, RAND>) // check on the MAC
7       AUTN = <SqnHSS XOR AK, MAC>
8       SNID = <'5G', idSN>
9       msgIn = < RAND, AUTN, SNID >
10      // Output
11      RES = f2(~k, RAND)
12      IK = f4(~k, RAND)
13      CK = f3(~k, RAND)
14      RES_star = KDF(<CK, IK>, <SNID, RES, RAND>)
15      K_seaf = KDF(KDF(<CK, IK>, <SNID, SqnHSS XOR AK>), SNID)
16      msgOut = RES_star
17    in
18    [St_1_UE(~tid, ~supi, ~idHN, ~k, ~sqn_root),
19     Sqn_UE(~supi, ~idHN, SqnUE, ~sqn_root, count),
20     In(msgIn)]
21    --[
22      // Open chains
23      Sqn_UE_Invariance(~supi, ~idHN, SqnHSS, ~sqn_root, count+dif),
24
25      // Auxiliary lemmas
26      Sqn_UE_Change(~supi, ~idHN, SqnHSS),
27      Sqn_UE_Use(~supi, ~idHN, SqnHSS),
28      KSEAF(K_seaf),
29
30      // Security properties
31      Running(~supi, idSN,<'SEAF','UE',<'RES_star', RES_star>>),
32      Running(~supi, idSN,<'SEAF','UE',<'K_seaf', K_seaf>>),
33      Running(~supi, idSN,<'SEAF','UE',<'supi', ~supi>>),
34      Running(~supi, ~idHN, <'HSS','UE', <'K_seaf', K_seaf>>),
35      Running(~supi, ~idHN, <'HSS','UE', <'RAND', RAND>>),
36      Secret(<'UE', ~supi>, 'key', K_seaf),
37      Secret(<'UE', ~supi>, 'supi', ~supi),
38      Commit(~supi, ~idHN, <'UE','HSS',<'AUTN', AUTN>>),
39      Commit(~supi, ~idHN, <'UE','HSS',<'supi', ~supi>>),
```

```
40      Commit(~supi, ~idHN, <'UE','HSS', <'K_seaf', K_seaf>>),
41      Commit(~supi, idSN, <'UE','SEAF',<'K_seaf', K_seaf>>),
42      Commit(~supi, idSN, <'UE','SEAF',<'RAND', RAND>>),
43      Honest(~supi),
44      Honest(~idHN),
45      Honest(idSN)
46      ]->
47      [St_2_UE(~tid, ~supi, ~idHN, ~k, ~sqn_root, idSN, K_seaf),
48      Out(msgOut),
49      Sqn_UE(~supi, ~idHN, SqnHSS, ~sqn_root, count+dif)]
```

After this rule is executed, the Subscriber can later do a key confirmation step. The rule for this step is not shown, but it is the reason why the new state St_2_UE needs to be stored.

We do not show the two alternatives for this Subscriber rule. Those are used in case either the MAC check fails, or the sequence number is not accepted because it is too small. The rule shown was the version that forced both checks to succeed, so there is a rule taking care of each eventuality.

12.2.7 Proof effort

In terms of proof effort, completing all the work of understanding the standard, protocol modeling, and verifying such a complex protocol takes many person-months. Concretely, we have written on the order of 300 lines of custom heuristics, which we elaborate on in Section 12.2.10.

The majority of the effort involved coming up with auxiliary lemmas, building upon each other, which are used as stepping stones to simplify the proofs of the desired properties. The auxiliary lemmas include three sources lemmas to solve partial deconstructions (see Chapter 8), which were manually found (as the work on 5G predates the work on --auto-sources), and four reuse lemmas, where two of the latter use induction.

We showcase one of the reuse lemmas here.

```
lemma sqn_ue_unique [reuse, hide_lemma=sqn_ue_src, hide_lemma=sqn_hss_src]:
" All supi HN Sqn #i #j.
  Sqn_UE_Use(supi, HN, Sqn)@i & Sqn_UE_Use(supi, HN, Sqn)@j
    ==> #i = #j "
```

This lemma shows that a Subscriber only uses a sequence number exactly once. The lemma encodes this by specifying that for every two instances of Sqn_UE_Use with the same Subscriber and Home Network and sequence number, happening at time points i and j, the two time points are actually the same.

Note that this lemma is marked reuse, and hides two of the reuse lemmas that precede it in the input file (not shown here) to improve performance. This is described further in Section 9.2.

12.2 Modeling 5G-AKA in TAMARIN

12.2.8 Executability

To increase confidence in our model's accuracy, we wrote four executability lemmas. These lemmas state that various expected executions are indeed possible in the model. These executions include runs with (or without) key confirmation, and with (or without) re-synchronization. The following is an example.

```
// This lemma shows a normal execution without resync.
// proof (automatic) (~30 sec)
lemma executability_honest[heuristic={executability_honest}]:
  exists-trace
  " Ex #i. SEAF_End()@i
    & not (Ex X data #r. Rev(X,data)@r)
    & (All supi HN sqn_root #i. Sqn_Create(supi, HN, sqn_root)@i
        ==> not (Ex #j. K(sqn_root)@j))
    & (All HN1 HN2 #j #k. HomeNet(HN1)@j &
            HomeNet(HN2)@k ==> #j = #k)
    & (All S1 S2 HN1 HN2 #j #k. Subscribe(S1, HN1)@j &
            Subscribe(S2, HN2)@k ==> #j = #k)
    & (All SNID1 SNID2 #j #k. Start_SEAF_Session(SNID1)@j &
              Start_SEAF_Session(SNID2)@k ==> #j = #k)
    & (All UE1 UE2 #j #k. Start_UE_Session(UE1)@j &
              Start_UE_Session(UE2)@k ==> #j = #k)
    & (All HN1 HN2 #j #k. Start_HSS_Session(HN1)@j &
              Start_HSS_Session(HN2)@k ==> #j = #k)"
```

The purpose of such lemmas is not to prove the absence of some undesired behaviors; rather, we aim to prove that certain expected normal behaviors are indeed possible within our TAMARIN model. This is why we specified an `exists-trace` lemma.

In this lemma, we require the protocol execution to have SEAF_End in the trace, which means the protocol has run to its conclusion to the Serving Network's satisfaction. Because we want to show there exists a normal execution, without adversary interference, we forbid any data reveals via Rev, and we disallow revealing the sequence number of any created mapping from the Subscriber to the Home Network. We model that a normal execution only requires a single instance of each entity (Subscriber, Serving Network, and Home Network) that each starts one session. All of these limitations help TAMARIN to find a nice, clean-looking execution without adversary involvement and with all parties just running the protocol once. The lemma verification succeeds and produces such an execution, which can then be inspected using TAMARIN's GUI.

As mentioned previously, proving executability lemmas helps catch modeling mistakes, which might otherwise be missed. For example, if a protocol is not executable, then all secrecy statements that require the protocol to have an executable run are vacuously true.

12.2.9 Properties

We have picked one property to look at in more detail. It turns out that this lemma is violated, meaning there is an attack for it. The lemma is as follows.

```
lemma weakagreement_ue_seaf_noRev [heuristic={weakagreement_ue_seaf_noRev},
    hide_lemma=sqn_ue_nodecrease, hide_lemma=sqn_ue_src, hide_lemma=sqn_hss_src]:
  " All a b t #i. Commit(a,b,<'UE','SEAF',t>)@i
       ==> (Ex t2 #j. Running(b, a, t2)@j)
            | (Ex X data #r. Rev(X,data)@r & Honest(X)@i) "
```

We model that the Subscriber has weak agreement with the Serving Network, under the assumption that no data was revealed for any party that is marked as needing to be non-compromised in the rule where the Commit is made. Note that the timepoint i used for the Commit is the same as that for the Honest fact in the right-hand side of the implication. The property requires that for any Commit there is a Running of the partner. However, this turns out to be false, as can be seen in the counterexample TAMARIN produces.

There are many more properties that this protocol should satisfy and they are modeled in the usual way for agreement properties. However, for space reasons we will not describe these further. The detailed results for the 5G-AKA protocol can be found in the publication [14].

12.2.10 Tactics and oracles

TAMARIN's built-in proof search will sometimes fail to find a proof in reasonable time and memory (or at all), even when a relatively simple sequence of proof steps exists. In such cases, the user can then guide TAMARIN interactively. Although this can be quite effective, it can also become tedious and the proofs are hard to reproduce. Hence, TAMARIN allows users to specify heuristics programmatically, by encoding user choices as tactics (see Section 16.3) or oracles (see Section 16.4). Essentially, these serve to prioritize proof methods, thereby guiding the proof search. Here we focus on an example and show how to develop an appropriate heuristic that can be specified using either mechanism.

For the lemma sqn_ue_invariance, we will describe what happens in two proof attempts: one using the default heuristic, and the other our dedicated oracle.

```
lemma sqn_ue_invariance [use_induction, sources, heuristic={sqn}]:
  " All supi HN Sqn sqn_root count #i.
    Sqn_UE_Invariance(supi, HN, Sqn, sqn_root, count)@i
       ==> sqn_root + count = Sqn"
```

In both attempts, we start with an induction and a simplify step, leading to one open case where we are left with two possible choices.

```
1. solve( (last(#i)) || ((count++sqn_root) = Sqn) )  // nr. 1
```

12.3 Conclusions and general insights

```
2. solve( Sqn_UE_Invariance( supi, HN, Sqn, sqn_root, count) @ #i ) // nr. 0
```

These have been prioritized by TAMARIN's default heuristic as shown above. As such, using option 1, the next proof step will resolve the case split between the inductive last time point and the form of the sequence number, which turns out not to be necessary (our oracle version will always just delay this option and is therefore more efficient). After solving option 1, only one case remains open, at which point the current second choice is the only proof step applicable, and thus must be solved. Solving what is currently option 2 results in three cases to analyze in both versions of the proof attempt, i.e., the one with and the one without the oracle. However, with the oracle, TAMARIN has used one fewer step and skips option 1 entirely.

Of the three resulting cases, we will discuss just the first case. There we get the following choices (order shown as given by the default heuristic).

```
1. solve( St_1_UE( ~tid, ~supi, ~idHN, ~k, ~sqn_root ) ▶₀ #i )
   // nr. 3 (from rule ue_receive_authReq_fail_freshness_send_sync_failure)

2. solve( !KU( f1(~k, <SqnHSS, RAND>) ) @ #vk.5 ) // nr. 10

3. solve( splitEqs(0) ) // nr. 2

4. solve( Sqn_UE( ~supi, ~idHN, Sqn, ~sqn_root, count ) ▶₁ #i )
   // nr. 4 (from rule ue_receive_authReq_fail_freshness_send_sync_failure
   // (loop breaker)
```

We note that in the oracle version, the skipped possible proof step is also there as a choice, but it is ignored. Both versions continue with the choice 1, solving St_1_UE. This leads to just one case with the previous choices 2-4 remaining in both. The oracle version will pick choice 4, resolving the source of Sqn_UE. This leads to four cases, which are immediately closed, finishing this sub-proof. In contrast, the standard heuristic would pick choice 2 above, resulting in ten open cases, which would require substantial reasoning to solve. Simply letting TAMARIN run from here, with the default heuristic, also does not finish the sub-proof within a reasonable time, i.e., a few minutes.

The choices explained here that can be taken manually are encoded either as oracles or tactics and used by TAMARIN to complete the proof quickly. Similar, manually derived, heuristics, encoded as oracles or tactics, are helpful in many other lemmas. Unfortunately, making the right choice is not easy. It requires experimentation and experience using TAMARIN to gain intuition into when specific sub-proofs are unlikely to be successful and could profit from manual intervention. We know of no easy way to automate this in TAMARIN, as otherwise we would have done so.

12.3 Conclusions and general insights

This case study illustrates the approach taken, and some of the modeling choices made, when modeling real-world protocols of considerable complexity. For such protocols, considerable time is required for constructing the proofs themselves, as when proof attempts fail, one must diagnose the reasons for this. This involves inspecting partial proofs in TAMARIN's GUI to identify those proof states that TAMARIN struggles with. Here one benefits strongly from TAMARIN's support for interactive theorem proving. Afterwards, to assist TAMARIN, reuse lemmas, induction, or even the development of oracles or tactics may be necessary.

We mentioned at this book's start that TAMARIN is a living system, undergoing evolution and improvement. This case study bears witness to this. While the overall approach taken is illustrative of how one models and verifies such protocols, support for different equational theories and proof automation has been improved since this case study was carried out, and this is documented elsewhere in this book.

For the 5G-AKA model in particular, we have seen that encoding natural numbers as multisets is not ideal, as the state becomes hard to read. This fact led to work that extended TAMARIN to support the natural numbers, together with support for reasoning about subterms. Subterm reasoning on numbers can be used to reason about ordering relations, for example, which number is smaller than or larger than another. And this in turn simplifies proofs requiring such orderings. Prior to these additions, e.g., in the 5G-AKA model, additional restrictions were used to specify such relations. Thus, we would use these features now if we were to redo this work and the resulting models would likely be faster to analyze and the modeling would be less error-prone.

Another point needing improvement is that the use of oracles in our model was time-consuming and difficult. It required understanding where proofs will fail to terminate, then selecting better alternative proof steps by hand that will lead to termination, and then encoding these choices as oracles to be used by TAMARIN. To simplify such processes, TAMARIN was recently extended with a new feature supporting tactics built into the theory file, which we would now use here.

Finally, the way we wrote the security properties in this case study differs slightly from how we presented such formulas elsewhere in this book. Namely, there are minor differences regarding how one annotates and specifies which parties must be honest, i.e., not compromised. We now suggest using these alternative formulations.

Overall, this example shows that there are clear benefits to the formal modeling and analysis of such complex, real-world protocols. Simultaneously, it shows the interplay between large-scale examples, and research on proof methodology and tool improvement.

Part V
Advanced Topics

Chapter 13
Observational Equivalence

In this chapter, we describe observational equivalence properties, and the workflows used to model and analyze them. Until now, all properties considered in this book were trace properties, meaning they are evaluated over individual traces. In contrast, observational equivalence describes a *hyperproperty* that compares two traces. We often call the workflow for reasoning about observational equivalence the *diff mode* of TAMARIN as this analysis is enabled using the flag `--diff`.

Support for reasoning about observational equivalence was added to TAMARIN in 2015 [15]. As a result, TAMARIN can now be used to analyze privacy-style properties formalized as observational equivalence, such as anonymity or unlinkability. This has numerous applications, such as reasoning about voter privacy (sketched in this section) or reasoning about how persons can be tracked as they roam about with devices such as RFID tokens or mobile phones. For example, reasoning about observational equivalence in TAMARIN was used to show that the current generation of mobile communication, the 5G standard, has a weakness whereby users' cellphones can be tracked [14]. TAMARIN found an attack whereby an active adversary can perform "presence tests" to track phones as they move over time.

13.1 Observational equivalence in TAMARIN

Unlike the properties discussed before, which are defined over a single trace, and thus called *trace properties*, observational equivalence is a hyperproperty comparing sets of traces. Consequently, the approach for analyzing observational equivalence in TAMARIN is to compare two different multiset rewriting systems and see whether the adversary can distinguish their behaviors.

To start, one enters the two systems as a *bi-system*, where one single input theory gives rise to two versions of the system. The systems are identical, except for terms that are wrapped under the distinguished `diff(x,y)` operator. This operator takes two terms as arguments where the first one is used in the so-called left instance of the bi-system, and the second in the right instance. This means that in the left instance diff(x,y) is replaced by x, and in the right instance by y. TAMARIN then explores all possible executions on each side, and for each complete trace checks that the same trace can be mirrored on the other side. This is done using an extra lemma, automatically added. This essentially ensures that an adversary cannot detect whether it is interacting with the left or the right instance.

More technically, after creating a theory file using the diff(x,y)-operator one starts TAMARIN with the command-line argument --diff to instruct it to use the mode for Observational Equivalence. This automatically adds the diff(x,y) operator to the allowed function symbols, and during loading adds the mentioned extra lemma, which is given as diffLemma Observational_equivalence in which the proof step rule-equivalence will be applied first.

In interactive mode, TAMARIN presents the user with two versions of the message theory, multiset rewriting rules, and precomputed sources: one version marked LHS for the left system, and one version marked RHS for the right system. These show the two different interpretations, based on the diff-terms.

Note that input files with diff-terms can still contain "normal" lemmas stating trace properties, on one or on both "sides". Lemmas can be annotated using left, right, or both to specify on which side they should be analyzed. By default, if no annotation is given, the lemma will be considered on both sides. The same holds for restrictions.

TAMARIN does separate precomputations for each side in trace mode, and for each side in equivalence mode, as equivalence mode uses slightly different reduction rules for normalization and termination. In particular, a new adversary deduction rule allowing the adversary to test equality between terms is added in equivalence mode. This ensures that the adversary can compare values whilst applying functions to the outputs on either side, similarly to *static equivalence* in the applied Π-calculus [1]. Moreover, a new final proof step, called MIRRORED is now available, that closes an exploration if it is a (complete) trace that can be mirrored on the other side. In the case that a trace is complete, but TAMARIN is unable to find a mirror, this means that either there is an attack, or TAMARIN was just unable to produce a mirror. It is up to the user to decide if this missing mirror is an actual attack or if the result is just inconclusive. This is a major difference to TAMARIN's trace mode: in diff mode, TAMARIN uses a sound, but incomplete, approximation of observational equivalence. It may thus fail to prove that two equivalent protocols are actually equivalent. In contrast, in trace mode TAMARIN uses no approximation.

13.1.1 A first example

To exemplify a very simple equivalence model and proof, we use an equational theory representing probabilistic encryption. Here, TAMARIN can prove that the two systems are indistinguishable, with the file available at **probEnc.spthy**.

```
theory probEnc
begin

functions: penc/3, pdec/2, pk/1

equations: pdec(penc(m,pk(k),r), k) = m

rule gen:
  [ Fr(~k) ]
--[ ]->
  [ !Key(~k), Out(pk(~k)) ]
rule enc:
  [ !Key(k), Fr(~r1), Fr(~r2), In(x) ]
--[ ]->
  [ Out(diff(~r1, penc(x, pk(k), ~r2))) ]

end
```

The use of diff(~r1, penc(x, pk(k), ~r2)) compares a fresh value to the encryption of an adversary-provided message using probabilistic asymmetric encryption under a public key for which the adversary does not know the private key. Here, under this equational theory, TAMARIN concludes that the adversary cannot distinguish both sides.

Other examples of successful verifications of equivalence include the RFID protocol by Feldhofer or a model of the decisional Diffie-Hellman property given TAMARIN's Diffie-Hellman theory [15]. Observational equivalence has been used to discover attacks against the TPM-Envelope protocol [15] and 5G-AKA [14].

13.2 Modeling and analysis workflow

When reasoning about observational equivalence, the main difference during modeling comes in the property specification, which is not done via explicitly user-defined lemmas as in trace mode. Instead, an automatically created equivalence lemma, diffLemma Observational_equivalence, is used to compare two systems, and the placement of the diff-terms defines the property. However, the placement of the diff-terms can be subtle, both to precisely capture the desired property and to avoid trivial attacks. In practice, one often needs several iterations before obtaining the desired model. In Section 13.3, we illustrate this process on a small example.

When it comes to analyzing the models, the same overall workflows described in Chapter 11 apply: one needs to debug syntax errors and warnings first, and handle partial deconstructions. However, there are some important differences.

First, interpreting TAMARIN's results, in particular attacks, differs from trace mode. We explain this in examples in Section 13.3.

Second, there are differences concerning the handling of termination and performance issues. Most of the strategies described in Chapter 11 remain valid, but some details change. For example, fine-tuning heuristics is often less effective for equivalence properties than for trace properties, as an equivalence proof necessarily computes (a representative set) of all executions. It is often more effective to fine-tune the model instead. For instance, in equivalence proofs, TAMARIN does not need to resolve a fact that only contains unconstrained variables (i.e., variables that do not appear elsewhere, and that are of type message), e.g., In(x) for an unconstrained x, or F(x). To make use of this, it is sometimes helpful to remove type annotations; this is in contrast to trace properties, where type annotations are typically helpful for TAMARIN.

Third, equivalence proofs tend to be much larger, and typically also grow more rapidly when the size of the model increases. Longer verification times are thus common.

Finally, restrictions, which tend to be efficient in trace mode, often have the opposite effect in equivalence mode, creating two possible problems: (i) their use can lead to spurious attacks, as TAMARIN internally uses some approximations, (ii) or their use can even lead to non-termination as TAMARIN continues to explore increasingly complex executions to determine whether the restrictions hold or not.

13.3 A second example: a voting protocol

As a second example, we show the development of the model and the analysis of a small, toy, voting protocol. We present this development in six steps where we iteratively improve both our model and our specification of its desired security property, after finding attacks on intermediate models.

The goal of this step-by-step guide is to help you understand and interpret different kinds of attacks in diff mode, as well as the process of specifying a meaningful equivalence property while avoiding trivial attacks. The full theory files for the examples given here are available as votingsimpleVx.spthy, where x is the version number of the following subsections.

The protocol in question is very simple. Each voter encrypts their vote using the voting server's public key, and sends the resulting ciphertext to the server, who decrypts all votes and announces the result. For simplicity, we assume that there are only two options: 'A' or 'B'. A security property we would like to verify is the secrecy of the votes.

13.3.1 Version 1, using deterministic encryption

Our first iteration will use deterministic asymmetric encryption for the voter to communicate their choice of 'A' or 'B' to the voting server (which is not yet modeled) by encrypting it under the server's public key. The two scenarios come in the form of the left instance and the right instance of the modeled bi-system.

This model, available at **votingsimpleV1.spthy**, uses asymmetric encryption defined as usual in its deterministic version:

```
functions: aenc/2, adec/2, pk/1

equations: adec(aenc(m,pk(k)), k) = m
```

A key for the server is generated by the following rule, where the associated public key is output to the adversary as well.

```
rule gen:
  [ Fr(~k) ]
--[ ]->
  [ !Key(~k), Out(pk(~k)) ]
```

The voter's choice is made in the next rule with the single diff-term diff('A','B'). This rule encodes the voter's choice and is annotated with Secret to be used below to check for secrecy (as usually done in trace mode). We will explain later why we use a diff-term here. The output is the asymmetric encryption of the vote under the server's public key.

```
rule voteDiff:
  let vote = diff('A','B')
  in
  [ !Key(k) ]
--[ Secret(vote) ]->
  [ Out(aenc(vote, pk(k))) ]
```

The Secret annotation is then used in a lemma encoding secrecy, as a trace property as we have introduced it earlier in the book.

```
lemma secrecy:
  "All v #i. Secret(v)@i ==> not Ex #j. K(v)@j"
```

When analyzing secrecy as defined in the above (standard) lemma, TAMARIN immediately reports violations on both sides of the bi-system. The reason is that both vote choices, 'A' and 'B', are publicly known choices. Hence these values cannot be secrets, unknown to the adversary. Naturally, in an election, everyone, including an adversary, knows all possible voting options.

The problem, of course, is that this is not really what we wanted to express. Ideally, we want to state that the choice *made by a certain voter* is secret, i.e., that we do not know whether this voter encrypted 'A' or 'B'.

Let us try again and reformulate the lemma using observational equivalence and diff-terms. The diff term placed in the voter's rule above does exactly this: it asks TAMARIN to verify whether an adversary can distinguish an instance of the protocol where the voter chooses 'A' from an instance where it chooses 'B'. In TAMARIN, this property is materialized using the built-in diffLemma named Observational_equivalence.

When we try to analyze this simple model, and prove the automatically generated diffLemma Observational_equivalence, we also get attacks. Intuitively, the problem is that the adversary can simply also compute the encryption of the two possible public choices under the server's public key and compare those ciphertexts with what the voter sends. As we have a deterministic encryption scheme, the adversary finds out if it is interacting with the left system or the right system.

Let us look at this issue in more detail. TAMARIN produces the attack graph shown in Figure 13.1, which shows a completed protocol execution. The execution ends with the adversary iequality rule, which allows the adversary to check whether two terms are equal. This rule is available only in diff mode, and is used here to compare the output of the voteDiff rule, with the constant 'A' encrypted under the server's public key created by the adversary. Note that this execution is found in the left-hand side instance of the bi-system, i.e., the version of the system where the voteDiff rule chooses 'A'.

To verify observational equivalence, TAMARIN checks whether the resulting completed execution shown above can also be done on the other side (here, the right-hand side), using the same choices by the adversary (i.e., here the adversary still encrypts 'A'). If so, the proof step MIRRORED would be applied, closing this branch. However, in this example, it results in a violation because this execution is only possible in the left instance. When TAMARIN attempts to mirror this execution on the right instance, this yields an impossible execution, as there the value 'B' is chosen by the diffVote rule, and thus the equality check at the end fails. This is because it requires aenc('A', pk(~k)) and aenc('B', pk(~k)) to be equal, which they are not as 'A' and 'B' are different underneath the encryption.

The above kind of issue is the essence of observational equivalence attacks: given a successful execution on one of the sides (left or right), it must be possible to have an execution where the adversary does exactly the same steps on the other side. As this is not possible here, an attack is reported. This also means that an attack in equivalence mode is just one graph, which corresponds to an execution that is possible on one side, but not on the other.

Note that after we find the first attack (using the usual 'autoprove', with button 'a'), we can examine all possible attacks by using the 'for all solutions' (button 'A') option. The attacks visible are very similar, once on the left with the adversary using 'A' as described above and once on the right using 'B'.

Examining our toy protocol further, an obvious improvement to avoid this attack is to use non-deterministic asymmetric encryption instead of the deterministic version. We will make this change in the next version.

13.3 A simple voting protocol

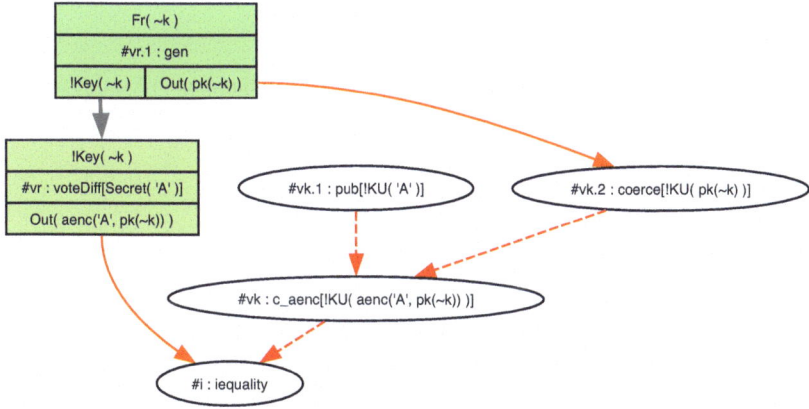

Fig. 13.1: Observational equivalence violation

13.3.2 Version 2, non-deterministic encryption

The main change here is to use non-deterministic asymmetric encryption, where a third parameter, representing the random values used during encryption, is added to the encryption function, and with the modified decryption equation just ignoring that parameter. The full file is available at **votingsimpleV2.spthy**. The resulting definition is as follows.

```
functions: penc/3, pdec/2, pk/1

equations: pdec(penc(m,pk(k),r), k) = m
```

The server key generation rule does not change from before. The voteDiff rule has the necessary minor change to create a fresh random value ~r1 and use it as an extra argument of encryption.

```
rule voteDiff:
  let vote = diff('A','B')
  in
  [ !Key(k), Fr(~r1) ]
--[ ]->
  [ Out(penc(vote, pk(k),~r1)) ]
```

Running this through TAMARIN yields a quick proof of equivalence of the theory. However, we have not yet modeled the voting server decrypting the votes and announcing the tally. To do this, we will add another rule that uses the server's private key to decrypt the received votes, and outputs the final tally. We then must re-run TAMARIN of course.

13.3.3 Version 3, adding a tallying authority

We now add the tallying authority, full file available at **votingsimpleV3.spthy**, modeled with the following rule.

```
rule authority:
  [ !Key(k),
    In(<penc(X, pk(k), r1), penc(Y, pk(k),r2)>) ]
  --[]->
  [ Out(<X,Y>) ]
```

This rule simply takes two messages encrypted with the election's public key and decrypts them, outputting the resulting tally in the clear. This means that the honest agent's rule's output can now be received and decrypted, however note that the adversary can also create their own encryptions to be passed to this rule.

The resulting theory produces 12 partial deconstructions, see Chapter 8, which we eliminate using `--auto-sources`, see Section 8.3 as parameter when loading the file with TAMARIN. The created `AUTO_typing_LHS` and `AUTO_typing_RHS` lemmas can be automatically proven.

As mentioned, the analysis with TAMARIN finds many attacks here (using "autoprove for all solutions" again to see all of them). We pick the attack shown in Figure 13.2 where the vote created by the rule `diffVote` is given to the tallying authority as the first, and an adversary-created vote as the second. The output of the tallying authority then is 'A' followed by the adversary's vote on the left-hand side system. The adversary then checks whether the tally contains an 'A'. This does not have a mirror in the right-hand side system as the voter's vote would be 'B' instead, and there would be no 'A' in the tally.

In a nutshell, by adding an arbitrary vote, the adversary obtains the final tally, which will contain the voter's vote. This vote depends on the side of the bi-system we are on, making them distinguishable: the adversary just needs to check whether the result contains an 'A' or a 'B'.

To ensure that we always get the same result, we can add another voter which always votes opposite: it votes 'B' if the first one votes 'A', and 'A' if the first one votes 'B'. One can also see this as the two legitimate voters swapping their votes: this way the resulting tally will always be one 'A' and one 'B' to hide what our voter of interest is actually doing. However, if the adversary could distinguish both sides, it can identify which voter voted 'A' or 'B', breaking vote secrecy.

13.3.4 Version 4, adding another voter with swap

We now add a second voter who always votes the opposite of our original voter, so the result is always one 'A' and one 'B' in a tally with the two voter's votes. As the model now becomes larger we use more let bindings to have an easier overview, and

13.3 A simple voting protocol

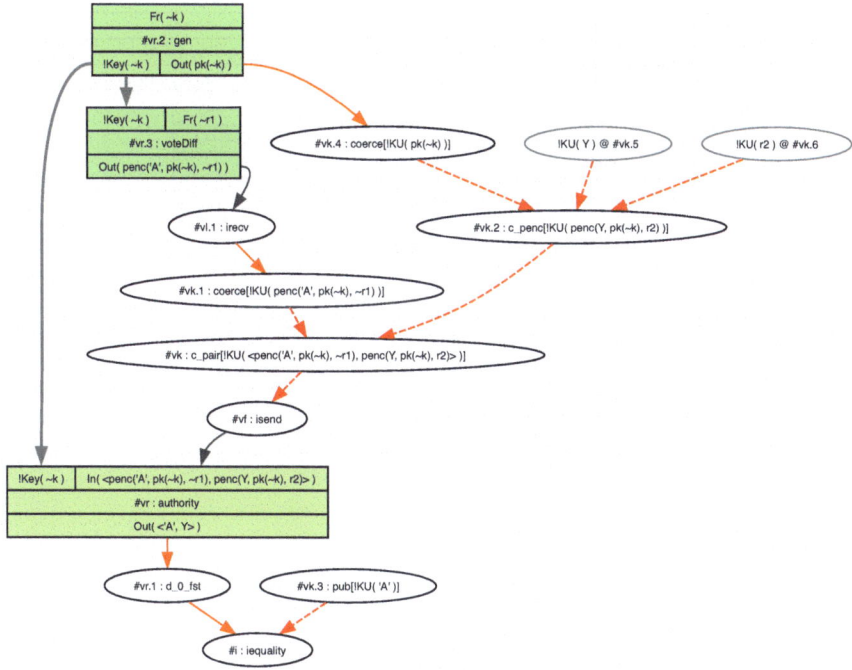

Fig. 13.2: Observational equivalence violation

thus we show some rules again despite just such syntactic changes. This full file is available at **votingsimpleV4.spthy**.

We first add new rules giving the existing voter as well as the new voter their respective long-term keys.

```
rule genVoterOther:
  [Fr(~k)]
--[]->
  [!VoterKeyOther(~k), Out(pk(~k))]

rule genVoterDiff:
  [Fr(~k)]
--[]->
  [!VoterKeyDiff(~k), Out(pk(~k))]
```

The main change to the model is to add a new rule that encodes the other voter's choice, additionally looking up its long-term key.

```
rule voteOther:
 let votecand = diff('B','A')
     vote = penc(votecand, pk(authorityk),~r1)
  in
  [ !Key(authorityk), Fr(~r1), !VoterKeyOther(~k) ]
--[ ]->
```

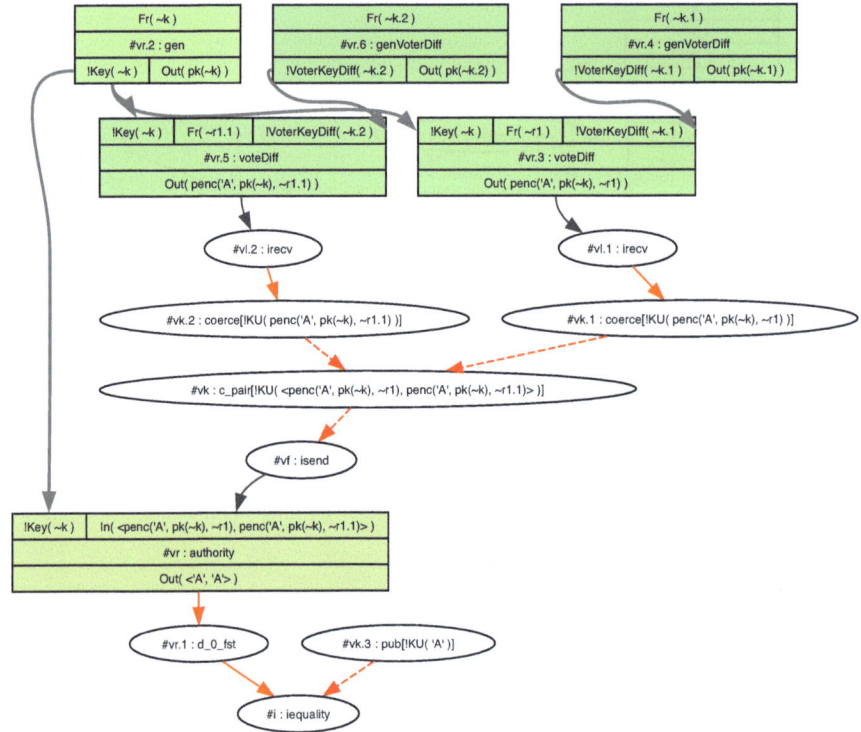

Fig. 13.3: Observational equivalence violation

```
[ Out(vote) ]
```

To ease comparison, we repeat here the rule for our voter of interest, extending the let binding.

```
rule voteDiff:
  let votecand = diff('A','B')
      vote = penc(votecand, pk(authorityk),~r1)
  in
  [ !Key(authorityk), Fr(~r1), !VoterKeyDiff(~k) ]
--[ ]->
  [ Out(vote) ]
```

The key difference between the two rules is that the new voter votes for the opposite candidate. However, we still find violations of the property, for example the attack shown in Figure 13.3. The problem here is that despite each voter having their own key, they make no use of it and the tallying authority does not check anything about it. Thus, the adversary can just send in one voter's vote twice, resulting in a pair of same votes, revealing which side we are on just based on the output. Here we chose the left-hand side and the voteDiff's vote and get two 'A' which cannot be

13.3 A simple voting protocol

mirrored, as there will be two 'B' on the right-hand side of the bi-system. This is not indistinguishable.

Obviously, to avoid this trivial attack, we must ensure that both votes are tallied. A way to ensure this is to have each party sign their vote, and for the tallying authority to check that the received votes are accompanied by appropriate signatures from the two different parties.

13.3.5 Version 5, adding signatures

Now we add signatures in the two vote-producing rules and a signature check using pattern matching in the tallying. The vote-producing rules now become the following.

```
rule voteOther:
  let votecand = diff('B','A')
      vote = penc(votecand, pk(authorityk),~r1)
      votesigned = <vote, sign(vote,~k)>
  in
  [ !Key(authorityk), Fr(~r1), !VoterKeyOther(~k) ]
--[ ]->
  [ Out(votesigned) ]

rule voteDiff:
  let votecand = diff('A','B')
      vote = penc(votecand, pk(authorityk),~r1)
      votesigned = <vote, sign(vote,~k)>
  in
  [ !Key(authorityk), Fr(~r1), !VoterKeyDiff(~k) ]
--[ ]->
  [ Out(votesigned) ]
```

Here the voters send out the pair of the actual vote and a signature on the vote, with the full file at **votingsimpleV5.spthy**.

We change the tallying rule to incorporate signature verification by pattern-matching on the two keys, and afterwards outputting the result.

```
rule authority:
  let voteA = penc(X, pk(k), r1)
      voteAsigned= <voteA, sign(voteA,kA)>
      voteB = penc(Y, pk(k), r2)
      voteBsigned= <voteB, sign(voteB,kB)>
  in
  [ !VoterKeyOther(kA), !VoterKeyDiff(kB), !Key(k),
    In(< voteAsigned , voteBsigned >) ]
--[ ]->
  [ Out(<X,Y>) ]
```

Here the tallied result is output as an ordered list, where the first vote is output as the first element of the list. TAMARIN finds attacks again. The reason, intuitively, is that the adversary can put in one chosen voter's vote as the first one to the tallying authority, then the first decrypted output is that voter's vote. An example of such an attack is shown in Figure 13.4, where the vote of rule `voteDiff` is input second to the tally and compared to 'A'. This fails on the other side as there would be a 'B'.

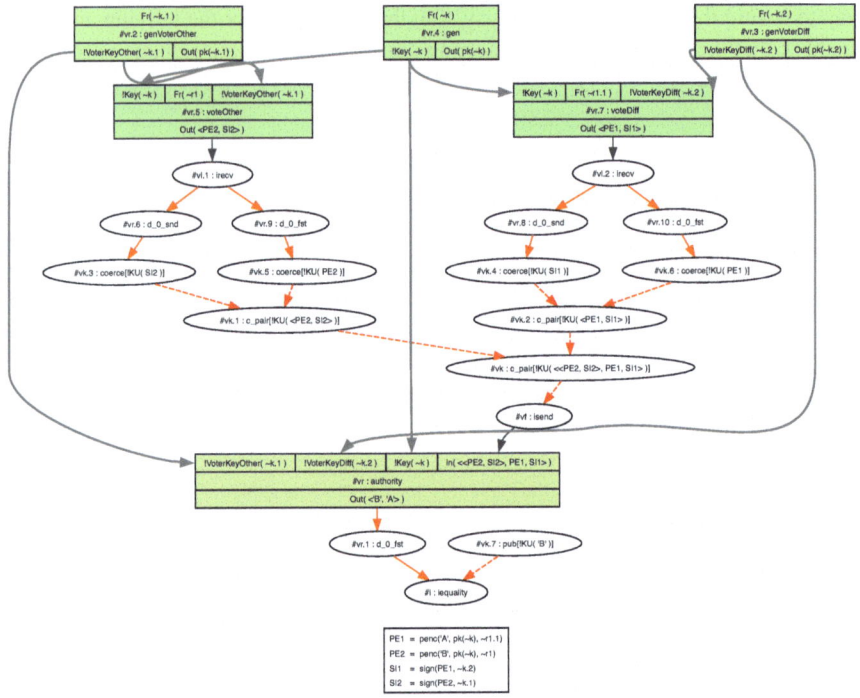

Fig. 13.4: Observational equivalence violation

Essentially, the order still leaks votes in this scenario. In practice, one would obviously publish the votes in random order to avoid this attack, e.g., using a mix-net. To model this we can output an associative-commutative multiset instead of an ordered list, so that the order is concealed. That is exactly what our last model does.

13.3.6 Version 6, order-concealing output

In the final model, available as **votingsimpleV6.spthy**, we include the built-in multiset with:

```
builtins: multiset
```

The rest of the model is unchanged except for the output of the tallying authority, which outputs the multiset of the votes rather than the ordered list. For this, we only show that last line of the rule, and not the whole rule.

13.3 A simple voting protocol

```
[ Out(X+Y) ]
```

This version is proven correct by TAMARIN. Essentially, we now have a voting system where the two voters vote opposite, each voter can only submit one vote, and the outcome is always the multiset of the two candidates 'A'+'B'. However, the adversary cannot distinguish which choice either of the voters makes. Of course, the model could be further refined and improved, for example by adding corrupted voters.

13.3.7 Summary

We have presented several versions of our toy voting protocol. Starting from the initial model, we discovered why we need an equivalence property rather than a trace property, and also how to specify the "right" scenario to avoid trivial attacks. We also learned a bit about practical voting protocols. In particular, one should use non-deterministic (randomized) encryption. Moreover, the tallying authority must take great care to not leak the order of votes, to not accept repeated votes by just one voter, and to check each voter's signature.

Chapter 14
Conditions on user-specified equational theories

In Section 3.1.4, we introduced equational theories and presented some examples of their use. As a reminder, the notation

```
equations:
  EXPR1 = EXPR2
```

is used to specify equational theories in models. When defining equations, one may name function symbols, as desired, but recall that some function names are reserved for use in built-in theories, as explained in Chapter 7. These functions may not be user-defined and include: one, exp, mult, inv, DH_neutral, pmult, em, xor, zero, and TAMARIN-internal functions, like mun. For the full list, see Chapter 20.

Due to fundamental theoretical limitations, TAMARIN cannot handle arbitrary equational theories. In this chapter, we explain the conditions that must be met by equational theories such that TAMARIN can reason with them. The conditions go beyond mere syntactic ones and are nontrivial to check. But for simplicity, we start with a syntactically defined class of equational theories that TAMARIN can handle.

14.1 Subterm-convergent equational theories

We first define the notion of *subterm-convergence*: An equation is *subterm-convergent* when its right-hand side is either a strict subterm of its left-hand side or alternatively a constant. We call an equational theory *subterm-convergent* when all of its individual equations have this property, and the theory itself is convergent. To ensure convergence (meaning confluence and termination), first confluence must be checked. This means that there cannot be two different terms that one term can rewrite to. Essentially, if the left-hand sides of all equations do not overlap (technically this means that there are no *critical pairs* between them), confluence is ensured. Then, due to the subterm-convergent property of all equations, termination is achieved for free, given confluence. That is, termination is immediately obvious as constants have no further steps, and there is a decreasing measure whenever the right-hand side is a subterm.

For example, `h(f(X),Y,Z) = f(X)` is subterm-convergent, whereas `h(f(X),Y,Z) = f(Y)` is not. Note that all syntactic built-ins from Section 7.1 are subterm-convergent, as can be easily verified.

We can now define a class of equational theories that is directly supported by TAMARIN. An equational theory is directly supported when it meets two conditions:

1. it is subterm-convergent, and
2. it is syntactically disjoint from the algorithmic built-ins from Section 7.2. That is, it may not use any function symbol that is already used by an algorithmic built-in.

At a technical level, such theories are supported by TAMARIN because subterm-convergence guarantees that the conditions in the next section are met. Specifically, subterm-convergence implies that the theory has the Finite Variant Property (FVP).

Not all equations needed in practice are subterm-convergent. We will next give an example of an equation used for unblinding blinded signatures. Although it is not subterm-convergent, it can still be added to TAMARIN, as we will show.

14.2 Beyond subterm-convergence

Equational theories that are not subterm-convergent must at least be convergent (see Section 6.7) and have the finite variant property (FVP), see [36]. Unfortunately, it is nontrivial for users to check either of these, and TAMARIN does not check whether the equational theories that users give it actually have these properties.

For general theories, checking the FVP requires checking confluence, termination, and then the FVP. There are tools for checking confluence; however they often leave a set of *critical pairs* for the user to check.[1] Similarly, there are tools for checking the termination of rewriting systems. However, integrating them would be difficult, and termination is undecidable in general. Finally, for checking the FVP, there has been work on tools for this, but they have not been integrated into TAMARIN as the necessary preconditions of confluence and termination are not checked anyway. Summing up, it is the modeler's responsibility to ensure convergence and the FVP by checking both these properties themself, either by hand or using other tool support, discussed below.

Note that if the equational theory lacks either convergence or the FVP, then TAMARIN will almost surely fail to terminate. Indeed, this may even happen when loading the theory. Moreover, TAMARIN's correctness proofs rely on these properties; hence TAMARIN's results are no longer guaranteed to be correct if the equational theory used is outside of this class.

---

[1] This check cannot be automated, at least without modifying the equational theory, which a procedure like Knuth-Bendix completion would require.

14.3 Current limitations for equational theories

One example beyond subterm-convergence is that of blind signatures, which are a special kind of signature where a party can choose a value and apply a blinding function to it to hide the signature's content. This blinded value is given to a signer who signs it, without knowing the hidden value. The initial party can then unblind the signature of the blinded value and receives a signature for the original value. Although it may not be obvious why someone would sign a value they do not know, blind signatures are a useful construct. For example, this operation was used in early electronic cash proposals such as Chaum's eCash [32].

The following equational theory models blinded signatures, as just described, available in the file **EquationalTheoriesFVPblindsig.spthy**.

```
functions: true/0, pk/1, sign/2, verify/3, blind/2, unblind/2
equations:
    verify(sign(m, k), m, pk(k)) = true,
    unblind( blind(m,r),r ) = m,
    unblind( sign(blind(m,r),k),r ) = sign(m,k)
```

This contains the additional `blind` and `unblind` functions along with their defining equations. Note that the equation representing the unblinding of a blinded signature is not subterm-convergent, as the right-hand side signature `sign(m,k)` does not appear on the left-hand side, but only `sign(blind(m,r),k)` is there. However, as the equations are convergent and have the finite variant property, TAMARIN can handle them. These equations are used, for example, in some models of voting protocols [57], as well as the eCash protocol just mentioned.

As mentioned, TAMARIN does not provide direct support to check for convergence or the FVP, but there are other dedicated tools available that can help with these tasks. To check whether a given theory is convergent, i.e., terminating and confluent, and has the FVP, one may proceed by checking each of these properties individually. To check termination, tools such as AProVe [66] and the Maude termination tool MTT [60] can be used. For confluence, the Maude Church-Rosser checker can be used [35, 61], although this tool may leave the user with some manual work resolving critical pairs. Finally, after establishing that a theory satisfies convergence, one can apply methods from [63] to check that it also satisfies the FVP.

14.3 Current limitations for equational theories

In the current version of TAMARIN, available at the time of writing (TAMARIN 1.10), there are various equational theories that users may desire for their models, which cannot be used.

14.3.1 Theoretical limitations

As equational theories are required to have the finite variant property to work with TAMARIN, this rules out those theories that lack this property. One example of this is the extension of Diffie-Hellman exponentiation that supports the combination of addition and multiplication in the exponent. When one adds the expected distributivity property, there is no representation of the resulting Diffie-Hellman extension that has the FVP. This also includes more precise models of ElGamal where addition in the exponent, or similarly multiplication not in the exponent, is needed. These cannot be represented.

For homomorphic operations (which are used in e-voting protocols for example) we do not have equational theories that have the FVP and they therefore cannot be represented. This includes homomorphic encryption and the combination of operators, such as xor and pairs. Another desirable extension is that of explicit division (used, for example, in identity-based protocols) or subtraction. These cannot be supported either, as the resulting equational theories do not have the FVP.

In some cases, when a theory is desired that is, in its full generality, outside of TAMARIN's scope, one can still work with approximations thereof. For example, for better approximations of elliptic curves, compared to the built-in Diffie-Hellman theory, see [47].

14.3.2 Associative-(commutative) operators

It may be interesting to consider equational theories with a new associative-commutative (AC) symbol, like the + from multiset or ∗ from Diffie-Hellman. However, users cannot add new symbols with the property of being AC. This is due to the necessity of normal form conditions and expanded variant computation that is built-in for the existing such symbols. For function symbols that just require associativity (A), such theories do not have the FVP and hence users also cannot add them.

Chapter 15
Advanced modeling of cryptographic primitives

In the symbolic model of cryptography, and in the examples we have seen until now in this book (notably in Chapter 7), there was exactly one symbolic model for each type of cryptographic primitive, such as symmetric encryption or signing.

Most of these models originated in the early days of model checking for security protocols, and have been the de-facto standard for decades. Around 2019, due to advances in TAMARIN's support for equational reasoning, property specification, and restrictions, it became feasible to reconsider the precision of these models and develop more fine-grained symbolic models for primitives such as signatures [74], Diffie-Hellman [47], Hash functions [33], Authenticated Encryption [31], and Key Encapsulation Mechanisms [39].

This chapter draws from these research works. We first illustrate the approach on the example of digital signatures, as developed in [74].

15.1 Digital signature schemes

We first present TAMARIN's default model for digital signatures when using builtins: signing, which defines the following function symbols and equations.

```
functions: true/0, pk/1, sign/2, verify/3
equations:
    verify(sign(m, k), m, pk(k)) = true
```

This equational theory specifies four functions.

1. true/0, modeling the constant true,
2. pk/1, modeling a function that, given a private signing key, yields the corresponding public verification key,
3. sign/2, modeling the signing algorithm of the signature scheme, and

4. `verify/3`, modeling the signature verification algorithm.

The theory also specifies an equation that formalizes how these functions interact: Given a message m and a private signing key k, if we sign m with k, then the verification of the resulting signature with respect to m and the corresponding public verification key `pk(k)` will succeed, represented by `true`.

Since we have no other equations involving `verify`, other than the equation just given, this equation specifies the only way that signature verification can succeed. There is no other combination of arguments that will be successfully verified. This implies, among other things:

- a signature can be verified against the exact same message and public verification key for which it was produced, and
- the signature verification algorithm will fail when given a verification key that does not correspond to the private signing key.

This is the standard model of a digital signature, which has been widely used in many symbolic modeling approaches, as it captures the main behavior of generic signature schemes.

However, it turns out that the above two properties are not implied by standard *cryptographic* definitions of signature scheme security, such as EUF-CMA or SUF-CMA [4, 68]. In fact they do not hold for many real-world digital signature schemes such as DSA, the original version of Ed25519, or several of the submissions to the NIST process for selecting post-quantum secure signature schemes [44]. Moreover, as summarized in [74], for many real-world signature schemes, it may be possible to:

1. given a signature, generate a new key pair that can also be used to verify the signature;
2. given a signature but not its message, produce another signature on the message for a key pair that was not generated with the honest key generation algorithm but by an adversary;
3. compute weak key pairs for which a single signature can verify against multiple messages; or
4. change some bits of a signature without affecting its validity.

In contrast, other signature schemes, such as the libsodium version of Ed25519 or the post-quantum secure Crystals-Dilithium, satisfy stronger properties that prevent these behaviors.

As one might expect, these behaviors can impact a protocol's security. If we implement a protocol with a signature scheme A that does not allow these behaviors, then the protocol might meet its security properties. In contrast, if we implement it with a scheme B that allows for some of these additional behaviors, then there might be an attack.

15.1 Digital signature schemes

In [74] it was shown how we can model several different classes of signature schemes, capturing their additional, often subtle, behaviors in detail. Two main modeling approaches are possible. The first focuses on finding attacks on protocols that rely on the behaviors possible with some (but not all) specific signature schemes. The second focuses on trying to prove a protocol's security property by only relying on the minimal guarantees that all digital signature schemes should offer, corresponding to EUF-CMA. We describe each of these in the following subsections.

15.1.1 Modeling signature schemes for attack finding

When we consider signature schemes that still meet the standard cryptographic definition EUF-CMA, the following, perhaps unexpected, behaviors have been identified in the literature [8, 28, 53, 89, 99, 105]:

1. key substitution attacks,
2. re-signing,
3. colliding signatures, and
4. malleability.

We explain next how to provide more detailed TAMARIN models for signature schemes for each of these classes. These can then be applied to any given TAMARIN protocol model that uses a concrete signature scheme. If an attack is found on a protocol property, this means that it is unsafe to use a signature scheme that allows for the additional behaviors modeled.

In Table 15.1 we give an overview of some common digital signature schemes and their associated TAMARIN models, which allow for finding attacks on protocols that exploit these additional, EUF-CMA conform, behaviors of the signature scheme. We provide the detailed TAMARIN models for each of these behaviors below. For more information on the advanced properties of these and other digital signature schemes, including post-quantum secure schemes, see [29, 44, 74].

The first three models below assume that the signatures built-in is already loaded, i.e., the following line is already present in the specification.

```
builtins: signing
```

The fourth model slightly deviates from the interface of the built-in signing, as it uses an additional argument in the signing function.

Here we only describe the models. Examples of concrete protocols that are vulnerable to each of these attack classes, and how these models help analyze them, are given in [74].

Signature scheme	Tamarin model
RSA-PKCSv1.5	{CEO/DEOgen [99], Re-signing [75], Colliding[†], Malleability [93]}
RSA-PSS	{CEO/DEOgen [99], Re-signing [82], Colliding[†], Malleability[†]}
DSA	{CEO/DEOgen [99], Re-signing[†], Colliding [110]}
ECDSA-FreeBP	{CEO/DEOgen [28], Re-signing[†], Colliding [105], Malleability [105]}
ECDSA-FixedBP	{Re-signing[†], Colliding [105], Malleability [105]}
Ed25519	{Colliding [26], Malleability [26]}
Ed25519-IETF	{Colliding [26]}

Table 15.1: Concrete digital signature schemes, and the corresponding TAMARIN models that model them more accurately [74]. For each case where a model is used and an attack is found, the citation refers to a known algorithm to compute the corresponding keys. In some cases (marked with [†]) no citation is given because there is no known algorithm to compute the corresponding keys; however the absence of the corresponding behavior is unproven, and hence it is prudent to assume it is possible and model the behavior.

15.1.1.1 Key/message substitution attacks

For most signature schemes, there is no explicit key or message binding. Namely, for any given signature, there may be more than one verification key and/or message that it can be successfully verified against. This type of behavior, or its absence, is known in the literature under various names, including Digital Signature with Key Selection (DSKS) and Exclusive Ownership. Here we use the exclusive ownership terminology, for which there exist two main variants: constructive (CEO) and destructive ownership (DEO). For signature schemes that allow these behaviors, we add the following functions, equations, and rule to the specification.

```
functions: CEOgen/1
equations:
  verify(sign(m, sk), m, pk(CEOgen(sign(m, sk)))) = true

functions: DEOgen/2 [private]
equations:
  verify(sign(m1, sk), m2, pk(DEOgen(m2,sign(m1, sk)))) = true

rule make_DEO_sk:
  [ In( m2,sign(m1,sk) ) ]
  --[ _restrict(not(m1=m2)) ]->
  [ Out( DEOgen(m2,sign(m1,sk)) ) ]
```

The CEOgen function represents an algorithm that can generate new private keys (or key pairs) that can also be used to verify a given signature. Similarly, the DEOgen function represents an algorithm that can generate new private keys (or key pairs) that can be used to verify a given signature with respect to a different message. We cannot directly model the fact that this must be a different message at the equational theory level as TAMARIN does not support conditional equations. Hence, we make DEOgen a

15.1 Digital signature schemes

private function, and only give the adversary access to this function through a rule make_DEO_sk. For rules, we can enforce that the message is different by adding an embedded restriction.

As a concrete protocol example, the MAC-based variant of the Station-to-Station (STS) protocol, which was proposed in [52], can be proven correct under the strongest signature scheme model. However, if we enable the CEOgen rule, TAMARIN automatically finds the attack that was found by manual inspection in [28].

15.1.1.2 Re-signing

Intuitively, one might expect that if someone can produce a signature on a message m with their signing key sk, they must know m. In practice, this is not the case for most common signature schemes. The underlying reason is that most signature schemes, as a first step, hash the message m to produce h(m), and subsequently use this hash in the signing function. If the signature reveals h(m), then the adversary can simply repeat the subsequent signing steps with its own signing key sk, producing a valid signature on m without actually knowing m.

For signature schemes where this is possible, we can simply add a rule that allows the adversary to "re-sign". Concretely, given a signature sign(m,sk1), but not the message m, the following rule allows the adversary to use any signing key sk2 that it knows to produce another signature on m.

```
rule: ReSign
  [ In( sign(m,sk1), sk2 ) ] -->
  [ Out( sign(m,sk2) ) ]
```

Given a concrete signature scheme, we can use Table 15.1 to determine whether to include the above rule in the protocol model.

15.1.1.3 Colliding signatures

Intuitively, one might expect for a given signature and public key that there exists at most one message for which the signature verifies. However, this is not the case for all schemes: for several schemes, it is possible for the adversary to produce a signature and public key that verify two messages of its choice. This was first shown in [105] for ECDSA. Similar behavior is possible for the original version of Ed25519 [26, 29], where for some signatures and public keys, verification passes for any message with high probability.

We model the worst case behavior, in which there are key pairs whose signatures verify with *any* message. We define an abstract function weak that models the signing keys of these pairs. We add an equation that models that signatures produced by this signing key for any message m1 can also be verified by the corresponding public key for any other message m2.

```
functions: weak/1
equations: verify(sign(m1,weak(x)),m2,pk(weak(x))) = true
```

15.1.1.4 Malleability

Finally, one natural distinguishing property between different provably secure signature schemes is *malleability*: if a signature successfully verifies, can we be sure that it was not changed? The basic cryptographic security definition for signatures, EUF-CMA, does not preclude that a signature can be modified and still verify successfully. Many standard signature schemes, including ECDSA and EdDSA, are malleable and allow such modifications.

We thus would like to model that given a signature, an adversary can produce a second signature that also verifies for the same message and public key. However, in our previous models, we used the built-in signature definition, in which signing had two arguments, and thus for any given message and signing key there was exactly one signature. In order to express that there can be multiple signatures for a given message and signing key, we must add an additional argument to the signing function that abstractly models the difference.

```
functions: verify/3, sign/3, pk/1, true/0
equations: verify(sign(m, r, sk), m, pk(sk)) = true
```

In practice, when signing messages in a protocol, we can instantiate the second argument r with any value, e.g., a constant, because verification ignores r and we only consider the fact that it is possible to produce a *different* signature for the same message and signing key. We can model this by an explicit mangle function.

```
functions: mangle/2
equations: mangle(sign(m,r,sk),repnew) = sign(m,repnew,sk)
```

This model gives the adversary the ability to modify signatures that continue to verify with the same message and key.

15.1.2 Modeling signature schemes for proving security

In the detailed signature models just presented, we focused on modeling specific additional behaviors, which is useful for finding attacks on protocols. However, we are usually more interested in proving that a protocol meets its properties, i.e., by relying on the properties of its underlying building blocks, such as a signature scheme, the protocol satisfies its properties.

As mentioned previously, the minimal security property that all provably secure signature schemes must meet is called EUF-CMA: Existential Unforgeability under Chosen Message Attacks. Informally stated, this property requires that for all verification keys produced by the scheme's key generation algorithm, the adversary

15.1 Digital signature schemes

cannot (with non-negligible probability) forge a signature that verifies using that key unless it knows the corresponding signing key. Additionally, to be useful, we require signature schemes to be correct: given a key pair produced by the key generation algorithm, if a signature was produced by the signing algorithm for the signing key, it should also verify with the pair's verification key. Note that correctness is not actually formally required by EUF-CMA.

We make two observations about the combination of EUF-CMA and correctness. First, these definitions do not guarantee any unique binding: given a signature, we cannot be sure that it can only be verified with respect to one message or one verification key. Second, the definitions do not specify what the result of the verification algorithm should be when given a verification key that was not produced by the key generation algorithm. In reality, the verifier typically cannot tell how verification keys were produced, and the verifier may be invoked with verification keys produced by an adversary. Thus, if we only know that a signature scheme is proven to be EUF-CMA and correct, we do not know what its verify algorithm will output for maliciously produced verification keys. So verify is *underspecified*.

In order to prove the security of a protocol that uses an EUF-CMA secure signature scheme, we would therefore like to model this underspecified verification function. In the modeling of the primitives we have seen so far, we have been using function symbols and equational theories to model, e.g., the verification function. In such models, the equational theories fully determine the binding properties and function outputs. These are therefore not suitable for modeling underspecified functions.

Modeling underspecified functions

Fortunately, we can model underspecified functions by taking another approach. Instead of using a function symbol in the term algebra and specifying additional relations through equational theories, we can instead use unrelated variables, and define their relationship using restrictions (see also Section 5.10.2 for details on restrictions). For example, consider the following model that produces traces with A and B facts.

```
theory UnderspecifiedExample begin

functions: h/1

rule HashPublic_Explicit:
  [ In($X) ]
--[ A(h($X))]->
  []

rule HashPublic_Restriction:
  [ In($X), In(Y) ]
--[ B(Y), _restrict( Y = h($X) ) ]->
  []

lemma ExplicitOnlyHashes:
```

```
    "All Y #i. A(Y)@i ==> Ex X. Y=h(X)"

lemma RestrictionOnlyHashes:
    "All Y #i. B(Y)@i ==> Ex X. Y=h(X)"

end
```

When either of the facts A or B occurs in a trace, its argument is the hash of a term. This is stated by the two lemmas, both of which are easily proved. The full file is available at **UnderspecifiedExample.spthy**. In the case of A, this holds because of the explicit constructor in the rule. In contrast, if we ignore the restriction in the second rule, B's argument could be *any* term that the adversary can produce. The purpose of the restriction in the rule `HashPublic_Restriction` is to bind $X and Y in such a way that in all traces that meet the restriction, $X acts as the "input" of an abstract function, and Y acts as the "output". In this sense, the model underspecifies the intended behavior before the restriction is applied, and we use the restriction to narrow the set of traces down to the desired one.

We can use this general approach to underspecify functions. For example, we can use restrictions to specify outputs for a subset of the domain, and leave the other outputs underspecified. This is exactly the approach we take to model an accurate signature verification function based on only its proven EUF-CMA guarantees. When verifying using an honestly-generated verification key, we will use the restriction to ensure it produces the expected output. In contrast, when verifying a signature using a key that was not honestly generated (e.g., because the adversary generated it) we will not specify whether signature verification returns `true` or `false`. However, in all cases, we will require that verification is deterministic, i.e., verify always returns the same result for the same inputs.

Concretely, this means that in TAMARIN models we will not use an abstract signature verification function, but will instead use actions and restrictions to model an underspecified verification function. In particular, we will introduce a `Verified` action that has four main arguments: the signature, the message we are verifying the signature against, the public key we are verifying the signature with, and the result of the verification algorithm (`true` or `false`). The full file is available at **acme-02-SVS.spthy**.

There is one technicality that we must solve: to formulate our restrictions, we must refer to the original message m and the public key pk(k) of the key used to produce the signature sign(m,r,k). A natural way to solve this would be to use pattern matching in the restrictions. Unfortunately, this approach does not work here because, as we will see later, the sign function will be reducible to model malleability. This implies that sign cannot directly occur in property specifications or restrictions, as explained in Section 5.1. We thus move extraction to the actions of the rules, with the help of two auxiliary functions e1 and e3 that extract the first (message) and third (signing key) argument from a signature, respectively.

```
functions: e1/1 [private]
functions: e3/1 [private]
```

15.1 Digital signature schemes

```
equations: e1(sign(x,y,z)) = x
equations: e3(sign(x,y,z)) = z
```

Note that we mark these functions as private. Recall from Section 3.1.2 that they cannot be used by the adversary, and we do not use them in the protocol, but they are only used to formulate the restrictions.

The final `Verified(sig,sigm,sigpk,verm,verpk,result)` action has six parameters: the first three `sig`, `sigm`, and `sigpk` correspond to the signature and the message and the public key it was intended to be verified with, `verm` and `verpk` denote the message and the public key we are verifying against, and `result` denotes the outcome.

In each rule in which a signature must be verified, we then annotate this with the following action.

```
Verified(sig,e1(sig),pk(e3(sig)),verm,verpk,true)
```

The second and third arguments here perform the intended extraction from the signature, which works around the technical limitations on the restrictions.

As mentioned before, EUF-CMA only considers guarantees for honestly generated public keys, whereas parties that verify signatures may not know how the public keys they use were generated. To model this distinction, we modify the PKI rules that we previously saw in Section 5.5 to include an `Honest` action that marks honestly generated keys.

```
rule Register_pk:
  [ Fr(~ltk) ]
  --[ Honest(pk(~ltk)) ]->
  [ !Ltk($A, ~ltk), !Pk($A, pk(~ltk)), Out(pk(~ltk)) ]
```

We can now add our restrictions that are direct representations of the correctness and EUF-CMA security guarantees for signature schemes. We take these restrictions directly from [74].

Correctness: This requirement follows directly from the requirement that an honestly generated public key, an honestly generated signature, and the correct message must verify as true.

```
Correctness:
  All sig, m, pk, t1, t2.
    Honest(pk)@t1 &
    Verified (sig, m, pk, m, pk, false)@t2
      ==> false
```

NoForgery: Here we state that if a signature verification does succeed against an honest public key, then the signature must have been honestly produced.

```
NoForgery:
  All sig, sigm, sigpk, verm, verpk, t1, t2.
    Honest(verpk)@t1 &
    Verified (sig, sigm, sigpk, verm, verpk, true)@t2
      ==> sigm = verm & sigpk = verpk
```

Consistency: We require that the verification procedure is a deterministic function. Namely, we specify that repeated calls to verify will always return a consistent answer.

```
Consistency :
  All sig, sigm, sigpk, verm, verpk, result1, result2, t1, t2.
    Verified(sig, sigm, sigpk, verm, verpk, result1)@t1 &
    Verified(sig, sigm, sigpk, verm, verpk, result2)@t2
      ==> result1 = result2
```

The preceding model now allows arbitrary verification behavior as long as the requirements for EUF-CMA are met. This allows for all key/message substitution attacks as well as colliding signatures. However, it does not cover malleability or re-signing, which are orthogonal aspects because they rely on the possibility of producing *different* signatures from existing ones, rather than unexpected verification behavior. Thus, for the full verification model, we additionally include the function symbols and equations for the malleability (Section 15.1.1.4) and re-signing (Section 15.1.1.2) behaviors.

Note that subsequent research in the computational setting, such as [29, 44], has formalized stronger computational properties for signature schemes. These can be used to formally prove the absence of the behaviors from Section 15.1.1 for a given signature scheme.

15.2 Advanced models of other cryptographic primitives

In this section, we briefly highlight some other cryptographic primitives for which more detailed symbolic primitives than the usual symbolic ones exist. We do not provide all details, but just the high-level ideas, and we refer the reader to the individual papers for the full modeling details.

15.2.1 Diffie-Hellman primitives, elliptic curves, and non-prime order groups

Diffie-Hellman exponentiation and its elliptic-curve counterpart are common building blocks of many security protocols, and involve operations on elements of a group of prime order. In computational analyses and proofs of such protocols, it is common to assume that all received values (for example, a Diffie-Hellman public key) are elements of the prime order group. We described the basic Diffie-Hellman built-in that captures such a model in Section 7.2.3.

However, in actual protocol implementations, such group elements are encoded in bitstrings, and not all received bitstrings may decode to a group element. In theory, the solution is simple: when receiving a bitstring, the recipient should check that

15.2 Other primitives

this corresponds to a group element, and reject the bitstring otherwise. Depending on the concrete group, such checks can require modular exponentiation, which is considered costly by implementers, and the benefit of performing these checks is not always clear to them. Because of this, many protocol implementations do not perform such checks, which allows adversaries to insert non-group elements. Any attacks that would result from such insertions are not covered by a basic Diffie-Hellman model or computational analyses that assume all values are group elements.

In [47], Cremers and Jackson explored the impact of different group encodings and embeddings on protocol security, and how to model these in TAMARIN. This leads to a range of different models depending on the specific properties of the Diffie-Hellman embedding or the properties of the actual elliptic curve that is used in an implementation.

The underlying technical idea is to represent elements of complex groups as triplets of the form (t, h, g^y). Here, t identifies the specific group to cater for models that involve operations on multiple distinct groups. Next, h and g^y represent the decomposition of a group element into the (non-prime order) cogroup element h and prime order subgroup element g^y. We introduce a constant gid for which we have that $gid^x = gid$ for all x. Given a group identifier t, this allows one to express the identity element as (t, gid, gid), regular prime order group elements as (t, gid, g^x), cogroup elements as (t, h, gid), and other supergroup elements as (t, h, g^x).

The full modeling details are given in [47]. To give a rough idea though, we show one aspect of the more advanced model. The previously mentioned triplets are encapsulated in an abstract function `ele`. Then, depending on the group details, we add different annotations and restrictions to the model. For example, to model nearly-prime order groups, each time a rule uses an exponentiation of an element to the power of y, we annotate the rule with an action fact `Raised` as follows.

```
rule Operate:
[ In(ele(t,oldh,n), State(y), In(newh)) ]
--[ Raised(t,oldh,newh,y) ]->
[ Out(ele(t,newh,n^y)) ]
```

In the `Operate` rule, the adversary can determine – by providing `newh` – what the outcome of the exponentiation is in the cogroup dimension. We use this to model all possible behaviors for the cogroup, and effectively allow the adversary to choose the cogroup details. However, the cogroup details do not change midway during an execution. To capture this, we add a consistency restriction that captures that whatever the adversary chooses, will have to be consistent within the trace.

```
restriction Consistency:
  "∀ t s r1 r2 y #i #j .
    Raised(t,s,r1,y)@i & Raised(t,s,r2,y)@j ==> r1 =r2"
```

Furthermore, for elements of the prime order subgroup (which are identified by the `gid` in the cogroup position of `ele`), the adversary cannot choose the result of the exponentiation to be outside of the prime order subgroup. We add a restriction to ensure that all exponentiations within the prime order subgroup result in elements of that subgroup.

```
restriction Identity :
  "∀ t newh y #i .
    Raised(t, gid, newh, y)@i ==> newh = gid"
```

For full details, see [47]. Using such more detailed models for specific group or curve choices enables TAMARIN to analyze a wider class of attacks for the protocol.

15.2.2 Hash functions

Hash functions are a core building block of security protocols. In the symbolic setting, as we have seen so far, hash functions are simply function symbols without any additional properties or equations specified. By default, this basic model means that the functions are considered to be collision-resistant (h(x)=h(y) ==> x=y), preimage-resistant (one cannot learn x from h(x), sometimes also called non-invertible), and the only way to construct h(x) is by knowing x and applying h.

The basic symbolic model is very similar to the computational definition of a so-called Random Oracle, also known as the ROM (Random Oracle Model) [25]. Informally, in the ROM, hash functions are modeled as oracles that given an input x produce a random output y, and when queried again with the same x return the same y. Thus, in this model, there is no connection between the input and output, except that the oracle behaves deterministically. In the majority of computational protocol proofs, hash functions are modeled as random oracles.

However, many deployed hash functions allow for more behaviors than either of these two idealized models. There are two main types of discrepancies. First, the idealized models assume that the only way to construct h(x) is by knowing x and applying h. However, this is not true for common hash functions, such as most versions of SHA-2, which are based on the Merkle-Damgård construction [90]. For example, in SHA-2, the input is split into fixed-size blocks, and (ignoring padding) h(b1,b2) is internally computed as h(h(b1),b2). This means that an adversary who knows h(b1) and b2, but not b1, can still compute h(b1,b2)[1]. This behavior is also known as a *length-extension attack*, as the adversary can extend a hash, for which it does not know the input, to produce a hash of any extension of this input. While length extension attacks are possible for many hash functions, they are neither possible in the basic symbolic model nor in the Random Oracle Model.

The second discrepancy is due to the way in which hash functions are commonly broken in practice: it is not the case that a hash function is considered either "completely secure" or "entirely broken." Rather, hash functions might still be pre-image resistant even if they are no longer considered collision-resistant. For example, SHA-1 is currently still considered to be pre-image resistant, but not collision resistant.

---

[1] In practice, this is complicated by the concrete padding scheme used, but we omit the details here.

15.2 Other primitives

Furthermore, if a hash function is no longer considered collision resistant, there are subtle variants of the attacks that may be possible depending on the concrete hash function. For example, for some hash functions, one might be able to construct a chosen-prefix collision, but not a chosen-suffix collision. Whether such a hash function is then still suitable for use in a protocol, depends on the protocol details.

In [33], the authors systematically analyze these discrepancies and create a family of symbolic models that can accurately capture various concrete hash functions or the properties that were proven for them. This leads to a hierarchy of hash function models, where the basic symbolic model is the strongest (most idealized) version. This allows them to analyze a range of protocols with TAMARIN and automatically discover known and new attacks, including the classical length-extension attack on the Flickr authentication protocol.

For example, one can model length-extension attacks by providing a rule of the following form, using pattern matching.

```
rule length-extension:
  [ In( h(b1) ), In( b2 ) ]
  -->
  [ Out( h(<b1,b2>) )]
```

If the adversary knows any hash value of the form h(b1) (even when it does not know b1), it can use this rule to create the hash of b1,b2.

We refer the reader to [33] for full details on the family of hash function models.

15.2.3 Authenticated Encryption with Associated Data

Real-world symmetric encryption schemes, such as AES, protect against an adversary trying to learn the message that was encrypted. However, they do not provide authentication: if we provide a random string to the AES decryption algorithm instead of a real ciphertext, it will not fail, but instead produce a (random looking) output. If we additionally want authentication, we could add a Message Authentication Code (MAC).

In many real-world scenarios, we often want both secrecy and authentication. For this purpose, a dedicated cryptographic definition exists, called Authenticated Encryption with Associated Data (AEAD). At its core, it provides secrecy and authentication for its input. Additionally, it may include "associated data" which is data that will also be authenticated, but not kept secret. For example, the associated data part may be used to identify a particular session at a recipient, such that the recipient can determine the right session and decryption key to use before starting decryption. In practice, modern protocols often do not use symmetric encryption primitives, but instead use AEAD constructions.

In [31], the authors explore the complex space of computational definitions for AEAD schemes. There are surprisingly many different computational security definitions for AEADs, which arise from the various key-binding and message-binding possibilities. Additionally, AEADs typically need some unique input per invocation (such as a nonce or a counter), which might be re-used in practical applications due to, e.g., memory or session resets, and fine-grained computational security definitions have been proposed to cover all these possibilities. [31] systematically explores these to arrive at a family of symbolic TAMARIN models for AEAD functions. Thus, given a protocol with a specific AEAD function, the modeler can pick the best symbolic model, and use this to get accurate analysis results.

In this case, the underlying idea is to extend the syntax from symmetric encryption (where enc has arity 2) to a more fine-grained model. We write enc(k,n,h,m) to represent the authenticated encryption of the message m with key k, where n is the explicit nonce (randomness) used in the encryption, and h is the (optional) auxiliary data that is only authenticated, but not encrypted. We can then model a new decryption function, as well as an extraction function for the associated data h that does not require knowledge of the key k.

Once this additional information is in place, we can then model the properties or weaknesses of different real-world AEADs by adding specific rules, equations, or function symbols. For example, to model an AEAD that is vulnerable to so-called nonce-reuse attacks, we add the following rule.

```
rule nonce_reuse:
[ In( enc(k,n,h1,m1)),
  In( enc(k,n,h2,m2)) ]
  --[ _restrict( not(h1=h2 & m1=m2) ) ]->
[ Out(k) ]
```

This rule models that if the adversary observes two ciphertexts that were the result of encrypting two different h,m pairs with the same nonce n and key k, then this leaks information about the key k. In our symbolic setting, we model the consequence of this information leakage as the adversary learning the key k.

For full details we refer the reader to [31].

Chapter 16
Reducing Proof-Construction Time

In this chapter, we describe the options available when verification fails to terminate, or simply takes longer than desired. In particular, we present different ways that the modeler can influence TAMARIN's reasoning heuristics to improve TAMARIN's efficiency and reduce the time it needs to construct proofs. Chapter 11 explains the overall workflows and provides some hints on which option is appropriate for which case.

During each analysis step, TAMARIN applies one of its proof rules, for example to refine a dependency graph or introduce case distinctions. In most cases, multiple rules are applicable and the rule chosen can make a difference in how quickly TAMARIN finds a proof, or whether it even finds a proof at all. TAMARIN uses heuristics to select among the applicable rules, as discussed in Section 6.4. While TAMARIN offers several built-in general-purpose heuristics (Section 6.6), users may wish to modify these heuristics based on the specifics of their model or even the current proof state. There are several ways to do this, which we consider next.

16.1 Changing priorities of facts using label prefixes

The easiest way to modify the order in which TAMARIN resolves certain facts is through their naming: one can change priorities by having their names start with L_ or F_. Facts starting with F_ are prioritized over others, i.e., solved *first*, whereas those prefixed by L_ are deprioritized, i.e., solved *last*, after all other facts. These prefixes do not change the ordering of these facts with respect to non-fact constraints.

For example, consider the case where we have an initiator process modeled by three rules I1, I2, and I3, which hand over state information using `State_I1` (between I1 and I2) and `State_I2` (between I2 and I3). Suppose that TAMARIN reaches a proof state where it has both an open constraint `State_I2` from an I3 rule instance, and some other constraint fact, say State_R2, from a responder process. In this case, the heuristics will determine which of these constraints will be solved first.

We can prioritize solving the initiator's preceding step by renaming the State_I2 facts in the file by F_State_I2. If TAMARIN now needs to choose between solving these facts, F_State_I2 will be prioritized over State_R2. Deprioritization proceeds analogously.

Essentially, this overrides locally the order in which state fact sources are explored by the heuristic. By exploring first the sources of a specific fact leading to, say, an initial key generation, often helps TAMARIN learn more about the overall system state. For example, exploring the previous state may yield information about whether keys were honestly generated, or not. This may lead to a direct contradiction to a property being proven, and thus closes a branch of the proof. Analogously, the L_ can be used to avoid, as much as possible, exploring the sources of other facts, for example, when this would cause large case distinctions.

Note that the prefix is considered to be part of the fact's name: F_State() and State() are two different facts and cannot be unified. Therefore, one must globally rename the fact in the model. Thus, when using this approach, one cannot control priorities in a fine-grained fashion. For example, one cannot prioritize a fact only in the premise of some of the rules that use this fact. The next section presents an approach that allows for more fine-grained control.

16.2 Changing priorities using + and - modifiers

The previous mechanism uses L_ and F_ to change the priorities of some facts across an entire model, namely, in each rule where the fact occurs. In some cases, we would like more fine-grained control, for example, to change the priorities of facts just within the context of some particular rules.

The modifier + (respectively -) modifies a fact in a rule to be prioritized (respectively to be delayed after all other facts) when this fact arises as a constraint from an instance of this specific rule. The annotation is given in square brackets after the fact name, when used within a given rule. For example, the fact T(x) has the normal priority, T(x)[+] would be solved with high priority, and T(x)[-] would be deprioritized.

This annotation can not only be used for state facts, but also for action facts when they appear in rules. Additionally, action facts in lemmas can be annotated, which then applies to all actions created from these lemmas in the exploration of a proof attempt.

Note that unlike the L_ and F_ prefixes, the minus and plus annotations are not part of the fact name. Hence facts with this annotation can be unified with other facts with the same name without annotations.

16.3 Tactics

Tactics are useful when one requires even more control over TAMARIN's heuristics. Compared to fact label prefixes and annotations just described, they have two main benefits. First, they offer far more flexibility to prioritize or de-prioritize proof methods that satisfy simple logical expressions built from pattern matching and fact name matching. Second, whereas the previous approaches affected the heuristics for all lemmas in the theory, users can specify which tactic should be applied on a lemma by lemma basis.

Intuitively, tactics work as follows. Users first specify from which base heuristic's order they want to start, by selecting one of TAMARIN's existing heuristics. They then use a tactic's predicates to modify the base order by specifying which proof methods should be prioritized or de-prioritized.

A TAMARIN theory can contain multiple tactics. Each tactic has a user-defined name, an optional pre-sorting heuristic, followed by a list of (de)priorization tactic formulas. The concrete syntax for these is the following:

- A tactic starts with the keyword `tactic:` followed by the tactic's name.

- This is optionally followed by the keyword `presort:` with an argument specifying one of the built-in heuristics, like s, c, i, etc., as defined in Section 6.6. This heuristic will be used to pre-sort proof methods before the tactic's prioritization is applied. By default, if no `presort` is specified, TAMARIN uses the s ("smart") heuristics to pre-sort the applicable proof methods.

- Zero or more `prio:` specifications, followed by zero or more `deprio:` specifications, and at least one of either of these must be given. Each `prio:` and `deprio:` specification is optionally followed by a {smallest} post-sorting indicator, and must include a tactic formula that selects proof methods to be prioritized or deprioritized. Tactic formulas are built from tactic predicates and the logical operators | ("or"), & ("and"), and not, with their standard interpretation.

There are two main tactic predicates that can be used in tactic formulas:

- `isFactName`: This predicate takes a string argument, which is interpreted as a fact name. The predicate holds if the proof method is a premise fact or an action fact whose name is equal to the argument.

- `regex`: This predicate takes a string argument, which is interpreted as a regular expression, using the Haskell PCRE (Perl Compatible Regular Expressions) syntax. The argument is matched against the string representation of the proof method.[1] The predicate holds if there is a match.

TAMARIN uses tactics to prioritize the proof methods its tries. Given a tactic, the proof methods that satisfy the first `prio` formula are given the highest priority, and

---

[1] The string representation of a proof method is visible in the GUI as well as the proof output, which can help to specify the correct regular expressions.

the proof methods that satisfy the last deprio formula are given the lowest priority. If multiple proof methods satisfy a formula, the original prioritization order between them is maintained, unless the {smallest} indicator is specified, in which case they are sorted by increasing length of their string representation. Proof methods that do not satisfy any of these formulas are left in their current order. Thus, after applying the tactic, the proof methods are reordered: first, the proof methods that satisfy the prio formulas, then proof methods that do not satisfy any formula in their original order, and then the proof methods that satisfy the deprio formulas.

The following snippet illustrates the syntax.

```
tactic: nameOfTactic
presort: heu
prio:
  PrioFormula1
prio:
  ...
prio {smallest}:
  PrioFormulaN
deprio:
  DeprioFormula1
deprio:
  ...
deprio:
  DeprioFormulaM
```

This tactic results in the following behavior:

1. All applicable proof methods are first sorted using the heuristic heu.

2. The applicable proof methods are returned in the following order:

    a. All applicable proof methods for which PrioFormula1 holds.

    b. ...

    c. All applicable proof methods for which PrioFormulaN holds, sorted by increasing length of their string representation.

    d. All applicable proof methods for which none of the prio or deprio formulas hold.

    e. All applicable proof methods for which DeprioFormula1 holds.

    f. ...

    g. All applicable proof methods for which DePrioFormulaM holds.

In the graphical user interface mode, all tactics contained in the current theory can also be inspected using the Tactic(s) link in the left-pane menu.

Tactics can be used like any other heuristic by specifying the tactic's name between braces, e.g., {nameOfTactic}. In practice, this can be used in three main ways.

First, when using TAMARIN on the command line, we can specify:

16.3 Tactics

```
tamarin-prover --heuristic={nameOfTactic} file.spthy
```

Second, we can specify a heuristic at the start of the theory, using:

```
heuristic: {nameOfTactic}
```

The previous two approaches apply to all lemmas in a theory. The third approach allows one to specify a different heuristic or tactic on a per-lemma basis. For example:

```
lemma test [heuristic={nameOfTactic}]: ...
```

By specifying multiple tactics within a single theory, we may use a different tactic for each lemma.

An example tactic

As a concrete example, we present a model for which the default smart heuristic fails to terminate, the consecutive heuristic C terminates in 162 steps, and our oracle terminates in just 10 steps. Our example is intentionally artificial and just for illustrative purposes. The input theory, available in full at **SourceOfUniquenessTactic.spthy**, starts with

```
theory SourceOfUniqueness begin

heuristic: {uniqueness}
```

where the included heuristic option {uniqueness} selects the tactic uniqueness, which is specified later in the theory, as the default heuristic for the theory. The rest of the theory includes the built-in symmetric encryption, and contains three rules. The first two rules each generate an encrypted term, and the third rule receives these terms. We intentionally add some complexity to this example by adding a restriction that forces multiple extra rule instances, and an ordering on action facts.

```
builtins: symmetric-encryption

rule generatecomplicated:
 [ In(x), Fr(~key) ]
 --[ Complicated(x) ]->
 [ Out(senc(x,~key)), ReceiverKeyComplicated(~key) ]

rule generatesimple:
 [ Fr(~xsimple), Fr(~key) ]
 --[ SimpleUnique(~xsimple) ]->
 [ Out(senc(~xsimple,~key)), ReceiverKeySimple(~key) ]

rule receive:
 [ ReceiverKeyComplicated(keycomplicated)
 , In(senc(xcomplicated,keycomplicated))
 , ReceiverKeySimple(keysimple)
 , In(senc(xsimple,keysimple))
 ]
 --[ Unique(<xcomplicated,xsimple>) ]->
 [ ]
```

```
// this restriction artificially complicates all occurrences of Complicated(x)
restriction complicate:
  "All x #i. Complicated(x)@i
    ==> (Ex y #j. Complicated(y)@j & #j < #i)
      | (Ex y #j. SimpleUnique(y)@j & #j < #i)"

lemma uniqueness:
  "All #i #j x. Unique(x)@i & Unique(x)@j ==> #i=#j"
```

Observe that, in this example, the xsimple argument of the receive rule is unique because every key in a (linear) ReceiverKeySimple fact is fresh and uniquely identifies a correspond encryption with a fresh xsimple. Thus, the lemma uniqueness intuitively holds: xsimple is a fresh value that is encrypted and can only be used once as the key required is fresh, and in a linear state fact.

Proving this lemma is difficult for TAMARIN and the default smart heuristic fails since it explores an ever-growing state. The consecutive heuristic C succeeds in 162 steps. In contrast, our tactic succeeds in 10 steps. Our tactic solves the ReceiverKeySimple state facts first, followed by solving encryptions of the form senc(xsimple) and senc(~xsimple), and lastly it solves KU(~key), before just using the default:

```
tactic: uniqueness
presort: C
prio:
    isFactName "ReceiverKeySimple"
prio:
    regex "senc\(xsimple" | regex "senc\(~xsimple"
prio: {smallest}
    regex "KU\( ~key"
```

The command tamarin-prover --prove SourceOfUniquenessTactic.spthy verifies the property in 10 steps.

16.4 Oracles

Oracles are programs that modify the order in which TAMARIN applies proof steps by modifying TAMARIN's baseline heuristic, similar to tactics. In contrast to tactics, which are part of TAMARIN's syntax, oracles are external scripts called by TAMARIN.

The oracle is used when the heuristic o or O is specified, e.g., through the command-line options --heuristic=o or --heuristic=O. The oracle's filename can be specified using the --oraclename=ORACLEFILE option. If no such filename is given, TAMARIN uses the default oracle filename ./oracle. Alternatively, the oracle program can be specified on a per-lemma basis, e.g., lemma lname[heuristic=O "ORACLEFILE"].

The difference between o and O is the pre-sorting of the proof methods provided to the oracle. O is the recommended heuristic, as it pre-sorts using the default smart

16.4 Oracles

heuristic s. That means that, as long as the oracle itself makes no changes to the ordering of proof steps, these steps are then ordered as by the default smart heuristic. The o heuristic does not pre-sort and leaves proof methods in the order they appear in the system, similar to the consecutive C heuristic, which returns proof steps in the order that their facts were created.

The oracle program receives from TAMARIN as input the list of possible next proof methods for the current constraint system, and it outputs to TAMARIN a sequence of numbers that is a reordering of some subset of the proof methods, as identified by their number in the input. The numbers output to TAMARIN are given the highest priority, in the order listed. Moreover, all remaining proof methods that the oracle does not list are appended at the end, in their original order. As a result, an oracle returning the empty sequence results in the default smart heuristics ordering (when using O) or in the order they appear in the constraint system (when using o). Note that an oracle program influences the heuristics, but has no effect on the correctness of TAMARIN's results as it cannot (accidentally or otherwise) suppress applicable proof methods.

To clarify this, suppose TAMARIN provides 5 possible proof steps, and the oracle decides that number 3 is best, and number 2 is second best, and it does not care about the rest. Then the oracle would return the sequence 3, 2 to TAMARIN, and the final ordering will be 3, 2, 1, 4, 5. As TAMARIN always applies the first highest-priority proof step, only the first step returned is really important. However, sorting all of them helps when inspecting a proof state in the GUI manually and is anyway a side-effect of giving a generic reordering of as many proof steps as one has identified in the oracle. The actual format is as follows. Proof methods match the regular expression (+) : (. +) where (+) is the method's index, and (. +) is the method. These methods have the same format as those visible in the GUI, without the solve(. . .) around it. The oracle calls are visible on the command line between START INPUT, START OUTPUT, and END Oracle call.

Consider again the SourceOfUniqueness example from the previous section. Instead of using a tactic, one can also use an oracle as follows, using the file at **SourceOfUniqueness.spthy**.

```
theory SourceOfUniqueness begin

heuristic: o "SourceOfUniqueness.oracle"
```

Here, the included heuristic option o selects the oracle option (purposely the one based on C, the consecutive heuristic), so it need not be passed on the command line later. The filename that follows names the oracle file to be used, which also does not need to be passed as argument. The remainder of the theory is the same as above.

```
builtins: symmetric-encryption

rule generatecomplicated:
 [ In(x), Fr(~key) ]
 --[ Complicated(x) ]->
 [ Out(senc(x,~key)), ReceiverKeyComplicated(~key) ]
```

```
rule generatesimple:
[ Fr(~xsimple), Fr(~key) ]
--[ Simpleunique(~xsimple) ]->
[ Out(senc(~xsimple,~key)), ReceiverKeySimple(~key) ]

rule receive:
[ ReceiverKeyComplicated(keycomplicated)
, In(senc(xcomplicated,keycomplicated))
, ReceiverKeySimple(keysimple)
, In(senc(xsimple,keysimple))
]
--[ Unique(<xcomplicated,xsimple>) ]->
[ ]

// artificially complicate occurrences of the event Complicated(x)
restriction complicate:
"All x #i. Complicated(x)@i
  ==> (Ex y #j. Complicated(y)@j & #j < #i)
    | (Ex y #j. Simpleunique(y)@j & #j < #i)"

lemma uniqueness:
"All #i #j x. Unique(x)@i & Unique(x)@j ==> #i=#j"

end
```

Similarly to the tactic from the previous section, the oracle prioritizes solving the ReceiverKeySimple state facts, followed by solving encryptions of the form senc(xsimple) and senc(~xsimple), and lastly KU(~key), before just using the default.

We can then use the following oracle script. The filename should be SourceOfUniqueness.oracle, and the file is available at **SourceOfUniqueness.oracle**, as specified in the theory, and the user must ensure that the script can be executed from the command line. On most systems this requires setting the script to be an executable file, and checking that python3 is present and can be found through /usr/bin/env.

```
#!/usr/bin/env python3

import re
import os
import sys
debug = True

lines = sys.stdin.readlines()
lemma = sys.argv[1]

# INPUT:
# - lines contain a list of "%i:goal" where "%i" is the index of the goal
# - lemma contain the name of the lemma under scrutiny
# OUTPUT:
# - (on stdout) a list of ordered index separated by EOL

rank = []        # list of list of goals, main list is ordered by priority
maxPrio = 110
```

16.4 Oracles

```
for i in range(0,maxPrio):
  rank.append([])

if lemma == "uniqueness":
  for line in lines:
    num = line.split(':')[0]
    if re.match('.*ReceiverKeySimple.*', line):
      rank[90].append(num)
    elif re.match('.*senc\(xsimple.*', line) or \
         re.match('.*senc\(~xsimple.*', line):
      rank[80].append(num)
    elif re.match('.*KU\( ~key.*', line):
      rank[50].append(num)
# an optional catch-all rank can be used, but is not required
#    else:
#      rank[40].append(num)

else:
  exit(0)

# Ordering all goals by ranking (higher first)
for listGoals in reversed(rank):
  for goal in listGoals:
    sys.stderr.write(goal)
    print(goal)
```

With the theory and oracle as above, the command tamarin-prover --prove SourceOfUniqueness.spthy verifies the property in just 10 steps.

One can use this oracle as a template, and simply add different lemma names to the one lemma listed here, or write separate cases below for a different ordering for other lemmas. This makes it easy to have specialized oracles per lemma, or allow multiple lemmas to use the same oracle steps.

One benefit of oracles over tactics is that oracles can be changed on the fly, for example, while exploring a proof in interactive mode, as they are external to the TAMARIN theory. In contrast, when changing a tactic, one needs to reload the theory. Oracles are more restricted than tactics for pre-sorting proof methods: oracles only allow pre-sorting with s or C, whereas tactics allow pre-sorting with any heuristic.

Note that the use of an oracle introduces an external dependency, namely, TAMARIN must be able to find and execute the oracle executable or script with the right interpreter. Specifying oracle paths and script interpreters is both system-dependent and release-dependent: oracles that work on one system can fail on other systems or after system updates. In practice, this can often be easily fixed. We describe some common error messages around the use of oracles and potential solutions in Section 11.4.

Chapter 17
Analyzing Protocol Families

TAMARIN's standard usage is to analyze the design of a given security protocol or perhaps accompany the evolution of that design, checking the protocol after each modification. But TAMARIN can also be used to compare protocols and even analyze families of related protocols. This can be used to determine the differences in the protocols' strengths with respect to the properties they meet, the adversaries they resist, or even where in the protocol run particular properties are established. Such an analysis supports protocol implementers in choosing the protocol variant that best matches the guarantees they need for their specific use case. For example, for resource-constrained devices one might be willing to sacrifice some security guarantees for less computation or communication. Alternatively one might trade off privacy for security or vice versa.

In [67], Girol, Hirschi, Sasse, Jackson, Cremers, and Basin used TAMARIN to analyze a large family of protocols, namely the protocols from the Noise Protocol Framework [98]. In this chapter, we use this as an example to show how one can analyze such a family in TAMARIN and the benefits of doing so.

17.1 Noise Protocol Framework

The Noise Protocol Framework [98] by Trevor Perrin describes a large set of security protocols, where keys used for authenticated encryption are computed from different combinations of Diffie-Hellman key exchanges, using varying combinations of static (long-term) and ephemeral (short-term) keys. The main motivation for the framework is that for different use cases, key distribution scenarios, and threat models, one might require a specific variant of a Diffie-Hellman key exchange. In this chapter, we will refer to such a Diffie-Hellman key exchange variant as a handshake. The Noise framework includes a high-level specification language that can be used to specify arbitrarily many different protocols, and the Noise Framework documentation provides 53 examples of specific protocols specified this way. These protocols

```
NN:                     KK:
    -> e                     -> s
    <- e, ee                 <- s
                             ...
                             -> e, es, ss
                             <- e, ee, se
```

Fig. 17.1: Two Noise handshakes, NN and KK, described in the high-level Noise language.

cover numerous scenarios ranging from handshakes between unidentified parties to handshakes between parties having pre-shared static asymmetric and symmetric keys. Some of these protocols are well known and are used in practice. For example, one such protocol is the key exchange protocol underlying Wireguard [55], which is a Virtual Private Network (VPN) that is part of the Linux kernel and used in multiple commercial VPN applications.

Let us briefly review how Noise protocols are defined, following the account from [67]. The protocols are constructed from a small set of primitives that we have: a Diffie-Hellman group, a hash function, a Key Derivation Function (KDF) (Section 12.2.2), and an Encryption with Associated Data (AEAD) cipher (Section 15.2.3). Each handshake is described by a pattern with two parts, pre-messages and messages. The former describe setup assumptions, like the keys that parties share using some public key infrastructure. The latter describes the operations that each party performs when sending or receiving handshake messages. Note that parties can have different kinds of keys that they use in the handshake: each party has a long-term static public-private key pair and/or an ephemeral public-private key pair.

Noise has its own custom language for describing and naming handshakes. We omit details and just illustrate it on two examples taken from [98]. Figure 17.1 provides examples in Noise syntax and Figure 17.2 gives the corresponding protocols in a more conventional MSC syntax. Note that we have used colors, which are not part of Noise's syntax, to suggest how parts of the two figures correspond to each other.

The first Noise handshake is named NN. In Noise's handshake names, 'N' indicates that no pre-shared static key is available, so 'NN' indicates this for both partners. This describes an unauthenticated Diffie-Hellman handshake built from two message patterns. In this handshake, there are no pre-messages sent, and hence only the second part is specified.

In the first message, the initiator generates an ephemeral private key e, and sends its ephemeral public key g^e, indicated by the key token e in the first message pattern. Each message sent ends with a payload, protected using AEAD under the best available key (not illustrated in the Noise syntax, this happens implicitly at the end of all message patterns). Here, p_1 is sent in the clear. In the second message, the responder generates and sends his own ephemeral key $g^{e'}$, indicated by token e in the second message pattern. The token ee means that when processing the second message, both parties

17.1 Noise Protocol Framework

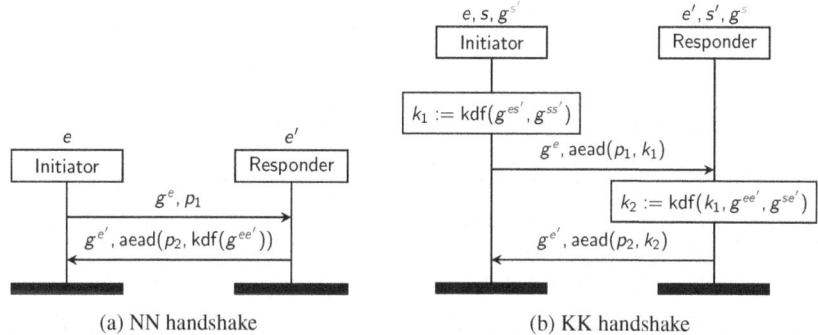

Fig. 17.2: MSCs for the handshakes of Figure 17.1. Here e, e' (respectively s, s') are ephemeral (respectively static) private keys and the p_i are payloads exchanged during the handshake. We name the parties along with the data they initially know. In transport mode, payloads are encrypted with the last key material used in the handshake. For legibility, we omitted the associated data of AEAD encryptions, which roughly corresponds to the hash of all preceding sent messages along with the public keys in pre-messages.

now derive a Diffie-Hellman term from their respective ephemeral keys. So, after the second message, the initiator knows its private key e and the responder's public key $g^{e'}$ and she can thus compute $g^{ee'}$. Symmetrically, the responder knows g^e and e' and can compute $g^{ee'} = (g^e)^{e'}$. The resulting shared value $g^{ee'}$ is used by both parties to construct a shared secret, which is the initial *current key*, and is used to protect payloads.

The second example, 'KK' is a Noise handshake for a kind of authenticated Diffie-Hellman key exchange, where the parties combine different keys using a KDF. Here 'K' means that a party already knows its communication partner's static public key. The ellipsis (...) indicates the end of the first part (pre-messages) and the start of the second part (handshake messages).

There are two pre-messages that contain the same static key token s, indicating that both parties already know their communication partner's static public key before starting the handshake. Namely, the initiator (respectively responder) knows its static private key s (respectively s') and its partner's static public key $g^{s'}$ (respectively g^s). In the first handshake message, the initiator

1. generates a fresh e (for key token e),
2. initializes the current symmetric key as empty,
3. computes the DH term $g^{es'}$ (DH token es) and combines it with the current symmetric key that can now be used,

4. computes the DH term $g^{ss'}$ (DH token ss) and again combines it with the current symmetric key (the resulting value is denoted as k_1 in Figure 17.2), and

5. sends g^e together with the first payload protected using AEAD under the current symmetric key k_1 with the transcript of all messages exchanged so far as additional data.

When receiving the corresponding message (i.e., the pair $\langle g^e, c \rangle$), where c is the encrypted payload), the responder performs the same computations and obtains the symmetric key k_1 and can therefore decrypt c.

For the second message, the responder generates and sends $g^{e'}$ (key token e), computes two DH terms corresponding to ee and se, and obtains the symmetric key k_2 accordingly, which importantly includes k_1 in the key derivation. Similarly, the message ends with the second payload protected by AEAD with the key k_2 and the hash of all previous communication steps as additional data.

Finally, message transport can start where all payloads are protected with AEAD using a derivative of the final symmetric key k_2 and empty additional data.

17.2 Analysis approach

Given that the Noise specification language can specify an arbitrary number of different protocols, it is desirable to support their systematic analysis and comparison. This is practically relevant for helping practitioners to determine which Noise protocol they should use for a given scenario and initial key distribution. It is also theoretically relevant. Since Noise offers an unbounded number of protocols, one may wonder if they are all useful or whether some Noise protocols are subsumed by others?

Carrying out a systematic comparison of the Noise protocols is, however, quite challenging. To start with, one must deal with the sheer number of protocols under consideration and analyze all of them with respect to different adversary models. Afterwards, one must make sense of the results, e.g., by comparing or visualizing them in some systematic way. Finally, for most classical protocols, one usually considers the security guarantees established after the entire protocol has executed. However, as we have seen already, for the Noise protocols, different messages may be sent encrypted with different keys and therefore come with different security guarantees. Hence a finer-grained analysis is necessary concerning when different guarantees are established.

Let us expand on this last point. The Noise protocols are designed for use in a variety of real-world settings with differing requirements. One such requirement is to minimize latency for message transmission: participants would like to send and receive messages as early as possible. For example, protocols may send messages during the early phases of the protocol's execution, where payloads are encrypted just using preliminary keys with relatively weak security guarantees. This is because

17.2 Analysis approach

sufficient keying material has yet to be exchanged to generate a session key with stronger security guarantees (where "stronger" means it can resist adversaries with more compromise capabilities). In summary, messages sent early on may satisfy security guarantees different from those sent later in the protocol's execution.

All of the above can be captured with appropriate lemmas, but this requires many lemmas. Namely, to characterize and compare the different protocols, one must prove (or find counterexamples to) a large set of lemmas, each of which makes a statement about the security properties of a Noise protocol after some combination of messages has been exchanged. Moreover, we also consider these properties with respect to a hierarchy of different adversaries, with different compromise capabilities, and we evaluate their respective impact on the protocol's resulting security properties. The combination of these factors, namely

- the Noise protocol considered,
- different combinations of properties checked (e.g., secrecy, authenticity, anonymity),
- the steps where the properties are checked, and
- the set of (atomic) adversary capabilities considered

leads to hundreds of thousands of *proof obligations* just for the 53 documented Noise protocols, where a proof obligation is a particular choice for each of these factors. Tackling this combinatorial explosion requires an efficient way to automatically and uniformly handle all of these relevant problems.

To tackle this problem, we built a special purpose tool, called Vacarme (meaning "lots of noise" in French) that uses TAMARIN as a subroutine for protocol classification. Given a Noise protocol, for a set of adversary capabilities (e.g., key compromise) and standard security goals (e.g., secrecy), Vacarme generates lemmas involving all combinations of the goals holding under the different subsets of adversary capabilities. These lemmas are quite detailed in that they also attribute each message in a Noise protocol with the maximal security guarantees it achieves in the form of the strongest threat models under which confidentiality, authentication, or anonymity holds. The precise statement of the lemmas and the details behind the analysis are rather technical and may be found in [67]. Here we restrict ourself to some remarks.

Proving each individual lemma builds directly on the following topics, covered earlier in this book:

- how to specify protocols in general;
- the built-in Diffie-Hellman equational theory (Section 3.1.4);
- how to specify security properties (Chapter 5) and threat modeling (Section 10.3) with a lattice of threat models; and
- how to use oracles and tactics.

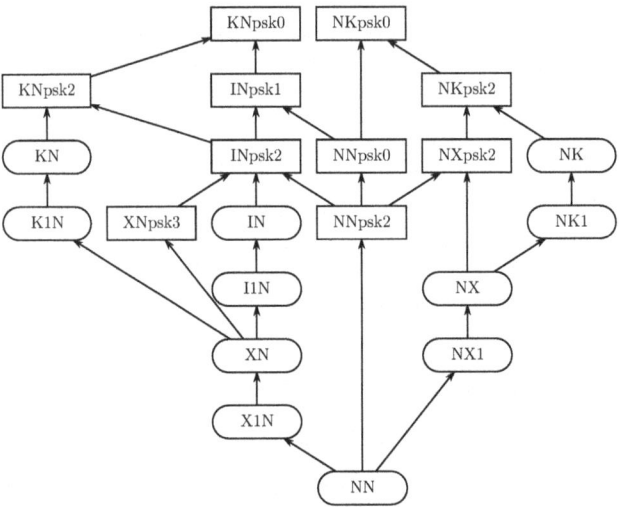

Fig. 17.3: Hierarchy of secrecy and agreement guarantees for the Noise protocols that do not require both the initiator and the recipient to have a static key. Here psk stands for the existence of a pre-shared symmetric key and is appended to a pattern name. A psk followed by a number delays the use of the psk until that message. Finally, psk0 indicates the use of the psk in the initial message. For ease of reading, variants with a psk are shown in rectangles, while those without psk are given in rounded rectangles.

The last point is particularly relevant as analyzing a very large set of lemmas requires full automation.

Even with automation, the only way to make the analysis feasible is to reduce the number of lemmas as much as possible, in a sound way. For this, Vacarme employs a dynamic filtering approach that reduced the number of TAMARIN lemmas analyzed to ca. 150,000. To do this, Vacarme not only starts TAMARIN runs and collects the results, it decides which other evaluations are to be given to TAMARIN, and which ones are unnecessary due to the properties and adversary capabilities under consideration. For example, if in one invocation TAMARIN determines that a given property fails, then Vacarme can immediately conclude that all logically stronger properties also fail, without rerunning TAMARIN. Also, a property proven with respect to one adversary model will hold for other adversary models with fewer capabilities. For this analysis, Vacarme carries out a generalized binary search over the space of adversary capabilities.

17.3 Example results for Noise

We give an example of one of the results of Vacarme's analysis in Figure 17.3. Vacarme outputs not only detailed analysis results, but it also generates protocol security hierarchies (see also [11]) like the one shown in the figure. The security hierarchy orders protocols for achieving both secrecy and agreement; however anonymity is not a goal, as including anonymity would lead to a completely different ordering. The protocols are all built from the Noise handshake patterns. Protocols lower in the hierarchy, like NN, are weaker than protocols higher in the hierarchy, like KN, for example. Also, we see that protocol patterns using a pre-shared symmetric key (with psk in the name) are stronger than those without. This is maybe not surprising, but visualizing these relationships helps provide a detailed understanding of the patterns.

This kind of large-scale analysis can provide fundamental insights into a particular design space, well beyond what is feasible by human analysis alone, thereby supporting designers in their protocol development and selection process. The analysis produced by Vacarme yielded fine-grained results: for each Noise protocol and each of its protocol steps, it established the strongest adversary under which it is secure. Moreover, the analysis showed that some Noise protocols offer clearly better security properties than others, while other protocols are simply incomparable.

Part VI
Outlook

Chapter 18
Impact in Practice

In this book, we have provided guidance on using TAMARIN and have given illustrations of its use. In this chapter, we turn to the question of how TAMARIN can be used on substantial, real-world protocols and, in particular, our experience with such large-scale verification efforts and the associated benefits.

The examples we give, TLS, 5G Authenticated Key Agreement, and EMV, are substantial in terms of both their specifications' size and complexity, and their practical relevance. TLS underlies most secure communication in the Internet between clients (computer, browsers, etc.) and servers, 5G is the predominant protocol used for cellular communication, and EMV governs most electronic payments made using credit and debit cards. Given the size of these specifications, we will only highlight what was accomplished and the lessons learned, and we provide pointers to the literature for further details.

Note that we presented 5G Authenticated Key Agreement previously, in Chapter 12. The emphasis there was on providing a case study on how to model and analyze a protocol of realistic size in TAMARIN. Here we focus on the practical relevance of this analysis.

18.1 TLS 1.3

Our first success story concerns the Transport Layer Security (TLS) protocol, which is probably the most used security protocol, world over. It underlies all secure internet connections that use HTTPS, where it represents the 'S', and many other applications that use TLS as their transport protocol. In the web setting, TLS is typically used to establish a unilaterally authenticated secure channel between a client, such as a web browser, and a server hosting a website or service. The TLS protocol is an Internet Engineering Task Force (IETF) standard, initially based on the Secure Sockets Layer

(SSL) protocol. It has evolved considerably since its first release as TLS 1.0 in 1999, leading to TLS 1.3 defined in RFC 8446 [101] in 2018.

The core TLS protocol is a key exchange protocol that supports numerous modes and options. For example, TLS contains a negotiation mechanism to agree on cipher suites and options such as mutual or unilateral authentication. Moreover, each option has many alternatives. The key exchange protocol produces symmetric keys for the transport layer protocol, which uses a symmetric cipher to encrypt and authenticate message payloads.

In addition to this core functionality, TLS also supports starting connections based on shared symmetric keys, resumption and rekeying mechanisms, out-of-band authentication, and even mechanisms to upgrade unilaterally authenticated connections to mutually authenticated ones. Furthermore, new versions of TLS must be backwards compatible with previous versions, while ensuring that parties agree to use the most secure option that they both support, even in the presence of a network adversary attempting so-called downgrade attacks.

18.1.1 TAMARIN analysis

TLS versions prior to 1.3 had been developed by engineers with little academic involvement. These older TLS versions were also plagued by numerous security vulnerabilities. When the development of TLS 1.3 started, the IETF reached out to several academic teams to help with its development and to ensure that they would achieve the most secure TLS protocol yet.

As part of this wider effort during TLS 1.3's development, Cremers, Horvat, Hoyland, Scott, and van der Merwe built several TAMARIN models of TLS 1.3 [45, 46]. This was a challenging process. Many aspects of the standard were initially underspecified and were rapidly changing. Moreover, the protocol's complexity was at the limits of what TAMARIN could handle at the time.

During the standard's development, which involved around 30 draft revisions, we incrementally built models of the standard as it evolved. The effort involved was several person-months, the majority of which were dedicated to understanding the details of the TLS 1.3 standard under development.

During our analysis of the transition between the 10th and 11th draft of the TLS 1.3 standard, we found an attack with TAMARIN on the proposed implementation of the "delayed authentication" mechanism to upgrade unilateral connections. The attack applies to clients and servers that use client certificates, and combines three modes: the initial key exchange, the resumption mechanism, and the delayed authentication mode. The attack allows malicious server owners (e.g., a web forum) to impersonate their clients towards other servers (e.g., the client's bank), violating the main goal of the delayed authentication mechanism [46].

18.1.2 Impact and lessons learned

The TAMARIN analysis directly helped prevent a broken mechanism for delayed authentication from being standardized and implemented. It also helped to clarify the exact guarantees for mutual agreement on the status of connections and it helped those involved in its standardization to gain confidence in the security of the final TLS 1.3 standard [101].

When TAMARIN found the attack described above, the individual modes had already been carefully scrutinized by designers and cryptographers. The attack was missed because it depends on subtle interactions between the modes. Notably, the attack involves at least 18 network messages, uses three modes, and involves the adversary feeding random values from one connection into the other. Such interactions are extremely difficult to find by human inspection.

Our interaction with IETF was very constructive. The standard was amended with protocol changes on the basis of our work, thereby avoiding the broken mechanism. We performed an in-depth analysis of the near-final standard, showing that it satisfies its main security properties [45]. Additionally, our analysis revealed several subtle behaviors and helped clarify the exact guarantees that the standard provides, which were then documented in the final standard.

18.2 5G-AKA

Our second success story revolves around the 5G-AKA protocol. We already described this case study in Chapter 12, but now repeat the key points, and show the TAMARIN features used. 5G is the latest generation of mobile communication technology, designed for higher data transmission, lower latency, and improved security. The 5G standard runs over thousands of pages of documentation. The most critical component for its security is 5G-AKA, the 5G key agreement protocol that is used by the mobile *user device* (namely its SIM card) and the customer's *home network* (the service provider one has a contract with) to agree on a shared key. All other keys are derived from this shared key. Hence the protocol's correctness is critical for the user's data security, the authenticity of messages and calls they receive, the connections they start, and for billing based on usage (call time or data).

5G-AKA is complex! Its complexity stems not just from the specification's size, but also the different contexts where the protocol can be used. For example, when roaming, the user device may connect to mobile networks (called *serving networks*) different from the service provider. The protocol then connects three parties, rather than just two, where only two parties, the user device and home network, initially share secrets. Other complexities arise due to technological and backwards compatibility constraints. For example, since older SIM cards lack the ability to create randomness, the protocol uses a counter to prevent replay attacks rather than fresh randomness.

However, to derive shared keys, both parties' counters must be equal and this requires a resynchronization sub-protocol that is used whenever messages are lost (e.g., in mobile scenarios when one travels through tunnels).

Some of the authors of this book had the opportunity of working with a company that was part of the industrial standardization body 3GPP, responsible for standardizing 5G-AKA. This collaboration gave us access to both the 5G specification and 5G specialists, and our focus was on 3GPP's TS 33.501 document. We built initial models for versions leading up to and including v0.7.1 with promising preliminary results. Unfortunately flaws were introduced in the following version, which we discovered using TAMARIN, and these were subsequently fixed prior to the final version, due to our disclosure. The resulting model with successful verification of properties (except privacy) was then for the protocol from v15.1.0 of Release 15 of TS 33.501. Additionally, we uncovered privacy problems that could not be fixed in the 5G standard as doing so would require a substantial protocol redesign.

18.2.1 TAMARIN analysis

5G-AKA was verified using TAMARIN by Basin, Dreier, Hirschi, Radomirović, Sasse, and Stettler [23]. This started with an in-depth reading of the relevant protocol documents, as well as discussions with those involved in its standardization. From there, we extracted an abstract version of the protocol, which we converted into an executable, analyzable TAMARIN model. This involved, among other challenges, handling complications that arose in the resynchronization protocol, the modeling of the sequence numbers for that, and the use of exclusive-or operations described in Chapter 14.

The majority of the effort spent was the several person-months needed to understand the specification; the time needed to subsequently formalize the resulting model was relatively short. Some additional person-months were needed for the verification, in particular writing proof strategies to help automate it. Along the way, we found flaws, which we then reported to the 3GPP. With one exception, these flaws were subsequently fixed in the standard. The final verification result is with respect to the corrected version.

The flaw in 5G that was not repairable concerned privacy, as previously mentioned. The privacy of the user's identity is violated for the 5G-AKA protocol by a fairly simple replay attack that exploits the resynchronization protocol. A further iteration (perhaps 6G?) should eliminate counter-based mechanisms to solve this problem. Nevertheless, 5G-AKA is still an improvement over 4G, as in 5G the adversary must be active and send messages to check if a specific user is nearby. In contrast, in 4G a passive adversary can simply listen to radio traffic and learn all the identifiers of users who are near its attack device using so-called IMSI catchers.

Follow-up work by Cremers and Dehnel-Wild [42] adapted the models to incorporate a more fine-grained view of the internal parties. This analysis revealed several unstated assumptions in the standard. If those assumptions are not upheld, flaws such as the incorrect attribution of customers for billing purposes are again possible.

18.2.2 Impact and lessons learned

The practical impact of our TAMARIN analysis [23] is that multiple mistakes in 5G-AKA were discovered and corrected. As a result, the protocol now standardized provides appropriate authentication and secrecy properties, which was not the case before. The most critical vulnerability found with TAMARIN, which was also fixed, was a protocol error that allowed the adversary to induce confusion between users for the home network. For example, the data or time that are used and should be billed to customer A could be incorrectly billed to another customer B. This disclosure led the authors and the publication [23] to be admitted to the "GSMA Mobile Security Research Hall of Fame" as CVD-2018 CVD#0012. The disclosure process to this industry consortium was unfortunately less straightforward than for TLS 1.3, where the IETF explicitly solicited academic input. Despite quickly finding the problem after the update from v0.7.1 and providing a fix that was ultimately used, it took months to get the problem fixed.

5G-AKA demonstrates that complex, large-scale industry protocols are directly within TAMARIN's scope. However, having a direct interface to the standardization body would help to better integrate TAMARIN's usage into the standardization process. As is currently still the case, the authors had to use an external vulnerability disclosure process. Hence it took a long time (over 6 months) after the information was provided before the proposed fix was finally applied, despite multiple intermediate versions being released. Furthermore, co-development of the standards and proofs would accelerate the feedback and improvement process as we were only able to analyze each version after it was made public.

18.3 EMV

Our third success story concerns EMV, which is the international standard for credit and debit card payments. This standard is used worldwide for payments with payment cards such as Mastercard, Visa, and American Express. Over 80% of all global payments use EMV and up to 98% in many European countries. For payments, each user has an agreement with a bank, receives a payment card, and can use it at merchants. This offers convenience, availability, and hopefully security. EMV supports both a contact version, where the card is inserted into a payment terminal (where a PIN is often needed), and a contactless version, where the card is simply held near the reader. A variation of contactless payments is when a mobile phone simulates a linked physical card.

EMV's complexity comes from the large number of parties supporting the standard, backwards compatibility with the billions of cards that were previously issued and are difficult to change, and the large number of terminals used at merchants, where change is also very slow. This means that legacy support must be considered throughout the protocol.

As EMV is the worldwide standard in card payments, it is an attractive attack target. Verifying its security claims is thus desirable, especially given that it is a complex protocol, no formal analysis was previously done prior to our analysis with TAMARIN, and older versions of the protocol exhibited numerous design weaknesses. Hence, one may expect that a formal analysis of EMV would uncover further issues requiring improvements.

18.3.1 TAMARIN analysis

Basin, Sasse, and Toro-Pozo used TAMARIN to analyze EMV [24]. Our formalization again started with a careful reading of the technical documentation. As we did not have access to experts who were involved in the protocol's development and standardization, as in the 5G case, we instead cross-checked our understanding using real-world transaction logs. In this way, we could create a model that matched both the documentation and actual usage. This modeling process was time-consuming and took over six person-months of work. Independently, we developed an app to check that any issues we found using TAMARIN would actually be exploitable in realistic scenarios.

The models developed [24] included the contact and contactless modes, and many different sub-protocols (required due to the aforementioned backwards compatibility), as well as the differences between the protocol used by Visa and the one used by Mastercard. For the contact setting, the complexity stems from the 24 different, in parts interworking, protocols and choices such as online or offline mode, with or without PIN, different encryptions of the PIN, etc. These include three major categories, SDA, DDA, and CDA, referring to the possible data authentication methods, which result in very different security properties. The protocols also use a wide range of cryptographic machinery including message authentication codes, signatures, exclusive-or, and certificates.

In the contactless case, there are 16 different versions of the protocol, split between the Visa and Mastercard groups. TAMARIN found novel attacks in the contactless setting against Visa's protocol due to the lack of authentication on the parameter stating whether or not a PIN must be entered for high-value transactions. This attack enabled us to bypass the PIN on transactions with Visa cards above the threshold that requires a PIN, which is, for example, typically 50 Euros in European countries.

18.3 EMV

We went further and developed and modeled fixes for this vulnerability and used TAMARIN to prove that the fixes suffice to protect card transactions by enforcing PIN use. In additional follow-up work by Basin, Sasse, and Toro-Pozo [18], we found using TAMARIN that Mastercard cards are vulnerable as well. This is due to a confusion attack whereby the datagrams sent by the Visa protocol and Mastercard protocol are interchangeable by a man-in-the-middle, which we also demonstrated in practice with our app. We extended our TAMARIN model to allow a mismatch between the payment network brand and card issuer brand, resulting in another 16 models, split between the Visa and Mastercard protocols. We again proposed fixes. However, during the disclosure process, Mastercard was able to activate another layer of detection in their payment network that provided an alternative way to eliminate the attack on Mastercard cards, which was effective immediately.

Our analysis of EMV built on the following topics, covered earlier in this book:

- how to specify a protocol in general;
- how to combine built-in and user-defined equational theories (Section 3.1.4);
- how to specify security properties (Chapter 5) and threat modeling (Section 10.3);
- how to use channels (Section 10.4; and
- the use of oracles (Section 16.4).

Our objective was to analyze all the 40 different versions (24 for the contact case and 16 for the contactless case) in a manageable way that is less error-prone than manually writing 40 models. To accomplish this, we generated the actual models from two base models: one for the contact case and one for the contactless case. This generation was done external to TAMARIN, using Makefiles. For every property of interest, our Makefile selects which of the 40 possible flows will actually be checked. Note that analyzing a property on all flows simultaneously would result in either everything being secure (which is not the case here) or TAMARIN returning the first found attack. In the latter case, this information is too coarse-grained and we therefore analyzed the different configurations independently. This determines, for each configuration, whether it is secure or can be attacked.

18.3.2 Impact and lessons learned

The work on EMV provides yet another example of how TAMARIN can be used to find attacks on a substantial, important, real-world protocol. The attacks discovered on EMV are based on subtle flaws that were buried in the standard for years. Moreover, we demonstrated that the attacks are practically feasible by exploiting the design flaws to conduct high-value transactions without using the card's PIN. As a side remark, for these attacks we used our own cards, paying for the purchased goods so as to avoid defrauding any merchant or bank.

Finding flaws in protocol designs is itself only part of the solution. The responsible parties and standardization bodies must also be convinced of their relevance if they are to be sufficiently motivated to actually fix their protocols. Unfortunately, and to our surprise, even with strong evidence produced by exhibiting the attacks on actual payment cards, and showing that the attacks are practical, not all vendors were willing to take the required actions.

18.4 Summary

These examples illustrate that tools for security protocol analysis have come a long way. We have advanced far beyond simple protocols where Alice authenticates Bob to substantial real-world protocols like those described in this chapter. The scaling has been in terms of the size, scope, and complexity of the protocols, as well as the complexity of the adversary model, the properties considered, and the comprehensiveness of the analysis. The real-world impact has been considerable: TAMARIN's use has progressed beyond the academic user community, and is now also embraced by numerous companies working on both proprietary protocols and public standards.

This scaling has been enabled by progress on numerous fronts. Algorithmic advances in computing with logical constraints and new algorithms for establishing observational equivalence have increased both the scope and size of protocols as well as the properties that TAMARIN can handle. This progress has been driven by increasingly challenging case studies, providing feedback on TAMARIN's limitations and priorities for improvements. At the same time, the success stories have raised the bar in terms of complexity and impact, further driving progress. Finally, although security protocol verification tools originated in the Formal Methods community, continued interaction with the cryptography community has helped to improve the level of detail that can now be captured in the protocol models.

There still remains much work ahead. From the technical perspective, pushing scalability even further remains a challenge. Possibilities here include improved automation using more intelligent and easily programmable proof strategies, support for an even greater range of cryptographic primitives, and enabling the reuse of proofs. Further work is also needed to increase TAMARIN's accessibility, including improvements to its user interface and better documentation. We hope this book will contribute to the latter.

References

[1] Abadi, M., Blanchet, B., Fournet, C.: The Applied Pi Calculus: Mobile values, new names, and secure communication. J. ACM **65**(1), 1:1–1:41 (2018). DOI 10.1145/3127586. URL https://doi.org/10.1145/3127586

[2] Abadi, M., Rogaway, P.: Reconciling two views of cryptography (the computational soundness of formal encryption). J. Cryptol. **20**(3), 395 (2007)

[3] Alur, R., Henzinger, T.A., Vardi, M.Y.: Theory in practice for system design and verification. ACM SIGLOG News **2**(1), 46–51 (2015). DOI 10.1145/2728816.2728827. URL https://doi.org/10.1145/2728816.2728827

[4] An, J.H., Dodis, Y., Rabin, T.: On the security of joint signature and encryption. Cryptology ePrint Archive, Paper 2002/046 (2002). URL https://eprint.iacr.org/2002/046. https://eprint.iacr.org/2002/046

[5] Arquint, L., Wolf, F.A., Lallemand, J., Sasse, R., Sprenger, C., Wiesner, S.N., Basin, D.A., Müller, P.: Sound verification of security protocols: From design to interoperable implementations. In: 44th IEEE Symposium on Security and Privacy, SP 2023, San Francisco, CA, USA, May 21-25, 2023, pp. 1077–1093. IEEE (2023). DOI 10.1109/SP46215.2023.10179325. URL https://doi.org/10.1109/SP46215.2023.10179325

[6] Baader, F., Nipkow, T.: Term Rewriting and All That. Cambridge University Press (1998). DOI 10.1017/CBO9781139172752

[7] Backes, M., Dreier, J., Kremer, S., Künnemann, R.: A novel approach for reasoning about liveness in cryptographic protocols and its application to fair exchange. In: 2017 IEEE European Symposium on Security and Privacy, EuroS&P 2017, Paris, France, April 26-28, 2017, pp. 76–91. IEEE (2017). DOI 10.1109/EUROSP.2017.12. URL https://doi.org/10.1109/EuroSP.2017.12

[8] Baek, J., Kim, K.: Remarks on the unknown key share attacks. IEICE Transactions on Fundamentals of Electronics, Communications and Computer Sciences **83**(12), 2766–2769 (2000)

[9] Baloglu, S., Bursuc, S., Mauw, S., Pang, J.: Provably improving election verifiability in Belenios. In: Electronic Voting - 6th International Joint Conference, E-Vote-ID 2021, Virtual Event, October 5-8, 2021, Proceedings, *Lecture Notes in Computer Science*, vol. 12900, pp. 1–16. Springer (2021). DOI 10.1007/978-3-030-86942-7_1. URL https://doi.org/10.1007/978-3-030-86942-7_1

[10] Barbosa, M., Barthe, G., Bhargavan, K., Blanchet, B., Cremers, C., Liao, K., Parno, B.: Sok: Computer-aided cryptography. In: SP, pp. 777–795. IEEE (2021)

[11] Basin, D., Cremers, C.: Know your enemy: Compromising adversaries in protocol analysis. ACM Trans. Inf. Syst. Secur. **17**(2), 7:1–7:31 (2014). DOI 10.1145/2658996. URL http://doi.acm.org/10.1145/2658996

[12] Basin, D., Cremers, C., Dreier, J., Sasse, R.: Tamarin book and supplementary material, including spthy files. https://tamarin-prover.com/book/

[13] Basin, D., Cremers, C., Kim, T.H., Perrig, A., Sasse, R., Szalachowski, P.: Design, analysis, and implementation of ARPKI: an attack resilient public-key infrastructure. IEEE Transactions on Dependable and Secure Computing **PP, Issue: 99**(3), 393–408 (2016). Http://dx.doi.org/10.1109/TDSC.2016.2601610

[14] Basin, D., Dreier, J., Hirschi, L., Radomirovic, S., Sasse, R., Stettler, V.: A formal analysis of 5G authentication. In: Proceedings of the 2018 ACM SIGSAC Conference on Computer and Communications Security, CCS '18, p. 1383–1396. Association for Computing Machinery, New York, NY, USA (2018). DOI 10.1145/3243734.3243846. URL https://doi.org/10.1145/3243734.3243846

[15] Basin, D., Dreier, J., Sasse, R.: Automated symbolic proofs of observational equivalence. In: Proceedings of the 2015 ACM SIGSAC Conference on Computer and Communications Security, pp. 1144–1155. ACM (2015). DOI 10.1145/2810103.2813662. URL http://doi.acm.org/10.1145/2810103.2813662

[16] Basin, D., Keller, M., Radomirović, S., Sasse, R.: Alice and Bob Meet Equational Theories, pp. 160–180. Springer International Publishing, Cham (2015). DOI 10.1007/978-3-319-23165-5_7. URL https://doi.org/10.1007/978-3-319-23165-5_7

[17] Basin, D., Radomirovic, S., Schmid, L.: Alethea: A provably secure random sample voting protocol. In: 31st IEEE Computer Security Foundations Symposium, CSF 2018, Oxford, United Kingdom, July 9-12, 2018, pp. 283–297 (2018). DOI 10.1109/CSF.2018.00028. URL https://doi.org/10.1109/CSF.2018.00028

[18] Basin, D., Sasse, R., Toro-Pozo, J.: Card brand mixup attack: Bypassing the PIN in non-Visa cards by using them for Visa transactions. In: 30th USENIX

Security Symposium (USENIX Security 21). USENIX Association (2021). URL https://www.usenix.org/conference/usenixsecurity21/presentation/basin

[19] Basin, D.A., Cremers, C., Horvat, M.: Actor key compromise: Consequences and countermeasures. In: CSF, pp. 244–258. IEEE Computer Society (2014)

[20] Basin, D.A., Cremers, C., Kim, T.H., Perrig, A., Sasse, R., Szalachowski, P.: ARPKI: attack resilient public-key infrastructure. In: Proceedings of the 2014 ACM SIGSAC Conference on Computer and Communications Security, Scottsdale, AZ, USA, November 3-7, 2014, pp. 382–393. ACM (2014). DOI 10.1145/2660267.2660298. URL https://doi.org/10.1145/2660267.2660298

[21] Basin, D.A., Cremers, C., Meier, S.: Provably repairing the ISO/IEC 9798 standard for entity authentication. Journal of Computer Security **21**(6), 817–846 (2013)

[22] Basin, D.A., Cremers, C.J.F., Miyazaki, K., Radomirovic, S., Watanabe, D.: Improving the security of cryptographic protocol standards. IEEE Security & Privacy **13**(3), 24–31 (2015). DOI 10.1109/MSP.2013.162. URL http://dx.doi.org/10.1109/MSP.2013.162

[23] Basin, D.A., Dreier, J., Hirschi, L., Radomirovic, S., Sasse, R., Stettler, V.: A formal analysis of 5G authentication. In: Proceedings of the 2018 ACM SIGSAC Conference on Computer and Communications Security, CCS 2018, Toronto, ON, Canada, October 15-19, 2018, pp. 1383–1396. ACM (2018). DOI 10.1145/3243734.3243846. URL https://doi.org/10.1145/3243734.3243846

[24] Basin, D.A., Sasse, R., Toro-Pozo, J.: The EMV standard: Break, fix, verify. In: 42nd IEEE Symposium on Security and Privacy, SP 2021, San Francisco, CA, USA, 24-27 May 2021, pp. 1766–1781. IEEE (2021). DOI 10.1109/SP40 001.2021.00037. URL https://doi.org/10.1109/SP40001.2021.00037

[25] Bellare, M., Rogaway, P.: Random oracles are practical: A paradigm for designing efficient protocols. In: Proceedings of the 1st ACM Conference on Computer and Communications Security, CCS '93, p. 62–73. Association for Computing Machinery, New York, NY, USA (1993). DOI 10.1145/168588.1 68596. URL https://doi.org/10.1145/168588.168596

[26] Bernstein, D.J., Duif, N., Lange, T., Schwabe, P., Yang, B.: High-speed high-security signatures. J. Cryptographic Engineering **2**(2), 77–89 (2012). DOI 10.1007/s13389-012-0027-1. URL https://doi.org/10.1007/s13389-012-0027-1

[27] Blake-Wilson, S., Johnson, D., Menezes, A.: Key agreement protocols and their security analysis. In: IMACC, *Lecture Notes in Computer Science*, vol. 1355, pp. 30–45. Springer (1997)

[28] Blake-Wilson, S., Menezes, A.: Unknown key-share attacks on the station-to-station (STS) protocol. In: Public Key Cryptography, Second International Workshop on Practice and Theory in Public Key Cryptography, PKC '99,

Kamakura, Japan, March 1-3, 1999, Proceedings, *Lecture Notes in Computer Science*, vol. 1560, pp. 154–170. Springer (1999). DOI 10.1007/3-540-49162-7_12. URL https://doi.org/10.1007/3-540-49162-7_12

[29] Brendel, J., Cremers, C., Jackson, D., Zhao, M.: The provable security of Ed25519: Theory and practice. In: 42nd IEEE Symposium on Security and Privacy, SP 2021, San Francisco, CA, USA, 24-27 May 2021, pp. 1659–1676. IEEE (2021). DOI 10.1109/SP40001.2021.00042. URL https://doi.org/10.1109/SP40001.2021.00042

[30] Bruni, A., Drewsen, E., Schürmann, C.: Towards a mechanized proof of selene receipt-freeness and vote-privacy. In: Electronic Voting - Second International Joint Conference, E-Vote-ID 2017, Bregenz, Austria, October 24-27, 2017, Proceedings, *Lecture Notes in Computer Science*, vol. 10615, pp. 110–126. Springer (2017). DOI 10.1007/978-3-319-68687-5_7. URL https://doi.org/10.1007/978-3-319-68687-5_7

[31] C.Cremers, Dax, A., Jacomme, C., Zhao, M.: Automated analysis of protocols that use authenticated encryption: How subtle AEAD differences can impact protocol security. In: 32nd USENIX Security Symposium, USENIX Security 2023, USA, August, 2023. USENIX Association (2023)

[32] Chaum, D.: Blind signatures for untraceable payments. In: Advances in Cryptology, pp. 199–203. Springer US, Boston, MA (1983)

[33] Cheval, V., C.Cremers, Dax, A., Hirschi, L., Jacomme, C., Kremer, S.: Hash Gone Bad: Automated discovery of protocol attacks that exploit hash function weaknesses. In: 32nd USENIX Security Symposium, USENIX Security 2023, USA, August, 2023. USENIX Association (2023)

[34] Cheval, V., Jacomme, C., Kremer, S., Künnemann, R.: SAPIC+: protocol verifiers of the world, unite! In: 31st USENIX Security Symposium, USENIX Security 2022, Boston, MA, USA, August 10-12, 2022, pp. 3935–3952. USENIX Association (2022). URL https://www.usenix.org/conference/usenixsecurity22/presentation/cheval

[35] Clavel, M., Durán, F., Hendrix, J., Lucas, S., Meseguer, J., Ölveczky, P.: The Maude formal tool environment. In: International Conference on Algebra and Coalgebra in Computer Science, pp. 173–178. Springer (2007)

[36] Comon-Lundh, H., Delaune, S.: The finite variant property: How to get rid of some algebraic properties. In: Term Rewriting and Applications, 16th International Conference, RTA 2005, Nara, Japan, April 19-21, 2005, Proceedings, *Lecture Notes in Computer Science*, vol. 3467, pp. 294–307. Springer (2005). DOI 10.1007/978-3-540-32033-3_22. URL https://doi.org/10.1007/978-3-540-32033-3_22

[37] Cortier, V., Delaune, S., Dreier, J.: Automatic generation of sources lemmas in Tamarin: Towards automatic proofs of security protocols. In: ESORICS (2), *Lecture Notes in Computer Science*, vol. 12309, pp. 3–22. Springer (2020)

[38] Cortier, V., Delaune, S., Dreier, J.: Automatic generation of sources lemmas in Tamarin: towards automatic proofs of security protocols. Journal of Computer Security (2022). To appear

[39] Cremers, C., Dax, A., Medinger, N.: Keeping Up with the KEMs: Stronger Security Notions for KEMs and Automated Analysis of KEM-based Protocols. In: CCS, pp. 1046–1060. ACM (2024)

[40] Cremers, C., Dax, A., Naska, A.: Formal analysis of SPDM: security protocol and data model version 1.2. IACR Cryptol. ePrint Arch. p. 1724 (2022). URL https://eprint.iacr.org/2022/1724

[41] Cremers, C., Dax, A., Naska, A.: Breaking and provably restoring authentication: A formal analysis of SPDM 1.2 including cross-protocol attacks. Cryptology ePrint Archive, Paper 2024/2047 (2024). URL https://eprint.iacr.org/2024/2047

[42] Cremers, C., Dehnel-Wild, M.: Component-based formal analysis of 5G-AKA: Channel assumptions and session confusion. In: 26th Annual Network and Distributed System Security Symposium, NDSS 2019, San Diego, California, USA, February 24-27, 2019. The Internet Society (2019). URL https://www.ndss-symposium.org/ndss-paper/component-based-formal-analysis-of-5g-aka-channel-assumptions-and-session-confusion/

[43] Cremers, C., Dehnel-Wild, M., Milner, K.: Secure authentication in the grid: A formal analysis of DNP3 SAv5. J. Comput. Secur. **27**(2), 203–232 (2019)

[44] Cremers, C., Düzlü, S., Fiedler, R., Fischlin, M., Janson, C.: BUFFing signature schemes beyond unforgeability and the case of post-quantum signatures. In: 42nd IEEE Symposium on Security and Privacy, SP 2021, San Francisco, CA, USA, 24-27 May 2021, pp. 1696–1714. IEEE (2021). DOI 10.1109/SP40001.2021.00093. URL https://doi.org/10.1109/SP40001.2021.00093

[45] Cremers, C., Horvat, M., Hoyland, J., Scott, S., van der Merwe, T.: A comprehensive symbolic analysis of TLS 1.3. In: CCS, pp. 1773–1788. ACM (2017)

[46] Cremers, C., Horvat, M., Scott, S., van der Merwe, T.: Automated analysis and verification of TLS 1.3: 0-RTT, resumption and delayed authentication. In: IEEE Symposium on Security and Privacy, pp. 470–485. IEEE Computer Society (2016)

[47] Cremers, C., Jackson, D.: Prime, Order Please! Revisiting Small Subgroup and Invalid Curve Attacks on Protocols using Diffie-Hellman. In: CSF, pp. 78–93. IEEE (2019)

[48] Cremers, C., Jacomme, C., Lukert, P.: Subterm-based proof techniques for improving the automation and scope of security protocol analysis. Cryptology ePrint Archive, Paper 2022/1130 (2022). URL https://eprint.iacr.org/2022/1130. https://eprint.iacr.org/2022/1130

[49] Cremers, C., Jacomme, C., Naska, A.: Formal analysis of session-handling in secure messaging: Lifting security from sessions to conversations. Cryptology ePrint Archive, Paper 2022/1710 (2022). URL https://eprint.iacr.org/2022/1710. https://eprint.iacr.org/2022/1710

[50] Cremers, C., Kiesl, B., Medinger, N.: A formal analysis of IEEE 802.11's WPA2: countering the kracks caused by cracking the counters. In: USENIX Security Symposium, pp. 1–17. USENIX Association (2020)

[51] Dax, A., Künnemann, R., Tangermann, S., Backes, M.: How to wrap it up — A formally verified proposal for the use of authenticated wrapping in PKCS#11. In: CSF, pp. 62–77. IEEE (2019)

[52] Diffie, W., van Oorschot, P.C., Wiener, M.J.: Authentication and authenticated key exchanges. Des. Codes Cryptography **2**(2), 107–125 (1992). DOI 10.1007/BF00124891. URL https://doi.org/10.1007/BF00124891

[53] Dolev, D., Dwork, C., Naor, M.: Nonmalleable cryptography. SIAM Journal on Computing **30**(2), 391–437 (2000). DOI 10.1137/S0097539795291562. URL https://doi.org/10.1137/S0097539795291562

[54] Dolev, D., Yao, A.: On the security of public key protocols. IEEE Transactions on Information Theory **29**(2), 198–208 (1983). DOI 10.1109/TIT.1983.1056650

[55] Donenfeld, J.A.: Wireguard: Next generation kernel network tunnel. In: 24th Annual Network and Distributed System Security Symposium, NDSS 2017, San Diego, California, USA, February 26 - March 1, 2017. The Internet Society (2017). URL https://www.ndss-symposium.org/ndss2017/ndss-2017-programme/wireguard-next-generation-kernel-network-tunnel/

[56] Donenfeld, J.A., Milner, K.: Formal verification of the WireGuard protocol. Technical Report, Tech. Rep (2017)

[57] Dreier, J., Duménil, C., Kremer, S., Sasse, R.: Beyond subterm-convergent equational theories in automated verification of stateful protocols. In: Principles of Security and Trust - 6th International Conference, POST 2017, Held as Part of the European Joint Conferences on Theory and Practice of Software, ETAPS 2017, Uppsala, Sweden, April 22-29, 2017, Proceedings, *Lecture Notes in Computer Science*, vol. 10204, pp. 117–140. Springer (2017). DOI 10.1007/978-3-662-54455-6_6. URL https://doi.org/10.1007/978-3-662-54455-6_6

[58] Dreier, J., Hirschi, L., Radomirovic, S., Sasse, R.: Automated unbounded verification of stateful cryptographic protocols with exclusive OR. In: 31st

IEEE Computer Security Foundations Symposium, CSF 2018, Oxford, United Kingdom, July 9-12, 2018, pp. 359–373. IEEE Computer Society (2018). DOI 10.1109/CSF.2018.00033. URL https://doi.org/10.1109/CSF.2018.00033

[59] Dreier, J., Puys, M., Potet, M., Lafourcade, P., Roch, J.: Formally and practically verifying flow properties in industrial systems. Comput. Secur. **86**, 453–470 (2019). DOI 10.1016/j.cose.2018.09.018. URL https://doi.org/10.1016/j.cose.2018.09.018

[60] Durán, F., Lucas, S., Meseguer, J.: MTT: The Maude termination tool (system description). In: International Joint Conference on Automated Reasoning, pp. 313–319. Springer (2008)

[61] Durán, F., Meseguer, J.: A Church-Rosser checker tool for conditional order-sorted equational Maude specifications. In: International Workshop on Rewriting Logic and its Applications, pp. 69–85. Springer (2010)

[62] Durgin, N., Lincoln, P., Mitchell, J., Scedrov, A.: Multiset rewriting and the complexity of bounded security protocols. Journal of Computer Security **12**(2), 247–311 (2004). URL http://dl.acm.org/citation.cfm?id=1017273.1017276

[63] Escobar, S., Sasse, R., Meseguer, J.: Folding variant narrowing and optimal variant termination. J. Log. Algebraic Methods Program. **81**(7-8), 898–928 (2012). DOI 10.1016/j.jlap.2012.01.002. URL https://doi.org/10.1016/j.jlap.2012.01.002

[64] European Payments Council: Guidelines on algorithms usage and key management. Tech. rep. (2009). EPC342-08 Version 1.1

[65] Gazdag, S., Grundner-Culemann, S., Guggemos, T., Heider, T., Loebenberger, D.: A formal analysis of IKEv2's post-quantum extension. In: ACSAC, pp. 91–105. ACM (2021)

[66] Giesl, J., Schneider-Kamp, P., Thiemann, R.: AProVE 1.2: Automatic termination proofs in the dependency pair framework. In: International Joint Conference on Automated Reasoning, pp. 281–286. Springer (2006)

[67] Girol, G., Hirschi, L., Sasse, R., Jackson, D., Cremers, C., Basin, D.: A spectral analysis of Noise: A comprehensive, automated, formal analysis of Diffie-Hellman protocols. In: 29th USENIX Security Symposium (USENIX Security 20). USENIX Association, Boston, MA (2020). URL https://www.usenix.org/conference/usenixsecurity20/presentation/girol

[68] Goldwasser, S., Micali, S., Rivest, R.L.: A digital signature scheme secure against adaptive chosen-message attacks. SIAM J. Comput. **17**(2), 281–308 (1988). DOI 10.1137/0217017. URL https://dx.doi.org/10.1137/0217017

[69] Graphviz. https://graphviz.org/

[70] Hirschi, L., Schmid, L., Basin, D.A.: Fixing the achilles heel of e-voting: The bulletin board. In: 34th IEEE Computer Security Foundations Symposium,

CSF 2021, Dubrovnik, Croatia, June 21-25, 2021, pp. 1–17. IEEE (2021). DOI 10.1109/CSF51468.2021.00016. URL https://doi.org/10.1109/CSF514 68.2021.00016

[71] Hülsing, A., Ning, K., Schwabe, P., Weber, F., Zimmermann, P.R.: Post-quantum WireGuard. In: IEEE Symposium on Security and Privacy, pp. 304–321. IEEE (2021)

[72] International Organization for Standardization, Genève, Switzerland.: ISO/IEC 9798-3:1998, Information technology – Security techniques – Entity Authentication – Part 3: Mechanisms using digital signature techniques (1998). Second edition

[73] ITU-T: Recommendation H.235 - Security and encryption for H-series (H.323 and other H.245-based) multimedia terminals (2003)

[74] Jackson, D., Cremers, C., Cohn-Gordon, K., Sasse, R.: Seems Legit: Automated Analysis of Subtle Attacks on Protocols that Use Signatures. In: CCS, pp. 2165–2180. ACM (2019)

[75] Jager, T., Kakvi, S.A., May, A.: On the Security of the PKCS#1 v1.5 Signature Scheme. In: Proceedings of the 2018 ACM SIGSAC Conference on Computer and Communications Security, CCS 2018, Toronto, ON, Canada, October 15-19, 2018, pp. 1195–1208. ACM (2018). DOI 10.1145/3243734.3243798. URL https://doi.org/10.1145/3243734.3243798

[76] Just, M., Vaudenay, S.: Authenticated multi-party key agreement. In: ASIACRYPT, *Lecture Notes in Computer Science*, vol. 1163, pp. 36–49. Springer (1996)

[77] Kiesl, B.: UT Tamarin. Available at https://github.com/benjaminkiesl/ut_tama rin

[78] Kirchner, C., Kirchner, H.: Equational logic and rewriting. In: J.H. Siekmann (ed.) Computational Logic, *Handbook of the History of Logic*, vol. 9, pp. 255–282. North-Holland (2014). DOI https://doi.org/10.1016/B978-0-444-51624-4.50006-X. URL https://www.sciencedirect.com/science/article/pii/B9 78044451624450006X

[79] Kremer, S., Künnemann, R.: Automated analysis of security protocols with global state. J. Comput. Secur. **24**(5), 583–616 (2016). DOI 10.3233/JCS-160556. URL https://doi.org/10.3233/JCS-160556

[80] Künnemann, R., Steel, G.: YubiSecure? Formal Security Analysis Results for the Yubikey and YubiHSM. In: Security and Trust Management - 8th International Workshop, STM 2012, Pisa, Italy, September 13-14, 2012, Revised Selected Papers, *Lecture Notes in Computer Science*, vol. 7783, pp. 257–272. Springer (2012). DOI 10.1007/978-3-642-38004-4_17. URL https://doi.org/10.1007/978-3-642-38004-4_17

[81] LaMacchia, B.A., Lauter, K.E., Mityagin, A.: Stronger Security of Authenticated Key Exchange. In: ProvSec, *Lecture Notes in Computer Science*, vol. 4784, pp. 1–16. Springer (2007)

[82] Lindenberg, C., Wirt, K., Buchmann, J.A.: Formal proof for the correctness of RSA-PSS. IACR Cryptology ePrint Archive **2006**, 11 (2006). URL http://eprint.iacr.org/2006/011

[83] Linker, F., Sasse, R., Basin, D.: A formal analysis of Apple's iMessage PQ3 protocol. Cryptology ePrint Archive, Paper 2024/1395 (2024). URL https://eprint.iacr.org/2024/1395

[84] Lowe, G.: Breaking and fixing the Needham-Schroeder public-key protocol using FDR. In: TACAS, *Lecture Notes in Computer Science*, vol. 1055, pp. 147–166. Springer (1996)

[85] Lowe, G.: A hierarchy of authentication specification. In: 10th Computer Security Foundations Workshop (CSFW '97), June 10-12, 1997, Rockport, Massachusetts, USA, pp. 31–44. IEEE Computer Society (1997). DOI 10.110 9/CSFW.1997.596782. URL https://doi.org/10.1109/CSFW.1997.596782

[86] Mauw, S., Smith, Z., Toro-Pozo, J., Trujillo-Rasua, R.: Distance-bounding protocols: Verification without time and location. In: 2018 IEEE Symposium on Security and Privacy, SP 2018, Proceedings, 21-23 May 2018, San Francisco, California, USA, pp. 549–566. IEEE Computer Society (2018). DOI 10.1109/ SP.2018.00001

[87] Mauw, S., Smith, Z., Toro-Pozo, J., Trujillo-Rasua, R.: Post-collusion security and distance bounding. In: Proceedings of the 2019 ACM SIGSAC Conference on Computer and Communications Security, CCS 2019, London, UK, November 11-15, 2019, pp. 941–958. ACM (2019). DOI 10.1145/3319535.3345651. URL https://doi.org/10.1145/3319535.3345651

[88] Meier, S.: Advancing automated security protocol verification. Ph.D. thesis, ETH Zurich (2013)

[89] Menezes, A., Smart, N.P.: Security of signature schemes in a multi-user setting. Des. Codes Cryptography **33**(3), 261–274 (2004). DOI 10.1023/B:DESI.00000 36250.18062.3f. URL https://doi.org/10.1023/B:DESI.0000036250.18062.3f

[90] Merkle, R.C.: Secrecy, authentication and public key systems. Ph.D. thesis, Stanford University (1979). URL http://www.merkle.com/papers/Thesis1979 .pdf

[91] Meseguer, J.: Conditional rewriting logic as a unified model of concurrency. Theoretical computer science **96**(1), 73–155 (1992)

[92] Millen, J., Clark, S., Freedman, S.: The interrogator: Protocol secuity analysis. IEEE Transactions on Software Engineering **SE-13**(2), 274–288 (1987). DOI 10.1109/TSE.1987.233151

[93] Moriarty, K.M., Kaliski, B., Jonsson, J., Rusch, A.: PKCS #1: RSA cryptography specifications version 2.2. RFC **8017**, 1–78 (2016). DOI 10.17487/RFC8017. URL https://doi.org/10.17487/RFC8017

[94] Ninet, T.: Formal verification of the Internet Key Exchange (IKEv2) security protocol. Ph.D. thesis, University of Rennes 1, France (2020)

[95] Paterson, K.G., van der Merwe, T.: Reactive and proactive standardisation of TLS. In: SSR, *Lecture Notes in Computer Science*, vol. 10074, pp. 160–186. Springer (2016)

[96] Peltonen, A., Sasse, R., Basin, D.: A comprehensive formal analysis of 5G handover. In: WISEC, pp. 1–12. ACM (2021)

[97] Perrig, A., Canetti, R., Tygar, J.D., Song, D.: TESLA Broadcast Authentication, pp. 29–53. Springer US, Boston, MA (2003). DOI 10.1007/978-1-4615-0229-6_3. URL https://doi.org/10.1007/978-1-4615-0229-6_3

[98] Perrin, T.: The noise protocol framework (2018). URL https://github.com/noiseprotocol/noise_spec/tree/ecdf084ece2bf92b16b1201b6ae5c99d23fb4151. (revision 34)

[99] Pornin, T., Stern, J.P.: Digital signatures do not guarantee exclusive ownership. In: Applied Cryptography and Network Security, Third International Conference, ACNS 2005, New York, NY, USA, June 7-10, 2005, Proceedings, *Lecture Notes in Computer Science*, vol. 3531, pp. 138–150 (2005). DOI 10.1007/11496137_10. URL https://doi.org/10.1007/11496137_10

[100] Radu, A.I., Chothia, T., Newton, C.J., Boureanu, I., Chen, L.: Practical EMV relay protection. In: 43rd IEEE Symposium on Security and Privacy, SP 2022. IEEE (2022)

[101] Rescorla, E.: The Transport Layer Security (TLS) Protocol Version 1.3. RFC 8446 (2018). DOI 10.17487/RFC8446. URL https://www.rfc-editor.org/info/rfc8446

[102] Schmidt, B., Meier, S., Cremers, C., Basin, D.A.: Automated analysis of Diffie-Hellman protocols and advanced security properties. In: 25th IEEE Computer Security Foundations Symposium, CSF 2012, Cambridge, MA, USA, June 25-27, 2012, pp. 78–94. IEEE Computer Society (2012). DOI 10.1109/CSF.2012.25. URL https://doi.org/10.1109/CSF.2012.25

[103] Schmidt, B., Sasse, R., Cremers, C., Basin, D.: Automated verification of group key agreement protocols. In: IEEE Symposium on Security and Privacy, pp. 179–194. IEEE Computer Society (2014)

[104] Smolka, G., Nutt, W., Goguen, J.A., Meseguer, J.: Order-sorted equational computation. In: H. Aït-Kaci, M. Nivat (eds.) Rewriting Techniques, pp. 297–367. Academic Press (1989). DOI https://doi.org/10.1016/B978-0-12-

046371-8.50016-X. URL https://www.sciencedirect.com/science/article/pii/ B978012046371850016X

[105] Stern, J., Pointcheval, D., Malone-Lee, J., Smart, N.P.: Flaws in applying proof methodologies to signature schemes. In: Advances in Cryptology - CRYPTO 2002, 22nd Annual International Cryptology Conference, Santa Barbara, California, USA, August 18-22, 2002, Proceedings, *Lecture Notes in Computer Science*, vol. 2442, pp. 93–110. Springer (2002). DOI 10.1007/3-540-45708-9_7. URL https://doi.org/10.1007/3-540-45708-9_7

[106] Team, T.M.: https://maude.cs.illinois.edu/wiki/The_Maude_System

[107] Team, T.T.: Tamarin Prover Manual. Available at https://tamarin-prover.com/manual/

[108] Team, T.T.: Tamarin Prover source code. Available at https://github.com/tamarin-prover/tamarin-prover

[109] Tree-sitter contributors: Tree-sitter. https://tree-sitter.github.io/tree-sitter/ [Online; accessed 24-February-2025]

[110] Vaudenay, S.: The security of DSA and ECDSA. In: Public Key Cryptography - PKC 2003, 6th International Workshop on Theory and Practice in Public Key Cryptography, Miami, FL, USA, January 6-8, 2003, Proceedings, pp. 309–323 (2003). DOI 10.1007/3-540-36288-6_23. URL https://doi.org/10.1007/3-540-36288-6_23

[111] Wesemeyer, S., Newton, C.J.P., Treharne, H., Chen, L., Sasse, R., Whitefield, J.: Formal analysis and implementation of a TPM 2.0-based direct anonymous attestation scheme. In: ASIA CCS '20: The 15th ACM Asia Conference on Computer and Communications Security, Taipei, Taiwan, October 5-9, 2020, pp. 784–798. ACM (2020). DOI 10.1145/3320269.3372197. URL https://doi.org/10.1145/3320269.3372197

[112] Whitefield, J., Chen, L., Kargl, F., Paverd, A., Schneider, S.A., Treharne, H., Wesemeyer, S.: Formal analysis of V2X revocation protocols. In: Security and Trust Management - 13th International Workshop, STM 2017, Oslo, Norway, September 14-15, 2017, Proceedings, *Lecture Notes in Computer Science*, vol. 10547, pp. 147–163. Springer (2017). DOI 10.1007/978-3-319-68063-7_10. URL https://doi.org/10.1007/978-3-319-68063-7_10

[113] Whitefield, J., Chen, L., Sasse, R., Schneider, S.A., Treharne, H., Wesemeyer, S.: A Symbolic Analysis of ECC-Based Direct Anonymous Attestation. In: IEEE European Symposium on Security and Privacy, EuroS&P 2019, Stockholm, Sweden, June 17-19, 2019, pp. 127–141. IEEE (2019). DOI 10.1109/EuroSP.2019.00019. URL https://doi.org/10.1109/EuroSP.2019.00019

[114] Wikipedia contributors: Extended backus–naur form — Wikipedia, the free encyclopedia. https://en.wikipedia.org/w/index.php?title=Extended_Back

us%E2%80%93Naur_form&oldid=1276703454 (2025). [Online; accessed 24-February-2025]

[115] Yu, J., Ryan, M., Cremers, C.: DECIM: detecting endpoint compromise in messaging. IEEE Trans. Inf. Forensics Secur. **13**(1), 106–118 (2018)

Part VII
Appendix

Chapter 19
Dependency Graph Examples

Below we provide the dependency graphs for the two attacks on the ISO-IEC four pass authentication protocol, discussed in Section 2.2.5. When the Message Sequence Charts (MSCs) for these attacks were presented, we had not yet provided the background for readers to understand the corresponding dependency graphs. We show the dependency graphs here and briefly comment on their relationships with the corresponding MSCs.

The correspondence between the MSC in Figure 2.4 and the first dependency graph in Figure 19.1 is as follows. The dependency graph presents strictly more information: it represents not only the actions of the agents involved in the protocol, it also includes detailed information on the adversary's actions. This includes both the messages sent by the adversary and also how the adversary derives the messages it sends. It also makes explicit that all messages communicated between protocol participants go over the adversary, i.e., participants do not communicate directly with each other as in the MSC. Finally, the information given in the nodes of the dependency graph is partially ordered, whereas the MSC totally orders the actions taken, which are the sending and receiving of messages. For example, in our dependency graph the Setup rule and the rule A1 can occur in any order. Note that, in the MSC, the setup of keys is implicit.

In the MSC, it is readily apparent what actions the participants in each role take, namely constructing and communicating messages, and how the actions are ordered. This ordering is determined simply by following the arrows denoting message communication. The sending and receiving of message is also represented in the dependency graph, where messages are sent (Out actions) and received (In actions) and state facts (e.g., StA1 and StA2) are used to order when sending and receiving can occur. This gives rise to a total ordering on the actions of any individual participant. However, the actions of all participants and the adversary are still partially ordered as some actions between participants or the adversary, can occur in parallel, as we have seen. For example, the steps taken by agent $B playing in the role A are linearly ordered as the application of A1 produces the state fact StA1, which is later consumed and replaced with StA2 when the agent $B takes its second step. Between these steps

© The Editor(s) (if applicable) and The Author(s), under exclusive license to Springer Nature Switzerland AG 2025
D. Basin et al., *Modeling and Analyzing Security Protocols with Tamarin*, Information Security and Cryptography,
https://doi.org/10.1007/978-3-031-90936-8

there is considerable parallelism possible, especially concerning the actions of the adversary.

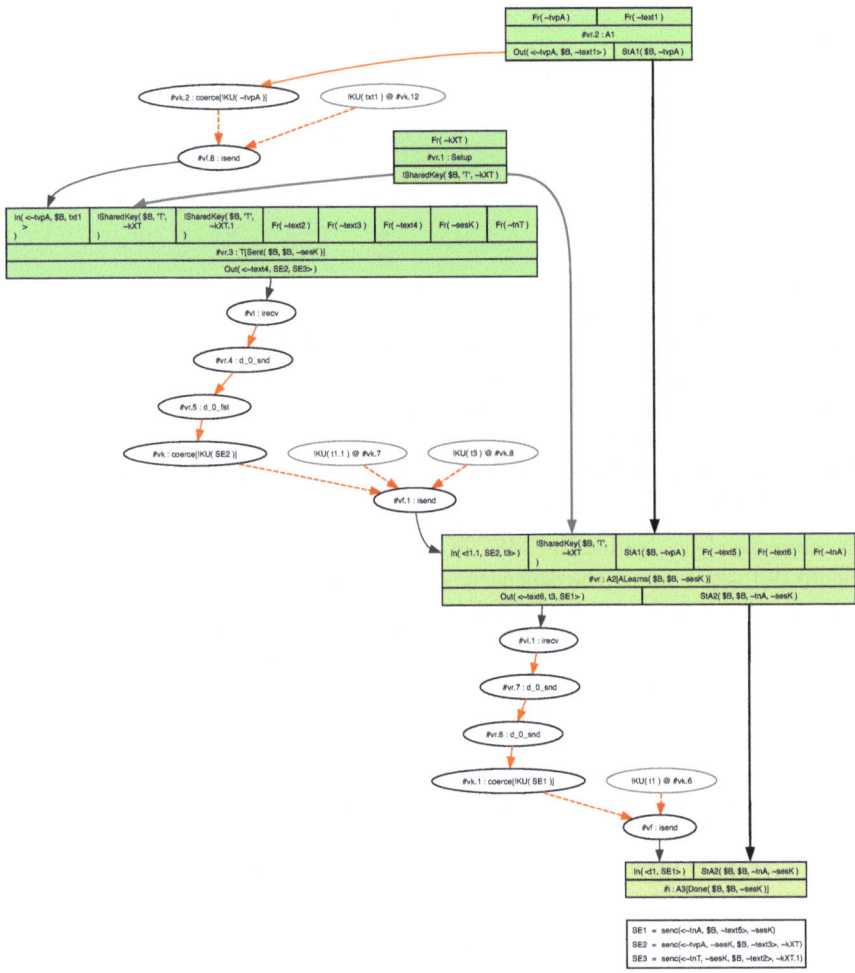

Fig. 19.1: Dependency Graph for Attack on `AauthenticatesB`

The reader may work out the relationship between the MSC in Figure 2.5 and the corresponding dependency graph in Figure 19.2 in a similar way.

19 Dependency Graph Example

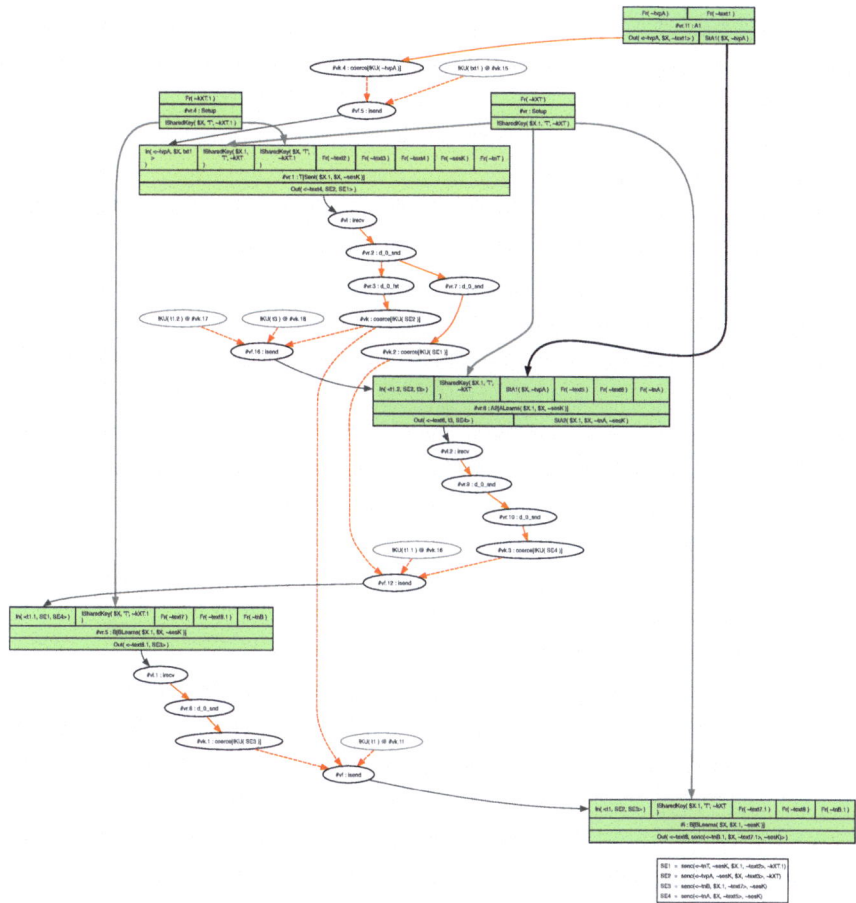

Fig. 19.2: Dependency Graph for Attack on `AauthenticatesB`

Chapter 20
Syntax

In this chapter, we provide an overview of TAMARIN's syntax in EBNF [114] notation. Our definition only covers the syntactic elements described in this book. It does not include, for example, the syntax for TAMARIN's SAPIC extension for process specifications. A complete, up-to-date syntax specification may be found in TAMARIN's manual [107]. In the TAMARIN source code repository [108] we provide the syntax files for the `tree-sitter` parser generator tool [109], which were used to generate the EBNF definition in the manual and can also be used to develop other parsers and tools for TAMARIN files.

Comments in TAMARIN's input language use conventions similar to the C language.

```
/* for a comment running over multiple lines */
// for a single line comment
```

All security protocol theories are named and delimited by `begin` and `end`. We explain the non-terminals used to define the command-line configuration and body items in the subsequent paragraphs.

```
theory            ::= 'theory' (ident)
                      ('configuration' ':' '"' commandline '"')?
                      'begin' _body_item* 'end'
_body_item        ::= preprocessor
                    | _signature_spec
                    | global_heuristic
                    | tactic
                    | _rule
                    | restriction
                    | _lemma
                    | formal_comment

commandline       ::= ('--auto-sources'
                    | ('--stop-on-trace' '=' _search_strategy))+
_search_strategy  ::= 'BFS'
                    | 'DFS'
                    | 'SEQDFS'
                    | 'NONE'
```

The purpose of `--auto-sources` is explained in Section 8.3. The `--stop-on-trace` options are explained in Section 6.1.2.

The preprocessor allows conditional blocks, including external files, and the definition of macros.

```
preprocessor     ::= ifdef
                   | define
                   | include
ifdef            ::= '#ifdef' _ifdef_formula _body_item*
                     ('#else' _body_item*)?
                     '#endif'
define           ::= '#define' ident
include          ::= '#include' '"' (param) '"'
_ifdef_formula   ::= ifdef_nested
                   | ifdef_or
                   | ifdef_and
                   | ifdef_not
                   | ident
param            ::= /[^"]*/
ifdef_nested     ::= '(' _ifdef_formula ')'
ifdef_or         ::= _ifdef_formula '|' _ifdef_formula
ifdef_and        ::= _ifdef_formula '&' _ifdef_formula
ifdef_not        ::= 'not' _ifdef_formula
```

Conditional blocks and the inclusion of external files are described in Section 10.2.3.

TAMARIN's syntax has the following three reserved keywords: `let`, `in`, and `rule`.

Identifiers always start with a letter or number, and may contain underscores after the first character. Although identifiers beginning with a number are valid, they are not allowed as the names of facts, which must begin with an upper-case letter.

```
ident ::= /[A-Za-z0-9]\w*/
```

Additionally, identifiers may not be one of three reserved keywords listed above.

Naturals are sequences of digits.

```
natural ::= /[0-9]+/
```

We next turn to the syntax definitions of equational theories, function symbol definitions, and predicates.

```
_signature_spec ::= built_ins | functions | equations | predicates | macros
```

Function definitions are given using the following syntax.

```
functions          ::= ('functions' ':'
                        _function_sym (',' _function_sym)* ','?)
_function_sym      ::= (ident) '/' (natural)
                        ('[' function_attribute
                          (',' function_attribute)*
                        ','? ']')?
function_attribute ::= 'private'
```

For equations, the syntax is:

20 Syntax

```
equations ::= ('equations' ('[' 'convergent' ']') ':'
               equation (',' equation)* ','?)
equation  ::= (mset_term: left) '=' (mset_term: right)
```

Note that the defined equations must be convergent, have the Finite Variant Property (FVP, Section 6.7), and not use fixed public constants in the terms. TAMARIN provides built-in sets of function definitions and equations. They are expanded upon parsing; one may therefore inspect them by pretty printing the file using `tamarin-prover your-file.spthy`.

```
macros ::= 'macros' ':' macro (',' macro)*
macro  ::= (ident)
           '(' (_non_temporal_var (',' _non_temporal_var)*)? ')'
           '=' (mset_term)
```

Macros are described in Section 10.2.2.

```
predicates    ::= ('predicate' | 'predicates') ':'
                  predicate (',' predicate)*
predicate     ::= (predicate_def) '<=>' (_formula)
predicate_def ::= (ident) '(' arguments? ')'
```

Predicates are described in Section 5.10.1.

```
built_ins ::= 'builtins' ':' built_in (',' built_in)* ','?
built_in  ::= 'diffie-hellman'
            | 'hashing'
            | 'symmetric-encryption'
            | 'asymmetric-encryption'
            | 'signing'
            | 'bilinear-pairing'
            | 'xor'
            | 'multiset'
            | 'natural-numbers'
            | 'revealing-signing'
```

The purpose of these builtins is described in Chapter 7, with further pointers provided in Table 7.1.

A global heuristic sets the default heuristic that will be used when proving lemmas. The specified goal ranking can be any of those discussed Section 6.6.

```
global_heuristic              ::= 'heuristic' ':'
                                  (_proof_method_ranking+)
_proof_method_ranking         ::= standard_proof_method_ranking
                                | oracle_proof_method_ranking
                                | tactic_proof_method_ranking
standard_proof_method_ranking ::= /[CIScis]+/
oracle_proof_method_ranking   ::= ('O' | 'o') ('"' param '"')?
tactic_proof_method_ranking   ::= '{' ident '}'
```

We describe oracles in Section 16.4.

```
tactic    ::= 'tactic' ':' ident presort?
              ((prio+ deprio*) | (prio* deprio+))
presort   ::= 'presort' ':' standard_proof_method_ranking
prio      ::= 'prio' ':' ('{' post_ranking '}')? _tactic_formula+
deprio    ::= 'deprio' ':' ('{' post_ranking '}')? _tactic_formula+
```

```
post_ranking      ::= 'smallest' | 'id'

_tactic_formula   ::= or_tacfor
                    | and_tacfor
                    | not_tacfor
                    | atomic_tacfor
or_tacfor         ::= _tactic_formula '|' _tactic_formula
and_tacfor        ::= _tactic_formula '&' _tactic_formula
not_tacfor        ::= 'not' _tactic_formula
atomic_tacfor     ::= tacfor_name ('"' param '"')*
tacfor_name       ::= 'regex'
                    | 'isFactName'
```

Tactics are described in Section 16.3.

Multiset rewriting rules are specified using the rule syntax given below. The protocol defined by a security protocol theory is given by the set of all multiset rewriting rules specified in the theory's body. The input language also supports some advanced features. For example, rule variants can be explicitly given. Furthermore, when the diff-mode is used to check for observational equivalence (Chapter 13), the left and right instances of a rule can be specified: when TAMARIN is called with --diff, it will accept diff_rule in addition to rule).

```
_rule             ::= rule
                    | diff_rule
rule              ::= simple_rule variants?
diff_rule         ::= simple_rule 'left' (rule) 'right' (rule)
simple_rule       ::= 'rule' modulo? (ident) rule_attrs? ':'
                      rule_let_block?
                      premise ('-->' | action_fact) conclusion
premise           ::= '[' _facts? ']'
action_fact       ::= '--[' _facts_or_restrictions? ']->'
conclusion        ::= '[' _facts? ']'
variants          ::= 'variants' simple_rule (',' simple_rule)*
modulo            ::= '(' 'modulo' ('E' | 'AC') ')'
rule_attrs        ::= '[' rule_attr (',' rule_attr)* ',' ? ']'
rule_attr         ::= rule_attr_color
                    | rule_role
                    | 'no_derivcheck'
rule_attr_color   ::= ('color=' | 'colour=') hexcolor
hexcolor          ::= ('"' ('#')? (/[0-9a-fA-F]{1,6}/) '"')
                    | (('#')? (/[0-9a-fA-F]{1,6}/))
rule_role         ::= 'role' '=' '"' (ident: role_identifier) '"'

_facts_or_restrictions ::= (_fact | embedded_restriction)
                           (',' (_fact | embedded_restriction))*
```

Rule variants, as well as left and right instances, are not intended to be specified by users. Instead, they are internally computed and output by TAMARIN when exporting a proof or parsed protocol specification. The color and role attributes are described in Section 6.5.

```
rule_let_block    ::= 'let' rule_let_term+ 'in'
rule_let_term     ::= (msg_var_or_nullary_fun | nat_var) '='
                      (mset_term)
```

The let-block allows more succinct specifications. The equations are applied in a bottom-up fashion. For example,

```
let x = y
    y = <z,x>
in [] --> [ A(y)]
```

is internally translated to

```
[] --> [ A(<z,y>) ]
```

For details of the definition of let-blocks, see Section 10.2.1. In general, it is good form to keep the set of variables on the left-hand side separate from the free variables on the right-hand side to avoid confusion.

```
embedded_restriction ::= '_restrict' '(' (_formula) ')'
```

Restrictions specify restrictions on the set of traces considered as described in Section 5.10.2. The formula specifying a restriction is available as an assumption in the proofs of *all* security properties specified in the security protocol theory. Restrictions can be either specified at the global level, or inside of specific rules as embedded restrictions Section 5.10.3.

```
restriction ::= 'restriction' (ident)
                restriction_attr?
                ':' '"' (_formula) '"'
```

In observational equivalence mode, restrictions can be associated to one side.

```
restriction_attr  ::= '[' ('left' | 'right') ']'
```

Lemmas specify security properties. By default, the given formula is interpreted as a property that must hold for all traces of the protocol specified by the security protocol theory. One can change this using the `exists-trace` trace quantifier.

```
_lemma ::= lemma
         | diff_lemma

lemma          ::= 'lemma' modulo? (ident)
                   diff_lemma_attrs?
                   ':' trace_quantifier? '"' (_formula) '"'
                   (_proof_skeleton)?
lemma_attr ::= 'sources'
             | 'reuse'
             | 'use_induction'
             | ('hide_lemma=' ident)
             | ('heuristic=' (_proof_method_ranking+: proof_method_ranking))

trace_quantifier ::= 'all-traces'
                   | 'exists-trace'

diff_lemma        ::= 'diffLemma' modulo? (ident)
                      diff_lemma_attrs?
                      ':' (_proof_skeleton)?
diff_lemma_attrs ::= '[' (diff_lemma_attr | lemma_attr)
                     (',' (diff_lemma_attr | lemma_attr))* ','? ']'
diff_lemma_attr  ::= 'left'
                   | 'right'
```

In observational equivalence mode, described in Chapter 13, lemmas can be associated to one side. For the two versions of the theory, called the left and the right theory (which defines which term is used from all `diff` occurrences), each lemma can be considered on either or on both sides, depending on the `left` or `right` annotation on the lemma.

A proof skeleton is a complete or partial proof as output by TAMARIN. It indicates the proof method used at each step.

```
_proof_skeleton ::= solved
                  | mirrored
                  | by_method
                  | method_skeleton
                  | cases
solved            ::= 'SOLVED'
mirrored          ::= 'MIRRORED'
by_method         ::= 'by' _proof_methods
method_skeleton   ::= _proof_methods (_proof_skeleton)
cases             ::= case ('next' case)* 'qed'
case              ::= 'case' (ident)
                          (_proof_skeleton)
_proof_methods    ::= (proof_method | step+)
proof_method      ::= 'sorry'
                  | 'simplify'
                  | ('solve' '(' constraint ')')
                  | 'contradiction'
                  | 'induction'
                  | 'rule-equivalence'
                  | 'backward-search'
                  | 'ATTACK'
step              ::= 'step' '(' proof_method ')'

constraint        ::= premise_constraint
                  | action_constraint
                  | chain_constraint
                  | eq_split_constraint
                  | disjunction_split_constraint
premise_constraint ::= _fact '▶' natural_subscript temporal_var
natural_subscript ::= ( '₀' | '₁' | '₂' | '₃' | '₄'
                      | '₅' | '₆' | '₇' | '₈' | '₉' )+
action_constraint ::= (_fact) '@'
                      ((temporal_var_optional_prefix)
                       variable)
chain_constraint  ::= '(' temporal_var ',' natural ')' '~~>'
                      '(' temporal_var ',' natural ')'
eq_split_constraint ::= 'splitEqs' '(' natural ')'
disjunction_split_constraint ::= (_formula) (('||' | '∥') (_formula))+
```

Formal comments may be used to provide explanation and context for models. In contrast to comments of the form /*...*/ and //..., formal comments are stored and output again when pretty-printing a security protocol theory.

```
formal_comment ::= (ident) ('{*' /[^*]*\*+([^}*][^*]*\*+)*/ '}')
```

We next turn to terms, as described in Section 3.1.2. When specifying terms, a common pitfall is the use of an undefined function symbol. This results in an error

20 Syntax

message pointing to a position slightly before the actual use of the function, due to grammar ambiguities.

We provide special syntax for tuples, multisets, xor, multiplication, exponentiation, and nullary and binary function symbols. An n-ary tuple <t1,...,tn> is parsed as an n-ary, right-associative application of pairing. Multiplication and exponentiation are parsed left-associatively. For the binary operator enc, one can write enc{m}k or enc(m,k). For nullary function symbols, there is no need to write nullary(), i.e., the brackets are optional. Note that the number of arguments of an n-ary function application must agree with the arity given in the function definition.

```
_term       ::= tuple_term
              | nested_term
              | nullary_fun
              | binary_app
              | nary_app
              | _literal
tuple_term  ::= '<' (mset_term: left) (',' (mset_term: right))* '>'
mset_term   ::= (nat_term) (('++' | '+') (nat_term))*
nat_term    ::= (xor_term) ('%+' (xor_term))*
xor_term    ::= (mul_term)
                (('XOR' | '⊕') (mul_term))*
mul_term    ::= (exp_term) ('*' (exp_term))*
exp_term    ::= (_term) ('^' (_term))*

nested_term ::= '(' mset_term ')'
nullary_fun ::= (ident)
              | ((ident) '(' ')')
binary_app  ::= (ident)
                '{' (arguments) '}'
                (mset_term)
nary_app    ::= (ident) '(' arguments ')'
arguments   ::= ((mset_term | temporal_var): argument)
                (',' (mset_term))*
_literal    ::= pub_name
              | fresh_name
              | _non_temporal_var

_non_temporal_var ::= pub_var
                    | fresh_var
                    | msg_var_or_nullary_fun
                    | nat_var

pub_var     ::= ('$' (ident) ('.' natural)?)
              | ((ident) ('.' natural)? ':' 'pub')
fresh_var   ::= ('~' (ident) ('.' natural)?)
              | ((ident) ('.' natural)? ':' 'fresh')

msg_var_or_nullary_fun ::= (ident) ('.' natural)? (':' 'msg')?

temporal_var ::= ('#' (ident) ('.' natural)?)
               | ((ident) ('.' natural)? ':' 'node')
nat_var      ::= ('%' (ident) ('.' natural)? (':' 'nat')?)
               | ((ident) ('.' natural)? ':' 'nat')
pub_name     ::= '''  /[^\n']+/  '''
fresh_name   ::= '~''  /[^\n']+/  '''
```

```
temporal_var_optional_prefix ::= ('#'? (ident) ('.' natural)?)
                               | ((ident) ('.' natural)? ':' 'temporal')
```

Facts are described in Section 3.1.5. The main reserved fact symbols are: In, Out, K, and _restrict. In and Out occur in left-hand and right-hand sides of rules and encode the built-in interface between the rules and the adversary-controlled network. K is used in property specifications to test whether the adversary can derive a specific term. In the context of a rule's action facts, _restrict is a reserved unary fact symbol that is used to specify rule-specific restrictions (see Section 5.10.3).

Furthermore, there are two facts internal to TAMARIN's search algorithm: KU and KD. These two facts are used internally by TAMARIN for the construction and deconstruction rules. KU-facts also log the messages deduced by construction rules.

```
_facts        ::= (_fact (',' _fact)*)
_fact         ::= (fact)
                | ('!' (fact))
fact          ::= ((ident) '(' arguments? ')' fact_annotes?)
fact_annotes  ::= '[' fact_annote (',' fact_annote)* ']'
fact_annote   ::= '+'
                | '-'
                | 'no_precomp'
```

Fact annotations can be used to change the priority of the corresponding goals in heuristics, or influence the precomputation step performed by TAMARIN, as described in Section 16.2.

Formulas are trace formulas as described in Chapter 5. Note that the language is slightly more liberal with respect to guardedness (Section 11.5), as it accepts a conjunction of atoms as guards.

```
_formula ::= quantified_formula
           | nested_formula
           | iff
           | imp
           | disjunction
           | conjunction
           | negation
           | _temporal_variable_operation
           | action_constraint
           | term_eq
           | subterm_rel
           | atom
           | predicate_ref
           | pre_defined

quantified_formula ::= ('Ex' | '∃' | 'All' | '∀') (_lvar+) '.' (_formula)
nested_formula     ::= '(' _formula ')'

iff         ::= (_formula) ('<=>' | '⇔') (_formula)
imp         ::= (_formula) ('==>' | '⇒') (_formula)
disjunction ::= (_formula) ('|' | '∨') (_formula)
conjunction ::= (_formula) ('&' | '∧') (_formula)
negation    ::= ('not' | '¬') (_formula)
```

20 Syntax

```
_temporal_variable_operation ::= temp_var_induction
                               | temp_var_order
                               | temp_var_eq
temp_var_induction ::= 'last' '(' temporal_var ')'
temp_var_order  ::= (temporal_var_optional_prefix)
                    '<' (temporal_var_optional_prefix)
temp_var_eq     ::= (temporal_var_optional_prefix)
                    '=' (temporal_var_optional_prefix)

term_eq         ::= (mset_term: left) '=' (mset_term)
subterm_rel     ::= (mset_term: left) ('<<' | '⊏') (mset_term)
atom            ::= '⊥' | 'F' | '⊤' | 'T'
predicate_ref   ::= (ident) '(' arguments? ')'
pre_defined     ::= ident
_lvar           ::= temporal_var
                  | _non_temporal_var
```

Chapter 21
Exercises

In this section, we present exercises that aim at improving the reader's practical understanding of the topics explained in this book. These exercises can be used as part of a tutorial or course where participants work, hands on, with TAMARIN. We have taken these exercises from different workshops and courses developed by ourselves and colleagues, with their permission. In particular, we thank Véronique Cortier, Alexander Dax, Sofia Giampietro, Xenia Hofmeier, Aurora Naska, Saša Radomirović, and Christoph Sprenger for their contributions here.

We will include solutions to selected exercises in Section 21.3.

21.1 Simple Protocols

We start with examples of smaller protocols, which we iteratively build in small steps. Later tasks will be more substantial. The project in Section 21.2 is even larger and leaves considerable flexibility to the reader.

21.1.1 Client-Server Key Transmission

We start with a simple one-message protocol where a client C sends a fresh key k to a server S, for which the client knows the public key.

$$1.\ C \to S : \{k\}_{pubS}$$

We consider the following subtasks, and make available the file **exercises/ClientServer.spthy** as a starting point.

1. Read the file and try to understand the protocol and how it is modeled.

2. Load the file in TAMARIN's interactive mode and study and prove all the stated properties. Which properties are analyzed, and what results do you obtain? What is the purpose of the lemma `Client_Server_can_finish`?

3. Prove the secrecy of the session key from the server's point of view. To do this, add the necessary annotations and lemma to the source file. What result do you obtain?

4. Allow for corruption by uncommenting the `Reveal_ltk` rule. Check all lemmas again. Which results change and why? Modify the lemmas so that they make sense again.

5. Currently the client does not know whether the server actually received his message and key. To allow the server to confirm the key's receipt, add a return message:

$$2.\ S \rightarrow C : h(k)$$

where $h(k)$ is the hash of the key received in the first message.

Hint: Include the builtin `hashing`, and modify the server and client rules.

6. Bonus: Can you now prove key confirmation from the client's point of view?

You can find the solutions to these subtasks in Section 21.3.1.

21.1.2 Needham-Schroeder Protocol

We consider a variant of the well-known Needham-Schroeder protocol and its correction proposed by Lowe. The protocol is found in the file **exercises/needham-schroeder.spthy**.

1. Load this file in TAMARIN's interactive mode and prove all the given properties. We suggest running TAMARIN using `--auto-sources` to avoid termination issues. Which lemmas are proven and which fail? Does TAMARIN find Lowe's attack? Can you help TAMARIN find that attack? *Hint: look at the lemma's source code.*

2. Read and understand the TAMARIN file. Modify it by applying Lowe's fix by adding "B"'s identity to the second message. What do you now observe? Do all properties hold?

You can find the solutions in Section 21.3.2.

21.1.3 Aliveness and Agreement - Separating Examples

Consider the following three simple protocols H1, H2, and H3:

21.1 Simple Protocols

H1(1). $I \to R : \{I, R\}_{\mathsf{sk}(I)}$
H1(2). $R \to I : \{I, R\}_{\mathsf{sk}(R)}$

H2(1). $I \to R : \{I, R\}_{\mathsf{sk}(I)}$
H2(2). $R \to I : \{I\}_{\mathsf{sk}(R)}$

H3(1). $I \to R : Ni, \{I, R\}_{\mathsf{sk}(I)}$
H3(2). $R \to I : \{I, Ni\}_{\mathsf{sk}(R)}$

Recall Lowe's hierarchy of authentication properties (in increasing strength): aliveness, weak agreement, non-injective agreement, and injective agreement. For each of the three protocols above:

- Determine the strongest property in Lowe's hierarchy that holds for I authenticating R and give an informal argument why it holds.
- Suggest an attack on the next stronger property (if any) showing that it fails to hold.
- Check your answers in TAMARIN.

Hint: For H3, include the nonce Ni in the agreement if possible.

You can find the solutions in Section 21.3.3.

21.1.4 Two message key exchange protocol (2MKEP)

We shall now model a two message key exchange protocol. We construct it in three steps with increasing complexity, using different abstractions, different security properties, and different adversary models.

21.1.4.1 2MKEP: start

We start by considering a very simple protocol: an initiator and a responder want to exchange secretly two random numbers, respectively mI and mR. For this, we assume that the initiator and responder *already* have a shared fresh symmetric secret key. Hence they can simply send each other encrypted messages, see Figure 21.1.

Using the skeleton file **exercises/2mkep-v1.spthy** and the following hints, model this protocol.

- Use TAMARIN's rewrite rules to model the setup of the shared symmetric key between initiator and responder. We do *not* allow either party to get compromised and reveal the key.

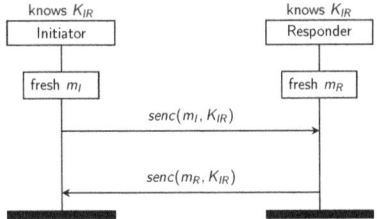

Fig. 21.1: 2MKEP: exchanging nonces with a pre-existing shared key

- Use TAMARIN's built-in symmetric-encryption theory for the encryption function, see Chapter 7. The given skeleton file already includes this built-in theory.

Write an executability lemma.

To ensure that your model behaves as expected, always write lemmas that guarantee that the parties executing the protocol can actually complete all their steps. This helps you detect typos and modeling errors, which may make some of the rewriting rules that model the protocol impossible to execute.

The skeleton file already includes such a lemma, lemma executable. This states that the initiator can finish her run of the protocol, sending the message mI and receiving the message mR from the responder, and the responder can finish his run, sending the message mR and receiving mI from the initiator. However, you must add the necessary action facts to the rules you write.

- Add the action facts FinishedI(..), for the initiator, and FinishedR(..), for the responder, to your model. In which rules should they be added?
- Once you have implemented the model and added the necessary action facts, load TAMARIN's interactive mode and verify your executability lemma.
- TAMARIN gives you a graphical output when it finds an execution. Try relating this graph to your model. Can you make sense of it?

Security Properties: Secrecy

The protocol should guarantee that no party other than the initiator and responder can obtain mI or mR.

- Thinking along the lines of the secrecy lemma in Section 5.3, add the following two action facts to the appropriate rules:

21.1 Simple Protocols

- `SecretI($I, $R, mI)`: Indicates that at this point the initiator (agent $I) believes mI to be a secret shared between her and the responder (agent $R).
- `SecretR($R, $I, mR)`: Indicates that at this point the responder (agent $R) believes mR to be a secret shared between him and the initiator (agent $I).

- Write a lemma `lemma secrecyI` stating that when the initiator finishes her role, exchanging a message mI (apparently) with the responder, then the message is a secret. Namely, it is only known by the initiator and responder, but not by any other agents, in particular not by the adversary.
- Write an analogous `lemma secrecyR`, referring to the message mR sent by the responder at the end of his role.

Once you have written these lemmas, load TAMARIN's interactive mode and verify both lemmas. Do they hold? What would you expect?

21.1.4.2 2MKEP: Public Key Infrastructure

In the previous task, we abstracted away (via a rule) how initiator and responder come to initially share a symmetric key. In reality, this is a crucial problem to solve. In this task, our solution is to assume that a public key infrastructure (PKI) is available.

We consider the straightforward idea where the initiator chooses a symmetric key K_{IR} and sends it to the responder, encrypting it with the responder's public key. See Figure 21.2.

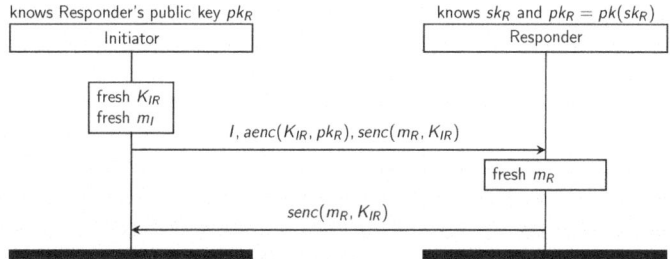

Fig. 21.2: 2MKEP: exchanging nonces using the PKI and a session key

We will make use of `asymmetric-encryption`, a built-in TAMARIN theory that models a public key encryption scheme, which we saw in Chapter 7. Using the skeleton file **exercises/2mkep-v2.spthy** and the hints below, model this version of the protocol.

- To use asymmetric cryptography, protocol agents must generate key pairs. Write a rule that allows an agent to generate a private/public key pair. For now, we do not allow agents to get compromised and reveal their secret keys.

- Model the rest of the protocol.
- Write an executability lemma to verify that your model is actually executable. For this, add suitable action facts and check that TAMARIN returns the expected protocol run, examining the resulting graph in interactive mode.

Security Properties: Secrecy

As in the previous task, this protocol should guarantee that no party other than the initiator and the responder can obtain mI or mR.

- Again, add the following two action facts to the appropriate rules:
  - SecretI($I, $R, mI): Indicates that at this point the initiator (agent $I) believes mI to be a secret shared between her and the responder (agent $R).
  - SecretR($R, $I, mR): Indicates that at this point the responder (agent $R) believes mR to be a secret shared between him and the initiator (agent $I).
- Write lemmas lemma secrecyI and lemma secrecyR checking the secrecy of the terms mI and mR. You may of course re-use the lemmas from the previous exercise.

Analyze both lemmas. This time, results should be different! While TAMARIN should still verify secrecyI, it should now falsify secrecyR.

Try to understand the attack graph TAMARIN produces. What happens if you do *not* make the agents' public keys available to the adversary in your PKI infrastructure rule? Verify that in that case TAMARIN proves both lemmas. Is it realistic to model a PKI that way?

Consider the differences

How do the results compare between these two exercises? Think about what has changed. One can of course further increase the level of detail of the model: for example, concretely modeling how the asymmetric encryption or the symmetric encryption is performed. Many things could go wrong there, too. In general, when modeling a protocol, choosing the right level of abstraction is hard, and this usually depends on whether or not you are interested in the details of its sub-protocols.

21.1.4.3 2MKEP: now with possible key leakage

The protocol in the previous task did not achieve the intended security properties. In particular, the responder had no guarantee that the initiator actually sent him the message. To fix this, we modify the protocol so that additionally the initiator signs

21.1 Simple Protocols

the message she sends, see Figure 21.3. TAMARIN has a built-in theory `signing` to model signature schemes, see Chapter 7.

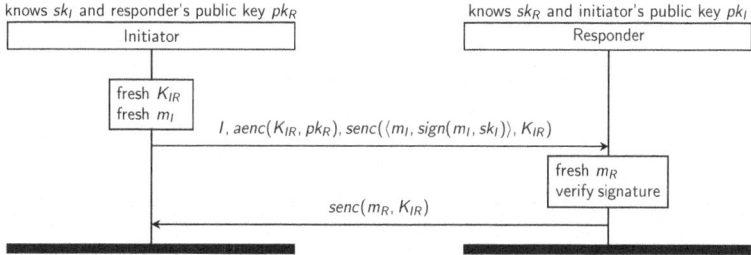

Fig. 21.3: 2MKEP: exchanging nonces using a PKI, session key, and signing

- Modify your previous model to include the initiator's signature.
- Check your executability lemma's resulting graph.
- Analyze both secrecy lemmas. This time TAMARIN should verify `secrecyI` and `secrecyR`. Check that it does!

Leaking Keys

If you think carefully, the verification results are surprising. The protocol should be vulnerable to a man-in-the-middle attack that compromises the secrecy of mR. Why does TAMARIN fail to find it?

Recall that while the adversary can use all the loaded function symbols (in this case `senc`, `sdec`, `aenc`, `adec`, `sign`, etc.), it cannot *execute* rules for its own benefit. In particular, the adversary cannot generate a private/public key pair using our PKI rule, and hence it cannot act as an agent. This is actually quite a restrictive adversary model, which we will now change.

- To fix this, write a rule that allows an agent to be compromised: the rule should take an agent's secret key and send it out on the network. In this way an adversary can use this key, *acting* like that agent afterwards.
- Analyze the secrecy lemmas. TAMARIN should now disprove both of them. Examine the attack graphs. They will probably show either the initiator or responder themselves leaking a key. This is not a real or sensible attack: of course the messages mI and mR will not be secret if either the initiator or responder themselves are compromised by the adversary. What we want to check, however, is that the messages mI and mR remain secret *if both the initiator and responder are honest*, but *all other agents may be compromised*.

- In the rule that reveals an agent's secret key, add an action fact (e.g., Compromised(..)) that documents that a certain agent has been compromised. Fix your lemmas SecretI and SecretR to exclude the case of the initiator and responder themselves being compromised.
- Run TAMARIN again in interactive mode. Does it now find the expected man-in-the-middle-attack?
- Observe how the reveal of keys has affected your executability lemma. Does the graph returned by TAMARIN still correspond to the standard protocol run that you would expect? If not, modify your executability lemma to exclude agents from being compromised. You should always check that your protocol is executable if everyone is honest, i.e., protocol executability should not require the adversary's help.

This concludes the 2MKEP example, for which we do not provide solutions.

21.2 A Large Protocol: PACE

We now present a task from a larger protocol project. In this task, we leave readers the freedom to design their own models from a blank canvas, i.e., no files are provided. Moreover, no solutions are given.

The PACE protocol is part of a protocol suite that is used for machine-readable travel documents throughout the world. These documents include electronic passports and identity cards. The PACE protocol establishes a secure channel between the terminal and the RFID chip on the passport or ID card. The protocol assumes that they initially only share a low-entropy secret and it uses a Diffie-Hellman key exchange to derive a strong session key. In practice, the low-entropy pre-shared secret may be either from a six-digit Card Access Number (CAN) or the Machine-Readable Zone (MRZ), which is a code printed on the document and optically scanned by the terminal.

In this part of the project, we develop the PACE protocol by a series of successive refinements. We start with a very simple challenge-response protocol for which we show an agreement property. With each refinement, we introduce additional features and possibly additional or stronger security properties. Our goal is to derive PACE and prove that it satisfies perfect forward secrecy for its session key as well as mutual agreement of the parties on the session key and other protocol elements.

21.2.1 A simple challenge-response protocol

Our initial protocol is the following simple MAC-based challenge response protocol P1 between an initiator I and a responder R.

21.2 A Large Protocol: PACE

$$I \rightarrow R : x$$
$$R \rightarrow I : [x]_{k(R,I)}$$

In this protocol, x is a nonce generated by I, $[M]_K$ denotes the MAC of message M with key K, and $k(R, I)$ is a symmetric long-term key shared by R and I. Make sure that the key $k(R, I)$ is uni-directional, i.e., $k(I, R) \neq k(R, I)$, meaning you do not use the same key when I sends to R as when R sends to I. Instead, there are two different keys, one for each direction.

Formalize this protocol in TAMARIN and prove that it satisfies the authentication property that I injectively agrees with R on the nonce x. Make sure that the intruder can also act as a regular protocol participant. This is theory *P1*.

21.2.2 Mutual authentication

The first refinement, protocol P2, combines two instances of P1, one initiated by I (generating and sending nonce x) and one initiated by R (generating and sending nonce y). These two instances are run in an interleaved manner such that the senders alternate and the resulting protocol has four messages. The property we wish to achieve is the agreement of each role with the other role on *both* nonces x and y.

1. Model the protocol P2 and analyze its desired security property in TAMARIN as the theory *P2a*. Can you find an attack?

2. If you have found an attack: describe the problem, propose a fix as the theory *P2b*, and try to prove the mutual injective agreement property. Iterate as needed until you succeed with a proof.

21.2.3 Introducing a session key

In the second refinement, we introduce a session key and a corresponding secrecy property. Instead of using the long-term key $k(I, R)$ for computing MACs, we compute MACs in both directions with the session key *Kir*, which is derived from the long-term key and the nonces x and y using a key derivation function kdf:

$$Kir = \text{kdf}(k(I, R), x, y)$$

At the same time, instead of computing the MACs of both nonces, we only MAC the other role's nonce (i.e., I computes the MAC of y and R computes the MAC of x).

1. Define the modified protocol in TAMARIN as the theory *P3a* and prove mutual agreement on x, y, and *Kir* as well as the secrecy of *Kir*. Note that you can declare the function kdf as a user-defined function in TAMARIN.

2. Give an informal justification of why we can include each role's own nonce in the agreement despite that nonce not being MACed. Compare with protocol P2.

21.2.4 Replace the password by a nonce

In this refinement, we replace the (low-entropy) password $k(I, R)$ in the session key Kir by a (high-entropy) nonce s generated by I, i.e.,

$$Kir = \mathsf{kdf}(s, x, y).$$

Moreover, we add the symmetric encryption of s with the hashed password $h(k(I, R))$ as a second (plaintext) component to the first message from I to R. We call this protocol P4.

Model the protocol P4 in TAMARIN as the theory *P4* and show that it satisfies the same properties as the protocol P3.

21.2.5 Introducing Diffie-Hellman: The PACE protocol

In the final refinement, protocol P5, we derive the PACE protocol by replacing P4's nonces x and y by Diffie-Hellman public keys g^x and g^y. A particularity of the PACE protocol is the choice of the generator g, which is defined by

$$g = \mathsf{map}(s, p).$$

Here, s is the nonce from P4 and p is a public domain parameter that, together with the mapping function map, ensures that g is a suitable group generator. We model map as a user-defined hash function, that is, without equational properties. The parameter p is added as an additional plaintext component to the first message. Furthermore, the hashed Diffie-Hellman secret

$$Kir = \mathsf{h}(g^{xy}).$$

now replaces the previous session key.

1. Transform your model of P4 into a model of the PACE protocol as described above and establish the same properties as for P4 (modulo the replacement of nonces by public keys) as the theory *P5ab*.

   Hint: Use "let $g = \mathsf{map}(s, p)$" in each protocol rule instead of storing g in state facts.

2. Strengthen the secrecy property of the session key Kir to perfect forward secrecy. Add this property to the theory *P5ab*.

21.3 Solutions

3. Explain how the protocol relies on the secrecy of the base g for the exponentiation. Would it still work with a public base? Justify your answer.

4. Remove any tags that you may have in your protocol so that the last two messages become unifiable. Find an attack on the secrecy or authentication property of the resulting protocol and fix it by ensuring that g^x and g^y differ. (Having unifiable messages in a protocol tends to make a protocol prone to attacks, but this is what PACE does.) This check can be specified in TAMARIN using a restriction. Specify this as the theory *P5d*.

This concludes the PACE example.

21.3 Solutions

Here we give examples of solutions to selected exercises.

21.3.1 Client-Server Key Transmission - Solutions

Here are our solutions for the protocol presented in Section 21.1.1, following the same subtask numbering. We provide a TAMARIN file containing the full solution in **exercises/ClientServerSolution.spthy**.

1. No further information, the model is commented.

2. As shown by lemma `Client_session_key_secrecy`, secrecy from the client's point of view holds.

   The lemma `Client_Server_can_finish` is an executability sanity check.

3. The property fails: nothing ensures that the message does not come from the adversary. To view this attack, take the solution file **exercises/ClientServerSolution.spthy**, comment out the rule `Reveal_ltk` (as in the initial task file), and comment out the line containing the LtkReveal in lemma `Server_session_key_secrecy`. Then load the resulting theory and inspect the attack on that lemma using TAMARIN's GUI.

4. Everything fails trivially. We must forbid LtkReveal for the concerned parties (even for executability to have a real trace), after which we get the previous results again. For this, we must modify all lemmas, which is already done in the solution file. We provide one example here, for secrecy from the client's point of view:

```
lemma Client_session_key_secrecy:
" All C S k #i.
  (
    /* If client 'C' has set up a session key 'k'
```

```
             with a server 'S' */
      Claim_Secret(C, S, k) @ #i
      /* and neither of the two communicating parties
         are compromised */
    & not (Ex #j. LtkReveal(C) @ #j) & not (Ex #j. LtkReveal(S) @ #j)
      /* the adversary cannot know 'k' */
      ==> not(Ex #j. K(k) @ #j)
    ) "
```

5. See **exercises/ClientServerSolution.spthy** for all the required changes.

6. Yes. This requires writing a lemma stating that if the client has finished, then the server knows the key. See the TAMARIN solution file from the previous subtask as well.

21.3.2 Needham-Schroeder Protocol - Solutions

Here are our solutions for the protocol presented in Section 21.1.2, following the same subtask numbering.

1. The sanity check and the typing lemma (i.e., the automatically generated sources lemma) hold.

   Secrecy fails, but TAMARIN finds a more complicated variant of Lowe's attack. One can uncomment parts of the lemma in the provided source code to get a nicer version.

2. Now all the properties hold, see **exercises/needham-schroeder-lowe.spthy** for the full solution.

21.3.3 Aliveness and Agreement - Separating Examples - Solutions

Here are our solutions for the tasks from Section 21.1.3. Specifically, see the TAMARIN input files **exercises/H1.spthy**, **exercises/H2.spthy**, and **exercises/H3.spthy**, which implement the three protocols. You can run TAMARIN on them to examine the results yourself. In short, this is what happens:

- H1. There is a reflection attack, so not even aliveness (or weak agreement if the Initiator is annotated with running) holds, see Figure 21.4.
- H2. Non-injective agreement holds, but injectivity fails as there is no nonce or timestamp, see Figure 21.5.
- H3. Injective agreement holds because of *Ni*.

21.3 Solutions

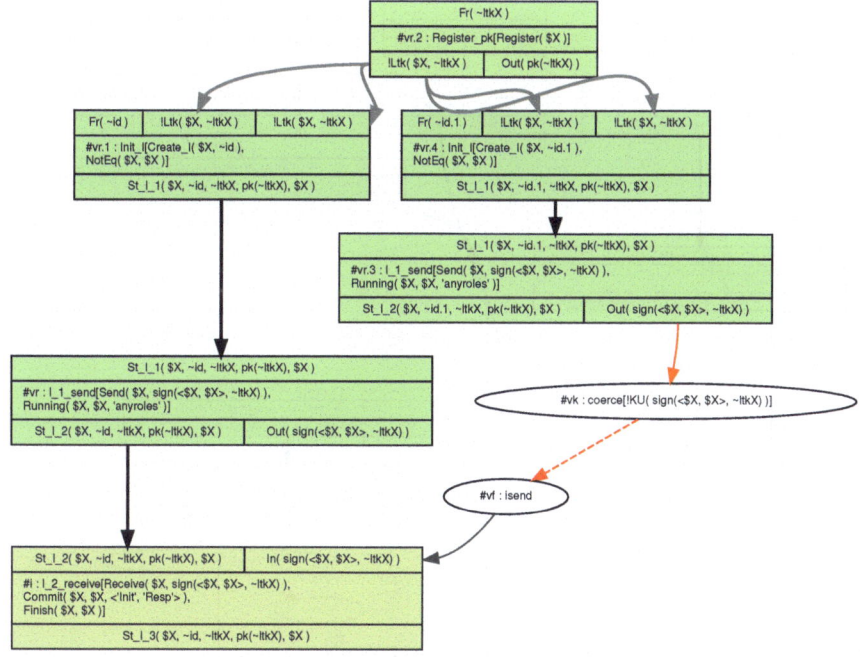

Fig. 21.4: Attack trace showing the reflection attack.

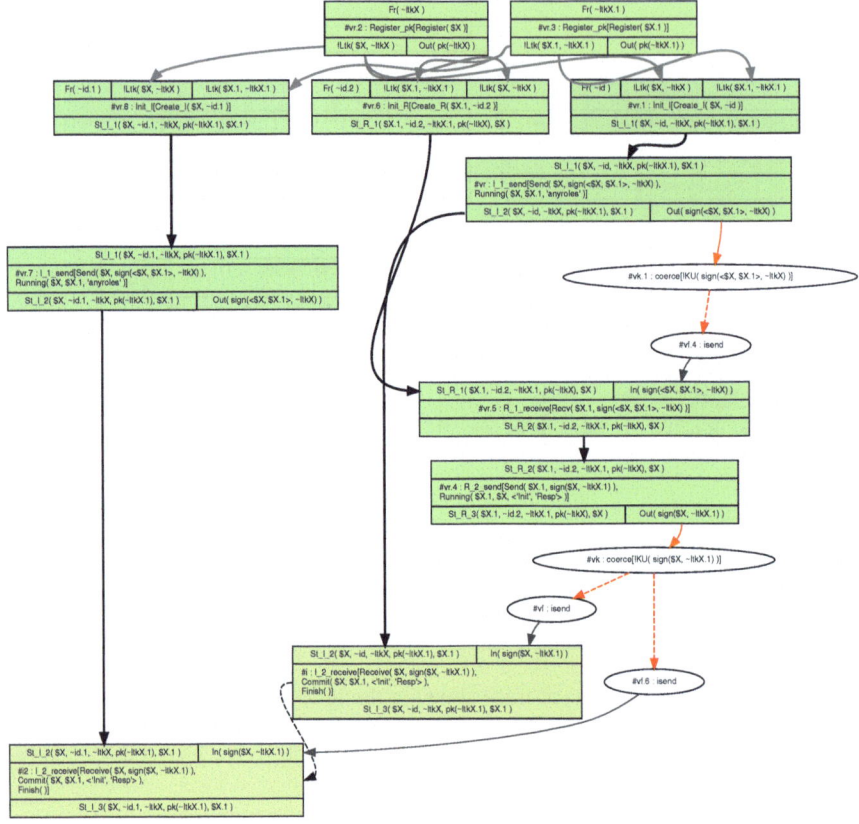

Fig. 21.5: Attack trace showing the violation of injectivity, i.e., a replay.

Index

∃, 55
∀, 55
+, 125
<, 55
⊏, 128
<<, 128
=, 34
   message equality, 55
   timepoint equality, 55
==>, 55
@, 55
[+], 250
[-], 250
#define, 162
#else, 162
#endif, 162
#ifdef, 162
$, 32
%+, 128
%1, 128
&, 55
_restrict, 74
~, 32
|, 55
^, 125, 127
1:nat, 128
5G-AKA, 195, 271

   in bilinear pairing theory, 127
   in Diffie-Hellman theory, 125

abstract function, 32
AC, 125, 234
action fact, 53
actions, 53
adec, 123
adversary deduction
   normal form conditions, 113
AEAD, 247
aenc, 123
agent
   compromised, 63
   honest, 63
   malicious, 62
   name, 12
agreement
   injective, 69
   non-injective, 68
   weak, 68
aliveness, 68
All, 55
analyzing protocol families, 259
anonymity, 217
applied-Pi calculus, 7
arity of function symbol, 32
associative operators, 234
associative-commutative operators, 234

associativity-commutativity, 125
asymmetric-encryption
    built-in, 123
at timepoint, 55
authentic channel, 167
authenticated encryption with associated data, 247
authentication property hierarchy, 66
auto-sources, 135
AUTO_IN_, 135
AUTO_OUT_, 135
AUTO_typing, 135

bad curve points, 244
bag, 35
bag built-in, 125
basic modeling, 151
before, 55
bi-system, 217
bilinear pairing built-in, 127
bilinear-pairing, 127
both lemma annotation, 218
branching, 50
branching in rules, 76
built-in, 121
    Diffie-Hellman, 35
    symmetric encryption, 34
builtins, 121

CEOgen, 238
certification, 8
channel
    authentic, 167
    confidential, 167
    secure, 167
chosen-prefix collision, 247
chosen-suffix collision, 247
colliding signatures, 239
collision resistant, 247
color annotation for rules, 101
command-line mode, 83
    workflow, 175
comment, 47
    multi-line, 47
common workflows, 171

compromised agent, 63
conditional block, 162
confidential channel, 167
confluent rewrite system, 107
conjunction, 55
constant, 32, 153
constraint solving algorithm in Tamarin, 92
convergent equations, 107
counter, 127
cryptographic protocol, 3

deconstructions, 131
deconstructor, 155
deduction
    normal form conditions, 113
define, 162
DEOgen, 238
dependency graph, 87
    traces, 90
    visualization, 101
deprio:, 251
design phase, 8
DH_neutral, 125, 127
diff, 217
diff mode, 217
Diffie-Hellman
    equational theory, 35
    simplified signed Diffie-Hellman protocol, 60
    small subgroup element, 244
diffie-hellman
    built-in, 125
diffLemma
    Observational_equivalence, 218
disjunction, 55
does not exist error, 185
DSKS, 238

EBNF, 295
eCK security model, 165
elliptic curve, 244
else, 162
"else" branch in rules, 76
em, 127
embedded restriction, 74

INDEX

EMV, 273
endif, 162
equality
  message variable, 55
  term, 34
  timepoint, 55
equation store, 109
equational theory, 7, 34, 107
equations
  convergent, 107
  on terms, 107
  orienting, 107
error, 179
  does not exist, 185
  exit 126, 186
  exit 127, 186
  no such file or directory, 185, 186
  permission denied, 186
  readCreateProcess, 185, 186
EUF-CMA, 236, 241
Ex, 55
Exclusive Ownership, 238
exclusive-or built-in, 125
execs function, 41
executability, 169
executions
  of global transition system, 40
exercises, 305
existential quantification, 55
existential unforgeability, 241
exit 126 error, 186
exit 127 error, 186
exp, 125, 127
explicit deconstructor, 155

F_ fact prefix, 249
fact, 19, 30, 35, 39
  injective, 158
  linear, 36
  persistent, 36
fact label prefixes for heuristics, 249
Finite Variant Property, 109
Formal Methods, 5
formula

semantics of trace formula, 56
Fr fact, 36
Fr rule, 38
fr sort, 32
free term algebra, 34
fresh, 32
  rule, 38
  value, 32, 153
  variable, 32
function
  underspecified, 241
function symbol, 31, 32
  injective, 34
  irreducible, 55
  private, 33
  reducible, 55
FVP, 109

$G^\sharp$, 39
getMessage, 124
global macro, 161
global transition system, 29, 39
graphical user interface, 81
  workflow, 171
gri, 39
ground term, 33
guarded lemma, 187
GUI, 81
  workflow, 171

h, 122
hashing, 122
hashing built-in, 122
heuristic lemma annotation, 105, 253
heuristics, 104
  fact label prefixes, 249
  oracle scripts, 254
  tactics, 251
hide_lemma annotation, 144
hierarchy of authentication properties, 66
Home Network, 196
  Identifier (idHN), 196
  public key (pkHN), 196
honest agent, 63
hyperproperties, 217

idHN, 196
IETF TLS 1.3, 269
if-then-else in rules, 76
`ifdef`, 162
impact in practice, 269
implementations, 8
implication, 55
`In`, 36
indistinguishability, 8
induction, 141
injective agreement, 69
injective fact, 158
injective function symbol, 34
interactive mode, 81
`inv`, 125, 127
invalid curve points, 244
irreducible function symbol, 55
`isFactName`, 251
ISO-IEC four pass authentication protocol, 14

K, 36, 38
K vs KU vs KD, 194
KD, 36
key infrastructure, 45, 60
key substitution attacks, 238
KU, 36

L_ fact prefix, 249
labeled operational semantics, 40
language syntax, 295
`last` timepoint, 142
`left` lemma annotation, 218
lemma
    semantics of trace formula, 56
    sources, 135
lemma annotation, 141
    `both`, 218
    `heuristic`, 105, 253
    `hide_lemma`, 144
    induction, 141
    `left`, 218
    reuse, 144
    `right`, 218
    sources, 135

    `use_induction`, 141
length extension attack, 246
`let`, 160
lfacts, 40
limit
    number of saturation steps, 134
    number of solved chain constraints, 134
limitations for equational theories, 233
linear fact, 36
local macro, 160
log, 30
loop, 49
loop breaker, 100

macro
    global, 161
    `let`, 160
    local, 160
    parameterized, 161
malicious agent, 62
malleability, 240
malleable signatures, 240
mangle, 240
memory exhaustion, 188
message, 30, 32, 33
    deduction, 38
    equality, 55
    ground, 33
message substitution attacks, 238
mirror, 218
`MIRRORED`, 218
model checker, 5
model quality control, 169
modeling language, 7
modeling state machines, 43
msg sort, 32
multi-core CPU, 179
multi-line comment, 47
multiset, 35
    `multiset` built-in, 125
    rewriting, 7
    rewriting rule, 30, 36

name of agent, 12
`natural-numbers`, 127

INDEX

natural-numbers built-in, 127
Naxos protocol, 165
negation, 55
network model, 38
no such file or directory error, 185, 186
no_precomp, 134
Noise protocol framework, 259
non-injective agreement, 68
non-interactive mode, 83
non-invertible, 34
non-prime order group, 244
nonce, 31
nonce-reuse attack, 248
normal form
    adversary deduction, 113
    term, 107
not, 55
number, 127
number used once, 31

observational equivalence, 7, 217
ONE
    in bilinear pairing theory, 127
    in Diffie-Hellman theory, 125
one-way, 34
OnlyOnce, 73
open chain, 136
--open-chains, 86
operational semantics, 40
oracle scripts, 254
order-sorted logic, 29
order-sorted term algebra, 31
orienting equations, 107
Out, 36

pairing, 33
parallelization, 179
parameterized macro, 161
partial deconstructions, 131
partner, *see* peer 63
pattern matching, 46, 47, 156
peer, *see* partner 63
permission denied error, 186
persistent fact, 36

pfacts, 40
pk, 123, 124
pkHN, 196
PKI, 60
pmult, 127
practical impact, 269
pre-computation, 131
pre-image resistant, 247
precomputations
    exclude facts from precomputation, 134
predicate, 55, 72
presort:, 251
prime order group, 244
prio:, 251
privacy, 8
privacy properties, 217
private function symbol, 33
property specification, 7
    K vs KU vs KD, 194
    syntax, 54
protocol, 3
    implementations, 8
    protocol family analysis, 259
    voting protocol, 220
pub sort, 32
public constant, 32
public key infrastructure, 45, 60
public variable, 32, 153

quote, 32

Random Oracle Model, 246
random value, 31
Raw sources, 135
re-signing, 239
readCreateProcess, 186
readCreateProcess error, 185, 186
recentness, 16
record, 30
reducible function symbol, 55
reducing proof-construction time, 249
Refined sources, 135
regex, 251
representing messages, 30

ReSign, 239
restriction, 72
  embedded, 74
reuse lemma annotation, 144
revealing-signing
  built-in, 124
revealSign, 124
revealVerify, 124
rewriting rule, 36
right lemma annotation, 218
role, 12, 29
role annotation for rules, 103
ROM model, 246
RTS, 179
rule, 30
  color annotation, 101
  multiset rewriting rule, 19, 30, 36
  role annotation, 103
  transition system rule, 29
rule-equivalence, 218
running Tamarin, 81

safety property, 7
sanity checking models, 169
SAPIC, 7
scope of variable, 32, 152
sdec, 123
secrecy, 8
secure channel, 167
security protocol, 3
semantics
  of TAMARIN's rules, 39
  of trace formula, 56
senc, 123
Serving Network, 196
session, 49
set of traces of rule set, 41
sign, 124
signature
  built-in, 124
  colliding, 239
  exclusive ownership, 238
  malleable, 240
  re-signing, 239
  substitution attacks, 238

signing built-in, 124
single quote, 32
small subgroup, 244
smallest, 252
SNname, 196
sort, 31
  fr, 32
  msg, 32
  pub, 32
sources, 131
  raw, 135
  refined, 135
sources lemma, 135
splitEqs, 109
standardization, 8
state machine, 14, 29
  modeling, 43
static equivalence, 218
$steps$, 40
Subscriber, 196
Subscriber Concealed Identifier, 196
Subscriber Permanent Identifier, 196
substitution, 33
subterm-convergence, 231
subterm-convergent equational theory, 231
SUCI, 196
SUF-CMA, 236
SUPI, 196
symbolic model, 31
symmetric encryption
  example, 34
symmetric encryption built-in, 123
symmetric-encryption, 123
syntax, 295
  property specification, 54

tactic:, 251
tactics, 251
term, 30, 33
  algebra, 31
  equality, 34
  ground, 33
  rewriting, 29
terminating

TAMARIN search, 188
  rewrite system, 107
theorem prover, 5
thread, 29, 44, 49
  identifier, 30
threat model, 38, 62, 163
threat modeling, 163
timepoint
  equality, 55
  precedence, 55
  variable, 55
TLS 1.3, 269
trace
  of execution, 41
  property, 53
traces and dependency graphs, 90
traces function, 41
transition, 39
  relation, 7, 40
  system, 7, 39
transition system rule, 29
true, 124
type annotation, 154

UE, 196
undecidability, 6
underspecified function, 241
universal quantification, 55
unlinkability, 217
use_induction, 141
User Equipment, 196
user-specified equational theory, 231

Vacarme, 263
variable, 32, 152
  fresh, 32
  public, 32
  scope, 32, 152
  timepoint, 55
variants, 108
verify, 124
visualization
  of dependency graphs, 101
voter privacy, 217
voting protocol, 220

weak, 240
weak agreement, 68
web interface, 81
WireGuard, 8, 260
workflow, 171
  command-line mode, 175
  GUI, 171

xor, 125

zero, 125

The manufacturer's authorised representative in the EU is Springer Nature Customer Service Centre GmbH, Europaplatz 3, 69115 Heidelberg, Germany. If you have any concerns regarding our products, please contact ProductSafety@springernature.com

Printed and bound by CPI Group (UK) Ltd, Croydon, CR0 4YY

26/03/2026

02078974-0003